BALZAC

BALZAC

BY

STEFAN ZWEIG

TRANSLATED BY WILLIAM & DOROTHY ROSE

With thirty-one vignettes

CASSELL · LONDON

CASSELL & COMPANY LTD
35 RED LION SQUARE, LONDON, WC1
Melbourne, Sydney, Toronto
Johannesburg, Auckland

This edition © Cassell & Co Ltd 1970
No part of this publication may be reproduced,
stored in a retrieval system, or transmitted,
in any form or by any means, electronic, ▪
mechanical, photocopying, recording or
otherwise, without the prior permission of
Cassell and Company Ltd.
First published 1947
Second edition second impression 1970

S.B.N. 304 93550 6

The vignettes in this book are reproduced from
engravings by the contemporary artists, *Gavarni,
Daumier, Vernier, Emy, Trimolet* and *Gagniet.*

Printed in Great Britain by
William Lewis (Printers) Ltd. Cardiff
1269

CONTENTS

v

INTRODUCTION

As THE EDITOR of this last posthumous work of my friend Stefan
Zweig, I should like to add a few words in explanation of the way in
which the book arrived at the stage of publication. The manuscripts entrusted to me by his relatives and heirs after the author's
death were of a very extensive nature. After seeing through the
press a volume of essays and lectures, which was published in 1943,
during the war, under the title *Zeit und Welt*, I began to examine
the material available for the biography of Balzac. The "large
Balzac", as Stefan Zweig used to call it in order to distinguish it
from his earlier and less ambitious writings on the subject, was to
be his *magnum opus*, and he had been working at it for ten years.
It was to be a summing up of his own experience as an author and
of what life had taught him. Balzac seemed to him to be a unique
theme, appropriate to his own special gifts and, as it were, destined
to be treated by him. Since his early days in Vienna he had been
deeply interested in Balzac's writings and in the Balzac legend, and
it may perhaps be recalled that Vienna played an important rôle
in the development of Balzac's European fame.

It was in Vienna that there practically originated the second
great wave of enthusiasm that finally established the French
novelist as a world-wide celebrity. It was in Vienna, during his
visit in the year 1835, that he had first won and enjoyed full
recognition from a European public. Hugo von Hofmannsthal was
the spokesman of the school of young Viennese writers to which
Stefan Zweig also belonged, and in his Introduction to Balzac's
collected works Hofmannsthal wrote the finest essay on the theme
of Balzac that is to be found in the German tongue. For these
young Viennese authors Balzac was not so much the great master
of the novel—which they regarded as a rather dubious form of
literature—but, more generally, "a teeming world of characters
. . . a great and infinitely plastic imagination, the greatest
imaginative realist since Shakespeare". Balzac was for them the
incarnation of creative literary power, a *potentiel de littérature*, so

to speak, that had never been fully exploited and was a constant
enticement to imitation and reverie. It was in this view of Balzac
that Stefan Zweig's conception was rooted, and something of the
youthful enthusiasm of those years can be seen in the present book.

While he was still trying out his strength, mainly as an inter-
preter of French literature, Zweig made a number of attempts to
say what he wanted to say about Balzac. First of all he published a
Balzac anthology with an Introduction, then various essays, and
finally the long essay on Balzac, which, together with those on
Dostoevsky and Dickens, formed the first volume of a series. The
"large Balzac" was to conclude the series of biographies which he
had systematically built up as a complement to the series of essays,
and was intended to crown his life's work.

The book was planned on a spacious scale and he occasionally
spoke of the possibility that it would comprise two volumes, but it
was destined to share the fate of the master's own work, the
Comédie humaine, and never to reach its projected span. Something
of Balzac's restlessness seemed to have infected his biographer. In
the preliminary draft of a supplementary chapter, which unfortunately remained in too fragmentary a state for inclusion in the
present volume, Zweig describes how, after Balzac's death, his
widow and her family were seized by a strange craving for extravagance, akin to that of Balzac himself, and recklessly squandered
the Ukrainian millions which they had hitherto so carefully preserved. When it was a matter of preparing his book on Balzac,
Stefan Zweig too became a spendthrift so far as time was concerned. He was no niggard either in the things of this world or in
the things of the spirit, but during his long years of authorship he
had forced himself to maintain a wholesome discipline in his
system of work. Without the economy of time that he was thus able
to achieve his literary output would inevitably have been far
smaller. But Balzac played havoc with Stefan Zweig's self-imposed
discipline. He kept adding to the files of material that he had
already accumulated, and I myself had occasion to observe him at
his labours and to lend him a helping hand. New vistas were continually opening up, and what he had already written was subjected
to constant revision. His magnificent collections of authors' manuscripts included one of the most precious of the volumes in which
Balzac had bound up his manuscript with the successive series of

proofs, and these entangled, unending proof corrections seemed to exert a mysterious, hypnotic effect on Zweig. Their influence extended to the manuscript of the biography. The core of the book, which was continually being copied out afresh by his indefatigable wife and collaborator, was a mere nucleus for further additions. The note-books and special files increased in number, lists and tables were prepared, the various Balzac editions and monographs in Zweig's possession were filled with underlinings, marginal comments, references and slips of paper. The small study of his house in Bath, into which he had moved shortly before the outbreak of war, became a Balzac museum, a depository of Balzac archives, a centre of information about Balzac.

When, in the summer of 1940, Stefan Zweig started on the voyage to America from which he was never to return, all this material had to be left behind. In the quietness of his refuge in the Brazilian summer-capital of Petropolis he finished his autobiography and his short story *The Royal Game*. Then, shortly before his death, he applied himself once more to his book on Balzac. At his request I sent him copies of some of his notes, but they arrived too late. They were returned to me unopened with a note written on the envelope to the effect that the addressee was dead. A copy of part of the manuscript, which he had taken with him, was found untouched when his papers were gone through by the two gentlemen who had been entrusted with their charge, his Brazilian publisher and the author Victor Wittkowski. He had tired himself out and felt that without the material he had left behind in London and Bath, and without his working copy of the manuscript, he could not bring the book to completion. In the darkening shadows of his last days he even suggested that it would probably be impossible to comprehend in his full stature such a gigantic figure as Balzac. No one who had tried to do so had yet succeeded.

When I first began to peruse the available material I doubted whether the book had been left as anything more than a torso. This, however, was not the case. The book had been finished. This is not to say that every chapter was complete or had been given its final shape, but essentially it had been brought to a conclusion. I shall not attempt here to give a detailed inventory of all the material that I used for the purpose of applying the finishing touches, since this would require a long article to itself, but I should like to say something about the text. The chief source was Zweig's working copy, on the cover of which he had already noted in English, "To be sent to the publisher". This was the third or, in some sections, the second version. He had revised this manuscript with the help of his wife, whose co-operation was by no means confined to the mechanical labour of copying. Her queries and marginal comments were clear and very much to the point, and frequently they provided a salutary counterpoise to his flights of lyricism. He was tempted at times by his theme to "sing an aria", as he put it. In this final version many changes and deletions had been made by Zweig himself. In other cases the decision had to be made by me, and I thought often of his quiet wife, Lotte, who had shared his work and his life with the almost passionate unobtrusiveness which was so peculiarly her own. It had seemed a matter of course that she should also join him in death.

The style and tone of the book have, of course, been left intact. Whole pages or intended insertions were sometimes missing, but these gaps it was possible to fill from the earlier versions and from the notes. The final chapters, of which only a rough draft was available, have been rewritten, and for this purpose I utilised the extensive apparatus in the way of files, note-books, annotated editions and slips to which reference has already been made above. The editions of Balzac which he used were the French critical edition of the collected works by Bouteron and the German version of the *Comédie humaine* published by the Insel-Verlag. Of this handsome production the Insel-Verlag had printed a special copy for him with the dedication, "This copy has been printed for Stefan Zweig", and the volumes had been his constant companions since 1908. I was able also to consult letters he had received from friends and helpers with reference to his work on Balzac, and I should like to take this opportunity of thanking, in the name of my departed friend, all those who aided him in his task.

Perhaps I may be permitted to add a word or two about the outward circumstances under which this book was produced. There were difficulties to contend with. The material was dispersed in various places, some of it in London, some in Bath, some deposited for safety at various banks. Whereas Stefan Zweig had been able to work at his manuscript during the early months of the war in comparative, though unreal, quiet, the period when I was engaged in its revision was one when the reality of the world conflagration had come very close indeed to the shores of England. It was a reality which compelled me to change my place of residence three times, having been bombed out on each occasion. Twice the working copy of the manuscript was literally torn out of my hands and flung across the room. The ceiling collapsed and buried the notes in rubble. Fragments of glass splinters and grains of plaster are still embedded in the pages. Even the front hall of Zweig's house in Bath, usually so quiet, was not spared its showers of splinters during one of the notorious "Baedeker raids". One bomb, which landed just in front of the wall of his study, luckily turned out to be a dud. The British Museum, to which I had recourse from time to time and which kept its hospitable North Library open throughout the war in such a praiseworthy manner, was likewise damaged in air-raids. My work was therefore carried on, to employ a typical English under-statement, under conditions that were not wholly normal. These experiences are mentioned here for no personal reasons, however, but merely as a documentary record.

This book, at least, was saved from the sinister forces which had exiled Stefan Zweig from his homeland and driven him to his death. It is not altogether what its author intended it to be, but I believe I can say with a clear conscience that it does form a worthy conclusion to his life's work. And in these times, when the slightest ray of hope means so much, it seems to me an auspicious omen that this last posthumous work of a good European and citizen of the world can now start on its journey unhindered and find its way to his friends in every country who remained loyal to him during the long years of spiritual blackout.

RICHARD FRIEDENTHAL.

London. *December*, 1945.

YOUTH AND EARLY EFFORTS

CHAPTER I

Childhood Tragedy

 man of Balzac's genius, en-
dowed with an exuberance of
imagination that puts it in his
power to establish and populate a universe of his own creation, is hardly likely to be a
stickler for the sober truth in
unimportant matters relating
to his private life. He will
subordinate everything to the
despotic sovereignty of his
creative will. And, character-
istically enough, this autocratic metamorphosis of various episodes
in his earthly existence began in the case of Balzac with the normally immutable basic fact of a man's civic career—that is to say,
his name. One day, when he was about thirty, he announced to the
world that his name was not Honoré Balzac, but Honoré de Balzac.
Furthermore, he declared that he had always possessed the full
right and entitlement to this predicate of nobility. Whereas his
father had only boasted in jest, and within his most intimate
domestic circle, of the possibility that he might be distantly related
to the ancient knightly family of Balzac d'Entragues, the powerful
imagination of the son challengingly exalted what had been but an
airy conjecture to the status of an incontrovertible fact. He signed
his letters and books in the name of "de Balzac", and even had the
arms of the d'Entragues family painted on the carriage in which he
travelled to Vienna. When unkind colleagues jeered at the conceit

of this self-ennoblement, he replied with a shameless air of candour that his father had established his aristocratic descent in official documents long before he, Honoré, was born. The predicate of nobility to be found in his birth-certificate was therefore no less valid than that of Montaigne or Montesquieu.

In this ungracious world of ours, unfortunately, matter-of-fact documents have an odious habit of displaying inquisitive hostility to the most flourishing of legends invented by poets; and it is an embarrassment to Balzac's reputation as a lover of the truth that the birth-certificate so triumphantly quoted by him happens still to be extant in the archives of the city of Tours. No trace of the aristocratic "de" is visible therein. Under the date "21 May, 1799" the parish clerk of Tours records with chilling clarity:

> Yesterday, the second of Prairial in the seventh year of the French Republic, there appeared before me, Pierre-Jacques Duvivier, the undersigned Registrar of Births, Marriages and Deaths, the citizen Bernard-François Balzac, proprietor, resident of this town, rue de l'Armée d'Italie, Section du Chardonnet No. 25, to notify the birth of a son. The said Balzac declared that the child is to receive the name of Honoré Balzac, and that it was born at eleven o'clock in the morning in his house.

Nor do the other relevant documents, such as those relating to his father's death or his elder sister's marriage, provide any proof of noble descent, which must therefore be regarded, together with all the genealogical digressions in which Balzac indulged, as a mere product of wishful thinking on the part of the great spinner of romances.

Yet even though, in the strict letter of the law, the various documentary attestations may have won their case against Balzac, his own sovereign will—his burning, creative will—has carried its point to glorious victory over the rigid veracity of the parchments. Whatever subsequent adjustments may be made in the cause of cold truth, poetry always triumphs over history. Though no French king ever bestowed a patent of nobility on him or any of his ancestors, when posterity is asked the name of the greatest French novelist it obeys his bidding and replies "Honoré de Balzac", not "Honoré Balzac", to say nothing of Honoré Balssa.

For Balssa, not Balzac, and certainly not de Balzac, was the correct surname of his proletarian ancestors. They possessed neither castles nor armorial bearings for their gifted descendant to paint upon his carriage doors. They did not ride forth in shining armour or take part in romantic tourneys, but drove their cattle out to the pasturage and tilled the soil of Languedoc in the sweat of their brows. Balzac's father, Bernard-François, was born 22 June, 1746, in a wretched stone cottage in the hamlet of La Nougayrié near Canezac as one of the numerous Balssas living there at that time. The only claim to fame ever acquired by any of these Balssas was of an extremely dubious nature. In 1819, the year in which Honoré left the university, his father's fifty-year-old brother was arrested on suspicion of having murdered a pregnant village girl, and after a sensational trial he was guillotined in the following year. It may perhaps have been the desire to place as great a distance as possible between himself and the memory of his notorious uncle which implanted in Balzac the first impulse to append the prefix of nobility to his name and invent for himself a different origin.

Bernard-François, the eldest of eleven children, had been destined by his father, an ordinary agricultural labourer, for the priesthood. The parish priest taught him to read and write, and even a certain amount of Latin, but the vigorous, energetic, ambitious youth showed little inclination for the tonsure and the vow of chastity. For a time he let himself drift in his native hamlet, helping out the local notary as a clerk or taking a hand in the work of the vineyards and behind the plough, but at the age of twenty he broke away for good. With the unyielding tenacity and driving force of the provincial, which were later to be depicted so powerfully and in such varying forms in the novels of his son, he burrowed his way into the life of the capital, inconspicuously at first, and lost among the innumerable young people who had come to Paris to make their fortunes without having any clear idea as to the way they were going to set about it or having any definite profession in view. In after years, when he had risen to be one of the notables of the province where he had settled, he asserted that he had been a secretary in the *conseil du roi* and even *avocat du roi* under Louis XVI, but this has long been unmasked as cheerful bombast on the part of the mendacious old story-teller, for none of the *almanachs du roi* records either a Balzac or a Balssa as having held such an office. It was the Revolution which carried this proletarian from the provinces, like so many others of his kind, on the crest of its wave, and he occupied some official position on the revolutionary municipal council of Paris, though he was wont to maintain a discreet silence about this particular stage of his career. It apparently enabled him to procure useful connections, however, and with his deep-rooted instinct for where money was to be made he found his way into that branch of the army where profits and perquisites would be likely to flow most abundantly, namely the department of war supplies and commissariat. From the commissariat golden threads stretched inevitably to the counting-houses of moneylenders and bankers. One day, after thirty years spent in obscure ways of making a living, Bernard-François once more changed horses and launched himself on a new career as first secretary in the banking firm of Daniel Doumerc in Paris.

At the age of fifty Father Balzac had at last accomplished the great metamorphosis—so frequently depicted by his son—which finally transformed a penniless, but restless and ambitious youth into a highly respected citizen, an upright member of "good society". Only now, with a modicum of capital and a secured position, had he reached the stage where he could take the next essential step which would turn the *petit bourgeois* into a bourgeois of the higher class before achieving the eventual longed-for consummation—a gentleman of private means. He would find himself a wife, a wife with a tidy dowry and of good bourgeois parentage. At the age of fifty-one, sound in wind and limb, of impressive appearance, skilled in drawing the long bow and a practised lady-killer, he cast his eyes upon the daughter of one of his chiefs at the bank. Anne Charlotte Laure Sallambier was thirty-two years younger than her wooer and possessed of somewhat romantic susceptibilities, but as a well-brought-up and dutiful daughter she obediently submitted to the advice of her parents, who proclaimed him to be a good catch. Though he was considerably her senior in years, his financial instinct was sound, and this was, in their view, the decisive factor. Having entered upon the married state, Father Balzac regarded it as beneath his dignity, to say nothing of not being sufficiently profitable, to continue to work for others. With a Napoleon in charge of the nation's fortunes, the business of war was likely to provide a speedier and more copious increase of revenue, so he made use of his old connections once more and, with the comfortable assurance of his wife's dowry to fall back upon in case of need, migrated to Tours as director of commissariat to the 22nd Division.

At this period, when their first son, Honoré, was born (on 20 May, 1799), the Balzacs were already prosperous and had been accepted as respected equals by the *haute bourgeoisie* of Tours. His commissariat duties appear to have provided Bernard-François with a good income, for the family, economising and speculating at the same time, now began to make something of a show. Very soon after the birth of Honoré they moved out of the narrow rue de l'Armée d'Italie into a house of their own. Until 1814, while the golden age of the Napoleonic campaigns lasted, they allowed themselves the provincial luxury of a private carriage and an ample staff of servants. The best society, even the aristocracy, frequented the house of the cottager's son who had once been a member of the red municipal council of Paris—among them the senator Clément de Ris, whose mysterious kidnapping was later to be described in detail in *Une ténébreuse affaire*, the baron de Pommereul, and Monsieur de Margonne, both of whom in after-years helped the struggling author in his most urgent need. Father Balzac was even called upon to take part in municipal activities and his opinion was asked when important decisions were to be made. In spite of his humble origin and obscure antecedents he had risen in this age of rapid careers and total upheaval to a position beyond reproach among the notables of the city.

Father Balzac's popularity is in every way comprehensible. He was a jovial man, of massive build, pleased with himself, with his success, and with the world in general. Though his speech was not distinguished by an aristocratic accent and though he cursed as lustily as any trooper and was not sparing of spicy anecdotes—some of his son's *Contes drolatiques* may perhaps be traced to this source—he was a magnificent spinner of yarns in which truth was frequently mingled with rhodomontade, constantly in good humour, and too shrewd in such changing times to burn his boats by irrevocably supporting either King, Emperor or Republic. Without having enjoyed the benefits of a sound schooling, he displayed a catholic interest in every direction and managed with the help of a varied taste in reading to accumulate an abundant stock of all-round knowledge. He even wrote a brochure or two, under such titles as *Mémoire sur le moyen de prévenir les vols et les assassinats* and *Mémoire sur le scandaleux désordre causé par les filles trompées et abandonnées*, though these works cannot of course be compared with those of his great son, any more than Father Goethe's Italian diary can be compared with Johann Wolfgang's *Italian Journey*. Bursting with health and filled with an undiluted joy in living, he was firmly determined to become a centenarian. After reaching the age of sixty he added a few illegitimate children to the four that had been born to him in wedlock, and in his eighties he was accused of being responsible for the pregnancy of a girl of loose reputation. No physician ever crossed his threshold in a professional capacity, and his determination to survive all his contemporaries was fortified by the fact that he was the recipient of an annuity from the so-called *Tontine Lafarge* which was increased proportionally whenever one of the other annuitants died. The same daemonic force which in the case of his son went to the myriad fashioning of life in a world of his own creation was concentrated by the father on his own physical survival. He had already outstripped all the other annuitants of the *Tontine Lafarge* and was drawing eight thousand francs a year when, at the age of eighty-three, he succumbed to a stupid accident. Otherwise, like his son, he might have achieved the impossible through sheer concentration of will.

❖⊃º⊂❖

If Honoré inherited his father's vitality and joy in telling stories, it was from his mother that he inherited his sensitiveness of feeling. Young as she was and though by no means unhappily married, she possessed the unfortunate quality of always feeling unhappy. Whereas her husband went through life cheerfully and unharassed, refusing to allow his wife's bickering and imaginary illnesses to disturb his imperturbable good-humour, Anne Charlotte Balzac was of that disagreeable type that displays its constant sense of injury in all the varied and scintillating hues of hysteria. She felt that she was not sufficiently loved, sufficiently respected or sufficiently honoured by any of the members of her family. She complained incessantly that her children were not sufficiently grateful to her for her noble self-sacrifice. Until the end of her life she never ceased to torment her already world-famous son with her "well meant" advice and lachrymose fault-finding. Yet she was by no means lacking either in intelligence or education. As a young girl she had been chosen to act as companion to the daughter of M. Doumerc, the banker, and this experience had endowed her with certain romantic inclinations. During those years she had imbibed a gushing enthusiasm for *belles lettres*, and in later life she showed a predilection for the mystic writings of Swedenborg and others. Her slight tinge of idealism was soon overshadowed, however, by an inborn apprehension with regard to money matters. Sprung from a typical Parisian *petit bourgeois* family, which filled its stocking sou by sou from a small hardware business, she brought into her marriage all the fusty, narrow instincts of her class, in particular a pedantic avaricé which was not incompatible with a greedy hankering for good investments and lucrative speculations. Bringing up children meant, so far as she was concerned, teaching them that spending money was a crime, while the earning of money was the most admirable of all virtues; urging them from the start to create for themselves a solid "position" in life or, if they were girls, to make a good marriage; affording them no personal freedom and keeping a strict eye on them all the time. With her importunate and watchful solicitude, with her peevish zeal for their alleged future welfare, she only succeeded in having a numbing effect on the whole family, in spite of her so-called good intentions. Years later, when he had long since grown to manhood, Balzac recalled how as a child he had always given a frightened start as soon as he heard her voice.

The measure of suffering inflicted on Balzac by this ill-humoured and inhibited mother of his, who coldly rejected any display of affection from her children, can be inferred from the bitter cry in one of his letters: "I have never had a mother." After this long passage of time it is hardly practicable to seek the hidden causes which induced Anne Charlotte Balzac to hold instinctively aloof from her first-born children, Honoré and Laure, though she spoiled the two younger ones, Laurence and Henri. Perhaps there was a transferred defensive reaction against her husband. It is, at any rate, certain that scarcely any mother can ever have shown such indifference and lack of affection towards her child. Hardly was her eldest son born before she had him removed from the house as if he were a leper. She was still in childbed at the time. The infant was handed over to the care of a nurse, the wife of a gendarme, with whom he remained until he was four years old. Even then, however, he was not permitted to return to his parents' house, spacious as it was, but was sent as a partial boarder to a family of strangers. Only once a week, on Sundays, was he allowed to visit his own family, as if they were distant relatives. They did not let him play with the younger children, he had no toys and received no presents. There was no mother to watch at his bedside when he was sick, and he never heard a tender word from her lips. When he nestled affectionately against her knee and wanted to embrace her, a stern rebuke checked any such attempt at intimacy as unseemly. At the age of seven the unwanted child was packed off to a boarding-school in Vendôme. Her sole desire was that he should be far away somewhere, far away in another town. When another seven years of almost unbearable discipline for the boy had come to an end with his return to his parents' house, she made life so painful for him ("*la vie si dure*", to use his own words) that when he reached the age of eighteen he turned his back of his own accord on an environment which had become intolerable.

Despite all the good nature which was such an indispensable part of him, he could never in his adult years forget the neglect he had experienced at the hands of his odd mother. Long afterwards, even after he had taken the tormentor of his childhood to live with him in his own house and his hair was already streaked with grey, he could not banish from his mind the memory of what she had done to him in those far-off years by the denial of her affection, and he poured out his heart to Madame de Hanska in a terrible cry of impotent revolt:

If you only knew what kind of a woman my mother is! She is a monster and a monstrous oddity at the same time. At the present moment she is engaged in driving my sister into the grave, after having been the ruin of my poor Laurence and my grandmother. She hates me for a number of reasons. She hated me even before I was born. I was on the verge of breaking with her; it had become almost a necessity. But I prefer to continue to suffer. It is a wound that admits of no healing. We believed she was mad and consulted a physician who has been on friendly terms with her for thirty-three years. But he said: "No! She is not mad. She is merely malicious." . . . My mother is the cause of all the ill that has befallen me in my life.

These words, bursting forth from him after many years, were his answer to the thousand secret tortures which had been inflicted on him at the most sensitive stage of his development by the very being who, by the laws of nature, should have been nearest to him and have shown him the tenderest devotion, yet who alone was to blame for his having suffered, as he himself phrased it, "the most dreadful childhood that has ever fallen to the lot of any man."

The six years which Balzac spent in the spiritual prison-house at Vendôme, the school of the Oratorian Brothers, are recorded in two very different documents,—the sober, official pages of the school register and the magnificent piece of literature entitled *Louis Lambert*. The school authorities merely made the prosaic entry:

No. 460, Honoré Balzac, aged eight years and one month. Has had smallpox, with no injurious after-effects. Constitution full-blooded, inclined to get overheated, and subject to occasional rises in temperature. Entered the school on 20 June, 1807, left on 22 August, 1813. Letters to be forwarded to Monsieur Balzac, his father, at Tours.

His schoolmates remembered him only as "*un gros enfant joufflu et rouge de visage*". All they could contribute to our knowledge of him at this time was some reference to his outward appearance or a few anecdotes of dubious authenticity. All the more moving, therefore, are the autobiographical pages of *Louis Lambert*, in which there is revealed to us the tragic inner life of a boy of genius whose torment was rendered doubly agonising by the very fact of his genius.

For this depiction of his own years of growth Balzac chose the device of the dual portrait. He is himself both Louis Lambert, the poet, and "Pythagore", the philosopher. Like the young Goethe in the figures of Faust and Mephistopheles, he split up his own personality, incorporating in two different characters the twin

fundamental aspects of his genius—the creative element which
formed living beings after the model of their prototypes, and the
regulating element which wanted to show the hidden laws working
themselves out in the great theatre of everyday life. In reality
Louis Lambert was a far truer picture of Balzac than was Pythagore, and the outward experiences at least of this seemingly
fictitious figure had been his own. Of the numerous reflections of
himself—Rafael in *La peau de chagrin*, d'Arthez in the *Illusions
perdues*, General Montereau in *L'histoire des treize*—none is so
complete and so palpably filled with personal experience as this
story of a child whose fate it was to be abandoned to the Spartan
discipline of an ecclesiastical boarding-school.

This institution, standing in the heart of the city of Vendôme
on the little River Loir, with its gloomy towers and massive walls,
presents even outwardly the appearance of a prison rather than
that of an educational establishment. From the day of entry the
two to three hundred pupils were subjected to strict monastic
discipline. There were no holidays and parents were allowed to visit
their children only in exceptional circumstances. During all those
years Balzac hardly ever went home, and in order to accentuate
the similarity to his own childhood experience he depicted Louis
Lambert as having neither father nor mother. The school fees,
which included not only tuition but also the cost of food and
clothing, were comparatively trifling, and the children were kept
unduly short of the barest necessities. Those who were not sent
gloves and warm underclothing by their parents—and thanks to
his mother's unconcern Balzac was among those who had to do
without these comforts—crept about in winter with frozen fingers
and chilblains on their feet. Particularly sensitive as he was both
physically and spiritually, Balzac-Lambert suffered more deeply
from the very outset than did his peasant school-mates:

> Accustomed to country air, to the freedom of an education that
> had been left to chance, to the tender care of an old man who
> had loved him dearly, to lie thinking in the sunshine, he found it
> exceedingly difficult to submit to the school regulations, to walk
> in file with other boys, to live within the four walls of a room
> where eighty young persons sat silently on wooden benches, each
> with a desk in front of him. His physical senses possessed a degree
> of acuteness which rendered them very delicate, and every fibre

of his being suffered under the constraint of this communal existence. The exhalations which poisoned the air, mingled with the odour of a classroom that was always filthy and in which the remains of the boys' meals were lying about, jarred on his sense of smell—the sense which more than all the others is closely linked with the cerebral system, so that any injury inflicted on it is bound to affect imperceptibly the organs of thought. Apart from these various contributions to the foulness of the air, there were lockers where each of us could keep his little treasures, such as the pigeons killed for feast-days or victuals that had been purloined surreptitiously from the refectory. There was also an enormous stone on which two buckets full of water were always standing, as a kind of trough at which we had to wash our hands and faces every morning, one after the other, in the presence of the teacher. From there we proceeded to a table where women combed our hair and powdered us. Our dormitory, which was only cleaned once a day, before we got up, was always dirty, and notwithstanding the numerous windows and high doorway, the air was always thick with the exhalations from the washplace, the corner where our hair was dressed, the lockers, the thousand occupations of each of the boys, and last but not least from our eighty bodies herded together. . . . The lack of the pure, fragrant air of the countryside in which he had lived hitherto, the change in his habits, the strict discipline—all this filled Lambert with sadness. With his chin propped on his left hand and his elbow resting on his desk, he whiled away the hours in his classroom with watching the green trees in the courtyard and the clouds in the sky. He appeared to be studying his lessons, but when the teacher noticed that his pen was not moving and the sheet of paper in front of him was still white, he would call out: "Lambert! You are idling."

The masters felt unconsciously that there was some force within this boy that resisted their influence. They did not realise that there was some process of an exceptional kind going on inside him, but were only aware that he was not reading and learning in the proper, normal way. They thought he was dull-witted or lazy, obstinate or dreamy, because he did not keep to the same jog-trot as the others, sometimes lagging behind and at others outstripping them with a single bound. In any case, none of the boys was whipped harder than he. He was constantly being punished. For him there were no hours of play or leisure. Imposition followed upon imposition, and he was kept in detention so frequently that during one period of two years he did not have more than six free days. Even more frequent and cruel was the physical chastisement, that *ultima ratio* of his stern preceptors, to which the greatest genius of his time was subjected:

This boy, so weak and yet so strong . . . drained the cup of both physical and spiritual suffering to the dregs. Chained to his desk like a galley-slave to his bench, beaten with rods and afflicted by illness, with every sense outraged, gripped as in a vice by an environment that was wholly repugnant to him, he was forced to yield his body that was merely his outward husk to the thousand tyrannies of the institution. . . . Of all our physical sufferings the most acute was undoubtedly that inflicted by a leather strap, about two fingers thick, which swished down upon our outstretched hands with all the strength and all the wrath that the teacher could bring to bear. In order to receive this punishment the culprit had to kneel down in the middle of the classroom, after having got up from his bench and walked to the teacher's desk under the curious and often mocking gaze of his schoolmates. These preliminaries heightened the torment for the more sensitive spirits, just as in olden days the procession from the gaol to the scaffold increased the ordeal of the condemned man. Some shrieked and wept hot tears both before and after the whipping, others endured the pain with a stoical expression, according to the character of each individual, but even the strongest-minded could scarcely suppress a convulsive twitching of his features as he waited for the first cut of the lash. Louis Lambert was singled out for innumerable thrashings, which he owed to a quality of his nature of which he was for long unaware. When he was suddenly jerked from his day-dreaming by the master's "Lambert! You are idling!" it often happened that he would flash at his interrupter a look of savage contempt that was charged with secret thoughts as a Leyden jar is charged with electricity. This exchange of looks must have given the master an uneasy feeling, and his resentment at the silent scorn in his pupil's eyes made him want to disabuse him of the habit. When the priest first became conscious of the contemptuous gleam that was like a lightning-flash aimed in his direction, he uttered the following comment which I have never forgotten— "If you don't stop looking at me like that, Lambert, you will get a thrashing!"

Not a single one of these harsh priests succeeded during all these years in discovering Balzac's secret. They saw in him only a pupil who lagged behind the others in Latin or in knowledge of vocabulary, and had no inkling of his uncanny capacity to grasp things before they were fully explained. They thought he was inattentive and uninterested, whereas they failed to realise that he was bored and fatigued by the lessons because they were too easy and that his apparent indolence was only exhaustion brought on by a *congestion d'idées*. It occurred to none of his teachers that this chubby-faced boy, this *"enfant gros et joufflu"*, had long since been carried away by his power of intellectual flight into other realms than the stuffy classroom, that he was the only one among all those young scholars who was in secret leading a dual existence.

This other world in which at the age of twelve and thirteen he had made his real home was the world of books. The librarian oi the polytechnic academy, who was giving him private lessons in mathematics—which is the reason why Balzac all his life possessed the worst head for figures to be found anywhere in the whole domain of literature—allowed the boy to take away any books he liked in order to read them at his leisure, though he could have had no idea of the immoderate extent to which the voracious young reader was taking advantage of the concession. These books were Balzac's salvation. They assuaged all the tortures and humiliations with which his years at school were oppressed. "If we had not been able to read the books from the library, which kept our minds alive, this system would have completely brutalised our lives." His actual life in school and playground faded into a twilight gloom, while his books gave him entry to a world that was for him now the only real one.

"From this moment," he says of Louis Lambert, his reflected image, "he developed a kind of ravenous hunger that he was unable to quench. He devoured books of every kind, he fed on works of theology, history, philosophy and science." In these secret hours of reading during his schooldays were laid the massive foundations of Balzac's later omniscience. A myriad facts and details were cemented together in his mind by a daemonically alert and prompt memory. Nothing perhaps illuminates the unique miracle of Balzac's perceptive faculty more clearly than his description of Louis Lambert's secret orgies of reading:

The assimilation of ideas through reading had in his case assumed phenomenal proportions. His eye took in seven or eight lines at a time, and their meaning was grasped by his mind with a rapidity that matched the swiftness of his eye. Frequently a single word sufficed to give him the sense of a whole sentence. His memory was marvellous. He could remember ideas acquired through reading no less accurately than those he had thought out for himself or heard in conversation. In short, his memory was not only of one type but of all types—memory for places, names, words, things, and faces. Not only could he remember anything he wanted to remember, but with his inward eye he saw them in the situation, the lighting, the colour in which they had once appeared to him in reality. He was gifted with this same faculty so far as the incomprehensible processes of reasoning were concerned. He remembered, to use his own expression, not only the way in which ideas were arranged in the book where he had first come across them, but also the states of his own soul at various periods far back in time. His memory, that is to say, possessed the incredible power of recalling the different stages through which his mind had passed and the whole activity which had contributed to its make-up—from the first thoughts which had entered it to the most recent idea that it had grasped, the most involved as well as the most simple. His brain, accustomed from an early age to the intricate mechanism which renders possible the concentration of human forces, absorbed from this rich storehouse an abundance of images which, in their remarkable clarity and freshness, constituted the nourishment of his mind during his hours of vivid contemplation. At the age of twelve his imagination, stimulated by continual practice, had developed to a pitch which enabled him to form such accurate conceptions of things he only knew about from books that their image could not have been more clearly present to his mind if he had, in fact, actually seen them. He either reasoned from analogies or else was endowed with a kind of second sight which enabled him to comprehend the whole orbit of Nature.

"When I read a description of the Battle of Austerlitz," he said to me one day, "I saw everything that was happening. The salvoes of the guns and the shouting of the soldiers rang in my ears and stirred me to the depths; I could smell the powder and hear the trotting of the horses as well as the voices of the men; I gazed down on the plain where armed nations were locked in battle, just as if I were standing on the hill of Santon, and the spectacle appeared to me terrible as a passage out of the Apocalypse.''

When every fibre of his being was concentrated in this way on what he was reading, he seemed to lose consciousness of his physical existence and functioned only by means of his inner faculties, whose scope became abnormally extended. To use his own expression, he "left space behind him.''

And after such ecstatic flights into the infinite, with their rapturous exhaustion of his spirit, the weary boy had to sit in his hated monastic garb with peasant lads whose dull brains plodded on laboriously in the wake of the teacher's discourse as if they were following the plough. With his mind still excited by the most esoteric problems, he was expected to keep his attention fixed on *mensa, mensam, mensae* and the rules of Latin grammar. Relying upon his superior intellectual capacity, which enabled him to learn a page by heart merely by scanning it once, he did not bother to listen to what the master was saying, but continued to reflect on the ideas that he had discovered in his books. This contempt for the actual physical world in which he lived generally cost him dear:

Our memory was so good that we never took the trouble to prepare our tasks. We only had to listen to our schoolmates reciting the French or Latin passages, or repeating the grammatical rules, in order to be able to do the same. Unfortunately, however, it sometimes occurred to the master to change the sequence in which he usually called upon the boys, and to call upon us first, and in that case we frequently did not even know what the task was. The most ingenious excuses did not avail to ward off the inevitable imposition, which was in turn neglected until the last possible moment. If there was a book that we wanted to finish reading or if we had lost ourselves in daydreams, the imposition was forgotten and this led to the infliction of further punishment tasks!

The precocious boy was subjected to increasingly severe chastisement, until at last he was not spared even the *culotte de bois*, the medieval stocks to which honest Kent was condemned in *King Lear*. Only when he experienced a nervous breakdown—the nature of the ailment which secured his release from the monastery school has never been discovered—was he able to leave this prison-house of his childhood where he suffered *"par tous les points où la douleur a prise sur l'âme et sur la chair"*.

◁◦▷

This eventual redemption from mental serfdom is preceded in the *Histoire intellectuelle* of Louis Lambert by an episode which is in all probability not wholly fictitious. Balzac describes how his *alter ego*, the imaginary Louis Lambert, at the age of twelve wrote a *Traité de la volonté*, a philosophical treatise on psycho-physical associations, which was snatched away from him by malicious schoolmates who resented his *"muette aristocratie"*. The most feared martinet among the teachers, the *"terrible père Haugoult"*, who was the scourge of his boyhood, heard the tumult, took possession of the manuscript, and disposed of it to a waste-paper dealer *"sans connaître l'importance des trésors scientifiques dont les germes avortés se dissipèrent en d'ignorantes mains"*. The scene is described with a moving faithfulness of detail, including the impotent fury of the outraged boy, which makes it unlikely that it could have been wholly invented. Did Balzac, however, undergo an experience of this kind with some youthful literary effort or did he really compose at this early age the *Traité de la volonté* whose idea and principles he sets forth in such detail? Was he already so precociously productive that he could venture to set his hand to a work of this sort? Was it Balzac, the real boy Balzac, who composed this treatise, or was it only the fictitious Louis Lambert, the spiritual brother of his imagination?

These are questions that can never be satisfactorily answered. It is certain, however, that in his youth—for the focus of a thinker's basic ideas is always to be found in his years of growth—Balzac did think of writing such a treatise before he gave concrete form to the innumerable aspects of the driving-power and constitution of the human will in the characters of his *Comédie humaine*. It would otherwise be too much of a coincidence that in his first novel, *La peau de chagrin*, the hero also works at a *Traité de la volonté*. The plan to discover the *"lois générales dont la formule sera peut-être ma gloire"* must have been the central idea, the *"idée mère"* which dominated Balzac's youth, and we have more solid grounds than mere speculation for assuming that the first incentive to study the psycho-physical relations between mind and body came to him during his schooldays. One of his masters, named Dessaignes, who like so many of his contemporaries had succumbed to the spell of the misunderstood theories of Mesmer and Gall, was the author of a work entitled *Etudes de l'homme moral fondées sur les rapports de ses facultés avec son organisme*. There can be no doubt that he communicated his ideas on this subject to his pupils and awakened in the only boy of genius that his class contained the ambition likewise to become a *"chimiste de la volonté"*. The popular conception at that time of a kinetic sovereign substance satisfied his unconscious urge to discover the method which lay behind the seeming disorder of the universe. Obsessed all his life by the overwhelming abundance of psychical phenomena, Balzac attempted long before the *Comédie humaine* to transform this grandiose chaos into an outwardly ordered system and to schedule its laws or components with a view to establishing the conditions underlying the activity of the spirit, just as Cuvier had done with regard to the animal kingdom. Whether, however, he set down his views in writing at such an improbably early age is hardly likely to be ascertained. That at any rate the rather confused axioms propounded in Louis Lambert's *Traité de la volonté* were not those of the twelve-year-old Balzac is proved by the fact that they were lacking in the first version of the novel (1832) and were only inserted in the later editions in a somewhat improvised manner.

❧◦❧

When he left school so suddenly at the age of fourteen, he saw his parents' house practically for the first time since he was born. His father and mother, who in the meantime had only received him on occasional visits as if he had been a distant relation, found him completely changed both outwardly and inwardly. In place of the chubby, robust, good-humoured *"enfant gros et joufflu"*, there returned after more than six years of monastic discipline a haggard, highly-strung lad with large, scared eyes. He returned like someone who had passed through a dreadful and unspeakable experience. His sister later described his bearing as that of a sleepwalker groping his way along with vacant gaze. He hardly heard when anybody asked him a question, but sat about in a

3

dreamy state and aggravated his mother by the reserve with which he concealed his secret feeling of superiority. Eventually—as in all the crises of his life—his inherited vitality gained the upper hand. He again grew cheerful and talkative, too much so in fact for his mother's liking. To supplement the education he had already acquired, he was sent to the grammar school at Tours, and when the family moved from Tours to Paris at the end of 1814 he entered the boarding-school of Monsieur Lepitre. This Monsieur Lepitre, when he was the Citoyen Lepitre in the days of the Revolution, had been a friend of Balzac's father when the latter was a member of the radical municipal council of Paris, and he had earned himself a tiny niche in history by being one of the leaders among those who took part in the attempt to rescue Marie Antoinette from the Conciergerie. Now he was merely the worthy head of an institution dedicated to the task of assisting young gentlemen to get through their examinations. In this boarding-school, too, with nobody to lavish on him the affection which he needed, the boy was pursued by the oppressive feeling of having been cast out and abandoned. And so he put the following words into the mouth of Rafael, the other reflection of his youthful self, in *La peau de chagrin*:

> The sufferings I had endured at home among my own family and at school were now renewed in a different form during my sojourn at the *Pension Lepitre*. My father had not given me any pocket-money whatsoever. My parents were completely content at the thought that I was being fed, clothed, and stuffed full of Latin and Greek. While living in boarding-schools I got to know some thousand or so schoolmates, but I cannot recall in any single case ever having come across a similar instance of utter unconcern on the part of a boy's parents.

Here also Balzac failed to distinguish himself as a "good pupil", evidently owing to his inward resistance, and his vexed parents sent him to yet another educational establishment, where he fared no better. In a class of about thirty-five boys he came thirty-second in Latin, a result which confirmed his mother in her suspicion that Honoré was a "*raté*", that he had turned out a failure. She therefore addressed to the seventeen-year-old lad, in the lachrymose, self-pitying tone which was to drive him to despair many years later when he was fifty, the following exemplary epistle:

My dear Honoré,

I can find no words strong enough to describe to you the grief which you are causing me. You are making me really unhappy, though I am doing all I can for my children and ought to expect that they should make me happy!

The good and worthy Monsieur Gancer has informed me that you have dropped down to the thirty-second place in translation!!! . . . He told me that you again behaved very naughtily a few days ago. So all the pleasure I had promised myself to-morrow has again been spoilt. . . .

We were to have met to-morrow at eight o'clock. We should have had our midday meal and supper together, and we could have had such a nice talk together and told one another all sorts of things. And now your lack of industry, your wantonness, your neglect of your studies compel me to leave you to your just punishment. How empty my heart is now! How long the journey will seem to me! I am keeping from your father the fact that you have got such a bad place in your class, for you certainly won't be allowed to go out on Monday, though your day off from school was intended to serve a useful purpose and by no means merely your personal pleasure. The dancing master is coming to-morrow at half-past four. I will have you fetched and taken back after your lesson. I should be remiss in the duty imposed on me by my love for my children if I were to treat you any differently.

In spite of his mother's sinister premonitions, however, and the denunciations she heaped on him, he managed by hook or by crook to complete his studies. On the 4th of November, 1816, he matriculated at the University as a student of jurisprudence.

This day, the 4th of November, 1816, ought rightfully to have signified the end of his servitude and the dawn of freedom for the young student. He should have been able to pursue his studies with a sense of independence and utilise his leisure hours as he felt inclined. But his parents had other views. A young man ought not to have any leisure hours. No minute of his time should be regarded as superfluous. He ought to earn money. It would be enough if he went to occasional lectures at the university during the day and studied the pandects at night. During the daytime he ought to have a profession as well. Not a single hour must be wasted in preparing himself for his future career. Not a single unnecessary sou must be expended. So while he studied at the University Balzac had to drudge as a clerk in the office of the advocate Monsieur Guyonnet de Merville, who was, by the way, the first of his employers for whom he willingly showed appreciation and whom he has gratefully immortalised under the name of Derville because he had the intelligence to recognise his clerk's quality and generously accorded the younger man his friendship. Two years later Balzac was handed on to a notary called Passez, a friend of the Balzac family, and therewith his future as an industrious citizen seemed assured. On the 4th of January Honoré, now at last launched on a "normal" path, obtained his baccalauréat. Soon he would assume the functions of partner to the worthy notary, and when Maître Passez grew old or died his young partner would take sole charge of the office. Then he would marry—into a wealthy family of good standing, of course—and thus finally do honour to his mistrustful mother, to all the Balzacs and Sallambiers, and to whatever other relatives he might possess. His biography would then have been something which only Flaubert could have written, as the exemplar of an honourable and normal bourgeois career. He would have been another Monsieur Bouvard or Pécuchet. But now the flame of revolt, subdued and smothered all these years, flared up in Balzac's breast. One day in the spring of 1819 he suddenly leapt from his stool in the notary's office and abandoned the dusty files that lay open on his desk. He had had enough of this kind of existence, which had never allowed him a day of freedom and happiness. For the first time in his life he held up his head and resolutely opposed his will to that of his family, declaring without more ado that he was not going to be an advocate or a notary or a judge or accept any official appointment whatsoever. He did not, in fact, want to enter any of the bourgeois professions. He was resolved to become an author and, by virtue of his future masterpieces, to achieve independence, wealth and fame.

CHAPTER II

Premature Questioning of Destiny

> My sufferings have added years to my life. . . . You cannot possibly imagine the kind of life I led until I was twenty-two.
>
> Letter to the duchesse d'Abrantès, in 1828.

Honoré's sudden announcement that he wanted to become an author, and not a lawyer, struck like a thunderbolt into the midst of his unsuspecting family. To give up an assured career! A Balzac, a grandchild of the highly respected Sallambiers, devoting himself to such a questionable craft as authorship! Where were the guarantees, where were the assurances that he would be able to earn a steady, reliable income? Literature! Poetry! This was a superfluous luxury in which a Vicomte de Chateaubriand could indulge, with his handsome château somewhere in Brittany, or a Monsieur de Lamartine, or the son of General Hugo, but not the insignificant offspring of a middle-class family. In any case, when had this undutiful youth ever shown the faintest sign of talent in that direction? Had anyone ever read a neatly composed essay of his? Had his poems ever been printed in the local news-sheet? Never! In all the various schools he had attended his place had been on the dunces' bench. He had come thirty-second in Latin, to say nothing of his performance in mathematics, which after all was the most important of the sciences for every honest business man.

Furthermore, the announcement came at an unpropitious moment, for the financial affairs of Father Balzac had just got into a somewhat tangled state. The Bourbon Restoration, which brought with it the cessation of the European struggle, had thereby dug up the roots on which all the petty blood-sucking parasites of war had fed throughout the lucrative Napoleonic years. For army contractors and war profiteers a bleak time had come. Father Balzac's fat salary of eight thousand francs had been cut down to a meagre pension, and to add to his difficulties he had been amply fleeced in the matter of the liquidation of the banking-house of Doumerc and in other speculative undertakings. The family could still be called comfortably off, and there were in any case, as we shall see later, a good few thousand laid away for a rainy day, but among the *petite bourgeoisie* it was an unwritten law, more strictly adhered to than any law of the State, that every reduction of income must be counterbalanced at once by a double measure of economy. The Balzacs had decided to give up their residence in Paris and to move to a cheaper locality, to Villeparisis, about twenty kilometres from the capital, where a reduction in their standard of living could be carried out less conspicuously. And this was the very juncture chosen by their simple-minded son, whom they had at last thought to be off their hands for good, to make the startling announcement not only that he wanted to become an author but that he expected his parents to finance him in his idleness.

It was out of the question! His parents were firmly agreed upon this point, and they rallied to their support friends and relations, who, of course, unanimously pronounced against the presumptuous whim of the young ne'er-do-well. Father Balzac was the one who exhibited the most equable temper in the matter. He did not like family scenes and eventually growled a good-natured, "Why not?" An old adventurer and gambler himself, who had changed his profession a dozen times and only settled down to a snug bourgeois existence late in his career, he could not summon up any fervent indignation at the extravagant ideas of his strange offspring. Honoré's favourite sister, Laure, was also on his side, though secretly. She had a romantic inclination for poetry, and the idea of having a famous brother was flattering to her vanity. What appeared as an honour in the dreams of the daughter, however, was in the eyes of the more prosaic mother a deep disgrace. How could she hold up her head before her relatives when they became apprised of the calamitous news that a son of Madame Balzac, née

Sallambier, had become a writer of books or a contributor to the newspapers? With all the loathing of the bourgeoisie for a way of living that lacked solid foundations she launched into the fray. Never! Never! This indolent wretch, who had never been any good at school, must not be allowed to indulge foolish fancies that could not earn him his bread. The fees and charges for his legal training had been paid in hard cash. Once and for all a stop must be put to such a ludicrous project.

Now, however, she encountered for the first time a strength of resistance which she had never suspected in her good-natured, easy-going son—the unbending, unshakable will-power of Honoré de Balzac, which, now that Napoleon was broken, had not its match in Europe. What Balzac wanted became for him the only reality, and when he had made up his mind he was able to achieve the impossible. Neither tears nor enticements nor entreaties nor fits of hysteria could persuade him to change his plans. He intended to become a great writer, not a notary—and the world is his witness that he attained his ambition. After a hard struggle which lasted for days the family reached a typically bourgeois compromise. The great experiment was set upon a sound basis. Honoré was to have his way. He was to be allowed to put to the test his ability to become a great and famous author, but how this was to be done was his own affair. The family would invest a strictly limited capital in the dubious undertaking. His parents would be prepared to subsidise Honoré's questionable talent for not more than two years, and if he had not become a great and famous author by the end of that period he would have to return to his stool in the notary's office, otherwise they would withdraw their support from their prodigal son. The father and his child drew up a strange contract. On the closely calculated basis of a minimum standard of living, the parents bound themselves to pay 120 francs per month, that is to say, four francs per day, towards their son's maintenance during his voyage in search of immortality. This was the best piece of business, more profitable than all his army contracts and financial speculations, to which Father Balzac had ever put his name.

The self-willed mother had for the first time been compelled to yield to a will stronger than her own, and we can imagine the despair with which she did so, for she was sincerely convinced that her son was ruining his life in the obstinate pursuit of a chimera. Her foremost task now was to conceal from the worthy Sallambiers the fact that Honoré had abandoned his respectable profession and was making this absurd attempt to stand on his own feet. In order to cover up his departure for Paris, she informed her relations that for reasons of health he had gone south to stay with a cousin. It was her hope either that he would soon discard as a passing fancy the ridiculous career he had chosen, or perhaps that her undutiful son would come to realise his foolishness, so that no one need hear of the unhappy escapade which was likely to damage his reputation, ruin his prospects of marriage, and lose him his legal clientèle. In preparation for all eventualities, however, she quietly made her plans. Since kindness and prayers were of no avail in dissuading this stubborn son of hers from embarking on the scandalous *métier* he had chosen, she must try cunning and tenacity. He must be starved out. He should see how comfortable things had been at home and how warm he had been in the well-heated notary's office. When he had to tighten his belt in Paris it would not be long before his grandiloquent schemes collapsed. When his fingers grew numb with cold in his garret, he would soon stop his stupid scribbling. Under the pretext of looking after his welfare as a mother should, she accompanied him to Paris in order to help him rent a room, but the room she selected for him was the poorest, the most wretched, the most uncomfortable lodging to be found even in the slums of Paris. Her object was to soften his determination and break his will.

❧⊃∘⊂❧

No. 9 rue Lesdiguières has long since been torn down, and this is a pity, for Paris would have had no finer monument to passionate self-sacrifice than this dismal garret, a description of which is to be found in *La peau de chagrin*. A dark, evil-smelling staircase led five flights up to a broken-down door roughly carpentered from a few planks. On opening this door one groped one's way into a low, dark attic that was icy cold in winter and scorching in summer. Even at a nominal rental of five francs a month—three sous a day—the landlady had not been able to find anyone willing to live in such a den, yet it was just "this hole, worthy to be compared with the leads of Venice", which his mother selected in order to inspire the budding author with a distaste for his new profession.

There could be nothing more detestable (Balzac wrote some years later in *La peau de chagrin*), than this garret with its dirty yellow walls that reeked of misery. . . .

The roof slanted almost to the floor, and the sky was visible through loose tiles. . . . My lodging cost me three sous a day and the oil I burnt at night cost another three sous. I looked after the room myself. I wore flannel shirts because I could not afford the two sous a day for laundry. I used coal for heating, the cost of which spread over the whole year worked out at about two sous a day. . . . All these outgoings together did not amount to more than eighteen sous, leaving me two sous for unforeseen expenses. I do not remember during this long and wretched sojourn in the Pont des Arts ever having paid for the water I used. I fetched it for myself every morning from the fountain in the Place St. Michel. . . . During the first ten months of my monastic solitude I lived in this way in poverty and seclusion, my own master and my own servant. With indescribable ardour I lived the life of a Diogenes.

With calculated solicitude Balzac's mother did nothing whatsoever to make this prison cell more comfortable and homelike. The sooner her son was driven by discomfort to return to a normal way of living, the better. So Balzac was provided only with the most indispensable articles necessary to furnish his garret, and these came from the family lumber-room—a hard, flat bed "like a miserable trestle", a small oak table covered with tattered leather, and two old chairs. That was all. A bed to sleep in, a table to work on, and somewhere to sit. Even his most passionate desire, to be allowed to hire a small piano, was not acceded to, and after a few days he had to write home begging for "white cotton stockings, grey worsted stockings, and a handkerchief". When he procured for himself a "*gravure*" and a "*glace carrée et dorée*", his mother wrote to Laure bidding her reprimand her brother for his "extravagance".

Balzac's imagination, however, was a thousandfold stronger than

the reality of his environment. His eye could invest the most unpretentious object with a lively interest and exalt the hideous.
Even the dismal view from his den over the grey roofs of Paris
afforded him consolation. To quote again from *La peau de chagrin*:

> I remember how I joyfully dipped my bread in my bowl of milk
> as I sat before my window and breathed in the fresh air. My eyes
> roamed over a landscape of brown, red and light grey roofs of
> slate or tiles covered with green or yellowish moss. At first this
> prospect struck me as monotonous, but soon I discovered
> peculiar beauties in it. There was the evening illumined by the
> rays of the sun, with the ill-fitting shutters of the windows out-
> lined as black hollows in this strange landscape, or the pale
> gleam of the street lamps which down below cast their yellowish
> reflections through the fog and with their faint accusing light
> mirrored the undulations of the crowded roofs on the pavements
> like a misty sea of architecture. Now and then queer figures
> emerged in the heart of this gloomy wilderness. Amid the flowers
> of some roof-garden I saw the sharp, hooked profile of an old
> woman watering her nasturtiums. Silhouetted in the crumbling
> frame of an attic window a young girl at her toilet thought that
> she was unobserved. I could only see her handsome brow and the
> long plaits that she was lifting into the light with graceful white
> arms. I gazed with pleasure at the ephemeral vegetation in the
> gutters of the roofs, pitiful weeds that some gust of wind had
> perhaps carried up to such a height. I studied the mosses and
> their colours vivified by the rain, which turned to dry velvet in
> the sun, brown with whimsical shadings. Finally the poetic and
> fleeting impressions of the day, the sadness of the mist, the
> sudden emergence of the sun, the silent magic of the night, the
> mysteries of sunrise, the smoke of the chimneys—all these
> happenings in the queer domain of Nature became familiar to
> me and kept me amused. I loved my prison-cell. I stayed there
> because I wanted to. These savannahs of Paris, formed out of
> the monotonous roofs that stretched like a vast plain above the
> abyss of life below, entered into my soul and mingled with my
> phantasies.

When he left his room on a fine day to indulge in the only pleasure he could allow himself, since it cost nothing, namely to stroll
along the Boulevard Bourdon towards the Faubourg St. Antoine
drawing fresh air into his lungs, this brief walk was a stimulus and
a spiritual experience:

One single passion snatched me from my studies—but was it not
really part of those studies? I began to observe the activity of
the Faubourg, its inhabitants, its characters. As badly dressed
as the workers of the quarter, indifferent to outward appearances, I mixed among them without their showing any reserve
towards me. I could join their groups, watch them shopping, and
listen to their discussions on their way home from work. Observation soon became a matter of intuition with me, I looked into
their souls without failing to notice externals, or rather I grasped
these external features so completely that I straightway saw
beyond them. My method of observation endowed me with the
capacity to share in the life of the individual in question just
as he lived it; it permitted me to put myself in his place in the
same way that the dervish in the *Arabian Nights* assumed the
form and the soul of the people over whom he uttered his magic
incantation. . . .

I understood these people's ways, I espoused their way of life,
I felt their rags on my shoulders, I walked with my feet in their
tattered shoes; their desires and their distress penetrated my
soul, or my soul passed into theirs. It was like a waking dream.
With them I flew into a passion at the employers who tyrannised
over them, or at the malicious trickery which compelled them
to return many times before they were paid their wages. I entertained myself by giving up my own habits, by transmuting
myself into somebody else in a kind of intoxication of my moral
forces, and by playing this game as often as I liked. To whom do
I owe this gift? Is it a kind of second sight? Is it a quality which
by abuse can border on madness? I have never explored the
sources of this power. I possessed it and I used it—that was all.
It mattered only that since that time I was able to analyse into
its component parts the elements of that compound mass which
we call "the people". I had analysed them and was able to
distinguish between their good and their bad qualities. I knew
well the importance to me of this Faubourg, this seminary of
revolutions, with its heroes, its inventors, its men of practical
wisdom, its rogues and criminals, its virtues and vices, all
hemmed in by misery, subdued by poverty, steeped in wine and
ruined by brandy. You cannot possibly imagine what innumerable adventures unfold themselves unnoticed in this city of
pain, what swiftly forgotten dramas! What terrible and yet what
beautiful things one sees here! Imagination cannot hold a candle
to the reality which lies hidden here and is never discovered. One

has to dive down too deeply in order to find these remarkable dramas, these tragedies or comedies, these masterpieces born of chance. (*Facino Cane.*)

The books in his room, the people in the streets, and an eye that was capable of penetrating everything, whether thoughts or happenings, these were enough to construct a world of his own. From the moment when Balzac began to write, there was nothing real around him but that which he had himself created.

◇⌒◦⌒◇

The first few days of his bitterly purchased freedom were employed by Balzac in preparing his abode for his literary labours, the dismal abode which was to be the scene of his immortality. He did not scorn to whitewash and paper the spotted walls with his own hands. He arranged the few books he had brought with him, fetched others from the library, piled into a neat heap the sheets of white paper which were to receive the masterpiece he was about to write, cut himself some pens, bought a candle for which an empty bottle provided the candlestick, and procured oil for the lamp that was to be the nocturnal sun shining in the infinite desert of his toil.

Everything was ready now—excepting for one not inconsiderable trifle. The hopeful writer had no idea what he was going to write about. His astonishing resolve to bury himself in a cave and not leave it until a masterpiece was perfected had sprung from a mere instinct. Now that he was ready to begin he had no definite plan of work, or rather, he was groping vaguely among a hundred unfermented plans. At the age of twenty-one he had not clearly made up his mind what he really was and what he wanted to become, whether a philosopher, a poet, a novelist, a dramatist, or a man of science. He was conscious of the force within him, but did not know in which direction to apply it: "I felt within myself the faith that I had an idea to express, a system to construct, a science to expound." But to what idea, what system, what literary *genre* was he to devote his genius? The magnetic pole of his spirit was as yet undiscovered, and the compass needle of his will was oscillating restlessly to and fro. He scanned the manuscripts he had brought with him. They were all fragments, none was complete, and he could not find among them the right springboard for his leap into immortality. There were a few pages with such labels as *Notes sur l'immortalité de l'âme*, or *Notes sur la philosophie et la religion*, which were partly lecture and reading notes and partly his own rough drafts in which the only thing that strikes the eye to-day is the memo: "I shall take this up again after I have finished my tragedy." There were also some scattered verses, the beginning of a rhymed epic called *Saint Louis*, preliminary sketches for a tragedy, *Sylla*, and for a comedy, *Les deux philosophes*. For a time he had planned a novel, *Coqsigrue*, an epistolary novel, *Sténie ou les erreurs philosophiques*, and another "*dans le genre antique*" entitled *Stella*. During an interlude he had worked on the draft of a comic opera, *Le corsaire*. As he proceeded with his disappointing survey Balzac grew more and more uncertain how to begin. Was it to be a system of philosophy, an opera libretto, a romantic epic, or a novel that would carry the name of Balzac out into the world? The primary need, however, was to write something, whatever it was, to bring something to completion that would make him famous and free him from dependence on his parents. With the furious zest that was part of his nature he delved into innumerable books with the dual aim of finding a theme and learning from others the technique of craftsmanship: "I did nothing but study and develop my style, until I thought I should lose my reason," he wrote to Laure. Gradually time began to press. Two months went by while he searched and tried his prentice hand, and the yield was pitifully meagre. So the plan to produce a philosophical work was postponed, presumably because it would have involved too much labour and not have been sufficiently profitable. He did not, on the other hand, feel that his powers were yet adequate for a novel. There remained the drama. It would, of course, have to be an historical, a neo-classic drama such as Schiller, Alfieri and Marie-Joseph Chénier had brought into fashion, something suitable for the Comédie Française. Once more he ploughed through dozens of volumes from the circulating library. He must have a theme! He would have given a kingdom for a theme!

At last his choice was made. On the 6th of September, 1819, he reported to his sister:

I have at long last decided to take *Cromwell* as my theme, because he provides the finest material in modern history. Since setting

to work on this theme and turning it over in my mind, I have
become immersed in it to the verge of losing consciousness of all
else. Ideas are accumulating in my brain, but I am being continually held up by my lack of talent for writing verse. . . . Listen,
sister, and tremble! I shall need at least another seven to eight
months to put the play into rhyme, to elaborate my ideas, and
then to polish the whole. . . . Oh, if you only knew how the
difficulties pile up in such a work! The great Racine—and this
should give you an adequate picture—spent two years polishing
his *Phèdre*, which is the despair of every poet. Two years! Two
whole years!—Think of it! Two years!

But now there was no going back: "Without genius I am lost!"
So he had to have genius. For the first time Balzac had set himself
a definite task and staked his unconquerable will on the issue.
When this will-power of his was brought into play, there was
nothing that could resist it. Balzac knew that he would finish
Cromwell because he was resolved to finish it and because it had to
be finished:

I am determined to complete my *Cromwell* even if I burst in the
attempt. I must have something ready before Mamma comes
and demands from me an account of the way I have spent my
time.

⋖〰∘〰⋗

Balzac threw himself into his work with that obsessed energy
which, as he once said, even his bitterest enemies had to admit.
For the first time he ordained for himself that monastic and even
Trappist seclusion to which he strictly adhered during every period
of intensive work throughout his life. Day and night he sat writing
at his table, and frequently he did not leave his room for three or
four days at a time. Even then he only went out to buy bread.
fruit and a further supply of coffee, which was the indispensable
stimulant for his overworked nerves. Gradually the winter drew on
and his fingers, always sensitive to the cold, threatened to grow
too numb to write in the draughty, unheated garret. Yet his
fanatical will did not yield. He did not stir from the table, where he
sat with his feet covered up in an old woollen rug of his father's
and his chest protected by a flannel waistcoat. From his sister he

begged "some old shawl" to wrap round his shoulders while he worked, and from his mother a cap which he asked her to knit for him. In order to save fuel, which was expensive, he stayed in bed for days at a time so that he could continue the writing of his immortal tragedy. None of these disagreeable concomitants of authorship was able to break down his resolution, and the only thing that made him tremble with apprehension was his expenditure on lamp-oil, because when the days grew short he had to light his lamp at three o'clock in the afternoon. Otherwise he did not mind if it was day or night. They both served him equally well for his work.

During all this time there were no pleasures, no women, no visits to restaurant or coffee-house, no relaxation whatsoever as a relief from his tremendous exertion. A natural timidity, which he was unable for a long time to throw off, kept him from seeking the company of women. In his various boarding-schools he had lived only among boys and he knew that he was awkward. He could not dance, had not learned to move in good society, and was aware that owing to his parents' economies he was badly dressed. Moreover, now that he was on the threshold of manhood, he looked unprepossessing no less in his physical appearance than in the neglect of his person. An acquaintance who knew him during those years even says that he was conspicuously ugly:

Balzac at that time was particularly and strikingly ugly, in spite of the intelligence which sparkled in his small eyes. A stout, thick-set figure, untidy black hair, bony features, a large mouth and defective teeth.

Since he had to turn over every sou three times before allowing it to leave his fingers, he lacked the most essential prerequisite for the making of friends. So far as the coffee-houses were concerned, which were the meeting places of young writers and journalists, he could do no more than stand outside and look at his own hungry face mirrored in the window-panes. Even the restaurants were closed to him. Of all the joys and splendours that the teeming city had to offer, every distraction, even the most fleeting, was beyond the reach of the voluntary hermit in the rue Lesdiguières.

One man alone took an occasional interest in the lonely writer. This was "*le petit père Dablin*". As an old friend of the family this

worthy citizen, a wholesale ironmonger by trade, made it his duty
to concern himself in some small degree with the fortunes of the
poor literary aspirant. Gradually there developed a touchingly
solicitous affection on the part of the older man for the forlorn
youth, and the friendship which sprang from this lasted for the
whole of Balzac's life. Though he was only a small suburban
merchant, this worthy man possessed a deep reverence for literature. The Comédie Française was his temple, and often when the
prosaic routine of his ironmongery was concluded for the day he
would take the young author with him to see a play. These evenings, when the splendour of Racine's verses was preceded by a
copious meal, provided the sole stimulant for the mind and body
of his grateful guest. Every week little Père Dablin bravely climbed
the five flights of stairs that led to the garret of his protégé, with
whom, as a means of self-education, he pored over Latin exercises.
Balzac, who had hitherto known in his own family only the ingrained instinct to save money and the petty ambition of the
petite bourgeoisie, recognised in him the hidden moral strength that
provides a purer motive force in such obscure figures of the middle
classes than is to be found in all the professional ranters and
scribblers of literature. And when later on, in *César Birotteau*,
Balzac intoned his Song of Songs in praise of the honest everyday
citizen, he added in gratitude a strophe in honour of this friend who
was the first to succour him, who with his "entirely inward power
of sympathy, that was both unrhetorical and unexaggerated" had
understood and assuaged the distress of his youthful uncertainties.
In the character of the kindly, modest, unassuming notary
Pillerault the lovable figure of "*le petit père Dablin*" has been
brought close to us. In spite of the narrow horizon with which his
daily life encompassed him, he realised intuitively that Balzac was
a genius ten years before Paris, the literary critics, and the world
in general had made up their minds to acknowledge him.

Yet though he could at intervals relieve the intensity of Balzac's
outward solitude, he could do nothing to lessen the fateful inward
uncertainty that tormented the literary novice. Balzac wrote and
wrote, with throbbing temples and fevered fingers, in an intoxication of impatience, for his *Cromwell* had to be finished in a few
weeks' time whatever the cost. But he experienced those lucid
moments, so terrifying to every beginner who has neither friends

nor advisers, when he was beset by doubts of himself, of his
capacities, of the work with which he was wrestling. Incessantly
he asked himself the question: "Have I enough talent?" and in
one of his letters he implored his sister not to mislead him by
sympathetic praise:

> By the sisterly love you bear me I conjure you never to say:
> "that is good!" when you write to me about one of my works.
> You must only point out my defects, and keep your praise to
> yourself.

In his youthful ardour he was resolved to produce nothing mediocre, nothing banal. "To the devil," he cried, "with the commonplace! One must become a Grétry, a Racine!"

Sometimes, it is true, when enveloped in the fiery cloud of
literary creation, he thought his *Cromwell* excellent, and he
proclaimed proudly: "My tragedy shall become the breviary of
kings and nations. I intend to make my début with a masterpiece
or break my neck in the attempt." Then came another access of
despair: "My distress all springs from the fact that I realise how
little talent I possess." Perhaps all his industry was in vain! For
what was the use of industry alone when it came to a work of
art? . . . "All the labour in the world is no substitute for a grain
of genius." The nearer his tragedy grew to completion, the more
did he torture himself with doubts whether it was going to be a
masterpiece or whether he had drawn a blank.

There was, unfortunately, little prospect that *Cromwell* would
turn out to be a masterpiece. Still unaware of the path that his
genius was to take, and with no experienced hand to guide him,
the novice had set off in the wrong direction. Nothing was less
suited to his still unfledged talent, unfamiliar as he was with the
ways of the world and the technique of the stage, than a tragedy,
and particularly a tragedy in verse. He must himself have been
aware that he had little gift for rhyme, and it was not merely
fortuitous that his verses, including the few poems that have
survived, are of such abysmally poor quality. The alexandrine in
particular, with its measured scansion, demands tranquillity,
deliberation and patience, that is to say, the very attributes which
were most inconsistent with the brimming nature of Balzac. He
could only think and write when his mind was allowed to soar,

4

when his pen could hardly keep pace with his words and thoughts. His imagination leapt from one associated idea to another and could not check its flight to count syllables and construct ingenious rhymes. Rigidity of form was bound to hamper the impetuous current of ideas, and the tragedy he produced in his effort to follow classic models was cold, imitative and empty.

Balzac had no time, however, to analyse his own temperament. He was in a hurry to get his tragedy finished, so that he could be independent and famous, and he urged his stumbling alexandrines along at all possible speed. His only desire was to reach the end, to learn what answer destiny would give to his question whether he was a genius or whether he was to return to his stool in the notary's office and continue to be a slave to his family. In January 1820, after four months of feverish toil, the draft was ready, and at the house of friends in L'Isle Adam he added the last touches and the final polish. In May he was back in Villeparisis with the completed manuscript in his scanty luggage and prepared to read it to his parents. The moment had come for the fateful decision whether to France and the world a new genius had been born in the person of Honoré Balzac.

His parents were awaiting the arrival of their problem child and his rhymed tragedy with impatient curiosity. Events had taken a slight turn in his favour. The family's financial situation had somewhat improved and the domestic atmosphere was more cheerful, due mainly to the fact that Laure, his favourite sister, had made an excellent match with a well-to-do civil engineer named de Surville, who was, moreover, of noble birth. Nor had the family been unimpressed by Honoré's unexpected fortitude during his fasting cure, an ordeal which he had survived without getting into debt to the extent of a single sou. This latter achievement was in itself a proof of character and determination, and a completed manuscript of two thousand lines testified by the quantity of paper alone that had been consumed in the process to the fact that Honoré's brusque renunciation of his solid prospects in the legal profession had not been dictated by a mere love of idleness. Père Dablin's cordial accounts of the young author's frugal way

of living had probably also contributed to the doubts now entertained by his parents whether they had not, after all, acted on
unfounded suspicion in dealing so hardly with their son. There
might be something behind this stubbornness of his, and if he really
was talented a première at the Comédie Française would be an
honour that the Sallambiers and the Balzacs would by no means
despise. Even his mother began to show a belated interest in
Honoré's play and offered to make a fair copy with her own hands,
so that when he came to read it in public the effect would not be
prejudiced by the innumerable corrections with which the manuscript was thickly strewn. For the first time in his life Honoré was
taken a little more seriously in the house of his parents.

The public reading, which was to decide whether or not Honoré
was possessed of genius, took place in May at Villeparisis, and it
was invested with the atmosphere of a little family celebration.
To complete the critical tribunal his parents invited not only their
new son-in-law de Surville, but a few influential acquaintances,
including Dr. Nacquart, who was to remain Balzac's lifelong
friend, physician and admirer. Little Père Dablin, of course,
refused to miss this strange première and made the two-hour
journey from Paris in the rumbling, old-fashioned stage-coach,
the *Coucou*.

It was, indeed, a strange première. The furniture in the drawing-
room had been solemnly rearranged for the occasion. In a semi-
circle of armchairs sat in eager expectancy the two parents, the
hypochondriac old Grandmamma Sallambier, and Laure with her
husband, who understood more about the building of roads and
bridges than the construction of alexandrines. Among the guests
the seats of honour were occupied by Dr. Nacquart, the Secretary
of the Royal Society of Medicine, and little Père Dablin. In the
background listened, though perhaps not very attentively, the
two younger children, Laurence and Henri. Facing this not conspicuously expert audience sat the newly fledged author, with a
small table in front of him and his small white hands nervously
fidgeting with his manuscript. He had smartened up his appearance, and his abundant mass of hair was swept back from his
forehead in a leonine mane. His little black eyes had for the
moment lost their fiery sparkle and roved restlessly from face to
face as if seeking an answer to an unspoken question. He began to

read hesitantly: "Act One, Scene One. . . ." But presently he got into his stride, and soon the torrent of alexandrines thundered and boomed, rippled and murmured through the hushed auditorium.

None of those present has left us a record of this strange and memorable performance, which lasted some three or four hours, or of the effect which it produced. We do not know whether old Grandmamma Sallambier managed to keep awake, or whether the two younger children had to go off to bed before the execution of Charles I. All we can be certain of is that the audience found itself somewhat embarrassed at having to pass authoritative judgment in the matter of Honoré's genius immediately the curtain had fallen on this rather fatiguing rehearsal. An old army contractor, a wholesale ironmonger, a civil engineer and a surgeon were not exactly the ideal critics that one would choose to express an opinion on the qualities of a tragedy in verse, and there is no doubt that they felt uncomfortable at having to decide whether the dramatic monstrosity to which they had just been listening had merely bored them personally or actually was a tedious production. In view of the general uncertainty on the subject, de Surville proposed that the work of the "new Sophocles"—as Honoré had somewhat prematurely pictured himself—should be submitted to a really competent authority. In this connection he recalled that the instructor in *belles lettres* at the polytechnic he had once attended was the author of some comedies in verse, and that these had even been produced on the stage. He was willing to use his good offices with Monsieur Andrieux, than whom there could be no better judge, since he was a duly licensed professor of literary history and had even been appointed in the meanwhile to a chair at the Collège de France.

Nothing impresses the worthy bourgeois more than a resounding official title. A man who had been appointed by the State to a professorial chair and who lectured at the Collège de France was bound to be possessed of infallible judgment. So Madame Balzac and her daughter made the pilgrimage to Paris and submitted the manuscript to the flattered professor, who appreciated being thus reminded of something which the world had long since forgotten, namely, that he was really a celebrated author. The opinion at which he arrived after reading Balzac's tragedy has since been confirmed by posterity. He thought it completely lacking in any

prospect of success, and it must be placed to his credit that he
did not frame his disappointing verdict in the form of a final and
forthright denial of Honoré's literary aptitude. He wrote very
courteously to Madame Balzac:

> It is far from my desire to wish to discourage your son, but I am
> of opinion that he could employ his time better than in writing
> tragedies and comedies. If he will give me the pleasure of paying
> me a visit I shall be happy to explain to him how, in my view,
> *belles lettres* should be studied and the benefit that can be
> derived from it without necessarily adopting poetry as a
> profession.   •

This was a "sensible" compromise that found a warm echo in
the hearts of Honoré's parents. If the lad wanted to keep on with
his writing, why not? It was at any rate better (and cheaper) for
a young fellow to sit at a writing-table than to lounge in coffee-
houses or spend his time (and money) in the company of loose
women. But it must, of course, be just as Professor Andrieux had
advised—not as a *"poète de profession"*, but purely as a literary
hobby side by side with a sound and lucrative calling. Honoré,
however, who despite the failure of his *Cromwell* still felt himself
to be a *"poète de vocation"*, glimpsed the danger. Some mysterious
instinct warned him that the task to which he was summoned was
too potent to be a mere side-issue in his life:

> If I take a job I am lost. I should become a clerk, a machine, a
> circus horse with prescribed hours for doing my thirty or forty
> laps in the ring, drinking, eating and sleeping. I should become
> merely a man intent on doing his daily round. And this is what
> people call living—this rotating like a mill-stone, this eternal
> recurrence of the eternally self-same things!

Without knowing of what it consisted, he felt that he had been
born to carry out a special task which would demand the full measure of his powers and even something in excess of the full measure.
He therefore refused the compromise and insisted on his bond.
The two trial years stipulated in the contract with his father were
not yet up. He had a full year left, and he intended to use it. With
uncurbed spirit and stubborn determination, as after every crisis
of disappointment throughout his life, more resolved than ever to
free himself from office drudgery and dependence on his family,
he returned to his voluntary prison-cell in the rue Lesdiguières.

CHAPTER III

The Novel Manufactory of Horace de St. Aubin & Co.

or some days, and even perhaps for some weeks, Balzac was unwilling to admit that his *Cromwell* was a failure. He discussed with his friend Dablin whether the tragedy ought not after all to be submitted to the Comédie Française, and the worthy ironmonger, who had few connections with the theatre, tried to enlist the services of an acquaintance of the actor Lafont in persuading the latter to interest himself in the work. Balzac would then pay Lafont a visit and do his best to wheedle him into showing it to the other members of the company. Suddenly, however, Balzac himself rebelled against the plan. Why should he take upon himself this unnecessary humiliation? A man who was conscious of the strength within him could bear even a heavy blow. *Cromwell* was finished and done with. It would be better to try again. He asked Dablin to cease his efforts, flung the manuscript into a drawer, and as long as he lived never cast another glance at this first misbegotten offspring of his youth.

His immediate need was to settle down to work again as soon as possible. His initial devastating failure had docked his arrogance somewhat. A year before, when he was writing his tragedy with mind aglow, he had given himself up to exuberant dreams, resolved to achieve fame, honour and freedom at one stroke. Now that he had fallen from the heights, the chief end he had in view was a practical one. He must throw off the yoke of dependence on his parents. The masterpieces, and the immortality they would bring, could wait. The first essential was to earn money by writing, money at any cost, so as not to have to render an account for every sou to his father and his mother and his grandmother as if it were given him in charity. The incorrigible optimist was forced to abandon his illusions and to think realistically. Balzac made up his mind to write something that would be a quick success.

But what kind of literature *was* having a quick success nowadays? He did not know, so he looked around and found that it was the novel. A new wave of novel-writing had struck the Continent, originating on the shores of England after the earlier, sentimental wave which had produced Rousseau's *Nouvelle Héloïse* and Goethe's *Werther* had spent its force. The Napoleonic age, like all years of war, had brought enough tension into people's daily lives, even more than enough, and they felt no urge to agitate themselves over the fate of fictitious individuals. The official journal, the *Moniteur*, had provided a surrogate for fiction; but with the return of peace and the Bourbons the public felt the need to have its soul thrilled by the adventures of others, to have its nerves tickled, to experience alternately the sensations of gruesome horror and sickly sentimentality. There was a demand for novels, for exciting, melodramatic, romantic, exotic novels, and the newly instituted reading-rooms and lending libraries could hardly quench the mass-hunger for this type of literature. A golden age had arrived for those authors who could mix without scruple in their witch's-kitchens tears and poison, corsairs and virtuous maidens, blood and incense, knavishness and nobility, sorcery and minstrelsy, boil them into a romantic-historical dumpling, and serve it up with an ice-cold sauce of the ghostly and the gruesome. There was, for instance, the English novelist Mrs. Ann Radcliffe, with her spooky tales of horror whose machinery rattled like a mill-wheel. The few Frenchmen who were smart enough to copy the industrious lady's technique had made a pot of money with their "*romans noirs*". Even on a higher plane, however, the historical and particularly the medieval setting was now all the rage. The knights of Sir Walter Scott had conquered more countries and defeated more opponents with their old-fashioned swords and shining armour than Napoleon with his cannon, while Byron's pashas and corsairs with their romantic melancholy were causing hearts to beat as furiously as once the communiqués announcing the victories of Rivoli and Austerlitz had done.

Balzac decided to trim his sails to the prevailing romantic wind and write an historical novel. He was not the first French author to be tempted by the popular success of Byron and Scott. Victor Hugo with his *Bug-Jargal, Han d'Islande* and *Notre Dame*, and Vigny with *Cinq-Mars* were soon to try their master hands in the same field, but they were already skilled in the art of composition and polished phrases because they had started as poets. When Balzac, on the other hand, began to write his novel *Falthurne* he was walking with uncertain steps in the path of imitation. From the wretched novels of Ann Radcliffe he borrowed an historical background, a conventional Neapolitan scene, and placed upon his stage all the indispensable characters to be found in a cheap sensational novel, first and foremost the ubiquitous witch, "*la sorcière de Sommaris, magnétiseuse*", Normans and *condottieri*, noble captives in chains and sentimental pages. The preliminary draft indicated battles, sieges, dungeons and the most improbable deeds of blood and heroism—more, for the time being, than the young author could cope with. Another novel, *Sténie ou les erreurs philosophiques*, also remained a fragment. It was written in letter form, in the style of Rousseau, and delineated in vague outline the favourite theme of Louis Lambert, the "*théorie de la volonté*". Part of this manuscript was inserted as padding in a later novel. Balzac had suffered his second defeat. He had come to grief in his attempt to write a tragedy and he had failed as a novelist. A year had gone by, then another six months, and at home the inexorable Atropos was waiting to cut the thin thread of his freedom. On the 15th of November, 1820, his parents gave notice that the room in the rue Lesdiguières would be vacated on the 1st of January, 1821. He must put an end to his scribbling! It was time to stop spending his parents' money and to begin earning money for himself!

To begin earning money for himself! There was nothing for which Balzac had been struggling more desperately than just that. During those months of solitary confinement in the rue Lesdiguières he had pinched and scraped, starved and slaved in order to secure his independence, but it had all been in vain. Now, at the eleventh hour, only a miracle could save him.

At such moments of extreme hopelessness and despair we always find in fairy tales that the tempter approaches his victim with a view to purchasing his soul. In Balzac's case the tempter looked by no means diabolic. He presented himself in the shape of a charming, amusing young man; his pantaloons were well-cut and his linen clean, and he did not want to purchase Balzac's soul but only the hand with which he wrote. Somewhere or other, perhaps in the office of the publisher to whom he was offering his novels or at the library or in an eating-house, Balzac had made the acquaintance of this youth, who was more or less of his own age and bore the aristocratic name of Auguste le Poitevin de l'Egreville. The son of an actor, he had inherited from his father a certain adroitness and compensated for his lack of literary talent by a versatile knowledge of the world. He had already managed to find a publisher for a novel called *Les deux Hectors ou les deux familles bretonnes*, the botching together of which was nearly completed, and this publisher had even paid him eight hundred francs in cash for the work, which was to appear in February in two volumes under the pseudonym Auguste de Viellerglé and to be sold by the bookseller Hubert in the Palais Royal. Balzac may have complained to his new-won friend of his own lack of success, and perhaps le Poitevin explained to him that the real cause of his misfortune was an excess of literary ambition. What had an artistic conscience to do with the writing of novels? Why take the work so seriously? These were presumably the arguments of the tempter. It was easy enough to write a novel. One had only to choose or purloin a subject, something historical since that was what the publishers were particularly keen about, and dash off the necessary few hundred pages with all possible speed—preferably in collaboration. He already had a publisher who would take their work. If Balzac felt that way inclined, they could write the next novel in partnership. Or better, the two of them could hash up the plot together and Balzac could write the stuff by himself, since he could do it more skilfully and quickly. Le Poitevin would look after the business side. So if Balzac agreed they would set up shop together and share fifty-fifty.

It was a degrading proposition. It would mean turning out blood-and-thunder stories by a fixed date, with a definite number of pages per book, and in collaboration with a totally unscrupulous and artistically unambitious partner. How different from his dreams of yesterday! He would be abusing his talent and perhaps ruining it beyond repair merely in order to scrape together a few hundred francs. A year ago he had wanted to make the name of Balzac immortal, to excel Racine, to expound to mankind a new theory of the omnipotence of the will. The price demanded by his tempter was his very soul, his artistic conscience. But he had no choice. He had to give up his room in the rue Lesdiguières, and if he returned home without having earned money by his pen his parents would not accord him a second lease of freedom. It would be better to walk his own treadmill than someone else's. So he came to terms with his tempter. In the case of their first novel, *Charles Pointel ou mon cousin de la main gauche,* which le Poitevin de l'Egreville had already begun, or perhaps merely sketched out, Balzac was to be regarded as a sleeping partner, though he did most of the work, and his name was not to appear on the title-page. The subsequent productions of the newly founded novel manufactory were to be signed by both members of the firm—A. de Viellerglé (an anagram of Egreville) and Lord R'hoone (an anagram of Honoré).

Therewith the pact with the devil was sealed. In Chamisso's famous story it was his own shadow that Peter Schlemihl sold to the Lord of the Underworld. Balzac was selling his art, his literary ambition, his name. In order to earn his freedom he sold himself into slavery. During the next few years his genius and his name were alike submerged in the obscurity of the galley.

❧

After concluding this transaction Balzac went home to his family in Villeparisis for a holiday. His room in the rue Lesdiguières had perforce been given up, and at Villeparisis he moved into the chamber which had been occupied by his sister Laure before her marriage. It was his firm resolve to obtain another *pied à terre* as soon as he had earned enough money to pay for it. In the meantime he installed his novel manufactory in the little room where his sister had formerly indulged her romantic dreams of her brother's future fame. He sat at his work night and day, piling one swiftly written sheet on another, for commissions were pouring in without respite thanks to the activity of his partner and agent, le Poitevin de l'Egreville. The weights were well balanced in this piece of clockwork: Balzac did the writing, le Poitevin disposed of the novels.

The family watched the new turn of events with satisfaction. After having seen the first contracts—eight hundred francs for the first book and rising rapidly to two thousand francs to be divided between the partners—they no longer found Honoré's occupation quite so absurd. Perhaps the ne'er-do-well would manage to stand on his own feet after all and cease to be a drain on their pockets. His father was particularly pleased by the fact that his son had apparently abandoned his idea of becoming a famous author, and by using a variety of pseudonyms had avoided bringing the honest name of Balzac into disrepute. "He is pouring water into his wine," the good-natured old gentleman said with complacency. "There is still time, and so I hope that he will get somewhere after all." Honoré's mother, on the other hand, who had the unfortunate gift of spoiling everything for her son by her importunate solicitude, regarded the novel manufactory established in her house as a family matter. Both she and his sister tried to pose as his critics and collaborators. She was not the last of his critics to lament his lack of style, but she was certainly the first to complain that Rabelais had corrupted him. She urged him to revise his manu-script carefully, and one can feel how weary he grew of this eternal tutelage. Soon we find the mother, who could not wean herself from her unwanted, lachrymose anxiety for her prodigal son, reporting as follows: "Honoré has such a conceited notion of him-self and his capacities that he hurts everybody's feelings." His elemental spirit was constricted in this household and the family atmosphere became unendurable. His sole desire was once more to have a room in Paris and to be free.

Driven by the urge to gain his independence he worked like a galley-slave. Twenty, thirty, forty pages, a whole chapter a day was his average output. But the more he earned, the more he wanted to earn. He wrote as a hunted man runs, with panting breath and bursting lungs, in order to escape from his family. At last he was working with such daemonic lack of restraint that even his mother grew frightened. "Honoré is working like a savage. If he

continues to live this sort of life for another three months I shall
have him on my hands as an invalid." Once he had got into his
stride Balzac flung the whole vehement energy of his being into
the work he was doing. Every third day his inkpot needed refilling
and he had used up ten pens. As he worked his powers gained
momentum with that driving obsession which was later to astonish
all his colleagues. He had probably already helped le Poitevin to
finish his first novel, *Les deux Hectors*, and before the year 1821
had reached its close he also took a hand in finishing *Charles Pointel*,
which appeared under the name of Viellerglé though it contained
whole passages from Balzac's *Sténie*. In the same year yet another
novel was ready, *L'héritière de Birague*, "*histoire tirée des manu-
scrits de Dom Rago, ex-prieur des bénédictins, mis au jour par ses
deux neveux M. A. de Viellerglé et Lord R'hoone.*" Even before this
four-volume work was out of the printer's hands, in February
1822, another four-decker trod close on its heels, *Jean Louis ou la
fille trouvée*, and this was likewise signed by the two worthy nephews
of the mythical prior. Balzac now seems to have had enough of a
firm in which he alone provided the head and the hand, the brain
and the heart. He swiftly dashed off a further novel, *Le Tartare ou
le retour de l'exile*, which also appeared in 1822 under the name of
A. de Viellerglé. Lord R'hoone, who was the real author, was not
even mentioned this time as a collaborator. Therewith the contract
seems to have lapsed. From now on Balzac published the products
of his factory under his own *nom de plume*. He was now the sole
owner of the business and he was resolved to make it the foremost
literary firm in France. In his early jubilation at the way he was
raking in money he triumphantly announced to his sister:

Dear Sister,
        I am working now like Henri IV's horse before it was cast
in bronze, and I hope that before the end of this year I shall have
made twenty thousand francs, which shall be the foundation-
stone of my fortune. I still have to deliver *Le vicaire des Ardennes*,
Le savant, *Odette de Champdivers*, and *La famille R'hoone* . . .
apart from a number of theatrical pieces.
    Lord R'hoone will before long be the man of the day, the most
prolific author in the world, the most charming companion, and
the ladies will love him as the apple of their eye. Then your little
Honoré will roll along in his own carriage, with head erect and

proud glance, and his pockets full of money. As he approaches one will hear the flattering murmur with which a public idol is greeted, and people will whisper: "That is the brother of Madame de Surville!"

One thing alone enables us to recognise in these poor productions the handiwork of the future Balzac, namely, the incredible speed at which they were written. Having already turned out some sixteen to twenty volumes either by himself or in collaboration with le Poitevin, he produced in this busy year of 1822 another three novels of four volumes each. They were *Clotilde de Lusignan ou le beau juif*, *Les centenaires ou les deux Beringheld*, and *Le vicaire des Ardennes*. It looks as if he were himself growing apprehensive that the public might not be able to stand up to a barrage like this, for in the case of the last two books he dropped the pseudonym of "Lord R'hoone" and signed himself "Horace de Saint Aubin". The new label cost the publisher considerably more than had that of the former firm. The eight hundred francs for each novel which he had had to share with his partner were screwed up by Lord R'hoone–Saint Aubin to two thousand francs for fifteen hundred copies. Five, perhaps ten, novels a year—which was child's play with such nimble and unscrupulous patchwork—and one of the dreams of his youth would be fulfilled. In a few more years he would be rich and his independence assured for ever.

⊷⊐○⊏⊶

Even the expert guild of *Balzacomanes* possesses no exhaustive record of the pseudonymous books written and published by Balzac during these years of servile drudgery. Yet the novels which appeared under the names of Lord R'hoone and Horace de Saint Aubin were only a minor part of his by no means reputable activity. He had no doubt had a hand in *Michel et Christine et la suite*, by his former partner Veillerglé, and wrote wholly or in part *Le Mulâtre*, which was published under the name of Aurore Cloteaux. No type of literary production, no commission, no kind of association was beneath his dignity between his twenty-second and thirtieth years. His swift pen was to be had cheaply and anonymously by whoever was prepared to pay for it. Like the public scribes who in the days of illiteracy used to sit in the streets of the

Paris suburbs and for a few sous composed whatever the passer-by desired, whether love-letters for servant-girls, complaints, petitions or denunciations, the greatest writer of the century offered his pen for hire with a cynical lack of scruple that an Aretino might have envied. He wrote books and brochures *ad lib.* for suspect politicians, obscure publishers, and slick agents, cheap ranges of goods in all styles and at all prices. He manufactured to order a royalist pamphlet, *Du droit d'aînesse* and cobbled together from borrowed sources an *Histoire impartiale des Jésuites,* while a melodrama called *Le nègre* was turned out with the same nonchalance as a *Petit dictionnaire des enseignes de Paris.* In 1824 the one-man firm, adapting itself to the change in public taste, switched production from novels to the so-called *Codes* and *Physiologies* which a shady *"courtier littéraire"* named Horace Raisson had brought into fashion. Month after month the mill ground out a series of other "Codes", with their forced wit to amuse the *petit bourgeois.* The *Code des gens honnêtes ou l'art de n'être pas dupe des fripons* was followed by *L'art de mettre sa cravate,* a *Code conjugal,* which was later expanded into a *Physiologie du mariage,* and a *Code du commis voyageur,* which was later to be useful for his immortal Gaudissart. All these "Codes", including a *Manuel complet de la politesse* which was signed by Horace Raisson and disposed of by him at great profit—some of these works sold over twelve thousand copies—came wholly or for the most part from Balzac's pen. This is capable of proof, but it is no longer possible to discover how many brochures, newspaper articles, and perhaps even commercial prospectuses he produced, for neither he nor his employers, who preferred to keep in the background, were inclined to acknowledge publicly the bastard offspring they had begotten in the dissolute by-ways of cheap publishing. All we can say without fear of contradiction is that not a single line of the innumerable pages scrawled by Balzac during his years of shame has the slightest connection with literature or art, and that one almost blushes at having to attribute them to him.

Prostitution is the only word that can be used for this kind of scribbling, and it was the worst kind of prostitution, since it was practised cold-bloodedly and solely with a view to making money quickly. He may, to begin with, have been swayed only by impatience to achieve his freedom, but once he had sunk deep enough and become used to easy profits, the descent grew steeper and steeper. After the large earnings which he drew from his novels he allowed his talents to be misused for lesser rewards, and there was no literary iniquity that he could not stomach. He was a harlot serving simultaneously two or three literary pimps. Even when his *Chouans* and *La peau de chagrin* had made him an outstanding figure in French literature, he continued—like a married woman secretly visiting a *maison de rendezvous* to earn some pin-money—to frequent his former low haunts and degrade the famous Honoré de Balzac to the status of a cheap hack for the sake of a few hundred francs. To-day, when his cloak of anonymity has become somewhat threadbare, we know that Balzac shrank from no literary sin. He patched other men's novels with scraps of his own and barefacedly stole other writers' plots and situations for his own works. With adroit impudence he undertook every kind of literary tailoring, in which the purloined material was pressed, lengthened, turned, dyed and modernised. He supplied anything for which there was a demand, whether in the way of philosophy, politics or *causeries*, always ready to meet his client's wishes, a brisk, skilful, unscrupulous workman, on call at any time and prepared to switch over to the production of any article that happened to be in fashion. It is pathetic to think of the kind of people with whom he associated in these dark years. He was the greatest story-teller of his age, yet he was nothing but the hireling of the scabbiest hole-and-corner publishers and wholesale book-hawkers of Paris. All this because he lacked self-confidence and was blind to his real destiny. It must forever remain a unique phenomenon in the annals of literature that even a genius like Balzac could lift himself out of the slough in which he had become bogged. We are reminded of Baron Munchausen's feat in drawing himself up from the swamp by his own pigtail. Some taint did, it is true, cling to his garments, a certain sickly perfumed odour from the dissolute haunts of literature he had been wont to frequent. *Semper aliquid haeret.* No artist can descend so deeply into the sewers with impunity. The lack of scruple demanded by the sensational novel, its lack of verisimilitude and its gross sentimentalities—these were elements that Balzac could never again wholly eliminate from his novels; but it was above all the glibness, the haste, the slick writing, habits contracted during the days of mass production, which permanently affected his style. Language is a jealous master and avenges itself inexorably on every artist who even occasionally treats it with unconcern. Balzac wakened too late to a sense of responsibility, and after he had reached maturity he would desperately plough through his manuscripts, galleys and page-proofs ten or twenty times; but it was too late to hoe out the weeds which had been allowed to take root with such impudent luxuriance. If Balzac's language and style remained irredeemably defective for the rest of his life, it was because he had been untrue to himself in the decisive years of his development.

In the ferment of his mind the young Balzac vaguely perceived that he was degrading his real self. He never put his name to any of these works, and later on, though with more audacity than success, he stubbornly disowned them. To the only intimate of his early years, the sister who had loyally supported his youthful ambitions, he refused even to show *L'héritière de Birague*, "because," as he said, "it is a real piece of literary *cochonnerie*." He gave her a copy of *Jean Louis* only on condition that she should "not lend it to a living soul, not even *show* it to anyone, and not talk about it, so that the copy does not go the rounds in Bayeux or anywhere else and damage my business." The word he used, *commerce*, proves decisively with what complete lack of illusion Balzac regarded his writing at this time. He was bound by contract to supply so many folios to the printer, and the quicker the better; all that mattered in the calculation of his fee was quantity and all that mattered to Balzac was the payment of his fee. In his impatience to start on a new tome as quickly as possible he cared so little for the artistic problems of composition, style, unity, and originality that he made his sister the cynical proposal, since she was not overburdened with work at home, that she should write the second volume of *Le vicaire des Ardennes* with the help of a short synopsis while he was dashing off the first. Hardly had he set up his factory before he was looking round for cheap hands. While acting as a "ghost" for others he was trying to enlist the services of a similar unseen collaborator for himself. Yet in the rare lucid intervals that came to him during his brutish labours he was pricked by a conscience that was not entirely atrophied:

O, my dear Laure [he groaned], I bless every day the good fortune which allowed me to adopt this free profession, and I am convinced that I shall yet make a good deal of money by it. But now that I am aware of my powers, as I believe, I am indeed sorry at having to expend the flower of my ideas on such absurdities. In my mind's eye I see something beckoning me and if only I could be assured as to my material situation . . . I would settle down to real work.

Like his Lucien de Rubempré, in whom he later depicted his own fall and eventual self-redemption, he felt a burning sense of shame, and stared with a shudder, like Lady Macbeth, at his stained hands:

My attempt to free myself by the bold stroke of writing novels —and what novels! Oh, Laure, how pitifully have my glorious projects collapsed!

He despised what he wrote and the brokers for whom he wrote. Only the uncertain presentiment that his superhuman efforts were bound in the end to lead to some great goal, to the achievement of fame, gave him the strength to bear the miserable serfdom into which he had voluntarily sold himself. As always, this most sincere of visionaries was rescued from reality by his illusions.

⋑∘⋐

Meanwhile Balzac had reached his twenty-third birthday. He had not yet lived or loved, but only toiled. He had never enjoyed the esteem or confidence of others, and no hand had been held out to help him. A despised helot at school, fettered to his family, he had sold the years of his early manhood for the shameful wage that was to provide his ransom. He laboured to redeem himself from the compulsion to labour, he drudged to free himself from drudgery, and this tragic paradox was to determine from now on the form and formula of his life. He was going round in a torturing circle. He was writing in order not to have to write any more; scraping money together, more money, and still more money, in order no longer to be forced to think of money; shutting himself off from the world in

5

order to conquer it more securely with all its countries, its women, its luxury and—the brightest jewel in its crown—the immortal fame it had to offer; economising in order to be able at last to squander; toiling, toiling, toiling day and night, cheerlessly and without pause, in order to live life as it should be lived. These henceforth were Balzac's dreams, the wild dreams that kept his nerves strung to a high pitch and dragged from him the last ounce of physical strength which enabled him to work as he did. His writings did not yet reveal the great artist, but they did make manifest the tremendous eruptive force which flung out continuously a fiery mass composed of human characters and human fates, landscapes, ideas and dreams. And, as in the case of a volcano, one is aware that this fiery flux was not merely an emanation from the surface but an explosive discharge from mysterious depths. An elemental force, confined and constricted, suffocated by its own superabundance, was seeking relief from the constraining pressure. Struggling frantically in his dark pit, he was striving to hammer his way through to light and air, the invigorating, seductive air of freedom. He turbulently demanded contact with life itself, instead of always having to construct merely a facsimile of life. He had won the strength to accomplish his work, and all he lacked was a smile from destiny. One single ray of light and everything would shoot up into blossom that was now threatening to wither and decay in the chill dungeon where it was shut out from the warmth of the sun:

If only someone would cast a magic beam on this frozen existence of mine! I have not hitherto enjoyed any of the flowering joys of life. . . . I go hungry, and there is nothing to satisfy my craving. But what does that matter? . . . I have only two passionate desires—love and fame. Neither has yet found fulfilment.

CHAPTER IV

Madame de Berny

Balzac had indeed not found fulfilment of his two "passionate desires". Neither love nor fame had yet come his way. All his tumultuous dreams had remained merely dreams, his fervent efforts had been in vain. The manuscript of *Cromwell* was yellowing in a drawer, concealed and forgotten amidst a mass of other worthless papers. The trashy novels that he had turned out *en masse* appeared and disappeared under false names, and among the thousands of authors who were writing books in France there was never mention of the name of Honoré Balzac. His talent was respected by nobody, and least of all by himself. It had not helped him at all that by stooping low he had managed to creep into the most disreputable section of the world of letters by the back-door. Nor was he getting any further by writing continuously day and night with the intent concentration of a starving rat that is determined to gnaw its way into the larder whence come the delicious odours that penetrate so tantalisingly to its very entrails. His most strenuous exertions had not brought him a single step forward.

The obstacle which stood in Balzac's way during these years was not a lack of strength, for that was dammed up within him and raging to find an outlet, but a lack of courage. He possessed the temperament of a conqueror and the resolute will to succeed. Even in his rare hours of depression he knew himself to be immeasurably superior to all his colleagues in intellect, knowledge, industry and intensive force, but owing perhaps to the impairment of his self-

reliance by the years of intimidation to which he had been subjected by his parents, he did not know how to provide the necessary
outlet for the intrepidity of his spirit. He says himself: "I possessed
courage, it is true, but only in my soul, not in my bearing." Until
his thirtieth year he did not venture, as an artist, to attack the
task which was commensurate with his genius, or, as a man, to seek
the society of women. Fantastic as it may seem at first sight, the
sensuous, impetuous Balzac of the later years was throughout his
youth almost morbidly shy.

Shyness, however, does not always spring from weakness. Only
the man who has found his balance can really be certain of himself,
and an excess of unused strength which does not yet know how to
apply itself may jog him restlessly between the opposite poles of
arrogance and apprehension. The young Balzac avoided women
not because he was afraid of falling in love, but on the contrary
because he was afraid of his own tempestuous nature. Furthermore,
he was late in reaching sexual maturity and speaks of a "stage of
incomplete puberty that was inordinately prolonged by overwork"
and a virility "which only hesitantly put forth its green shoots".
Yet the stocky, broad-shouldered young fellow with the thick,
almost negroid lips was later to become so suffused with this potent
force that it endowed him with the strongest sexual capacity that
a man can possess, the capacity to be indiscriminate. Neither his
senses nor his imagination needed the charm of youth or beauty in
a woman. This sorcerer who had such control over his own will that
during his lean years he could write out a menu on his table and
believe that he was savouring caviare and *vol-au-vent* as he chewed
a slice of stale bread, this man could see a Helen in every woman,
even in Hecuba, as soon as his will-power came into play. He was
inhibited neither by loss of youth, nor faded beauty, nor corpulence,
nor any other female blemishes such as would have induced a
fastidious amorist to copy the renunciatory gesture of Joseph. He
loved any woman whom he wanted to love and took whatever he
desired to take. Just as he was willing to hire out his pen promiscu-
ously to anybody who required it, so he was ready to make love
to any woman who could help rescue him from dependence on his
parents, without being concerned whether she was pretty or ugly,
stupid or quarrelsome. His first wooing—like his books—was
anonymous:

Look around [wrote this strange idealist to his sister in his twenty-second year] and see if you can find me some rich widow with a fortune . . . and sing my praises to her—an excellent young man, twenty-two years of age, of good appearance, with vivacious eyes, full of fire! And the finest dish in the way of a husband that has ever been cooked by the gods.

Like the volumes sold in the booksellers' shops of the Palais Royal, Honoré Balzac was offered cheaply on the marriage-market in those days, the reason being that he set very little value on himself. He was not to acquire a higher appreciation of his own worth until he had found someone to give him encouragement. If a publisher or a critic had promised him success, if a woman had smiled at him, he would have cast off his shyness like a cloak. But fame spurned him and women ignored him, so he strove to possess himself of the next best thing, money, and therewith his freedom.

It is not really surprising that women did not give him any particular encouragement. "A very ugly young man" is the way Vigny begins his description of Balzac, and he neglected his personal appearance no less than he abused his talents. Even his masculine acquaintances noted with distaste the thick grease on his mane, the decaying teeth, the way he dribbled when he spoke quickly, his unshaven chin and his untied shoelaces. The old local tailor at Tours, who was commissioned to turn his father's worn-out suits for him to wear, was unequal to the task of cutting the fashionable waist and fullness over the hips after allowing for the bull-like neck and massive shoulders. Balzac knew that his short legs and general awkwardness would make him look ridiculous if he tried to copy the mincing gait of the dandies of the day or ventured on to the dance-floor, and this feeling of inferiority in the company of women drove him back time and again to his work and his solitude. What was the use of a fiery eye if it timidly took cover under its lids as soon as a handsome female approached? What was the use of his vaunted intellect or knowledge or his inner exuberance if shyness kept his lips sealed, if all he could produce in his embarrassment was a few stuttering words, whereas others who were a thousand times more stupid could insinuate themselves with supple phrases? He knew that he could talk with infinitely greater accomplishment, that his virility and powers of seduction were immeasurably more potent than those of the pretty, ogling youths in their well-cut coats and neat cravats. In his unquenched hunger for love he would have been prepared to barter all his future works, his intelligence and his art, his intellect and his knowledge, for this other art which understood so well how to lean over a woman with a tender air and a sparkle in the eye, and to feel the delicious shudder that rippled through her shoulder. Yet not the faintest gleam of success fell to his lot, a gleam that his mounting power of imagination would at once have fanned into a flame capable of illuminating a whole world. His glance meant no more to women than his name did to publishers, and Balzac himself has depicted his early mood of despair at this failure in *La peau de chagrin*:

> My soul, hampered and hindered time and again in its effort to seek expression, retired more and more within itself. Frank and unaffected as I was by nature, I was bound to appear cold and affected. . . . I was shy and awkward; I doubted whether my voice could make the slightest impression; I was repelled by my own self; I was aware of my ugliness and was ashamed. Despite the inner voice which always supports a man of gifts in his moments of despair, and which called out to me: "Courage! Keep on!", despite the sudden flashes of revelation which illumined my solitude and showed me the powers I possessed, despite the hope I drew from a comparison of the popular works of the day with the works of art created by my own imagination—in spite of all this I remained uncertain as a child. I was a prey to the wildest ambition, I believed that I was destined for great things, yet at the same time I was aware of my insignificance. . . . Among the young people of my own age I met a group of swaggerers who strutted along with head erect, uttered meaningless phrases, and would sit down at a woman's side without any feeling of constraint. These were the ones who impressed me most —with the outrageous things they said, the way they nibbled the knobs of their canes, their whole affected babble. In their conversation they prostituted the prettiest women, asserting that they had slept with every one of them or at least acting as if they had, yet at the same time they gave themselves superior airs and pretended that such pleasures really meant nothing to them. In their eyes the most virtuous, the most chaste woman was an easy prey, to be vanquished by a simple word, by a daring little gesture, by the first bold look. I declare to you upon my word of honour and my conscience that at that time it seemed to me less

difficult to acquire power or literary fame than to win the favour
of a young, intelligent and charming lady of rank. . . . There
were plenty of women in those days whom I worshipped from
afar, for whom I would have gone through fire and water. They
could have torn my soul in pieces. I would have shunned no
sacrifice and no torture. Yet they belonged to dolts whom I
would not have tolerated as porters at my gate. . . . There is no
doubt that I was too simple for this mannered company, who
moved in an artificial light and clothed their thoughts in conventional phrases or fashionable expressions. I understood
neither how to let my silence speak for itself nor how to chatter
and yet say nothing. So at last I was forced to conceal within
my own breast the fire that was consuming me. Yet I was
possessed of a soul such as no woman could fail to appreciate,
filled with the romantic enthusiasm for which they yearn. I
really did contain within me the power of which those blockheads
only bragged; but all women treated me treacherously and
cruelly. . . . Oh, to have the feeling that one is made for love
and destined to make a woman happy, and yet never to find a
single one, not even a courageous and noble Marceline or some
elderly marquise! To have to carry treasures about with one in a
beggar's knapsack and meet nobody, not even a child or a
curious young girl, who wants to admire them! I was often in
such despair that I was near to putting an end to my life.

Even adventures of the lighter sort, in which young men usually
find a substitute for the love-affairs they only experience in
imagination, were denied to him. In the little town of Villeparisis
he was under the eye of his parents, while in Paris his meagre
monthly allowance had been insufficient to invite even the poorest
grisette to supper.

But the higher the walls of the restraining dyke, the more
strongly do the waves beat against them until the breach is made.
For a time Balzac was able to suppress his desire for women and
caresses by the monastic discipline of fasting and exercises, which
in his case consisted of a phenomenal absorption in his work. In his
novels he revelled in surrogates for the reality that was beyond his
reach and intoxicated himself with his sweet and sentimental
heroines. This outlet for his imagination, however, only served
to feed the inflammable substance that was waiting for the kind-
ling spark. It was a vicious circle of desire. The youthful stage of

confused, tormented, cloudy dreaming was over. Balzac could bear his solitude no longer. He wanted to live, to love, and to be loved. And when Balzac made up his mind to get what he wanted he could create an infinite universe out of a grain of dust.

Dammed-up passions are wont, like other natural forces, such as air, fire, and water, to break through in an unexpected quarter when the pressure has reached its climax. Balzac's decisive experience began in Villeparisis, almost in the shadow of his parents' home. It so happened that a married couple named de Berny not only had a residence in Paris adjoining that of the Balzac family's *pied à terre*, but also a country-house at Villeparisis. This led to a friendship which the bourgeois Balzacs counted as no small honour. Monsieur Gabriel de Berny, the son of a governor and himself a former counsellor at the imperial court, was of aristocratic descent. His wife, who was very much younger, was less blue-blooded but a far more interesting character. Her father, Philippe Joseph Hinner, sprung from an old German family of musicians in Wetzlar, had been a special protégé of Marie Antoinette, who found him a wife in the person of one of her ladies-in-waiting, Marguerite de Laborde. After Hinner's early death, in his thirtieth year, the connection with the royal house became even closer, for his widow married the Chevalier de Jarjailles, the most courageous of royalists, who when the hour of danger arrived proved his devoted loyalty by returning at the risk of his life from Coblence and braving every hazard to rescue the Queen from the Conciergerie. The spacious country-house of the de Bernys was enlivened by seven children, handsome boys and girls, and invested with an atmosphere of laughter, games and witty conversation. Monsieur Balzac did his best to entertain his neighbour, who with increasing blindness had grown somewhat morose and odd, while Madame Balzac became a close friend of Madame de Berny, who was about her own age and likewise of a somewhat romantic temperament. Laurence was the constant playmate of the de Berny girls, and when Honoré arrived he too was found a fitting occupation to cement the family friendship. His parents thought that he might as well do something useful to pay for his board and lodging, so in the intervals of writing novels he was set to work giving lessons to his younger brother Henri; and as Alexandre de Berny was about the same age as Henri, nothing was more natural than that he too should take advantage of this opportunity to obtain private tutoring. So Honoré, who welcomed any pretext to turn his back on his parents' house, spent more and more of his time in the comfortable and cheerful home of the de Bernys.

⊷∘⊶

It was not long before Monsieur and Madame Balzac noticed that one or two strange things were happening. In the first place, Honoré was wandering over to the de Bernys even on days when he was not due to give a lesson, even spending whole afternoons and evenings there. Furthermore, he was paying greater attention to his toilet, holding himself less aloof, and growing manifestly more amiable. His mother found an easy answer to the puzzle. Honoré was in love, and there could be no doubt on whom his choice had fallen. Madame de Berny had a pretty young daughter named Emmanuèle, of whom Balzac wrote twenty years later: "She was an enchanting beauty, an exotic flower!" His parents smirked with satisfaction. This wasn't so bad, and it was the most sensible thing the unpredictable fellow had done so far! The de Bernys were not only far superior to the Balzacs in social status, but they were also very well off, and with a wife from such influential circles Honoré would at once obtain a lucrative position that would at the same time be more reputable than turning out novels by the dozen for insignificant publishers. So they encouraged this gratifying intimacy with a secret twinkle in their eyes, and Madame Balzac was probably meditating pleasurably on the good round sum that the bride would bring with her as her dowry. She dreamt of a marriage contract between the young couple that would be adorned with the signatures of all the relatives of the two families.

It was unfortunate for Honoré's mother that with her narrow bourgeois instincts, honestly concerned though she was for her son's advancement, she never really understood him. This time, too, she guessed completely wrong. It was not the charming young girl but the mother, who was already in fact a grandmother, Laure de Berny, who had cast her spell over Balzac. It was normally not within the bounds of probability that a woman of forty-five, who had given birth to nine children, should still be capable of inspiring passion in the breast of a young man. It was the most improbable of all the possibilities. There are no portraits by which we can judge whether Madame de Berny was beautiful in her earlier years, but there is no doubt that at the age of forty-five she would have long since ceased to be regarded as the goal of any normal man's erotic desires. Though the delicate melancholy of her features may have been attractive, her figure had attained a matronly amplitude. Her feminine charm had been completely absorbed in the tender qualities of the mother. It was, however, this very motherly quality, so yearned for by Balzac during all the years of his childhood and denied him by his own mother, that he had been seeking for and had now found in the form that answered to his wants. The mysterious instinct which accompanies every genius on his path like a guardian angel had made him aware that the power within him needed guidance and direction, a loving and understanding hand to release the inward tension, refining the coarseness of his fibre without damaging the tissue, offering encouragement while, without malicious criticism, pointing out his defects in a helpful, collaborative spirit, trying to enter into his thoughts and not ridiculing his exuberant dreams as arrant foolishness. The compulsive urge to unfold and to impart his thoughts to others, which his mother had regarded as a monstrous presumption, could now at last be satisfied. This woman, who was about the same age as his mother, gave him a feeling of confidence as she listened to him, her bright, shrewd eyes lit with kindly interest, while he spoke of the fiery projects that filled his waking dreams. It was she who with delicate understanding would correct the little aberrations due to awkward and ungainly traits, to tactlessness and lack of self-control, handling him gently and carefully, helping to form and educate him; and by her attentive deference alone she restored his failing self-confidence. In his *Madame Firmiani* he describes the happiness he derived from this intellectual contact:

> Have you ever had the good fortune to meet a woman whose melodious voice lends her words an enchantment which equally invests her whole bearing? A woman who knows when to speak

and when to be silent, who claims one's attention with a perfect sense of delicacy, who chooses her words with felicity and speaks a language that is remarkable for its purity? Her teasings are like caresses, her criticism does not wound; she does not handle things in a quarrelsome spirit, but is content to guide a conversation and to bring it to a close at the right moment. She behaves with smiling charm, her courtesy is not forced, and she can make an effort without becoming over-anxious. The respect one renders her is never more than merely a sweet shadow; she never tires you, but when you leave her you are satisfied both with her and with yourself. And you find all the things with which she surrounds herself stamped with the same pleasing grace. Everything in her house flatters the eye, and the air you breathe is like the air of home. This woman is natural. All she does is effortless, she does not show off, she expresses her feelings simply because she feels sincerely. . . . She is both tender and cheerful, and her sympathy is displayed in a way that is particularly agreeable. You will love this angel so ardently that even if she were to make a mistake you would be ready to admit that she is right.

It was a new and different atmosphere into which he was entering. His intercourse with this circle taught the young Balzac, who had a unique feeling for the relation of people to their epoch, to sense the living spirit of history in the present. At Laure de Berny's baptism the duc de Fronsac and the princesse de Chimayes had stood sponsor, representing such exalted godparents as the King and Queen of France. She had received the names of Louise after Louis XVI and Antoinette after Marie Antoinette. In the house of her step-father, the Chevalier de Jarjailles, she had heard that paragon of loyalty tell the story of how he had smuggled himself into the Conciergerie at the risk of his life and received from the hands of the condemned Queen the letters she had written to Fersen. Perhaps she had shown him the grateful letter from the Queen which, together with the handkerchief steeped in blood from her scaffold, the family preserved as its most precious treasure, the last moving letter which said: "We have cherished a beautiful dream, that is all. But it meant a great deal to me to have received this further proof of your devotion." What memories these were, stimulating his imagination with a thousand details, intensifying his will to shape and create! One thinks of Balzac's forlorn youth, his dreary years at school and in the wretched garret of the rue Lesdiguières, the eternal petty laments he had had to listen to at home about high rents, rates of interest, investments and annuities, with the parental exhortations to start earning money and to settle down, and then one pictures him listening to this tender, gentle voice telling stories of a dying monarchy and the horrors of the Revolution. When his impatient curiosity grew importunate, he was not rebuffed, but answered with a look of maternal affection. In such discourse his imagination took wings, his heart expanded, and from this gentle tuition the impetuous poet gratefully gained his first insight into life.

⋘○⋙

That was how it began in the case of Madame de Warens when she took the young Jean-Jacques Rousseau into her house. She too had wanted merely to afford some guidance and direction to an awkward, immature, tempestuous young man. She too had no other thought or purpose but to impart her experience to someone who lacked it. But the relations between teacher and pupil can easily and imperceptibly be transmuted into an emotion that tends to the erotic. Without deliberate intent, affectionate tuition changes to affection, respect turns to devotion, and the desire for intimate association becomes desire for more secret intimacies. Madame de Berny, like Madame de Warens, allowed herself to be deceived at first by the shyness of her ardent young pupil and thought it was only respect for her years and her superior social status. She had no inkling of the daemonic forces that she was liberating as she gradually encouraged his self-reliance, of the glowing, long-suppressed fires that a mere look could kindle. She could not possibly suspect that her age meant nothing to a man of Balzac's intense imagination, which could make her, a mother and a grandmother, once more desirable. His will to love, his unique will, achieved the miracle:

> The first time I saw you all my senses were excited and my imagination caught fire. I believed that in you I had found the perfect being . . . though I could not say what kind of a being. But at last, completely possessed by this notion, I disregarded all else and saw in you only this one single perfection.

Admiration turned to desire, and now that Balzac had summoned up the courage to desire he would brook no resistance.

Madame de Berny was startled. In her earlier years she had by no means been a saint. Shortly after her marriage, more than twenty-two years before, she had had her first passionate love-affair, with a black-haired young Corsican, and this was not likely to have been her last. Malicious rumour in Villeparisis even whispered that the last two children born to her belonged only in name to her elderly, half-blind husband. It was therefore no puritan prudery that was being shocked by a young man's passion. She realised the absurdity of beginning a *liaison* at the age of forty-five, under the eyes of her grown-up children, with a man who was younger than her own daughter. What was the point of succumbing once more to the sweet temptation when one knew that such a love could not endure? In a letter which has not come down to us she attempted to confine Balzac's emotional exuberance within the limits of friendship. Instead of passing over in silence the difference in their ages she emphasised it. Balzac's reply was vehement. He was not timorous like his tragic hero Athanase Granson in the *Vieille fille*, who

> feared the curse of ridicule that the world would cast over the love of a young man of twenty-three for a woman of forty.

He was determined to overcome her resistance and cried almost angrily:

> Good heavens, if I were a woman, if I were forty-five and still desirable—oh, I would behave differently from you! What a problem it is to be a woman who is entering upon the autumn of her years and refuses to pluck the fruit which exiled Adam and Eve from paradise!

For the very reason that she loved this ardent young man, Madame de Berny made things difficult for her importunate wooer. For weeks and months she resisted with all her force. This was Balzac's first love-affair, however, and he exerted all his strength of purpose. He needed a first, decisive victory for the sake of his own self-confidence, and a weak woman, disappointed and unhappy in her marriage, already kindled by the flame of his desire, was unequal to the strain of resisting a will that was to be powerful enough to conquer the world. One sultry August night the inevitable happened. In the darkness the back-gate that gave entry to the park of the de Bernys' country-house was softly opened. A tremulous touch guided the awaited lover into the house, and there began that

> night of surprises, so full of delights! That night, which the happy being who is part child, part man can enjoy only once in his life and which will never return.

Nothing can remain secret for long in a small town, and Honoré's frequent visits to Madame de Berny soon gave rise to lively speculation and spiteful talk. There were tense scenes in the de Berny household, since it could not be other than painful for the three young daughters still at home to see their father being betrayed, and they did all they could to make the unwelcome lover's sojourn in the house disagreeable. Madame Balzac was even more deeply affected when she at last began to gain an inkling of the truth. She had completely neglected her son during the decisive years of his development, deliberately suppressing his childish affection for her, destroying his confidence in himself, and trying to keep him at arm's length in humble subjection. Now, when she realised that he had found in Laure de Berny a helpful friend and adviser, everything in fact that she herself should have been to him as his mother, and a mistress as well, this domineering woman was seized by a kind of wild jealousy. In order to remove him from the proximity of his mistress, she forced him to leave Villeparisis in the spring of 1822 and go to stay with his sister, Madame de Surville, in Bayeux. She accompanied him to the stage-coach so as to give him no opportunity for escape at the last moment. Whereas she had formerly looked on his writing of novels as nothing but a means of earning money, she now tried to assume the rôle of his literary mentor. She asked him to submit his manuscripts to her for criticism before sending them to the publisher. But it was too late. Balzac had learned to distinguish between his mother's way of criticising and that of Madame de Berny. He showed the same indifference to her belated and artificial interest in his work as he did to her fits of hysteria. He had lost his fear of her, and with his fear he had lost his respect. "I had asked Honoré to give me his word," she wrote angrily to her daughter, "that he would revise his manuscripts carefully. I had told him to submit them to somebody with more experience of writing than he had himself. . . . Honoré acted as if nothing I said to him was of the slightest importance. He did not listen to me. Honoré is so sure of himself that he refuses to submit his manuscripts to anyone."

Now that she felt him slipping out of her control she tried to keep him by force, but her power was broken. Balzac's first success with a woman had given him his manhood. His self-confidence asserted itself defiantly, and she who had so abused his youth was compelled to recognise that the power of terror which she had exercised over him for two decades was destroyed forever. When she denounced him to his sister she was unconsciously denouncing her own impotence, but all her reproaches came too late. Balzac had freed himself from dependence on his parents. He had recovered from his unhappy youth as one gets over an illness. He was glorying in the imperious sensation of his own power. The centre and focus of his life was no longer the house of his parents, but that of Madame de Berny. No entreaties, no reproaches, no fits of hysteria at home, no secret gossip and whispering in the town could break his resolve to devote himself freely and passionately to the woman who loved him. "Honoré," his mother wrote wrathfully to her daughter, "will not admit how indiscreet it is to visit her house twice a day in this manner. He does not see what is being put so clearly in front of his eyes. I wish I were two hundred leagues away from Villeparisis! He hasn't room in his head for anything but this *affaire*, and he does not understand that he will one day grow tired of this entanglement if he lets himself become so excessively absorbed in it."

⋘○⋙

It was his mother's last hope that he would soon weary of this "*passion qui le perd*", that he would soon give up this absurd love for a woman of forty-five or, to be quite accurate, now forty-six. Once more, however, she was compelled to realise how little she had ever understood him. Far from having any corrupting effect on him, his love for Laure de Berny helped him to find himself.

By awakening the man in this nostalgic "being who was part child, part man", it slowly and without undue abruptness liberated the great novelist that was latent in the hasty scribbler. Through Laure de Berny's *"conseils d'expérience"* Balzac became the true Balzac. Later he acknowledged:

> She was my mother, friend, family, companion and adviser. She made me a writer: she gave me the sympathy I needed when I was young, she guided my taste, she wept and laughed with me like a sister, she came to me every day like a healing sleep that allays one's pain. . . . Without her I would doubtless have died.

She did for him everything a woman can do for a man:

> When great storms threatened to submerge me, she kept my head above water by her encouragement and acts of sacrifice. . . . She stimulated in me the pride which protects a man against all the baseness of the world. . . . If I survive I owe it to her. She was everything to me.

And when this *amitié amoureuse*, which continued on a basis of physical intimacy for a whole decade, from 1822 to 1833, subsided gradually into a mere *amitié*, Balzac's attachment and loyalty became sublimated and, if anything, strengthened. Everything that Balzac wrote about Laure de Berny during her life and after her death constitutes a single rapturous hymn of gratitude for the *"grande et sublime femme, cet ange d'amitié"*, who had awakened in him the man, the artist, and the creator. She had given him courage, freedom, and a sense of outward and inner security. Even the idealised portrait of Madame de Mortsauf in *Le lys dans la vallée* he called only a *"loin reflet d'elle . . . une pâle expression des moindres qualités de cette personne"*, and he confessed in shame that he would never be able to express fully what she had been to him, *"car j'ai horreur de prostituer mes propres émotions au public"*. But the extent to which he felt this association with Laure de Berny as an unparalleled stroke of good fortune in his life has been recorded by him in his immortal saying: "There is nothing that can match the last love of a woman who is giving a man the fulfilment of his first love."

His association with Madame de Berny was the redeeming and decisive factor in Balzac's career. She not only liberated the man who had not yet found his true self and the artist who had almost given up hope, but more than that, she determined for the rest of his life the type of woman with whom he was to fall in love. Henceforth Balzac was to seek in every woman the maternally protective guide and helpmate that had given him so much happiness in this prototype. He needed women who did not make claims upon his time, overworked as he was, but had the leisure and the capacity to offer him relaxation when his work was done. What he required as the essential prerequisite for love was both social and spiritual distinction. Understanding meant more to him than passion. The only women who could meet his demands were those to whom he could look up because they were more experienced than he and also, strange to say, older. *La femme abandonnée* and *La femme de trente ans* were not only titles he gave to novels, they were also the heroines of his own life, mature women disappointed in life and love. They no longer expected anything from existence and felt it as a gracious favour from destiny that they should once more be desired and allowed to serve the great writer as companions and helpmates. The cocotte, the harlot, the so-called daemonic woman, or the literary snob never held any charm for Balzac. Superficial beauty never seduced him and he was not tempted by youth. He even emphasised his "deep distaste for young girls" because they ask too much and give too little. "The woman of forty," he said, "will do everything for you—the woman of twenty nothing." In all his love experiences he unconsciously longed only for a recurrence of that manifold love, complete in all its aspects, which he had found in the one woman who had been everything to him—mother and sister, friend and tutor, mistress and companion.

CHAPTER V

Business Interlude

alzac's first request to destiny had been fulfilled. The help of a loving woman had been granted him, and thanks to the self-reliance he had thereby acquired he had achieved his spiritual independence. When he had won material independence also, he would be ready to enter upon his true vocation, to undertake the work he was to do.

Until he was twenty-five Balzac cherished the hope of gaining this material independence slowly and tenaciously by his hackwork, but in the last days of the winter of 1824 he suddenly made up his mind to launch out on a new venture. It was to be a black day in his life's calendar, the ill-fated day when he entered the shop of the publisher and bookseller Urbain Canel, 30 Place St. André des Arts, with a view to offering him his latest novel, *Wann-Chlore*. Not that he met with an unwelcome reception. On the contrary, the publishing and bookselling firm of Canel was well aware that the wholesale and retail novel-writing firm of Horace de Saint Aubin delivered its goods punctually and was able to satisfy the public demand for murder and bloodshed, sentimental intrigue and exotic atmosphere. Monsieur Canel accepted Balzac's manuscript without more ado. Unfortunately, however, he also took the opportunity of revealing to him the other business projects that he had in mind. He confided to Balzac that he had hit on a promising idea of publishing books suitable for Christmas, confirmations and *nouveaux riches* bourgeois households. There was still a good demand for the French classics, but sales had hitherto suffered for the reason that these esteemed gentlemen had written too much. The collected works of Molière or Lafontaine, for instance, ran in their extant editions to a large number of volumes and took up too much room in the average middle-class household. The brilliant thought had now occurred to him of publishing the collected works of all the classic writers each in a single volume. By the use of small print and two columns to the page the whole of Lafontaine or Molière could easily be brought within two covers. If these volumes were furthermore adorned with pretty vignettes they would be bound to sell like hot cakes. The plan had been worked out to the last detail, and the Lafontaine volume was, as a matter of fact, already in hand. To enable this grandiose undertaking to be launched in fitting style one trifling item was still lacking—the necessary capital.

Balzac, with his eternal visionary enthusiasm, was immediately enraptured with the scheme and proposed to Canel that he should himself become a partner in the project. There was no intrinsic reason why he should rush into such dubious business adventures. His own business of turning out novels was flourishing quite tolerably well, thanks to his indefatigable labours and lack of literary scruple. With an equipment consisting merely of a bundle of goose-quills and a few reams of paper per month he was earning a pretty regular income of a few thousand francs a year. His newly acquired self-reliance, however, had brought with it a taste for a higher standard of living. The lover of a great lady did not want to continue living in a garret, and the small room he was now occupying on the fifth floor of the rue de Tournon was too cramped and unworthy of him. It was also humiliating, fatiguing, inglorious and, in the long run, futile to keep on working at his treadmill, writing books that were paid for line by line, page by page, and volume by volume. Why not take the bold leap that would bring him a fortune? Why not risk a couple of thousand francs on a safe speculation of this kind? He could still continue to turn out the stupid novels, newspaper articles and all the rest of the anonymous stuff which flowed with so little effort from his facile pen. The genius of Beaumarchais had not been prejudiced by the fact that he had published the works of Monsieur de Voltaire as a sideline, and had not even the great humanists of the Middle Ages been proof-readers and technical advisers to publishing firms? The earning of money, by whatever method, never appeared to Balzac as a disgrace, but only as evidence of a versatile mind. It was foolish only if one earned too little money by too much work, and the clever thing to do was to acquire a great deal of money by one swift *coup*. At last the time had come to acquire the capital that would enable him, with resolute concentration on his central purpose, to create a work of art which he could sign with his own name and answer for to the world and to posterity.

Balzac did not take long to make up his mind. Whenever he heard of a stroke of business to be done, his imagination overruled his reason in calculating the pros and cons, and speculation gave him a pleasurable thrill such as he felt when writing and creating. He never rejected a business opportunity on the score of literary pride. He was ready to deal in anything, from books and pictures to railway shares, from real estate to timber and metal. His sole ambition was to find an outlet for the forces within him and thrust his way forward; the goal and the means were of no concern. He was bent solely on achieving power. Even at the age of thirty he was still trying to decide whether to go in for politics or to become a journalist, just as Goethe for a long time hesitated whether to become a painter or a poet and Wagner was uncertain whether he wanted to be a dramatist or a musician. If the opportunity had offered Balzac might equally well have become a business man or a slave-dealer, a speculator in real estate or a banker. It was mere chance that directed his genius into the channel of literature, and if in 1830 or 1840, or even 1850, he had been offered the choice between becoming a Rothschild or the creator of the *Comédie humaine*, it is very doubtful whether he would not have elected to be a leading light in the world of finance rather than in the world of letters. Every project that came his way, whether in the business or the literary sphere, excited his imagination because of its apparently unlimited possibilities. He could not see without becoming subject to hallucinations, he could not tell a story without exaggerating, he could not work out an arithmetical calculation without becoming intoxicated by the figures. Just as he was able to survey in his mind's eye all the intricacies of a plot as soon as an idea for a novel occurred to him, he could not help seeing a vast and inevitable profit in every speculation by which he was attracted. Monsieur

Canel had only to speak of his scheme for one-volume editions of the classics for Balzac to imagine himself holding magnificently bound books in his hand, printed on snow-white paper and adorned with vignettes, the first volume, the second volume, the whole series—though only the first two folios of the first volume had yet been set up in print. He saw the public thronging to the bookshops in Paris and the provinces, reading and fondling the new volumes in châteaux and in cottages. He saw the counter of Monsieur Canel piled high with orders and porters groaning under the heavy packages which were being sent out every day and every hour to all points of the compass. He saw the till overflowing with thousand-franc notes and himself living in a splendid house with his tilbury at the door. He saw the furniture with which he was going to surround himself, the sofa covered with red damask which he had seen the previous day at an antique dealer's on the left bank, the damask curtains at the windows, the decorative statuettes on the chimneypiece, and the pictures on the wall. It went without saying, he declared to Monsieur Canel, who stood in silent astonishment at such enthusiasm, that he would contribute the trifling two or three thousand francs to which his share would amount. Furthermore, he would write prefaces to the *Lafontaine* and *Molière* which would for the first time explain to France who these men were. It would, in fact, be the finest series ever published, the greatest success of all time.

As Balzac left the shop he felt that he was already a millionaire. Monsieur Urbain Canel had acquired a partner for a small business speculation and Balzac in his dreams had acquired a fortune.

The strange story of this undertaking would have been a fitting subject for Balzac's own pen. It had not been his intention, apparently, to become deeply involved. His share in the whole affair did not amount originally to more than fifteen hundred or two thousand francs, that is to say, no more than he earned by one of the potboilers he was able to turn out so rapidly. But everything Balzac touched inevitably assumed vast proportions. When he wrote the first *Scènes de la vie privée* he was unaware that he was beginning the great epic work of his age, the *Comédie humaine*. When he accepted a modest share in Monsieur Canel's publishing scheme he had just as little inkling of the financial responsibility he was about to shoulder.

The first contract, signed in the middle of April 1825, was quite harmless. Balzac merely became a partner in a small consortium which was to provide the seven or eight thousand francs required to defray the cost of publishing a volume of Lafontaine. It is not known how these four men were brought together. Apart from Balzac they were a physician, a pensioned officer, and the bookseller, whose financial contribution probably consisted of the sum he had already laid out. All four were men of modest means prepared to contribute about fifteen hundred francs apiece in what promised to be a lucrative transaction. Unfortunately their co-operation for the purpose of exploiting Lafontaine's fables was not long-lived. From an extremely choleric letter written by the physician it is to be inferred that their very first discussions were conducted in a violent tone which very nearly led to blows, and by the 1st of May Balzac's three partners, all cautious business-men, had withdrawn their support and left the only idealist among them to carry the whole weight on his own shoulders.

Balzac had been driven a step further than he had intended to go. He was now the sole owner of a *Lafontaine* which had not yet been set up in type and had to defray the whole cost of production himself, amounting to nearly nine thousand francs. This was for him a relatively huge sum, and the question is, where did the money come from? Did he knock off another two or three novels in his leisure hours, or did he manage to persuade his parents to place the capital at his disposal? A glance at the account books solves the mystery. The invoices are accompanied by three promissory notes in the name of Madame de Berny, who had apparently succumbed to the spell of his enthusiasm. For a second time she tried to smooth his path.

Balzac's temperament, however, got the upper hand. It would have been logical to await the success of the Lafontaine volume before tackling the next author on his list, but his ingrained optimism vanquished his reason. He could no longer think or work or live on a small scale. The young student who had counted every sou had become the impatient besieger of destiny. So Molière had to follow swift on the heels of Lafontaine. Two books could be sold with more facility than one, so away with all pettifogging business scruples!

Balzac again made use of his ardent powers of persuasion, and this time it was Monsieur d'Assonvillez, a friend of his family, who declared his readiness to advance five thousand francs for the printing of the *Molière*. So before a single copy had been disposed of, Balzac had invested fourteen thousand francs of other people's money at his own risk. With feverish haste he went ahead with the preparation of the two volumes, with too feverish a haste, in fact, for the wholesalers craftily took advantage of his inexperience and enthusiasm to supply him with paper that was soiled from being kept too long in stock. Devéria's vignettes, on which Balzac had placed such high hopes, turned out badly. In order to compress the whole of Lafontaine in one volume the type had to be so small that it was fatiguing even to good eyesight, and the prefaces which Balzac hurriedly dashed off added nothing whatever to the attractiveness of volumes that were already æsthetically unattractive.

From the business point of view the result was a foregone conclusion. In his anxiety to net the maximum profit Balzac had fixed the price per volume at twenty francs. This frightened the booksellers, so the first thousand copies, instead of being the harbingers. of innumerable further impressions, as Balzac had fondly dreamed, remained in the printer's stockroom unwanted either by the booksellers or the public. Of a work designed for mass consumption the total number of copies sold at the end of a year amounted in all to twenty. Printers, binders, paper-makers and others had to be paid in cash. In order to give himself breathing space Balzac reduced the price to thirteen francs a volume. Even this did not help. He went down to twelve francs, but there were still no orders. At last he disposed of the entire stock at remainder prices, and was once more swindled. After a year's desperate struggle the catastrophe was complete. Instead of acquiring the fortune of which he had dreamed, Balzac was in debt to the tune of fifteen thousand francs.

❧⊙❧

Any other man would have capitulated after a failure of this magnitude, but Balzac was not yet strong enough to accept a defeat as final. Later on, when one of his plays met with public dis-

approval, he would compensate for his lack of success by writing a
novel that stirred the world. When his creditors were in full cry
after him and the *huissiers* were lying in wait for him at his door, he
would amuse himself by making fools of them and would boast of
his debts as if they were triumphs. But at the age of twenty-six he
had neither previous success to uphold him nor a reputation which
in itself was a guarantee to his creditors. He had not yet become the
Napoleon of literature, who could afford to accept an occasional setback. Perhaps out of shame at having to make an admission of
failure to his parents, who had always doubted his abilities, or
perhaps because he did not want to confess to Laure de Berny that
he had lost his whole stake at the first throw, he again doubled the
stake. The only way he saw to retrieve his losses was to risk more
capital. There must have been some error in his first calculation,
and Balzac thought he knew what it was. It was bad business to be
merely a publisher, because one was cheated by expensive printers
who skimmed off the cream. Neither the writing of books nor the
publishing of books was a lucrative business, but only the printing
of books. Only by launching out on a bold, comprehensive venture,
in which he himself did the writing, selecting, printing, and publishing, could his abilities find their full scope. So he resolved to make
good his failure with Lafontaine and Molière by undertaking all the
various processes essential to the production of books. Following
well-established precedent, he tried to make his bankrupt business
solvent by extending it. Balzac started on the second lap of his
business career. He decided to set up a printing-works.

In an enterprise of this nature certain provisos had to be fulfilled
which in Balzac's case were lacking. In the first place he knew
nothing about the technique of printing. Secondly, he did not
possess the royal licence which in those days was necessary before
one could become a printer. Thirdly, he did not possess either the
premises or the machinery. Fourthly, he had no capital with which
to acquire the licence, the premises, and the equipment, to say
nothing of both skilled and unskilled assistants. When a man has
made up his mind to start a business on unsound foundations,
however, he only too frequently finds that malicious Fortune gives
him a helping hand at the outset. Balzac succeeded in enlisting the
services of an expert compositor named André Barbier, to whom
his attention had been drawn while the *Lafontaine* was in the press,

and he persuaded him to take over the technical direction of the
Imprimerie Honoré Balzac. The licence to print was obtained
through the good offices of Monsieur de Berny, who wrote a letter of
recommendation to a Minister and to the President of Police. We
can surmise what tender hand guided the pen of the supplanted
husband:

> This young man has been known to me for a long time. The
> correctness of his convictions and his knowledge of literature are
> in my view a guarantee that he is fully aware of the obligations
> which will be imposed on him by such a profession.

This recommendation sufficed, and Honoré Balzac (not yet calling
himself Honoré *de* Balzac) was granted an official licence to carry
on the trade of printing.

Once in possession of his letters patent there was no difficulty in
finding a printing press for sale, and he came upon what he wanted
in the rue des Marais, a dark narrow alley on the left bank, later
called the rue de Visconti. On the ground floor of a house next to
the one in which Jean Racine died in 1699 and Adrienne Lecouv-
reur in 1730 there was a dirty little printing establishment whose
owner, a certain Monsieur Laurence *aîné*, had long wished to dispose of a business that was bringing him in a very meagre profit.
He was happy to meet a prospective purchaser who offered him a
good price, or at least who promised to pay him a good price and
provided adequate guarantees.

Three of the four provisos had been fulfilled without much
trouble. The fourth was considerably more difficult, for purchase
was easier than payment. Balzac needed from fifty to sixty thous-
and francs—thirty thousand to acquire the concession and the
business, twelve thousand for Barbier, his technical manager, who
did not appear completely convinced of his employer's qualifications for a commercial career and demanded this sum as security,
and the rest for sundries such as essential replacements, which were
likely to be heavy since much of the plant was antiquated and the
business had been neglected by its former proprietor. With nothing
to his name but fifteen thousand francs' worth of debts, the prospect of raising another fifty to sixty thousand did not look promising. Luckily for him, or rather unluckily, he succeeded in finding
solid guarantors where they were least to be expected. His parents,

neither of whom had ever been disinclined to yield to the chance of a tempting speculation and whose liquid assets amounted at the time to some two hundred thousand francs, had capital available for investment and, surprisingly enough, they raised no objection to their son's new venture. Printing was a good sound trade, not a frivolous affair like writing books, and Honoré's eternal optimism was presumably persuasive enough to convince his father and mother of the sunny prospects that lay ahead. A family council agreed to capitalise his allowance of fifteen hundred francs, and on the strength of his parents' guarantee a friend of theirs named Madame Delanoix advanced thirty thousand as working capital. The remainder seems again to have been provided by the self-sacrificing Madame de Berny. On the 4th of June, 1826, Balzac duly informed the Ministry that he had set up in business as a printer:

> I, the undersigned owner of a printing-works in Paris, hereby announce that I am transferring my residence and place of business to No. 17 rue des Marais, Faubourg St. Germain.

The third act of the tragi-comedy had begun.

❧

This strange printing establishment has often been described, and many vivid pages of the *Illusions perdues* and *La maison du chat qui pelote* cast a sharp light on the activity that went on behind the darkened windows. The rue des Marais wound its narrow, crooked way between St. Germain-des-Prés and the Quai Malaquais. No ray of sunshine ever penetrated to its cobblestones. The tall entrance-gates that led to the courtyards of its houses indicated that in the seventeenth century they had looked down upon visitors rolling through in their carriages to call on aristocratic occupants. But tastes and values had changed in the course of two hundred years. The nobility, whether of blood or of wealth, had long since moved to less gloomy, more congenial quarters, and small craftsmen had set up their shops in the shabby alley whose dismal aspect was enhanced by soot, dirt and age.

The house in which Balzac and Barbier set up their printing press did not even possess the advantages that had survived from the street's former connection with the aristocracy. It had been built on the site of an earlier spacious house and impudently pushed its way forward beyond its more polite neighbours, its fore-part even stretching right up to the roadway. It had been cheaply constructed for utilitarian purposes, and the ground-floor consisted of a single large room used as a workshop, from which an iron spiral staircase led up to the first storey, where the new proprietor proceeded to install himself. This private lodging contained an ante-chamber, a dark kitchen, a small dining-room with a chimney-piece in the Empire style, and a combined study and sitting-room with a little alcove.

It was Balzac's first real home and he furnished it with loving care. Instead of papering the walls he hung them with light-blue percale, arranged his books in their handsome bindings, and provided himself with a variety of small, cheap articles—all with a view to delighting the eye of his faithful helpmeet, who visited him day after day during these most difficult years: "She came every day, like a healing sleep that allays one's pain."

This little sanctuary, which Balzac built into the rocking barque of his business venture like a cabin, was no mere pandering to a frivolous taste for luxury, for he took his new occupation very seriously. From early morning till late at night he stood in shirt-sleeves and with open collar among his twenty-four workmen in the hot room that reeked of oil and damp paper, sweating and strug-gling like a Trojan to feed the seven hungry printing-presses. No detail was too unimportant, no work too undignified, for him to attend to personally. He corrected the galleys, helped with the type-setting, did the costing, and wrote out the invoices with his own hand. He was always squeezing his somewhat corpulent body through the crowded room, past machines and piled-up bales, either to urge one of the workmen to greater efforts or on his way to the tiny office with its glass partition, where he would haggle with book-sellers and paper-suppliers for every sou. None of those who came to give an order or present a bill to this bustling master printer, who received them among the rattling, creaking presses with his hands still black from oil and ink, could ever have had the faintest presentiment that the stout, industrious little man in front of them with the filthy matted hair and persuasive tongue was or was about to become the greatest writer of his age.

During those years Balzac really had bidden farewell to his lofty

ambitions. He threw himself body and soul into his new profession
of printing. His one aim in life was to keep his presses going and to
build up a flourishing business. Gone were his visions of bringing
the French classics to the hearths and hearts of the people. He
printed whatever came his way, without trying to pick and choose.
The first piece of work turned out by his firm was of no very high
literary merit, but merely a prospectus entitled *Pillules anti-
glaireuses de longue vie, ou grains de vie*. The second was a speech in
defence of a murderess, printed by an ambitious lawyer at his own
expense. The third was a puff for a quack medicine, *Mixture brésili-
enne de Lepère, pharmacien*. Then came a motley array of whatever
his clients happened to provide—brochures, prospectuses, editions
of the classics, poems, advertisements, catalogues and amusing
trifles. He printed one only of the works that came from his own
pen, a *Petit dictionnaire des enseignes de Paris par un batteur des
pavés*, which he had presumably dashed off for some publisher at a
time when he urgently needed some ready cash.

Things went badly from the start, and it must have been with
mixed feelings that Balzac read through the proofs of a booklet
sent to him for printing. It was called *L'art de payer ses dettes et de
satisfaire ses créanciers . . . ou manuel du droit commercial à l'usage
des gens ruinés*. The art of satisfying his creditors was one which
he never succeeded in mastering. The very first financial transaction in which he engaged showed how the same qualities can produce opposite effects in different fields of activity. The optimism
and power of imagination which enabled him in the sphere of art
to create a new world led inevitably to his ruin when he launched
into business. He stumbled over the first step. In order to increase
his working capital he had sold his stocks of *Lafontaine* and *Molière*
at a considerably reduced price to the bookseller Baudouin, receiving twenty-two thousand francs for the whole two thousand five
hundred copies. This worked out at less than nine francs a copy
instead of the twenty he had originally fixed. He needed the money
urgently, however, and signed the contract without attaching any
importance to the fact that Baudouin, instead of paying him
twenty-two thousand francs in cash, preferred to give him twenty-
seven thousand in drafts on two booksellers, one of whom lived in
the provinces. Balzac saw only the extra five thousand francs and
snapped at the bait without noticing the hook. The hook was not

long in making its presence felt. At the very moment when he presented the drafts to the two booksellers for payment they both went bankrupt. Deeply in debt as he was, he could not afford to wait until the bankruptcy proceedings had taken their course, and decided to recoup himself as best he could by taking over the stocks of the provincial bookseller. So instead of ready money he received vast quantities of worthless volumes, old editions of Gessner, Florian, Fénelon, and Gilbert, which had been collecting the dust in a provincial warehouse for years. It was fit subject for a comedy. With the capital provided by Madame de Berny he had published his two editions of the classics; since these found no sale he had got rid of them for less than half the original price in order to obtain a further supply of capital; now instead of the expected ready money he found himself with another stock of books on his hands that were equally unsaleable. He had exchanged one lot of waste paper for a different lot that was worth far less. It was like the story of Lucky Hans in the old German fairy-tale, who spent his accumulated wages on a cow, then bartered the cow for a goat, the goat for a goose, and finally the goose for a mill-stone, which rolled into the water and left him with nothing.

Tied up in great bales the works of these once popular authors were stored in the printing-room to gather dust. Unfortunately, the workmen wanted to be paid in hard coin and Balzac could not settle his weekly wage-bill with volumes of Fénelon, Florian, and the rest. Soon the merchants who supplied the firm with paper got wind of the way things were going and ruthlessly refused Balzac's promissory notes, which had not yet acquired their future value as autographs. They insisted on immediate settlement of their accounts, and the little glass-screened office did not provide a safe refuge from their clamorous dunning. Balzac appeared less and less frequently in the printing-room, and particularly as the week-end approached his absences grew more and more prolonged. He wandered from door to door seeking extension of the time allowed him for payment and exploring the possibilities of a loan from bankers, friends or relatives. During those months, when he was struggling in desperation to keep his head above water, he experienced personally all the scenes of humiliation which he was later to describe so unforgettably in *César Birotteau*.

He fought with the strength of a Samson, but had to give up in the end. By the summer of 1827 he had lost everything; there was not even a sou in the till to pay his workmen. He had had no more success as a printer than as a publisher, or as the author of a tragedy in verse. Only two logical possibilities remained, either public bankruptcy or private liquidation.

Balzac chose a third possibility. Like his immortal counterpart, Napoleon, he was not content to accept defeat and remain exiled on Elba, but tried his luck at Waterloo. Undeterred by his past experiences, he once more tried to salvage a bankrupt undertaking by enlarging it. When his publishing business was about to disappear beneath the waves he attached a printing press to it as a lifebuoy, and when that too began to sink he attempted to keep it afloat by adding a type-foundry. The tragic part of this enterprise, as of all Balzac's enterprises, was that the basic idea was perfectly sound. Balzac was partly a visionary and partly a hardened realist, with the clear insight of a lawyer or a man of business. His project of a one-volume edition of the French classics was in itself by no means foolish. It was carried out later in a more efficient way and proved a success. Nor was his printing venture intrinsically wrong-headed. The demand for reading-matter was rapidly on the increase. His third scheme, that of the type-foundry, was even particularly promising. He had heard of a new printing process, the so-called *fonterreotypie*, invented by a certain Pierre Deréchail, which was said to achieve better results than were obtainable by the normal method of stereotyping—"without the employment of a crucible for casting the matrices and without the necessity to reverse and correct the cast pages". Balzac was immediately fascinated. With far-seeing vision he realised that in the age of industrialisation which was then beginning every process leading to the simplification and cheapening of production would bring decisive results, and that the greatest profits of the century would ensue from such inventions. As is proved by his novels, he never lost interest in the problem of invention. It is not merely fortuitous that David Séchart in the *Illusions perdues*, a story which mirrors Balzac's own experience as a printer, is concerned with a process in the manufacture of paper which brings in millions. Balthasar Claes in *La recherche de l'absolu*, César Birotteau, the inventor of the *pâté sultane*, the painter Frenhofer, the musician Cambara—all these seek to enhance by a novel combination of forces the results that have hitherto been achieved. No great writer of his age since Goethe took such a lively interest in the progress of science as did Balzac, and he had the foresight to anticipate the inevitable evolution by which hand-setting and casting by hand must in the near future yield to mechanical improvements as a consequence of the enormous growth in numbers of the reading population. The new printing process appeared, at any rate, to offer a promising start. With the impatience of the eternal optimist and a desperation born of his pending bankruptcy, Balzac seized the new opportunity held out to him.

On the 18th of September, 1827, when the printing firm was already on its last legs, a new company was formed which included Barbier and a certain Lorant, the liquidator of the bankrupt type-foundry of M. Gillet Fils, 4 rue Garoncière. In December the first circulars were sent out. Apparently Lorant was supplying the equipment, Barbier taking over the management, and Balzac handling the advertising for the new process. There was to be no more toiling and moiling at the petty jobs that came the way of the small printer. The new undertaking was to be carried on in the grand style. Balzac prepared a magnificent album in which speci-mens of all the new types that his firm would be able to supply were neatly set out, together with the vignettes and ornamental cuts that would be available to printers or publishers thanks to the new process. Hardly were the preparations for the new catalogue completed when Barbier suddenly announced his intention to withdraw from the partnership. The ship threatened to sink before it had left port. Once more Madame de Berny came to the rescue in this dangerous crisis. She persuaded her husband to give her a power of attorney over his property and took over Barbier's share. The nine thousand francs which she threw after the money she had already lost rendered the barque temporarily seaworthy again.

It was, however, too late. The splendid album with its variety of types to tempt prospective buyers and clients was not ready in time, and the firm's creditors, alarmed at the retirement of Barbier, who seemed to them to be the only reliable partner, began to besiege the house. Paper-merchants and booksellers demanded payment of their accounts, money-lenders called in their loans, and the workmen wanted their wages. Nobody paid any heed to Bal-zac's assurances that the money would begin to roll in when the

new enterprise was solidly on its feet. Nobody would accept any
more promissory notes either from the firm of Balzac and Barbier,
or the firm of Balzac and Lorant, or from Honoré Balzac himself.
On the 6th of April, 1828, the third consortium, which was to have
lasted for twelve years, had to declare itself insolvent. Balzac was
bankrupt, triply bankrupt, as a publisher, as a printer, and as the
owner of a type-foundry.

The bad news could no longer be concealed from Balzac's
parents, who would have to be informed at once unless their first
intelligence of their son's failure and the stigma of bankruptcy on
the name of Balzac was to come to them from the newspapers. The
tidings of collapse burst on their ears like a thunderclap. His
mother tried at first to keep the loss of their invested capital a
secret from her husband, who was now eighty-two years of age, and
in this she was for a time successful. But then came the inexorable
question whether the family was simply to drop the prodigal son
or whether a further sacrifice should be made to rescue his reputation as a business man.

Madame Balzac, who had refused her son any pocket-money
whatsoever at school and had scolded him for his extravagance
when he hung a small engraving on the wall of his room, could
hardly be expected to touch the family savings, though these were
still fairly considerable. She was, however, also concerned for her
good name and filled with apprehension of public gossip. That the
name of Balzac should appear under the heading *Bankruptcies* in
all the newspapers would shame her before her relatives and neighbours. So, doubtless in desperation, she declared her readiness to
make a further financial sacrifice in order that the public disgrace
of insolvency might be averted.

A cousin, Monsieur de Sédillot, undertook at her request the
difficult task of liquidation. Balzac had so confused the accounts
of the companies with their individual liabilities that it took Monsieur de Sédillot about a year to disentangle the balance-sheets
and, partially at least, to satisfy the creditors. His first sensible
step was completely to eliminate Balzac from the process of
winding-up. Visionaries and hatchers of grandiose schemes were of

no use in a task which required meticulous accuracy. His melancholy labours did not come to an end until the middle of 1828. The
printing firm, on which debts to the tune of over a hundred thous-
and francs were outstanding, was acquired by Barbier for sixty-
seven thousand, which represented for the Balzac family a sheer
loss of from forty to forty-five thousand francs. Madame de Berny,
who had invested altogether forty-five thousand francs on her
lover's behalf, received the type-foundry as security, a very in-
adequate first instalment, and handed it over to her son Alexandre.
For the time being all those who had put their trust in Balzac's
business genius lost heavily, but by the irony of fate both undertakings began to pay their way as soon as Balzac had vanished from
the scene and they could be carried on with the sober and patient
judgment which a commercial enterprise demands. Balzac returned
to the only sphere of activity where his imagination could bring
fruitful results, the sphere of art.

❦❧

When Monsieur de Sédillot had finished patching up the affairs
of the two firms, it was left to Balzac to draw up his own personal
balance-sheet. From the material point of view it was devastating.
He was twenty-nine years of age and less independent than ever.
At the age of twenty-nine he was nearly a hundred thousand francs
in debt to his parents and Madame de Berny. For ten years he had
worked in vain, without pause, without relaxation, without diversion. He had accepted every form of humiliation, written thousands
of pages under pseudonyms, and had been chained to an office desk
from morning till night except when he was hunting around for
clients or wrestling with creditors. The debts he had accumulated
during his three years in business were the rock of Sisyphus which
for the rest of his life he was again and again to trundle up the hill
with straining muscles, only to see it go crashing down again before
he had reached the summit. This first false step condemned him to
lifelong indebtedness, and his youthful dream of one day being able
to devote himself freely and independently to creative work was
destined never to be fulfilled.

The material side of the balance-sheet, however, was outweighed
by an incomparable asset. What he had lost as a man of business he

7

had gained as a man of letters. The entry on the credit side was in a more valuable and universally recognised currency. These three years of toil, of incessant wrestling with the forces of reality, taught the romantic, who had hitherto been content with delineating pale shadows copied from fashionable models, to see the actual world with all its daily dramas, any one of which, as he said later, was as moving as a Shakespeare tragedy and as intense as one of Napoleon's battles. He had learned the tremendous, the daemonic significance of money in our materialistic age, and he knew that the struggles waged around a bill of exchange or a promissory note, the tricks and stratagems employed in small shops no less than in the great counting-houses of Paris, involved as great a play of psychological forces as did the adventures of Byron's corsairs or Sir Walter Scott's blue-blooded knights. By labouring with workmen, battling with usurers, and desperately bargaining with wholesale merchants he had acquired an immeasurably greater knowledge of social conditions and contrasts than his famous contemporaries Victor Hugo, Lamartine, or Alfred de Musset, who sought only the romantic aspects of life, its exalting and grandiose elements; whereas he had also learned to see and portray the cruelties inherent in poverty, the ugliness in humble lives, the secret power that lay dormant in men. The imagination of the young idealist was enriched by the clear-sightedness of the realist, the scepticism of a man robbed of his illusions. No magnificence would henceforth impress him, no romantic drapery deceive him, for he had looked deeply into the working of the social machine, perceiving the snares with which debtors were bound hand and foot and the meshes which offered a means of escape. He knew how money was made and how it was lost, how lawsuits were conducted and how men got on in the world, how to squander and how to save, how others were cheated and how one cheated oneself. As he later so rightly said, it was only because he had tried so many ways of making a living in his youth and learned to see their causal connections that he was able faithfully to portray his own epoch. His greatest masterpieces, the *Illusions perdues*, *La peau de chagrin*, *Louis Lambert*, and *César Birotteau*, the great epics of the middle classes, of the stock exchange, and the business world, would have been unthinkable without the disappointments he had experienced during these years. Only now, after his imagination had become fused and interpenetrated with reality, was it possible for the wondrous substance of the Balzac novel to emerge as the most perfect compound of realism and fantasy. Only after he had failed to achieve success in the world of actuality was the artist in him sufficiently mature to fashion a world of his own to set beside it.

CHAPTER VI

Balzac and Napoleon

"What he began with the sword, I shall consummate with the pen."

 n view of such a complete collapse of his rash speculations, it would have been logical to expect that Balzac's self-confidence must have been buried under the ruins of his extravagant hopes. But as his plans came toppling down like a house of cards he felt only one thing— that he was free to begin anew. The vitality he had inherited from his father, and perhaps from a whole line of sturdy peasants, was not affected in the slightest degree by the catastrophe, and he had no intention of mourning in sackcloth and ashes for the money he had lost. In any case, it was not his own money that had vanished, and throughout his life the very size of his debts made them appear as unreal as were the fortunes that he acquired in his imagination. Defeat was never able to shake his elemental optimism. That which broke the back of weaker men merely scratched his skin: "In every period of my life my courage triumphed over my misfortunes."

For the time being, however, it seemed desirable, if only on grounds of decency, to hide his light under a bushel. Moreover, there were sound reasons for not having his own front door at which unwelcome creditors could knock. Like a redskin in one of the novels of Fenimore Cooper that he liked so much, he practised for a time the craft of covering up his tracks, and since he wanted to stay in Paris both to earn his living and to be near Madame de Berny it was necessary for him to change his lodgings occasionally and refrain from registering his address with the police.

His first hiding-place was in the house of Henri de Latouche, with whom he had struck up a friendship in recent months. Latouche knew his way about in the newspaper world of Paris, and he took the younger man under his wing. More receptive than creative, with a feminine talent for sympathetic understanding and criticism, he was agreeable and kind during the years of his success, but withdrew into embittered reserve when disappointment came his way. Comparatively ungifted himself, his flair for talent in others gave him a share in their immortality. It was he who rescued for posterity the poems of André Chénier, whose brother had kept them jealously locked away in a desk for a quarter of a century, and he inspired some of the most beautiful French lyrics ever written, wonderful stanzas by Marceline Desbordes-Valmore, whose unfaithful lover he had been. It spoke for his keen insight that he offered friendship and hospitality to a bankrupt printer on the verge of thirty who had not yet published a single line that showed promise of his future genius, and more than anyone else encouraged and exhorted him to try his luck once more in writing.

Balzac did not stay very long with his amiable but very loquacious friend. In order to work as he was accustomed to working, that is to say, day and night without pause or interruption, he needed complete seclusion, a cell of his own, however small. So that he might enjoy the tranquillity he needed for his new start, the de Survilles gave him permission to use their name, for if he were to rent a lodging under his own name his bell would be ringing all day long and there would be no respite from creditors, messengers and bailiffs. In March 1828 an unknown tenant, a certain Monsieur de Surville, moved into a little house in the rue de Cassini, and for nine years this was to be Balzac's headquarters, the four or five rooms of which he populated with innumerable characters summoned up by his creative imagination.

The rue de Cassini offered many advantages from the point of view of situation. It was a suburban street, inhabited by obscure citizens, and no one would expect to find an author, particularly an author of reputation, living near to the *Observatoire* on the extreme edge of the town:

> It is no longer Paris, and yet it is still Paris. The district has something of the square, the street, the boulevard, the fortifications, the gardens, the avenue, and the high road; it is in the provinces

and yet it is also in the capital; there is something of all this, yet nothing of all this; it is a desert.

Like a robber knight swooping down from his castle, Balzac could descend at dusk upon the "Paris at my feet which I intend to conquer". On the other hand, he could pull up the drawbridge and thus prevent surprise by unwelcome visitors. Only two friends, apart from Latouche, knew the whereabouts of his secret lair. They were the painter Auguste Borget, who occupied the lower storey, and Madame de Berny, who probably helped him to choose it. It was not only just round the corner from her own residence, but possessed an unusual amenity. A narrow back-staircase led up from the yard straight to a hidden door which opened into Balzac's bedroom, so that however frequent her visits they could do no harm to her reputation.

This lodging was expensive only in comparison with the rue Lesdiguières. The three rooms he occupied—sitting-room, study, and bedroom, together with an engaging little bathroom—cost him no more than four hundred francs a year. Balzac, however, was an adept in the art of turning something cheap into something expensive. Scarcely had he moved into his new quarters when he succumbed to a passion for furnishing it sumptuously. Like Richard Wagner, who also remained in debt all his life, he wanted to enjoy a foretaste of luxury in his surroundings while he was still toiling to make his fortune. Whenever Wagner changed his place of abode his first step was to send for the upholsterer to put up velvet curtains, cover the furniture with damask, and lay down thick carpets, so that he might have the right atmosphere for musical composition. In the isolation of his study Balzac needed an ornate, an over-ornate *milieu*, which was, in fact, too crowded for good taste. He took a delight in furnishing his rooms to provide the stylised setting that appealed to his temperament, just as in his novels he built up the environment of his characters with a wealth of detail that required the combined knowledge of an architect, an upholsterer, a tailor and a connoisseur so that he might see them in the round. It was not yet possible for him to acquire the more costly requisites, such as Italian bronzes, gold snuff-boxes, a carriage adorned with a coat of arms. and all the various tawdry elegancies for which he sacrificed his sleep at night and the best part of his health for a period of twenty years. In the rue de Cassini

he limited himself for the time being to the cheaper superfluities,
hunting through the shops of bric-à-brac and antique dealers to buy
ornaments that were completely unnecessary. The few articles of
furniture that he had managed furtively to rescue from his creditors in the rue des Marais were supplemented by clocks, candelabra,
statuettes, and knick-knacks such as normally cheer the female
heart. Not only his parents but also his friend Latouche found
this feminine taste for odds and ends ridiculous in a penniless
writer:

> You haven't changed at all. You pick out the rue de Cassini to
> live in and are never there. You go about everywhere, except to
> the place where a useful sphere of activity awaits you and where
> you could earn a living. Your heart clings to carpets, mahogany
> chests, sumptuously bound books, superfluous clocks and copper
> engravings. You chase through the whole of Paris in search of
> candelabra that will never shed their light upon you, and yet
> you haven't even got the few sous in your pocket that would
> enable you to visit a sick friend.

Perhaps he needed this superabundance in his outward surroundings to balance the superabundance within him. His study he kept
bare and monastic, and it always remained so. It contained the
little table which he took about with him whenever he moved, and
to which he seemed superstitiously attached, the candlestick that
was so necessary since he worked mainly by night, and the cup-
board for his papers and manuscripts. The salon, however, had to
be coquettishly attractive, the bedroom and even more the bathroom voluptuous. On emerging from the dark, ascetic cell in which
he worked he wanted to feel warm, sensuous colours about him,
delicate stuffs and a golden cloud from the paradise of wealth,
something that would lift him above the world of everyday, so that
he should not wake too abruptly from his dreams.

The question is, where did he obtain the money for his new
acquisitions? He was not earning anything, and he was in debt to
the tune of sixty thousand francs, on which he had to pay interest
at the rate of six thousand a year. He had only barely managed in
the rue Lesdiguières, when he had scrubbed out his own room and
fetched water from six streets away in order to save the sou for the
water-carrier, so how was he able to purchase luxuries as well as
necessities now that he had such a weight of debt on his shoulders?

The heroes of his novels, the de Marseils, the Rastignacs, and Mercadet, help to explain the paradox. Again and again they defend the thesis that having no debts or only small ones makes a man economical, while huge ones make him extravagant. When he had a hundred francs a month Balzac turned each franc seven times before he spent it. When he was burdened with a debt that to him was of astronomical proportions, it was all the same whether books he loved were bound in cheap linen or in red morocco, whether he paid off another few hundreds to his creditors or added a few further thousands to the original debt. His heroes argued—and so did Balzac—that everything would turn out all right if one became famous, or married a rich wife, or had a stroke of luck on the stock exchange. Alternatively, if success did not crown one's efforts, one's creditors would not be particularly affected by the little extra indebtedness. Balzac, however, was resolved to be successful. The real struggle was only just beginning, as he well knew, and it would not be a matter of petty skirmishes with exiguous fees as the guerdon of victory. The victory this time would be decisive. On the mantelpiece of his study stood the only ornament he allowed as relief to the bareness of the room, a plaster statuette of Napoleon, and Balzac felt the conqueror's gaze as a challenge to himself. As a spur to his efforts he took a piece of paper and wrote on it: "*Ce qu'il n'a pas pu achever par l'épée, je l'accomplirai par la plume.*" "What he began with the sword, I shall consummate with the pen." He pasted the slip on the base of the statuette, and it remained there as a continual exhortation to exert himself to the utmost until he too had scaled the heights as Napoleon had done, the greatest man of his time, who had likewise waited year after year in a Paris garret before carving out an empire with his naked sword. Balzac sat down at his table, with his pen as his only weapon and a few reams of virgin paper as his only ammunition, resolved to conquer the world.

Balzac now had the great advantage of knowing both his capacity for work and what he wanted to work at. The bitter struggle of the past ten years had made him aware of his strength, and he realised that the essential condition for decisive success was resolute concentration on his goal. The power of will could achieve miracles only if he did not vacillate and dissipate his efforts in different directions. Singleness of purpose, devotion to one exclusive passion—this alone was the source of power and must irresistibly ensure success. Belatedly he grasped the reason for his lack of success in business. He had not thrown himself into it body and soul; he had not concentrated on it with every fibre of his being; he had not chased after every sou and every order with the passionate instinct of the real business-man. Instead of straining every nerve and applying every thought to the furthering of his printing venture, he had employed part of his time in reading books and writing. If he was once more to embark on a literary career he must devote himself to it more wholeheartedly than hitherto. The conditions were favourable. He had acquired a practised hand with his numerous pseudonymous books, and through his many-sided contact with life he had gathered sufficient material for an endless gallery of portraits. He had served a hundred masters and performed every task that came his way. With the approach of his thirtieth year his apprenticeship was over. If he threw himself into his work with the whole power of his will he could become his own master.

His new feeling of responsibility towards himself and his work was manifested in the decision to publish his next book under his own name. So long as he concealed his identity behind pseudonyms, with no other purpose but speed and a quick return for his labours, he was able to take his obligations lightly, since praise or blame was meted out to an imaginary Monsieur de Saint Aubin or Viellerglé. When, however, it was a matter of putting a new brand on the market under his own label, when it was a matter of pushing his way through the crowded throng of books and writers of books, he was no longer content to be looked upon as one of the hacks who were turning out the popular sensational novels of the day. The Balzac of 1828 had made up his mind to enter the lists with open visor and match swords with the most famous and successful of historical novelists. He was resolved not only to equal but to excel Sir Walter Scott. The preface to his new book was the fanfare with which he opened the tournament:

It is not the author's intention to limit himself to a narrative style in which facts are tediously paraded and the action revealed step by step as one demonstrates a skeleton whose bones have been carefully numbered. The great lessons which speak to us from the open book of history must nowadays be depicted in a way that everybody can understand. This method has been followed for some years by writers of talent, and the author wishes to join their ranks. He has attempted in the present book to reproduce the spirit of an age and to bring to life an historical episode. He prefers to offer living speech rather than a documentary record, the battle itself rather than a report of the battle, and instead of epic narrative he has chosen dramatic action.

For the first time since his premature attempt at a rhymed tragedy, Balzac had set himself a task which called for the exercise of all his powers, and the world was soon to receive with astonishment the fruits of his intense absorption.

Balzac had long been working at the theme which he was to choose for his first real novel. Among his numerous papers are some sketches for a story to be called *Le gars*, dealing with an incident in the revolt of the Vendée against the French Republic. Certain episodes had been intended for another of his pseudonymous works with a Spanish background. His enhanced feeling of responsibility, however, had made him realise the insincerity and faultiness of the historical documentation in his earlier historical novels, and that if he chose a contemporary theme it would not be enough merely to surround his characters with cardboard scenery. He would have to see the environment in its true perspective and bring it to life. In his former stories of the Middle Ages only the specialist was capable of detecting his slips, but the fighting in the Vendée was not far removed in time from his own age. Numerous eye-witnesses were still living who had fought in the *compagnies des Bleus* or with the peasant troops of Cadoudal. So this time Balzac set to work with admirable thoroughness. He borrowed contemporary memoirs from the libraries, studied the military reports, and made extensive extracts. For the first time he discovered that it was just the little, apparently insignificant, but veracious details which gave a novel its convincing vividness. Without truth and sincerity there could be no art, and characters could never spring to life if they were not rooted in their environment. They had to be shown in their kinship with the soil and the *milieu*, breathing the very air of their epoch.

With his first individual and characteristic novel Balzac the realist came upon the scene.

For two or three months Balzac studied and read, searching through all the available memoirs and poring over maps in order to pin-point as accurately as possible the various troop movements and military operations. Even to the keenest imagination, however, a printed text can never be a substitute for the immediate impressions conveyed by direct observation. Balzac soon realised that the journey of Mademoiselle de Verneuil could only be made sufficiently vivid if he took the stage-coach over the same route as his heroine. He would be able to produce the atmosphere and the living tints of the landscape only if he were to put his imaginative vision to the test of reality.

As luck would have it, one of the old republican soldiers who had taken part in the campaign against the Chouans happened to be living in retirement at Fougères, which had been the scene of military operations at that time. This Baron de Pommereul was, moreover, an old friend of the Balzac family. Such a favourable coincidence had to be exploited, even if it meant borrowing the money for the journey or doing a little more pot-boiling (and even the Balzac experts have not been able to track down all the hack-work to which he put his hand in the intervals of writing his more solid books). With impetuous candour he made his excuses to Baron de Pommereul for having, on account of his precarious financial position, to invite himself to stay at the latter's house. And de Pommereul, who was probably thoroughly bored in his remote country abode and, like every old warrior, was glad to find someone prepared to lend a willing ear to his stories of past campaigns, replied by return of post that Balzac would be welcome.

His luggage was scanty. He was not yet impelled by vanity, as happened in later years, to select the gaudiest and most expensive of a hundred and thirty waistcoats. Nor could he yet travel in his own carriage, accompanied by a liveried footman. A very modestly, not to say shabbily dressed young man climbed up to one of the cheaper seats on the public stage-coach, and even this was a luxury he could not afford the whole way. The last part of the journey had

to be made on foot for reasons of economy, and having to step out
on the highway on his own short legs did not exactly improve his
already somewhat dilapidated toilet. When, dusty and perspiring,
he knocked at the door of General de Pommereul's house, he was at
first taken for a tramp, but this painful impression was soon
effaced. His youthful buoyancy asserted itself almost before the
first introductions had been made, and he relinquished himself to
the cheerful feeling of having at last found good quarters with
board and lodging assured for the next few weeks. Madame de
Pommereul has left us a record of this first meeting which gives
us a vivid picture of the vitality that radiated from him:

> He was a short young man with a thickset figure that was
> emphasised by his badly-cut suit. His hat was deplorable, but as
> soon as he removed it and one saw the expressiveness of his face
> everything else was forgotten. After that it was his face alone
> that I saw. Anyone who has not seen him can have no concep-
> tion of what a forehead he has, and what eyes! An expansive
> brow, which had a luminous look; golden-brown eyes, as full of
> expression as what he said. His nose was thick and square, his
> mouth enormous and always twisted in a laugh in spite of his
> defective teeth. He wore a heavy moustache and very long hair
> thrown back over his shoulders. At that time, and particularly
> when he first arrived, he had on the whole a rather lean look as
> though he had not had enough to eat. . . . In his whole manner,
> his movements, his bearing, and the way he spoke, there was so
> much good-nature, naivety, and frankness that one could not help
> liking him as soon as one saw him. But his most prominent
> characteristic was his constant good-humour, which was so
> exuberant that it became infectious.

He was so well fed by the de Pommereuls that he did not lose his
"newly acquired embonpoint and fresh colour" until he had been
back in Paris for some weeks.

Instead of the fortnight he had originally planned to stay he
remained for two months. He listened to de Pommereul's reminis-
cences, made notes and wrote. He forgot Paris, forgot his friends,
forgot even Madame de Berny, to whom he had made a solemn
vow that he would send her a diary with a record of his daily
impressions. He lived in the state of absorbed concentration which
with him was always to precede successful achievement, intent only

upon his work, and after a few weeks he was able to submit several chapters of his new novel to Latouche in Paris.

Latouche, who had a dowser's instinct for discovering talent, divined at once the promise of a great writer. His confidence, honest and sincere though it may have been, was expressed unfortunately in a material form. He decided to "put his money" on what he regarded as a future favourite, and knowing that Balzac could not afford to refuse, offered him a thousand francs for the copyright of a still unfinished novel. Balzac had no choice. Though he had formerly pocketed from fifteen hundred to two thousand francs for books dashed off with very little effort, he could not in his present situation resist an offer of a thousand francs in cash. The transaction was concluded, and, as is usual in such circumstances, it meant the end of their friendship. Latouche experienced an unpleasant surprise. Accustomed to regarding Balzac as a rapid worker, who delivered the agreed quantity of murder, poison, and sentimental dialogue punctually to the day, he was annoyed to discover that this time Balzac had to be sent reminders. He would not hand over his manuscript until he himself was satisfied with it. Then came a further cause of delay. When the manuscript had at last been extracted from the procrastinating author and set up in print, the proofs came back with so many corrections and alterations that it had to be set up afresh. Latouche raved that he was losing time and money over these constant emendations, but Balzac was not to be hurried. The artist's feeling of responsibility had begun to assert itself. For the first time he felt what he owed to the name Honoré Balzac, which he was resolved to render immortal, and in contrast to the unconcern with which throughout his life he regarded his business and other material debts, this was an obligation which he did not intend to ignore.

◈⊃◦⊂◈

In mid-March, 1829, the publishing firm of Canel brought out *Le dernier Chouan ou la Bretagne en 1800* in four volumes by Honoré Balzac—still not *de* Balzac. Its success did not come up to expectations, and not without reason. The arrangement and coherence revealed for the first time the master hand of a great novelist; the scene was unfolded with great skill; the military details were full of movement; the characters of General Hulot and of the spy Corentin were modelled directly from life; and his sense of the political background, which was to stamp the impress of their time so incomparably on the later novels, enabled him to draw the figure of Fouché, who exercised a lifelong fascination over Balzac, from the shadows in which this powerful counterpart of Napoleon had always deliberately lurked. Only the plot itself betrayed the former writer of sensational novels. The character of Mademoiselle de Verneuil, transferred from his pseudonymous story *Le guitariero*, which had been published two or three years before, did not ring true. The Paris critics, who in spite of all the boosting efforts of Latouche and Balzac were rather lukewarm, pointed to the "*dévergondage du style*", and Balzac himself could not but admit that his years of careless scribbling had made him slovenly. Even five years later, after he had polished the style for a new edition with the greatest possible care, he wrote to Baron Gérard when sending him a copy of his "ancient work in its revised form"— "Do what I will, I am afraid the hand of the novice will always be recognisable." Nor was the public particularly enthusiastic about the would-be French Sir Walter Scott. By dint of great effort 445 copies were sold in the first year. Premature confidence in Balzac's genius once more had to be paid for in hard cash. Pure chance enabled Balzac to make up for this semi-success. While he was still working on *Le dernier Chouan* the publisher Levasseur, who had succeeded in finding out where he lived, called on him and reminded him none too gently of the sum of two hundred francs advanced a year before for a *Manuel de l'homme d'affaires* which Balzac had undertaken to write. Balzac had long since forgotten the transaction, but Levasseur insisted on fulfilment of his contract. Unwilling to interrupt his serious work in order to turn out a popular booklet, Balzac offered his creditor an alternative. Among his old manuscripts he had a *Code conjugal*, which he had begun to set up in print at his own works under the title *Physiologie du mariage*. If Levasseur were agreeable he was prepared to revise this old book in payment of his debt. Levasseur, who probably knew that there was no chance of getting his two hundred francs back from the penniless author, accepted the proposition.

Balzac set to work, and when he had finished very little of the original work remained. He had been reading a great deal of

Rabelais in recent years, and instead of the cool wit of his former model, Laurence Sterne, he employed a style that was full of verve and gusto. Madame de Berny and a new acquaintance, the duchesse d'Abrantès, provided him with amusing anecdotes, and the book compiled in this way to pay off a forgotten debt turned out to be a sparkling, witty, smooth piece of writing which provoked discussion because of its impudent paradoxes, cynical charm, and humorous scepticism. The discussion, both good-humoured and ill-humoured, was very soon forthcoming, and it ensured the immediate success of the book. Women in particular, who were later to be Balzac's most determined standard-bearers, were at the same time irritated and entertained. They sent him letters of praise or condemnation, in tones either flattering or critical; but in any case the book was the sole topic of conversation in all the salons during the next few weeks. Balzac had not yet made his way, he was not yet famous, but one thing had been achieved. The Parisians' curiosity had been titillated by the young author. People sent him invitations, he had to order well-cut suits and resplendent waistcoats from his tailor, and the duchesse d'Abrantès presented him to Madame Récamier, whose salon was at that time the chief clearing-house for literary works in the capital. When visiting the rival firm of Mesdames Sophie and Delphine Gay he made the acquaintance of his already famous colleagues Victor Hugo, Lamartine, and Jules Janin. One last effort and his second request from life would be fulfilled. He would be not only loved, but famous.

⊸⊃o⊂⊷

The way was not yet open, but a breach had been made in the dykes, and with all the force of a pent-up flood Balzac's tremendous creative energy came pouring out like a cataract. Once Paris had become aware of the young writer's versatility, which was able to bake a solid dish like an historical novel and a piquant pasty like the *Physiologie du mariage* simultaneously in the same oven, he was almost bewildered with success and the commissions that began to come in thick and fast. Those who commissioned him to write, however, had no inkling of the volume and variety of this conjurer's repertoire or of the reverberating echo that would thunder back in answer to their first tentative call.

Balzac's output in the two years 1830 and 1831, after his name had begun to have a certain value, is almost unparalleled in the annals of literature. He turned out short novels, stories, newspaper articles, *causeries, feuilletons,* and political commentaries. If one reckons up the seventy authentic items from his pen that were printed in 1830 (to say nothing of those he probably published under other names) and the seventy-five items printed in 1831, he must have produced the equivalent of nearly sixteen printed pages a day, without taking into account alterations in the proofs. There was no periodical or newspaper in which his name did not suddenly appear. He contributed a motley collection of articles to *Le Voleur, La Silhouette, La Caricature, La Mode, La Revue de Paris,* and dozens of other publications. He discoursed in easy style on the *Philosophie de la toilette* or the *Physiologie gastronomique,* wrote one day on Napoleon and the next an *Etude des moeurs par les gants,* put on philosophic airs in observations on *Saint Simoniens et Saint Simonistes,* or indulged the *Opinion de mon épicier,* studied *Le claqueur* or *Le banquier,* scoffed at a *Manière de faire une émeute,* and discussed the *Moralité d'une bouteille de champagne* or the *Physiologie du cigare.*

Such versatility and wit were not in themselves remarkable in Paris journalism. It is, however, astonishing that in this brilliant pyrotechnic display there should be found perfect masterpieces which, though as yet only in small compass and dashed off in the space of a single night with the same speed as his more ephemeral writings, have successfully survived their first century. *Une passion dans le désert, Une épisode sous la terreur, El Verdugo, Sarrasine*—these revealed the hitherto unknown writer at one stroke as an unexcelled master of the art of the short story. The further he advanced along his chosen path, the more he realised what he could do. *Vires acquirit eundo.* His powers grew as he went. With his genre pictures of Parisian society, such as *Etudes de femmes, La femme de trente ans,* and *La paix du ménage,* he created an entirely new type, that of the "misunderstood wife" who had been disillusioned by marriage and was pining away as though from some mysterious malady on account of the coldness and unconcern of her husband. These stories, weighted with sentimentality and marred by a lack of realism and objective truth which makes them too sickly-sweet for our modern taste, found an enthusiastic public. The innumerable disappointed women in France and elsewhere who felt themselves to be misunderstood thought they had discovered in Balzac the physician who could diagnose their sorrows. He alone, who excused every lapse if it was due to love and dared to maintain that not only "the woman of thirty" but even the woman of forty, and she in particular owing to her maturer knowledge and discernment, had the strongest claim to love—he alone understood them. They regarded him as their advocate, who defended their infractions of the laws of the state and of bourgeois morality, and many a Madame d'Aiglemont saw her own reflection in his idealised portraits. His *Scènes de la vie privée*, which appeared in April 1830, were read with equal enthusiasm not only in France but in Italy, Poland, and Russia. With the watchword he had coined, "the woman of thirty", he proclaimed the right to love of the woman who had passed her first youth.

Yet even a more sober tribunal than that of his female readers, who with narcissist tendencies indulged their self-pity by identifying themselves with their favourite characters in fiction, could not fail to be amazed at the versatility and concentrated force of this young author who had leapt at one bound into the literary arena. Scarcely one of his already famous contemporaries had written anything to match the succinct descriptive power of *L'auberge rouge*, and in *Un chef d'oeuvre inconnu*, after having astonished the critics by the breadth of his talent, Balzac revealed the depth of his genius. His fellow-artists in particular felt that the urge to perfection, which is the innermost secret of all art, had never before been forced up with such frenzy to the pitch of tragedy. A dozen facets of his genius had each begun to reflect from its limited surface something of the light within, but the only true gauge of his genius is to be found in his breadth, abundance, and diversity. The full measure can be judged only by the total sum of his achievement.

Balzac first showed his true mettle in *La peau de chagrin*. It was in this story that he disclosed what he was aiming at—the novel as a cross-section of society, the upper classes mingled with the lower, poverty and riches, want and extravagance, the genius and the bourgeois, the Paris of lonely garrets and crowded salons, the power of money and its impotence. The keen observer and acute critic had begun to impose a sense of truth on the reluctant, sentimental romanticist. One romantic feature of *La peau de chagrin* was

8

the idea of transplanting an oriental fairy-tale from the *Arabian Nights* to the Paris of 1830. Further romantic traits are perhaps to be seen in the figures of the cold Countess Feodora, who prefers luxury to love, and her antithesis Pauline, the girl capable of a love that is boundless and altruistic. But the realism of the Bacchanalia, which shocked his contemporaries, and the autobiographical scenes which described his own student years sprang directly from personal experience. The arguments of the doctors and the philosophy of the usurer were not mere reproductions of conversation overheard in the salons, but the sublimated essence of real characters. After ten years of vain groping Balzac had discovered his true vocation as the historian of his own age, as the psychologist and physiologist, painter and physician, judge and literary creator of the monstrous organism calling itself Paris, France, or the world. If his first discovery was his own enormous capacity for work, the second and no less important one was the purpose to which this energy should be applied. When Balzac had found his purpose he had found himself. Hitherto, with explosive forces dammed up within him, he had felt only that these forces were irresistible, but they were eventually to carry him up in his comet-like career soaring high above the turbid throng of his contemporaries:

> There are some vocations which one must obey, and there is an irresistible power driving me on to the achievement of power and glory.

Yet just as Goethe, even after the success of *Werther* and *Götz von Berlichingen*, still did not dare to admit to himself that his talent was for literature and for literature alone, so Balzac was not convinced even after *La peau de chagrin* that literature was his true vocation and destiny. He was, in fact, one of those gifted beings whose genius would have displayed itself in any form they had chosen. It is possible to think of him as having become a second Mirabeau, a Talleyrand, another Napoleon, the greatest picture-dealer in the world, or a prince of speculators. That was why he was by no means persuaded in his earlier years that he was born to be a writer, and Gautier, who knew him well, was possibly not far wrong when he said: "He did not possess a gift for literature. In his case there was an abyss between thought and form, an abyss which, especially in the initial stages, he despaired of being able to bridge." Writing was not a necessity to him, and he never felt it to be his mission. He regarded it only as one of the many possible alternative ways in which he might attain the wealth and fame that would enable him to dominate the world: "He wanted to become a great man, and he did so by emitting constant currents of that force which is more potent than electricity." His real genius lay in his will-power, and it may be called either chance or Fate that this will-power found its outlet in literature. His books were being read in every country in the world, and even the aged Goethe had expressed to Eckermann his benevolent astonishment at such outstanding talent, while the editors of reviews and other journals were trying to tempt him with the highest fees, yet still Balzac remained unconvinced. A year before he had written: "The postage on a letter, a ride in an omnibus, these represent a dreadful expense for me, and I stay at home so as not to wear out my clothes." Now he was being offered dazzling commissions, yet still he regarded literature as merely one of many possibilities. As late as 1832 we find him writing to his mother: "Sooner or later I shall make a fortune, either as a writer, or in politics, or in journalism, either by a wealthy marriage or by some big business *coup*."

For a time he was fascinated by the idea of entering politics. The revolution of July 1830 had put the middle-classes in power again and there was plenty of scope for forceful young men. A deputy in the French Chamber could rise as swiftly as a twenty-five or thirty-year-old colonel of the Napoleonic era. Balzac almost made up his mind to abandon literature for politics. He flung himself into the "*sphère tempestueuse des passions politiques*" and attempted to secure election for the constituencies of Cambrai and Fougères. He wanted to stand at the helm, to "*vivre la vie du siècle même*", and if the electors had been more kind this might have been the path that his ambition would have chosen. He might have become the political leader of France instead of Thiers, or he might even have become a second Napoleon.

Fortunately the voters decided otherwise in both constituencies, but the other danger still remained. He might yet find "*une femme et une fortune*", the "*richissime veuve*" for whom he hankered all his life. This would have brought out the hedonist in him and effaced the worker, since—though he did not yet know it—his tremendous achievement could only be wrung from him by the

equally tremendous pressure of circumstance. For a widow with
thirty or forty thousand francs a year Balzac would at any time,
even when he was at the height of his fame, have been prepared to
surrender himself to a life of ease. "I could willingly resign myself
to a state of domestic bliss," he confessed to his friend Zulma
Carraud, and he described to her his dream of living in the country
where he would only "*faire de la littérature amateur*"—write a book
occasionally when he felt like it.

Providence was wiser than Balzac's inmost wishes and denied
him their premature fulfilment, for it wanted more from him than
this. It barred the way that would have enabled him to prostitute
his gifts on a ministerial bench, it refused him the fortune he
dreamed of winning by some *coup* on the Stock Exchange, and it
kept out of his reach all the rich widows after whom he chased.
It changed his early passion for journalism into a loathing for all
newspaper writing, and chained him to the desk from which his
genius could dominate not merely the Chamber of Deputies, the
Stock Exchange, or an elegant scene of domestic though luxurious
bliss, but the whole world. With the ruthless discipline of a gaoler
it drove him back again and again to his work in his prison cell,
frustrating every endeavour to break out into a world where he
could enjoy the unrestricted delights of freedom, love, and power,
and for every attempt to escape it loaded him with a double weight
of chains. In the midst of his early fame he must have been seized
by some dark foreboding of the crushing burden he was about to
assume. He fought against it, he tried to evade it, he never ceased
to long for the miracle that would snatch him at one stroke from
his bondage, he continued to dream of a great gamble, of a wealthy
wife, of a magic twist of Fate. But it was not granted him to escape
his destiny; it had been ordained that he should create, and so the
pent-up force within him had to construct for itself a world of such
scope as had hitherto been unknown in literature. Its dimensions
could not be measured, its horizon knew no limits. Hardly had he
begun his task when he realised that this abundance and superabundance which was streaming forth from him must be articu-
lated systematically if either he or his readers were to have any
possibility of commanding a view of the whole vast domain. If
literature was to be his field of activity he would not pile one book
haphazardly on another, but link them together in a hierarchy of

all earthly passions and all the forms that life could assume. When sending the first of these novels to a friend, he wrote: "The ground-plan of my work is beginning to take shape." He had conceived the fruitful notion of making individual characters reappear in different books and thus, instead of a disconnected series of novels, creating a complete literary history of the age which would embrace all classes, professions, ideas, emotions, and social conditions. In the preface to the edition of his *Romans et contes philosophiques* he got Philarète Chasles, whose hand he guided, to prepare the public for the reception of his literary innovation. A comprehensive history of the times was planned, and this first volume was only—

> the first picture in a great series of frescoes. The author has set himself the task of delineating the society and civilisation of our epoch, which, with its overheated imagination and the pre-dominance of individual egotism, appears to him to be decadent. It will be seen how the author is continually able to mix new colours on his palette . . . how he depicts every stage of the social scale in turn. He introduces us to one figure after another —the peasant, the beggar, the shepherd, the citizen, the cabinet minister, and he will not shrink from limning a portrait of the priest, or even the King himself.

At the age of thirty Balzac did not yet realise the extent of the task he had undertaken. He was not aware that in writing the *Comédie humaine* he was to be the instrument for recording an epic cycle which was being dictated by the age itself. At the moment when the artist in him began to dominate, the great vision was already present in his mind, but twenty years of immeasurable and incomparable toil were hardly to suffice for its shaping.

BALZAC AT WORK

CHAPTER VII

The Man of Thirty

From 1831 onwards, after he had reached the age of thirty and appeared before the world with his first substantial book, Balzac became once and for all Honoré de Balzac. The period of tedious effort and devious development was finished. As a man, an artist, and a character he had come to the end of his years of growth. No further decisive change took place either in his physical appearance, in his development as an artist, or in his moral outlook. His vitality had found its direction, the creative writer had set himself his task, the ambitious architect had drafted the tentative plan of his future structure, and with his *courage de lion* Balzac threw himself into the work that lay before him. So long as his pulse still beat the rhythm of his daily work went on without pause and without slowing down. From the moment when he settled down to a task the dimensions of which were, in fact, boundless, death alone could set a limit to his Promethean will. Balzac at work is perhaps the most grandiose example of creative continuity to be found in modern literature. Fed like a mighty tree from the eternal sources of the earth, he stood erect in all his massive strength until he was felled by the axe, thrusting out branch after branch towards the sky and, immovably rooted, patiently fulfilling his organic destiny—to grow, to flower, and to bear ever finer fruits.

Despite all his creative innovations Balzac himself did not change. If one compares his portraits at the age of fifty with those at thirty, one finds only trifling differences—a streak or two of grey in his hair, shadows under the eyes, a sallow tint in his former fresh colouring, but the general appearance is exactly the same. At thirty his essentially individual characteristics had assumed their ultimate form. The "short, lean, pale young man" in whose unpretentious appearance the only positive feature was a vague resemblance to the young Buonaparte before the days of his glory had reverted, oddly enough, to the "chubby child with round cheeks". As soon as he had anchored himself to his writing-table the highly strung, uncertain, impatient, happy-go-lucky elements in his make-up yielded to a breadth and ease abounding in a sense of strength and confidence. He was drawing his own portrait in the character of d'Arthez when he wrote:

> The expression in d'Arthez' eyes, which had once shone with the fire of a noble ambition, had grown tired with the coming of success. The thoughts which had invested his brow with grandeur had faded, his once slim figure had grown corpulent. The golden hue of good-living suffused his face, which in his youth had shown the sallow tones painted by poverty—the tones which indicated a temperament exerting all its forces to fight continually until success had been achieved.

The first and, as in the case of most artists, deceptive impression made by his physiognomy is that of a healthy, pleasure-loving, and jovial good-humour. Despite the smooth, taut forehead, above which his usually not overclean mane of hair was piled up, the soft flesh of his face, with its greasy skin, sparse moustache, and broad, indeterminate features, gives the impression of belonging to a man fond of comfort and good-living, of sleeping long hours, of eating much and working little. Only when one looks at his shoulders, broad as those of a weight-lifter, the shoulders of his own Vautrin, when one looks at the muscular, bull-like neck which he could keep bent over his work for twelve or fourteen hours at a time without wearying, when one looks at the athlete's chest, only then does one gain some conception of the massive force that lay in this man. The forceful element in him begins below the soft, flabby chin. His body is carved out of bronze. Its dominating quality, as in his writing, lies in its massiveness, in its breadth, in its indescribable vitality.

Every attempt to discern the presence of genius in Balzac's face must therefore be vain and misleading. The sculptor David d'Angers tried to give the impression of genius by heightening the brow and moulding it with jutting bulges, as if the writer's thought were pushing its way out through the confining skull. The painter Boulanger tried to conceal the obtrusive paunch with a white monkish robe and to tauten his whole bearing. Rodin did the same by giving him the ecstatic look of a man startled out of tragic hallucinations. All three artists seemed to feel that this countenance, with its lack of striking features, must be strengthened in order to make the genius within it recognisable, in order to smuggle in daemonic or heroic elements, and Balzac himself made the same attempt when he again drew his own portrait in the character of Z. Marcas:

> His hair was like a mane; his nose was short and compressed, furrowed at the tip and with broad nostrils like a lion. His forehead too was leonine and divided into two powerful bulges by a great cleft.

The truthful observer must ruthlessly admit that Balzac—like all really representative national geniuses, such as Tolstoy or Luther—looked like a man of the people, that his face was, as it were, the epitome of the faces of innumerable humble folk of his homeland. Balzac's face was definitely commonplace, even plebeian. In France particularly the highest intellectual achievement is found in two types, the one aristocratic and subtly sublimated, as in Richelieu, Voltaire or Valéry, the other expressing the force and vitality of the people, as in Mirabeau or Danton. Balzac belonged wholly to the elemental type, not to the aristocrats or decadents. If a blue apron were tied round his waist and he stood behind the bar of a *bistro* in the south of France, his cheerful figure would be indistinguishable from that of any illiterate innkeeper pouring out wine and chatting with his customers. As a peasant behind the plough, as a water-carrier in the street, as a tax-collector, or a sailor in a Marseilles brothel Balzac would not have looked out of place. In shirt-sleeves or carelessly dressed he appeared genuine and natural. When he tried to be elegant and gave himself aristocratic airs, with his hair pomaded and holding a lorgnon in front of his eyes to ape the dandies of the Faubourg St. Germain, he looked as if he were wearing a disguise. As in his art, his strength lay not in artifice, when he ventured into a philosophical or sentimental sphere in which he was untrue to himself, but in being natural. His dominating physical qualities, too, were his vitality, his vivacity, his strength.

It is not the function of a portrait to give visual expression to these qualities. It should be like a still extracted from a living film, a split second of inaction, an interrupted movement, and we can no more deduce his physical and mental exuberance from his various portraits than we can deduce the unparalleled and versatile productivity of his genius from a single page of his writings. A fleeting and superficial glance at Balzac's face tells one nothing. The reports of all his contemporaries are agreed on this point. When his short, stoutish figure, still panting from the effort of climbing the stairs, entered a room wearing a brown coat that was badly buttoned, shoes that were half unlaced, and an untidy mane of hair, and threw itself into an armchair that creaked dangerously under its weight, the first impression was devastating. Could this coarse, greasy plebeian who reeked of perfume be our Balzac, the minstrel of our most secret emotions, the advocate of our rights? These were the questions that the astonished ladies asked themselves, and the other authors present squinted complacently into a mirror to confirm the fact that they looked far less bourgeois and far more intellectual. Many a smile was hidden behind a fan, while the gentlemen exchanged malicious glances at the expense of their commonplace but dangerous literary rival. As soon as Balzac began to speak, however, the first painful impression vanished, for a sparkling torrent of wit electrified the atmosphere. All eyes were drawn towards him as he talked of a hundred things, discoursed on philosophy or sketched out political schemes, drew on his large repertoire of anecdotes or told stories, both true and invented, which grew more and more fantastic and incredible as he went on. Golden sparks of playful good-humour flashed from his dark eyes as he boasted, scoffed, laughed, and intoxicated himself and his listeners. When he was able to scatter his bounty there was nobody to compare with Balzac.

His physical vitality cast a spell as unique as that which fascinates the reader of his books. Everything he did seemed to have a tenfold intensity. When he laughed the pictures on the walls trembled, when he spoke the words came cascading forth and made one forget his bad teeth. When he travelled he threw the postillion a further tip every half-hour, urging him to whip his horses to greater speed, when he made financial calculations the thousands and millions tumbled over one another pell-mell, when he worked there was no difference between day and night as he sat writing round the clock and blunted a dozen pens in the process. When he ate—this is how the gossip-writer Gozlan describes the scene:

> . . . his lips quivered, his eyes shone with happiness, his hands twitched with pleasurable anticipation at sight of a pyramid of beautiful pears or peaches. . . . He was magnificent in his flamboyant, Pantagruelian way; he had removed his cravat and his shirt collar was open; with a fruit knife in his hand he laughed, drank, and carved into the juicy flesh of a large pear. . . .

Nothing was more foreign to Balzac's nature than pettiness. He possessed the childlike good nature that we generally attribute to giants, and nothing could shake it. Though he was aware that his colleagues felt embarrassed in his all-too-massive presence and that they whispered to one another behind his back of his lack of style and a hundred other malicious calumnies, he had a friendly word for each of them, dedicated his books to them, and mentioned them all somewhere or other in his *Comédie humaine*. He was too magnanimous for enmity, and nowhere in his writings is there to be found any polemic against an individual. When he tormented his publishers and kept them on the curb, it was not in order to squeeze a few extra francs out of them, but from a desire to play with them and show that he was the master. When he lied, it was not in order to deceive, but to indulge his exuberant imagination and his sense of humour. He knew that people were making mock of what they regarded as his childish ways, but this only induced him to exaggerate them. He would tell his friends some tall story and observe with his quick, keen eyes that they did not believe a word he said, but would hawk it all round Paris next morning, yet this only made him season his stories even more strongly. It amused him to see that the others thought him rather a freak, that he did not fit into their conventional scheme of things, and in anticipation of the caricatures of which he was later to be the butt he caricatured himself with Rabelaisian gusto. What harm could they do him, anyway?

He was pervaded by the consciousness that in the muscles under his skin and the grey cells of his brain he was stronger than them all, so he let them have their way.

Balzac's self-reliance was based on his sense of strength, both physical and intellectual, and not on the fame or success that came to him, for so far as his literary achievement was concerned he remained uncertain of himself even after he had published *La peau de chagrin*, *Père Goriot*, and a dozen other imperishable masterpieces. His vigorous confidence in his own vitality did not spring from a weighing of the pros and cons, from introspection, or from judgment of others. It was something elemental. He enjoyed the feeling of abundance within him, and had no use for apprehensive self-criticism or introspective analysis. As he wrote to the duchesse d'Abrantès:

> In my five foot two inches there is compressed every imaginable contrast and contradiction. If anyone likes to call me vain, extravagant, stubborn, frivolous, inconsistent in my thinking, dandified, careless, indolent, lacking in due reflection and not sufficiently painstaking, without perseverance, loquacious, tactless, ill-bred, rude, subject to odd changes of mood, he will be no less right than anyone else who says that I am thrifty, modest and courageous, tenacious, energetic, carefree, industrious, steadfast, taciturn, full of refinement and courtesy, and always cheerful. It can be asserted with equal truth that I am a poltroon or a hero, a clever fellow or an ignoramus, extremely talented or stupid. Nothing will surprise me. I myself have finally resolved to believe that I am merely an instrument, the plaything of circumstance.

Whatever food for thought, praise, or mockery he might give to others, he went on his way with head erect, brave, cheerful, and unconcerned, taking all the buffetings that fortune had to offer. In the consciousness of his strength he could afford to be negligent. Though his vanity may have been childish, it was never petty. He had the carefree assurance of a man who is slightly tipsy.

Such a broad-based, generous nature was bound to be extravagant, and Balzac was prodigal in every respect but one. He was perforce economical of the time he spent in other people's company. He once said that he had "only one hour a day to give to the world", and there was no room in his life for social intercourse. The people with whom he had close ties of attachment can therefore be counted on one's fingers. Hardly more than ten were really intimate with him and even these, with the exception of the most important figure of all, had already come into his life by the time he was thirty. His circle of friends widened very little in later years, just as he added very little to his experience of the world or to his artistic development. What he had to absorb he had already absorbed. Henceforth he had time for no new friendships, but only for his work, and only the men and women of his own creation were real and important to him.

In his narrow but constant circle of friends the women took the foremost place. Nine-tenths of his letters, perhaps even more, were written to women. Only with them could he yield to his *"besoin d'épancher le coeur trop plein"*, his irrestible longing to pour out his heart from time to time in confession. Only to women could he *"se mettre à nu"*, and after months of silence he would suddenly erupt with a tempestuous urge to communicate his thoughts and feelings, frequently to a woman whom he had never seen or with whom he had merely a fleeting acquaintance. He never addressed an intimate letter to a man, and he never brought himself to speak of his inner conflicts or the problems of artistic creation even to the greatest and most celebrated of his contemporaries, such as Victor Hugo or Stendhal. Accustomed as he was to monopolising a conversation, hardly waiting to hear what the others might have to say in his impatience to continue with his fantasies and rodomontade, he had little interest either in maintaining a correspondence with his fellow-authors or in conversing with them. He did not need the stimulus of friendship, but the exact contrary. He needed an easing of his inward tension. If, therefore, he wrote chiefly to women it was not only, as he remarked scoffingly to Théophile Gautier, because *"cela forme le style"*, but from a profound and perhaps partly subconscious desire to find the woman who would understand him. Worn out with work, harassed by his obligations, living under a crushing weight of debt, caught up again and again in the current of his *"vie torrentielle"*, he yearned incessantly for a woman who would be a mother, sister, mistress and helpmate as Madame de Berny had been during his years of development. It was not an inclination for amorous adventure that kept him continuously searching, but on the contrary a passionate need of tranquillity.

One must not be deceived by the *Contes drolatiques* with their boisterous priapic sensuality. Balzac was never a Don Juan or a Casanova. What he wanted was a woman who would give him the bourgeois contentments, *"une femme et une fortune"*, as he candidly admitted. A man of his imagination and active intellect did not need the further mental and emotional excitement of cheap adventures. Half unconsciously, though sometimes with clear insight, he was seeking the woman who could satisfy both poles of his being, redeeming his work from the curse of having to serve as a means of earning money without prejudicing it by the claims she made upon him, gratifying his physical desires while at the same time rescuing him from his financial and material difficulties. If possible, she should also gratify his naive snobbery by being of aristocratic descent.

This was the dream of his life, though it was never to find fulfilment. He found the object of his search only piecemeal, sometimes the one half, sometimes the other; but never—or too late—both together. Even his first liaison with Madame de Berny was condemned to incompleteness because, as he once said, the Devil had so cruelly deranged the clockwork of the years. At the age of twenty-three he had found in her a guide and comforter, who had rescued him in the hour of danger and loved him passionately, but the discrepancy in their ages, which had not seemed unnatural when he was most in need of her, was bound in the course of time to appear incongruous. At the age of thirty even Balzac, who was capable of seeing the Helen of his dreams in any woman, found it embarrassing to be the lover of a woman of fifty-three. Hard as it was for Laure de Berny to resign herself to the inevitable, as it is even for the wisest of women so long as she is in love, the sensual element in their relationship gradually ebbed.

Before this transformation was complete, however, Balzac had already sought and found satisfaction elsewhere for the sensual side of his nature, and the ageing Madame de Berny's jealousy was perhaps enhanced by the fact that his new friend was likewise in the autumn of her years and that her physical charms were therefore somewhat faded. The duchesse d'Abrantès was the widow of General Junot and when Balzac first met her, at Versailles in 1829, a rather dilapidated monument to past glory. She was excluded from the Bourbon court, taken little notice of in society, and so

hopelessly in debt that she had to make money out of her reminis-
cences and dug up old scandals, either real or invented, which she
sold year after year and volume by volume to the publishers.
Nevertheless she found no difficulty in detaching Balzac from the
rather too maternal apron-strings of Madame de Berny, for she
appealed to two of the strongest elements in his nature—the
insatiable thirst of the artist to study history in its living springs
and the insatiable snobbishness which was his deep-seated weakness. Titles and noble names always exercised a spell over him, and
the triumphant sensation of being the friend and even the lover
of a duchess, the successor in her bed if not of the Emperor himself,
at any rate of one of his generals, the successor of Murat, King of
Naples, and Prince Metternich, was bound to divert him for a time
at least from the arms of Madame de Berny, whose mother, after all,
had only been a lady-in-waiting to Marie Antoinette.

The vanity and ardour of the eternal plebeian in Balzac launched
him into an adventure which presumably did not present any
considerable difficulties from the start. What an advantage for a
future *"historien de son temps"*, whose imagination needed only a
spark for the illumination of a whole horizon, to be able to lie *entre
deux draps* with a woman who knew all the secrets of history! The
duchesse d'Abrantès had met Napoleon at the house of her mother,
Madame Permont, when he was still the slim young Captain
Buonaparte. She had not only stood in the front row among the
newly created princes and princesses at the Tuileries, but had
witnessed what went on behind the scenes while the history of the
world was being unfolded. If all Balzac's novels with a Napoleonic
milieu, such as *Une ténébreuse affaire* or *Le colonel Chabert*, are
steeped in documentary detail, this is due to his connection with
the duchesse d'Abrantès, in which genuine love played a very
minor rôle compared with mutual sensuality and intellectual
curiosity. As a love affair it did not last long, but a certain com-
radely attachment remained. They were both heavily in debt, eager
to taste what life had to offer, and soon diverted to other passions,
but they tried to help one another in a spirit of good fellowship for
some considerable time after their transient ardour had cooled
down. She introduced him to Madame Récamier and other
aristocratic acquaintances, while he assisted her in the parcelling
out of her memoirs to the publishers and perhaps secretly took a

9

hand in the writing of them. Gradually she faded out of his life, and when years afterwards she was found dead in a wretched garret in Paris he described her end in a startled tone which betrays the fact that she had completely passed out of his mind and his association with her had been nothing but a fleeting though ardent episode in his life.

⊸∘⊷

About the time when his liaison with the duchesse d'Abrantès was in its early stages another woman, Zulma Carraud, entered Balzac's life, and with her he formed the best, the noblest, the purest, the most valuable and, despite periods of separation both in space and time, the most lasting of his friendships. Of the same age as his favourite sister Laure, Zulma Tourangin had married a captain of artillery named Carraud in 1816. Carraud was a man of *"austère probité"*, a brave officer whose sterling merits failed to receive the recognition they deserved. During the Napoleonic wars, while his comrades were carving out brilliant careers on the battlefield or rising to dazzling heights in the Ministries, he had the misfortune to spend years as a prisoner of war in the English hulks. When at last he was exchanged it was too late. No suitable employment could be found for an officer without influence who had lacked the opportunity during his captivity to pull strings or win military decorations. For a time he was posted to small provincial garrisons, until eventually he was put in charge of the state powder factory, and he and his wife led a quiet existence within the narrow limits of a remote provincial town. Zulma Carraud, who was not particularly pretty and afflicted with a slight limp, had a great respect for her husband's integrity of character and felt the deepest compassion for him in the ill-starred destiny which had so prematurely cut short his ambition and soured his life, but it cannot be said that she loved him. She kept house for him and her son, and since she was gifted with brains and a sense of tact that bordered on genius, she was able, even in the limited society available to her, to gather round her a small circle of sincere if comparatively humble friends, including a certain Captain Periolas to whom Balzac later became particularly attached. It was this Captain Periolas who provided him with important details for his stories dealing with military life.

Zulma's meeting with Balzac at his sister's house was a stroke of luck for both of them. For Zulma, with her humanity of outlook and an intellect far above that of any other member of her circle, or even many of Balzac's celebrated fellow-writers and critics, it was a profound spiritual experience to encounter in her small world a man whose literary genius was as immediately evident to her as his radiant and overflowing humanity. For Balzac it was a piece of good fortune that he had a house to go to where, exhausted by work and harassed by creditors, he could find solace without being subjected to rapturous admiration or put on show. There was always a room ready for him where he could work undisturbed, and in the evening he found warm-hearted friends waiting for him with whom he could talk without restriction and enjoy a completely intimate atmosphere. He could relax in shirt-sleeves, so to speak, without fear of being a burden, and in the consciousness that a refuge was always at his disposal after the strain of his labours, he dreamed for months ahead of his excursions to the various garrison towns, whether St. Cyr or Angoulême or Frapesle, where the Carrauds happened to be stationed.

It was not long before Balzac realised the spiritual quality of this obscure woman, with her genius for devotion and sincerity, and a deep platonic friendship grew up between them. There can be no doubt that Zulma Carraud was not indifferent to the physical attraction exerted by such a personality as Balzac, but she kept herself in rein. She knew that no other woman could do so much for Balzac's restless character, capable as she was of complete self-effacement while at the same time unostentatiously allaying his difficulties and smoothing his path. On one occasion she wrote to him: "I was the woman destined for you by Fate." And he wrote in turn: "I needed a woman like you, an unselfish woman." He confessed to her that "A quarter of an hour spent with you in the evening means more to me than all the joys of a night in the arms of those beauties . . ."

Zulma Carraud, however, was too clear-sighted not to realise that she lacked the sexual attraction to satisfy for long a man whom she placed so high above all others. In any case, a nature like hers would have found it impossible to deceive or abandon a husband who was so entirely dependent on her for his happiness. So she set out to offer him a friendship, *"une bonne et sainte amitié*", as he says, free from any selfish vanity or ambition and untroubled by erotic undercurrents: "I should not like even a grain of egoism to enter into our relationship." Since she could not offer him both guidance and love, as Madame de Berny had done, she preferred to keep both spheres separate so as to be a more perfect helpmate in his difficulties, "*un oeil de plus pour vous*", and she cried: "*Mon dieu!* Why did not Fate cast my lot in the city where you have to dwell? I should have given you everything in the way of affection that you could have desired. I should have taken up my abode in the house where you lived. . . . It would have been happiness in two volumes." Such an opportunity of dividing up one's life into the physical and the spiritual did not come their way, however, so she sought another way out: "I will adopt you as my son." She wanted to make it her life task to think for him, care for him, and advise him. Like all the women who loved this childlike genius, who did not know how to manage his own life, she felt the need to mother him.

Balzac could, in fact, have had no more honest or capable adviser either as man or artist than this unknown woman whose destiny it was to live buried in the provinces and tied in the bonds of a banal marriage. In 1833, at a time when Balzac's work was a fashionable sensation but had not yet found real understanding, she wrote to him with that accent of unflinching sincerity which characterised everything she said:

> You are the first writer of the age and, in my opinion, the most important writer of all times. You can be compared only with yourself, and beside you everything else appears shallow.

It is true that she immediately went on to say:

> None the less I have my doubts about adding my voice to strengthen the chorus of the thousands who are singing your praises.

For an unerring instinct prompted her to be afraid of the fashionable, the sensational element in Balzac's success. It was just because she was aware of his greatness of heart, because she loved the "Balzac who is essentially good at heart", who "hides himself behind all his muslin curtains, cashmere shawls, and bronze statuettes", that she feared the danger to his talent and his character that might arise from his social success in the salons and his material success with the publishers. She was anxious that his highest potentialities should be fulfilled: "I am obsessed by the desire to see you perfect." This perfection was to be something other than—

a fashionable or salon success (which I regret, since it spoils you for the future). Perfection—it is that upon which your true fame must rest, the future fame of which I am thinking and which is as important to me as if I bore your name or stood so close to you that it would shed its light on me too.

She imposed upon herself the duty of being his artistic conscience because, though she realised his greatness and his goodness, she was not blind to his dangerous tendency to yield in childish vanity to the flatteries of society. At the risk of losing his friendship, which was the thing she valued most in life, she told him with the utmost honesty of her misgivings no less than of her approbation, conscious though she was that she was thereby dissenting from the adulation showered upon the fashionable author by princesses and other society ladies.

Nowhere are there to be found more sensible judgments and criticisms than hers, and even after a century every word of praise or disapproval uttered by this wife of an artillery captain in Angoulême is more cogent than all the critiques of Sainte-Beuve and the other professional reviewers. She admired *Louis Lambert, Le colonel Chabert, César Birrotteau,* and *Eugénie Grandet,* while having a lively distaste for the over-scented salon stories such as *La femme de trente ans,* quite justly calling *Le médecin de campagne* "too viscous and overburdened with ideas", and being repelled by the exaggerated pseudo-mysticism of *Séraphita.* With astonishing lucidity she perceived every danger that threatened his prospects of permanent success. When he tried to enter politics she anxiously warned him: "The *Contes drolatiques* are more important than a Minister's portfolio." When he turned to the Royalist Party, she exhorted him:

Leave the protection of such interests to the people around the Court and do not throw in your lot with them. You will only soil the reputation you have hitherto earned honestly.

Defiantly she declared that she would always remain faithful to her love for the poor, who are so disgracefully calumniated and exploited by the greed of the rich, for I myself belong to the people. It is true that socially we are included among the aristocracy, but we have always preserved our sympathy for the people, who are suffering from oppression.

When she saw the damaging effect on his work of the tempestuous haste in which he wrote, she warned him:

> Do you really call it literature when you write as if you had a knife at your throat? How can you create a really perfect work if you hardly allow yourself time to put it on paper? Why this hurry, merely in order to provide yourself with such luxuries as would befit a *nouveau riche* baker, but not a genius? The man who could portray a Louis Lambert really ought not to find it necessary to acquire English carriage-horses. . . . It grieves me, Honoré, to see you not being true to your own greatness. Oh! so far as I am concerned you could have bought the horses, the carriage, and the Persian hangings—but you should not have given some crafty fellow the opportunity to say of you: "You can buy him for money at any time!"

She loved his genius, but she feared his weakness. So she watched with apprehension while he wrote furiously, allowed himself to be requisitioned by the salons and, with a view to impressing the "high society" which she despised, surrounded himself with an unnecessary luxury that drove him into debt. With a foresight that was all too justified she implored him: "Do not use yourself up so prematurely!" With her strong French feeling for liberty she would have liked to see the greatest writer of the century independent in every respect, independent of praise or blame, of public opinion or the need for money, and she was plunged into despair at seeing him continually falling into new servitude:

> A galley slave—that is what you will always be. You are crowding ten men's lives into one and burning yourself up in your greed. Your fate throughout your life will be that of Tantalus.

It was a prophetic comment!

It says much for the integrity of Balzac, who was far shrewder than all his little vanities might lead one to imagine, that at a time when princesses and duchesses were enveloping him in the incense of their flattery he not only accepted these hard and often violent reproaches, but again and again thanked her for her honesty.

You are my public [he wrote to her], and I am proud to know you, you who are giving me the courage to perfect myself.

He thanked her for helping him "to hoe the weeds from my fields. Every time I have seen you I have carried away with me some gain that has benefited my life." He knew that her warnings held no ignoble motive, no jealousy or intellectual arrogance, but were actuated only by the most sincere solicitude for the immortal soul of his art, and he allotted her a special place in his life: "My feeling for you cannot be compared with any other; nothing can match or even resemble it." Even when, later on, he poured out his soul to another woman, to Madame de Hanska, whom he fetched from the Ukraine to be his personal confessional box, it did not shake "this privileged priority in my heart which will always remain unchanged." He only grew more silent towards his whilom friend, perhaps from a certain discomfort and some secret sense of shame. Whereas in his effusions to Madame de Hanska and other women he dramatised himself, his debts, and his labours, he knew that he could not utter a word of untruth to Zulma Carraud without her being aware of it, and unconsciously he felt himself more and more inhibited in his confessions to her. Years went by without his visiting the quiet study in her house which she had placed at his disposal, and the only time that she came to Paris—heaven alone knows at what sacrifices—he was so engrossed in his work that he did not open her letter and left her waiting a fortnight for an answer that never came. But shortly before his death, in the year when, already a doomed man, he was at last, after sixteen years, able to lead Madame de Hanska home as his bride, he paused for a second to review his past life and acknowledged to himself that Zulma had been the most significant, the most sincere, and the best of all the women he had known. He took up his pen to write to her: "I have never ceased to think of you, to love you, and even here to talk with you."

Balzac, the eternal romancer and exaggerater, did not exaggerate when he set his relationship to Zulma Carraud above all the others and apart from them as the purest of his friendships. All the other relationships—with the exception of his association with Madame de Hanska, which dominated his later years—were more or less episodic. He revealed his sure psychological insight when, of all the celebrated women he knew, he became particularly attached to the noble Marceline Desbordes-Valmore, to whom he dedicated one of his greatest works and whom he visited in her attic in the Palais Royal, in spite of the hundred steps up which he had to pant—no small achievement in view of his weight. With George Sand, whom he called his *"frère George"*, he was linked by a kind of cordial comradeship which had in it no tinge of erotic intimacy—a rare exception in those days. His pride protected him from becoming listed as the fourteenth or fifteenth in her catalogue of lovers and sharing the honours of her bed with half the literary world of Paris, including Alfred de Musset, Sandeau, Chopin, and Sainte-Beuve. In the background were a few ephemeral shadowy figures, such as the unknown "Marie", with whom he had a brief liaison and who probably bore him a child, and a certain "Louise" whose other name is equally unknown. Balzac maintained a masterly discretion behind a façade of apparently carefree loquacity where intimate relationships with women were concerned.

Even more rare were his friendships with men. Nearly all those to whom he was closely attached were obscure, unimportant people. If he needed women with whom he could relax, he needed male friends on whom he could rely. Like Goethe, Beethoven, and most men of creative mind who have resolved to devote themselves to the production of some comprehensive work, Balzac did not choose friends of outstanding intellect who would stimulate and spur him on to artistic creation and competition. He was content with men to whom he could turn in the brief intervals of his labours and who were ready at any time to help him. What he sought was a kind of family relationship. We know little of Monsieur de Margonne, in whose château in Sachez a comfortable room where he could work was placed at Balzac's disposal on about a dozen occasions when he wanted to get away from Paris. And his real friends were by no means men of the quality of Victor Hugo, Lamartine, Heine or Chopin, though he knew them all personally, but an ironmonger, a physician, an obscure painter, and a tailor. *Le petit père* Dablin had been his indispensable companion since the years in the rue Lesdiguières. With Auguste Borget he shared for a time the house in the rue de Cassini. Doctor Nacquart looked after his health until the day of his death and helped him on occasion not only with advice of a specialist nature in connection with his novels, but also in case of need with a few hundred francs to patch up the gaping hole in his pocket which he never succeeded in mending. Buisson, the tailor in the rue de Richelieu who had learned to respect Balzac's genius before it was discovered by the critics of Paris, not only allowed him credit for as long as he liked, but also lent him money and provided him with a place of refuge in his house when he had no other channel of escape from less discerning creditors. To lend money to a man with Balzac's sense of gratitude was not a bad piece of business, and the worthy tailor at any rate received adequate repayment of the debt owing to him, however large it may have been, with a couple of lines in the *Comédie humaine*: "A suit made by Buisson is enough to enable one to play a royal rôle in any salon." This line or two of publicity at once made Buisson the tailor of all those who wanted to cut a good figure in society. Great men have another means of payment besides that which is normally regarded as legal tender. They can confer immortality on their creditors.

This small circle of friends was practically complete when Balzac began to write the works which have won him his fame. At the age of thirty his receptive period had come to a close. He no longer needed stimulus, discussion, extensive reading, fresh knowledge or new friends. He was ready; and what he had to give in the way of genius and wit, warmth and intensity, belonged in future to his work. He once said that a great tree dries up the soil around it. "*Un grand arbre ressèche le terrain autour de lui.*" In order that it may blossom and bear fruit, it draws into itself all the strength within reach. Though he possessed hundreds of acquaintances, Balzac took no one else into his inner circle—with the exception of Madame de Hanska, who became the central figure and the real focus of his life.

CHAPTER VIII

Black Coffee

Sudden success is always dangerous for an artist. In 1828 Balzac was a literary hack, bankrupt, up to the eyes in debt, a poor devil who confessed that he stayed at home to save his clothes. Two or three years later he was one of the most famous writers in Europe, with a public in Russia, Germany, England, and the Scandinavian countries, with journals and reviews clamouring for contributions from his pen, courted by all the publishers, snowed under with letters from admiring readers. Overnight one of the ambitions of his youth had been fulfilled, *la gloire*, the dazzling fame which carried his name round the world on radiant wings. Even a more sober-minded person than Balzac could not have helped being intoxicated by such success, and Balzac was far from being sober-minded. He had lived too many years in obscurity, poor and hungry, filled with impatient despair, observing in fleeting moments of envy that it was always the others, never himself, but always the others, who were acquiring riches, women, success, the luxuries and lavish windfalls of life. With his sensuous nature, it is comprehensible that he should desire to exploit the stir he had made and taste the pleasures which the world had to offer. He wanted to breathe in the fame that had come to him, taste it on his tongue, touch it with his fingers, perceive it with all his senses, to feel the cosy warmth of applauding crowds, the sweet breath of flattery. Now that the world was aware of his talent, he wanted to show himself to the world. He was weary of humiliations and rebuffs, of the years

of servitude and financial embarrassment, and he was ready to yield to the seductive temptations that fame brought with it, to the delights of luxury and extravagance. He knew that the world was now his stage, so he decided to appear before his public and play a rôle in society.

No less remarkable than Balzac's genius as a writer was his lack of aptitude for the rôle of society lion. It is a peculiar feature of the human brain that even the highest degree of intellectual capacity and the most varied accumulation of experience are unable to overcome a man's innate disabilities. However clear an insight one may have into one's own temperamental defects, one has no power to eliminate them. Diagnosis is not the same thing as cure, and we can see again and again how the wisest of men are unable to control their small follies, which are the butt of other people's ridicule. Conscious though he was of the childishness of his snobbery, he was unable to suppress this worst of his weaknesses. The man who was producing the greatest creative work of the century, and could have walked in the presence of kings and princes with the unconcern of a Beethoven, suffered from an absurd mania for the aristocracy. A letter from a duchess of the Faubourg St. Germain meant more to him than Goethe's praise. He would perhaps rather have become a Rothschild, living in a palace with servants, carriages, and a gallery of masterpieces, than have acquired immortality, and for a genuine patent of nobility signed by Louis Philippe he would have sold his soul. If his father had been able to step from the peasantry into the world of the prosperous *bourgeoisie*, why should he himself not take the further step into the aristocracy? The epoch of startling and brilliant careers had only just passed, but was there any reason why it should have come completely to a close? If a Murat, a Junot, and a Ney, sons of craftsmen and coachmen or grandsons of innkeepers, could become dukes through ordering cavalry charges and bayonet attacks, and if financiers, profiteers on the Stock Exchange and industrial magnates were even now being ennobled, why should not he too be able to rise into the "higher" strata of society? The same vigour which sixty years before had urged Balzac's father to exchange a thatched cottage in La Nougayrié for the wider opportunities of Paris was perhaps unconsciously now spurring on his son to rise still higher; but it is ludicrous that he should identify this higher goal with entry into a hitherto exclusive circle and not

with his own creative achievement. It is an attitude of mind that
cannot be analysed rationally. We are faced with an incomprehensible paradox. In order to climb into a "higher" sphere of society
he submitted to humiliations all his life. In order to live in luxury,
he condemned himself to forced labour. In order to appear elegant,
he made himself look absurd. Unconsciously he was himself a living
proof of the law which he demonstrated a hundred times in his
novels—that a master in one sphere can be a bungler when he
ventures into another for which he is not fitted.

Balzac dressed himself for the part he was to play in society. In
the first place, he could not appear merely as Monsieur Balzac.
That would sound too bourgeois in the Faubourg St. Germain. So
on his own authority he attached to it the predicate of nobility,
and beginning with *La peau de chagrin* all his books were published
under the name Honoré *de* Balzac. Woe to anyone who dared to
deny him the right to this title. The doubter would be told that it
was really out of pure modesty that he called himself merely "de
Balzac", since he was a descendant of the marquis d'Entrague. To
render this latter assertion more credible he had the arms of the
d'Entrague family engraved on his cutlery and painted on his
carriage. The next step was to change his style of living completely.
People would only believe, so he argued, that Honoré de Balzac was
a great writer if he lived up to his reputation. Unto him that hath
shall be given, and in a world where only appearances count one
must produce the effect of having much if one wants to be given
much. If Monsieur de Chateaubriand could possess a château,
Girardin keep two riding horses, and even Jules Janin or Eugène
Sue maintain a carriage, there was all the more reason why Honoré
de Balzac should drive out in a tilbury with a liveried footman
behind so that people should not rate him as the lesser writer. He
rented the second floor of the house in the rue de Cassini, bought
opulent furniture, and no dandy was to be able to say that his
clothes were richer and more expensive than those of Honoré de
Balzac. He had specially chased gold buttons made for his blue
dress-coat, while the worthy Buisson supplied him with silk and
brocade waistcoats on credit. And thus, with his leonine mane
thickly pomaded and a small lorgnon coquettishly poised in his
hand, the newly fledged author made his entry into the salons of
Paris *pour se faire une réputation*—as though his reputation were

not already assured both among his own generation and the generations yet to come.

The result of Balzac's personal impact on Parisian society was disappointing, and it had unfortunate repercussions on his fame as a writer. His attempt to turn himself into a dandy was a complete failure. The salons to which he had access at this stage of his career were not those of the Faubourg St. Germain, nor was he yet invited to the great embassies, and his entry into society was limited to the literary drawing-rooms of Madame Delphine Gay and her daughter and of Madame Récamier, ladies who tried to compete with the aloof official aristocracy by cultivating the aristocracy of letters. Even in these less exalted circles, however, the effect of Balzac's ostentatious elegance was catastrophic. His very physical appearance destroyed any hope he might have entertained of cutting an aristocratic figure. Neither Buisson's tailoring, nor gold buttons, nor lace cravats could disguise the thick-set, stout, red-cheeked plebeian who spoke in such a loud voice without letting others get a word in edgeways and burst into a room like a cannon-shell. His temperament was far too exuberant to be kept in check by a discreet reserve of manner that did not come natural to him. Twenty years later Madame de Hanska found cause to complain that he stuffed his knife into his mouth when he ate and that his noisy bragging jarred on the nerves of the very people who were most sincerely anxious to admire him. She deplored his reverberating peals of laughter and the "tempestuous deluge of eloquence" which drowned everyone else's remarks in its flood. None but an idler, intent only on externals, possesses the time and the perseverance to appear elegant at all times—which is in itself a kind of art—and Balzac, who was merely tearing himself away from his work for an hour or so, betrayed the haste with which he had decked himself out for the occasion. The ill-matched colour scheme of his coat and trousers drove Delacroix to despair, and what was the use of a gold lorgnon when the nails of the fingers in which it was held were dirty? His shoe-laces would come undone and trail loosely over his silk stockings, and when he grew heated the grease from his pomaded hair dripped on to the frills of his collar. Balzac wore his elegance as a lackey wore his livery. His taste inclined more and more to the extravagant rather than to the discreet; he made expensive things look cheap and gave luxury the appearance of ostentation, and the combined effect—as is proved by the innumerable caricatures of which he was the subject—often compelled even his feminine admirers to conceal a smile behind their fans.

Yet the more Balzac felt that his attempt at elegance was not a success, the more he tried to overdo it. If he could not cut a good figure he would at least provide a sensation. If he could not produce a pleasing and striking effect by an air of unobtrusive distinction, at least his extravagances should become as celebrated as the writings by which he had acquired his fame. If he was to become a butt for people's scoffing, he would at least give them adequate cause to scoff. So after his first failure he invented a grotesque device which, as he said jestingly, was to make him more famous than his novels had done. He procured himself a stick as thick as a club and encrusted with turquoises, about which he spread the strangest rumours, such as for instance that he kept in the knob a portrait in the costume of Eve of a mysterious mistress who belonged to the highest circles of the aristocracy. When he entered the box of the "Tigers" at the *Théâtre des Italiens* with this Hercules club in his hand (which had cost him seven hundred francs that he never paid), the whole audience stared at it hypnotically, and Madame de Girardin was inspired by the remarkable object to write a novel called *La canne de Monsieur de Balzac*. Yet the ladies remained uncured of their disillusionment and none of them selected as her protégé this troubadour who had sung their praises, while the lions of the Paris salons, the models for his Rastignacs and de Marsays, whom he so deeply admired, felt that they had no need to fear the ponderous, elephantine competition of the new candidate for social honours.

Balzac enjoyed no greater success with his colleagues in the world of letters, who watched with a certain disquiet the fat pike that had suddenly made its appearance in their carp pond. Many of them still remembered only too vividly the shady past that had preceded his sudden rise to fame, but surprised by his talent and disturbed by his prolific output they would have been prepared to accept him as one of themselves. Unfortunately Balzac spurned their advances. Despite his good nature and generous enthusiasm for the achievements of others, he deliberately adopted an arrogant attitude towards his literary colleagues in particular. Instead of accepting their readiness to meet him on friendly terms he treated them brusquely, kept his hat on his head when he entered a room, and refused to be placed on the same footing as themselves in the world of letters. Instead of diplomatically indulging the little vanities of his fellow-writers, he loudly emphasised his firm objection to being lumped together with an Alexandre Dumas, a Paul de Kock, an Eugène Sue, a Sandeau or a Janin. He offended them by bragging of the high fees he was able to command, and he put the journalists' backs up into the bargain. Few authors have been so indifferent to the possibilities of favourable critiques and the publicity that journalists have it in their power to dispense. He let them feel that he did not need their favours, and just as he tried by the rather vulgar flamboyance of his dress to impress himself on society as "a man apart", so in his naive and incautious sincerity he underlined continually that he was not to be measured by the same standard as the others. Even though he did this in the most casual way imaginable, with a hearty laugh and in playful good spirits, the Parisians regarded his attitude as a provocation.

Balzac's weaknesses were too evident not to offer a hundred points of attack to the nimble wit and malice of those who were ready to take advantage of them, and the newspapers all bubbled over with mocking humour at his expense. The greatest writer of his age became the favourite butt of mordant notices and impudent caricatures. On no one does "society" take a more bitter revenge than on the man who despises it yet cannot do without it. Balzac himself was not particularly affected by his failure. He was too vigorous, too full of spirits and a sense of his own superiority to notice pinpricks, and he answered the smirks and scoffs of dandified bores or snobbish blue-stockings with the boisterous guffaw of a Rabelais. Magnanimous and creative even in his wrath, he countered the spitefulness of exasperated journalists and the smaller fry of literature not with petty polemics, but with the grandiose fresco painting of literary corruption in the *Illusions perdues*. His genuine friends, on the other hand, were pained to see a man of Balzac's genius placed by his little snobbish weaknesses in a humiliating situation which for the time being justified the gibes of which he was the target. Zulma Carraud, in her remote

provincial town, realised sooner than he did himself that the fruits
of Paradise he hoped to pluck in Parisian society would before
long turn to ashes in his mouth, and she implored him not to be an
actor "in a world which demands a hundred times more from you
than it can give in return." In friendly warning she cried to him:
"Honoré, you are now a celebrated author, but you are destined
for something higher. Mere fame is nothing to a man like you. You
should set yourself a higher goal! If I had the courage I would say
to you: 'Why are you, out of pure vanity, wasting your unusual
intelligence in such a foolish manner? Give up this life of elegance. . . .'" Balzac, however, was to learn the lesson of bitter
experience before the intoxication of early fame yielded to a sober
realisation of the truth of his own law that one cannot be a master
in two spheres at once, and that destiny intended him not to strut
in a transient world of men and women who would soon forget him,
but to immortalise this same world with its heights and its depths
by the creative power of his pen.

We can turn to innumerable contemporary descriptions of Balzac
as he was at this time. Some are merely amusing, others are witty;
some are condescending, others are malicious or even venomous;
but they all view him in the narrow, misleading perspective of
Parisian society and journalism. We are shown Balzac in his blue
coat with its chased gold buttons, and carrying his massive jewel-
encrusted club, Balzac *en pantoufles*, Balzac driving in his tilbury
with groom and footman, Balzac strolling along the boulevard and
reading all the shop signs to find names for his characters, Balzac
the collector of bric-à-brac who hunted through the antique shops
in the hope of picking up a Rembrandt for seven francs or a bowl
by Benvenuto Cellini for twelve sous, Balzac the terror of his
publishers and the bugbear of the compositors, Balzac the braggart
and hoaxer who preached chastity as the essential prerequisite for
creative work and Balzac the lover who changed his women more
frequently than he changed his shirt, Balzac the gourmand who
could devour three dozen oysters at a sitting and follow it up with
a steak and poultry, Balzac the visionary who talked of the
millions he would derive from his mines, his hothouses, and his

business interests, yet had to hide himself under a false name for
weeks at a time because he was unable to pay a bill of a thousand
francs.

It is not mere chance that three-quarters of the pictures of Balzac
which have come down to us are not portraits but caricatures, or
that his contemporaries have recorded countless anecdotes about
him, yet have not bequeathed to us a single accurate and important
biography. It is clear from all this that the effect on the Parisians
of Balzac's personality was to make them regard him not as a
genius but as an eccentric, and in a certain sense they may have
judged rightly. He was bound to appear eccentric in public because,
in the real meaning of the word, he diverged from his orbit as soon
as he quitted his room, his writing-table, and his work. The essential
Balzac was invisible to the Gozlans, the Werdets, and the Janins,
to the idlers and the strollers on the boulevards, because they only
knew him during the "one hour a day" he had to give to the world,
and not during the other twenty-three hours of his creative solitude.
When he went out among his fellow-men it was like the brief
respite allowed to a prisoner when he walks in the prison yard for a
breath of fresh air. Or, like the ghost that on the last stroke of
midnight has to vanish back to the dark regions whence it came, so
Balzac had to return to his labours after his interlude of uncurbed
exuberance; and none of those who indulged in irony at his expense
had any inkling of the greatness of his work or the austere discipline
under which it was carried out. The essential Balzac was the one
who in twenty years, apart from numerous dramas, short stories
and essays, wrote seventy-four novels of which almost every one
is of the first rank. And these seventy-four novels contain a world
of their own, with all the different landscapes, streets, houses, and
characters required to populate it.

This is the only standard by which Balzac can be measured. In
his work alone can the real Balzac be recognised. The man whom
his contemporaries regarded as a foolish eccentric possessed the
most disciplined artistic intelligence of the age. While they jeered
at him for his extravagance he was an industrious ascetic with the
steadfast, persevering patience of an anchorite. Those who chose
the middle way and were secure in their consciousness of being
normal human beings scoffed at him for his tendency to exaggeration, but he produced more from that creative mind of his than all

10

his colleagues put together. He was perhaps the only one of whom it could truthfully be said that he worked himself to death. His calendar was different from that of his contemporaries. Their day was his night and their night was his day. His real life was lived in a world of his own, a world that he had made himself, and the real Balzac was seen and heard only by the four walls of the room in which he wrote. No contemporary could have written his biography, which is contained in his books themselves.

❧⊙❦

Let us take a day in Balzac's working life, a day typical of thousands.

Eight o'clock in the evening. The citizens of Paris had long since finished their day's work and left their offices, shops or factories. After having dined, either with their families or their friends or alone, they were beginning to pour out into the streets in search of pleasure. Some strolled along the boulevards or sat in cafés, others were still putting the finishing touches to their toilet before the mirror prior to a visit to the theatre or to a salon. Balzac alone was asleep in his darkened room, dead to the world after sixteen or seventeen hours spent at his desk.

Nine o'clock. In the theatres the curtain had already gone up, the ballrooms were crowded with whirling couples, the gambling-houses echoed to the chink of gold, in the side-streets furtive lovers pressed deeper into the shadows—but Balzac slept on.

Ten o'clock. Lights were being extinguished in houses here and there, the older generation were thinking of bed, fewer carriages could be heard rolling over the cobbles, the voices of the city grew softer—and Balzac slept.

Eleven o'clock. The final curtain was falling in the theatres, the last guests were turning homewards from the parties or salons they had been attending, the restaurants were dimming their lights, the last pedestrians were disappearing from the streets, the boulevards were emptying as a final wave of noisy revellers disappeared into the side-streets and trickled away—and Balzac slept on.

Midnight. Paris was silent. Millions of eyes had closed. Most of the lights had gone out. Now that the others were resting it was time for Balzac to work. Now that the others were dreaming it was time for him to wake. Now that the day was ended for the rest of Paris his day was about to begin. No one could come to disturb him, no visitors to bother him, no letters to cause him disquiet. No creditors could knock at his door and no printers send their messengers to insist on a further instalment of manuscript or corrected proofs. A vast stretch of time, eight to ten hours of perfect solitude, lay before him in which to work at his vast undertaking. Just as the furnace which fuses the cold, brittle ore into infrangible steel must not be allowed to cool down, so he knew that the tensity of his vision must not be allowed to slacken:

My thoughts must drip from my brow like water from a fountain. The process is entirely unconscious.

He recognised only the law which his work decreed:

It is impossible for me to work when I have to break off and go out. I never work merely for one or two hours at a stretch.

It was only at night, when time was boundless and undivided, that continuity was possible, and in order to obtain this continuity of work he reversed the normal division of time and turned his night into day.

Awakened by his servant knocking gently on the door, Balzac rose and donned his robe. This was the garment which he had found by years of experience to be the most convenient for his work. In winter it was of warm cashmere, in summer óf thin linen, long and white, permitting complete freedom of movement, open at the neck, providing adequate warmth without being oppressive, and perhaps a further reason why he had chosen it was because its resemblance to a monk's robe unconsciously reminded him that he was in service to a higher law and bound, so long as he wore it, to abjure the outside world and its temptations. A woven cord (later replaced by a golden chain) was tied loosely round this monkish garment, and in place of crucifix and scapular there dangled a paper-knife and a pair of scissors. After taking a few steps up and down the room to shake the last vestiges of sleep from his mind and send the blood circulating more swiftly through his veins, Balzac was ready.

The servant had kindled the six candles in the silver candelabra on the table and drawn the curtains tightly as if this were a visible symbol that the outer world was now completely shut off, for

Balzac did not want to measure his hours of work by the sun or the stars. He did not care to see the dawn or to know that Paris was waking to a new day. The material objects around him faded into the shadows—the books ranged along the walls, the walls themselves, the doors and windows and all that lay beyond them. Only the creatures of his own mind were to speak, and act, and live. He was creating a world of his own, a world that was to endure.

Balzac sat down at the table where, as he said, "I cast my life into the crucible as the alchemist casts his gold." It was a small, unpretentious, rectangular table which he loved more than the most valuable of his possessions. It meant more to him than his stick studded with turquoises, more than the silver plate that he had purchased piece by piece, more than his sumptuously bound books, more than the celebrity he had already won, for he had carried it with him from one lodging to another, salvaged it from bankruptcies and catastrophes, rescued it like a soldier dragging a helpless comrade from the turmoil of battle. It was the sole confidant of his keenest pleasure and his bitterest grief, the sole silent witness of his real life:

> It has seen all my wretchedness, knows all my plans, has overheard my thoughts. My arm almost committed violent assault upon it as my pen raced along the sheets.

No human being knew so much about him, and with no woman did he share so many nights of ardent companionship. It was at this table that Balzac lived—and worked himself to death.

A last look round to make sure that everything was in place. Like every truly fanatical worker, Balzac was pedantic in his method of work. He loved his tools as a soldier loves his weapons, and before he flung himself into the fray he had to know that they were ready to his hand. To his left lay the neat piles of blank paper. The paper had been carefully chosen and the sheets were of a special size and shape, of a slightly bluish tinge so as not to dazzle or tire the eyes, and with a particularly smooth surface over which his quill could skim without meeting resistance. His pens had been prepared with equal care. He would use no other than ravens' quills. Next to the inkwell—not the expensive one of malachite that had been a gift from some admirers, but the simple one that had accompanied him in his student days—stood a bottle or two of ink in reserve. He would have no precaution neglected that would serve to ensure the smooth, uninterrupted flow of his work. To his right lay a small notebook in which he now and then entered some thought or idea that might come in useful for a later chapter. There was no other equipment. Books, papers, research material were all unnecessary. Balzac had digested everything in his mind before he began to write.

He leaned back in his chair and rolled back the sleeve of his robe to allow free play to his right hand. Then he spurred himself on with half-jesting remarks addressed to himself, like a coachman encouraging his horses to pull on the shafts. Or he might have been compared to a swimmer stretching his arms and easing his joints before taking the steep plunge from the diving-board.

Balzac wrote and wrote, without pause and without hesitation. Once the flame of his imagination had been kindled it continued to glow. It was like a forest fire, with the blaze leaping from tree to tree and growing hotter and more voracious in the process. Yet swiftly as his pen sped over the paper, the words could hardly keep pace with his thoughts. The more he wrote the more he abbreviated the words so as not to have to think more slowly. He could not allow any interruption of his inner vision, and he did not raise his pen from the paper until either an attack of cramp compelled his fingers to loosen their hold or the writing swam before his eyes and he was dizzy with fatigue.

The streets were silent and the only sound in the room was the soft swish of the quill as it passed smoothly over the surface of the paper, or from time to time the rustle of a sheet as it was added to the written pile. Outside the day was beginning to dawn, but Balzac did not see it. His day was the small circle of light cast by the candles, and he was aware of neither space nor time, but only of the world that he was himself fashioning.

Now and then the machine threatened to run down. Even the most immeasurable will-power cannot prolong indefinitely the natural measure of a man's physical strength. After five or six hours of continuous writing Balzac felt that he must call a temporary halt. His fingers had grown numb, his eyes were beginning to water, his back hurt, his temples were throbbing, and his nerves could no longer bear the strain. Another man would have been content with what he had already done and would have stopped

work for the night, but Balzac refused to yield. The horse must run
the allotted course even if it foundered under the spur. If the
sluggish carcase declined to keep up the pace recourse must be had
to the whip. Balzac rose from his chair and went over to the table
on which stood the coffee-pot.

Coffee was the black oil that started the engine running again,
so for Balzac it was more important than eating or sleeping. He
hated tobacco, which could not stimulate him to the pitch necessary
for the intensity with which he worked:

> Tobacco is injurious to the body, attacks the mind, and makes
> whole nations dull-witted.

But he sang a paean in praise of coffee:

> Coffee glides down into one's stomach and sets everything in
> motion. One's ideas advance in column of route like battalions of
> the *grande armée*. Memories come up at the double bearing the
> standards which are to lead the troops into battle. The light
> cavalry deploys at the gallop. The artillery of logic thunders
> along with its supply waggons and shells. Brilliant notions join
> in the combat as sharpshooters. The characters don their cos-
> tumes, the paper is covered with ink, the battle has begun and
> ends with an outpouring of black fluid like a real battlefield
> enveloped in swathes of black smoke from the expended gun-
> powder.

Without coffee he could not work, or at least he could not have
worked in the way he did. In addition to paper and pens he took
with him everywhere as an indispensable article of equipment the
coffee-machine, which was no less important to him than his little
table or his white robe. He allowed nobody else to prepare his
coffee, since nobody else would have prepared the stimulating
poison in such strength and blackness. And just as in a sort of
superstitious fetishism he would use only a particular kind of paper
and a certain type of pen, so he mixed his coffee according to a
special recipe, which has been recorded by one of his friends: "This
coffee was composed of three different varieties of bean—Bourbon,
Martinique, and Mocha. He bought the Bourbon in the rue de
Montblanc, the Martinique in the rue des Vieilles Audriettes, and
the Mocha in the Fauborg Saint-Germain from a dealer in the rue
de l'Université, whose name I have forgotten though I repeatedly

accompanied Balzac on his shopping expeditions. Each time it involved half-a-day's journey right across Paris, but to Balzac good coffee was worth the trouble."

Coffee was his hashish, and since, like every drug, it had to be taken in continually stronger doses if it was to maintain its effect, he had to swallow more and more of the murderous elixir to keep pace with the increasing strain on his nerves. Of one of his books he said that it had been finished only with the help of "streams of coffee". In 1845, after nearly twenty years of over-indulgence, he admitted that his whole organism had been poisoned by incessant recourse to the stimulant and complained that it was growing less and less effective, while it caused him dreadful pains in the stomach. If his fifty thousand cups of strong coffee (which is the number he is estimated to have drunk by a certain statistician) accelerated the writing of the vast cycle of the *Comédie humaine*, they were also responsible for the premature failure of a heart that was originally as sound as a bell. Dr. Nacquart, his lifelong friend and physician, certified as the real cause of his death "an old heart trouble, aggravated by working at night and the use, or rather abuse, of coffee, to which he had to have recourse in order to combat the normal human need for sleep."

The clock struck eight at last and there came a tap at the door. His servant, Auguste, entered with a modest breakfast on a tray. Balzac rose from the table where he had been writing since midnight. The time had come for a brief rest. Auguste drew back the curtains and Balzac stepped to the window to cast a glance at the city which he had set out to conquer. He again became conscious that there was another world and another Paris, a Paris that was beginning its work now that his own labours had for the time being come to an end. Shops were opening, children were hastening to school, carriages were rolling along the streets, in offices and counting-houses men were sitting down at their desks.

To relax his exhausted body, and refresh himself for the further tasks that awaited him, Balzac took a hot bath. He usually spent an hour in the tub, as Napoleon had liked to do, for it was the only place where he could meditate without being disturbed—meditate without having immediately to write down the substance of his thoughts, surrender himself to the voluptuous pleasure of creative dreaming without the necessity for simultaneous physical effort. Hardly had he resumed his robe, however, when steps could be heard outside the door. Messengers had arrived from his various printers like Napoleon's despatch-riders sent during the battle to maintain contact between the command post and the battalions that were carrying out his orders. The first arrival demanded a fresh instalment of the current novel, the still damp manuscript of the night that had just passed. Everything that Balzac wrote had to be set up in print at once, not only because the newspaper or publisher was waiting for it as for the payment of a debt that was due—every novel had been sold before it was written—but because Balzac in the trance-like state in which he worked did not know what he was writing or what he had already written. Even his keen eye could not survey the dense jungle of his manuscripts. Only when they were in print and he could review them paragraph by paragraph, like companies of soldiers marching past at an inspection, was the general in Balzac able to discern whether he had won the battle or whether he had to renew the assault.

Other messengers from the printers, the newspapers or the publishers brought proofs of the pages he had written two nights before and sent to press on the previous day, together with the second or third proofs of earlier instalments. Whole piles of freshly printed galleys, often five or six dozen of them still damp from the press, overflowed his little table and claimed his attention.

At nine o'clock his brief respite was at an end. His form of rest, as he once said, consisted of a change of task. But correcting proofs was not an easy business so far as Balzac was concerned. It involved not merely the elimination of printers' errors and slight emendations of style or content, but the complete re-writing and re-casting of the original manuscript. In fact, he regarded the first printed proofs as a preliminary draft, and to no task did he devote more passionate energy than to the gradual shaping of his plastic prose in a sequence of proof-sheets which he scrutinised and altered time after time with a keen sense of artistic responsibility. In everything that concerned his work he was tyrannical and pedantic, and he insisted on the galleys being printed according to rules that he himself laid down. The sheets had to be specially long and wide, so that the printed text looked like the pip on an ace in a pack of playing-cards. The margins to right and left, above and below, were vast blank spaces for corrections and alterations. Moreover, he would not accept proofs printed on the usual cheap yellowish paper, but demanded a white background against which every letter could stand out clearly.

Balzac sat down again at his little table. The first swift glance—he possessed the gift of his Louis Lambert of being able to read six or seven lines at once—was followed by a wrathful stab of the pen. He was dissatisfied. Everything he had written on the previous day, and the day before that, was bad. The meaning was obscure, the syntax confused, the style defective, the sequence clumsy. It must all be changed and made clearer, simpler, less unwieldy. The frenzy with which he attacked the square of printed text, like a cavalry-man charging at the solid phalanx of the enemy, can be seen from the savage jabs and strokes from his spluttering pen that stretch right across the sheet. A sabre-thrust with his quill and a sentence was torn from its context and flung to the right, a single word was speared and hurled to the left, whole paragraphs were wrenched out and others plugged in. Soon the normal symbols used as directions to the compositor no longer sufficed, and Balzac had to employ symbols of his own invention. Before long there was not enough room in the margins for further corrections, which now contained more matter than the printed text. The marginal corrections themselves were scored with symbols drawing the compositor's attention to supplementary afterthoughts, until what had once been a desert of white space with an oasis of text in the middle was covered with a spider's web of intersecting lines and he had to turn the sheet over to continue his corrections on the back. Yet even that was not enough. When there was no more space for the symbols and criss-cross lines by which the unhappy compositor was to find his way about, Balzac had recourse to his scissors. Unwanted passages were removed bodily and fresh paper pasted over the gap. The beginning of a section would be stuck in the middle and a new beginning written ; the whole text was dug up and raked over; and this chaotic mass of printed text, interpolated corrections and alterations, symbols, lines, and blots went back to the printer in an incomparably more illegible and unintelligible state than the original manuscript.

In the newspaper and printing offices laughing throngs gathered round to examine the astonishing scrawl. The most experienced compositors declared their inability to decipher it, and though they were offered double wages they refused to set up more than *"une heure de Balzac"* a day. It took months before a man learned the science of unravelling his hieroglyphics, and even then a special proof-reader had to revise the compositor's often very hypothetical surmises.

Their task, however, was still only in its initial stages. When Balzac received the second set of galleys, he flung himself upon them with the same rage as before. Once more he would tear apart the whole laboriously constructed edifice, bestrewing each sheet from top to bottom with further emendations and blots, until it was no less involved and illegible than its predecessor. And this would happen six or seven times, except that in the later proofs he no longer broke up whole paragraphs but merely altered individual sentences and ultimately confined himself to the substitution of single words. In the case of some of his books Balzac re-corrected the proof-sheets as many as fifteen or sixteen times, and this alone gives us a faint idea of his extraordinary productivity. In twenty years he not only wrote his seventy-four novels, his short stories, and his sketches, but he re-wrote them again and again before they finally appeared in print.

Neither financial need nor the entreaties of his publishers, who alternated between friendly reproaches and legal action, could dissuade Balzac from pursuing his expensive system. On numerous occasions he forfeited half his fee, and sometimes the whole of it, because he had to pay the cost of corrections and re-setting out of his own pocket. But it was a matter of artistic integrity, and on this point he remained inexorable. The editor of a newspaper once printed an instalment of one of his novels without waiting for the final proof or obtaining Balzac's *imprimatur*, with the result that Balzac broke off relations with him forever. To the outside world he appeared frivolous, slipshod and covetous, but as an artist he waged the most conscientious and unyielding struggle of any writer in modern literature. Because he alone knew of the energy and self-sacrifice that went to the perfection of his work in his secluded laboratory, where his painstaking absorption was invisible to those who saw only the finished product, he treasured his proof-sheets as the sole faithful and reliable witnesses. They were his pride, the pride not so much of the artist as of the worker, the indefatigable craftsman. He therefore compiled one copy of each of his books, made up of the successive layers of revised proofs in their various stages, together with the original manuscript, and had it bound in a massive volume that sometimes comprised about two thousand pages as compared with the two hundred or so of the published novel. In some cases the manuscript was merely attached instead of being bound in with the proofs. As Napoleon distributed princely or ducal titles and coats of arms to his field-marshals and other loyal adherents, Balzac presented these volumes from the vast realm of the *Comédie humaine* to his friends as the most precious gift he had to bestow:

> I offer these volumes only to those who love me. They are witnesses to my lengthy labours and to that patience of which I have spoken to you. It was these dreadful pages on which I spent my nights.

Most of them were given to Madame de Hanska, but Madame de Castries, the Countess Visconti, and his sister were also among the recipients. That the few people singled out for such an honour were fully conscious of the value of these unique documents may be judged from the reply of Dr. Nacquart when he received as a reward for his years of friendship and medical care the volume containing the proof-sheets of *Le lys dans la vallée*:

> This is a truly remarkable monument, and it should be made accessible to all who believe in the perfection of beauty in art. How instructive too it would be for the public, which believes that the productions of the mind are conceived and created with as little effort as they can be read! I wish my library could be set up in the middle of the Place Vendôme, so that those who appreciate your genius might learn to estimate at their true value the conscientiousness and tenacity with which you work.

With the exception of Beethoven's notebooks there are hardly any documents existing to-day in which the artist's struggle for expression is more tangibily demonstrated than in these volumes. The elemental force with which Balzac was endowed, the titanic energy that went to the making of his books, can here be studied more

vividly than in any portrait or contemporary anecdote. Only by
knowing them can we know the real Balzac.

The three or four hours during which he worked at his proofs,
which he jokingly called "*faire sa cuisine littéraire*", took up the
whole forenoon. Then he pushed aside the pile of papers and
refreshed himself with a light lunch, consisting of an egg, a sand-
wich or two, or a little pasty. He was fond of good living and the
heavy, greasy dishes of his native Touraine, the tasty *rillettes*, the
crisp capons and the red juicy meat, while he knew the red and
white wines of his home province as a pianist knows his keyboard;
but while he was working he denied himself every luxury. He was
aware that eating makes a man sluggish, and he had no time to be
sluggish. There was no time even for an interlude of rest, and he
very soon moved his armchair up to the little table again, either to
continue correcting proofs or to jot down memoranda, work at an
article or two, and write letters.

At last, towards five o'clock, he laid aside his pen for the day. He
had seen nobody and had not even cast a glance at a newspaper,
but now he could ease off a little. Auguste served supper and he
would sometimes receive a visit from a publisher or a friend, but
generally he remained alone with his thoughts, which perhaps
revolved round the work he was to do during the coming night. He
never, or hardly ever, went out into the street, for he was too
fatigued. At eight o'clock, when others were going out to seek their
pleasures, he went to bed and fell asleep at once. His sleep was deep
and dreamless. Like everything else he did, it was characterised by
an extreme intensity. He slept in order to forget that all the work
he had already done would not relieve him of the work which was
to be done on the morrow, and the morrow after that, until the
last hour of his life. At midnight his servant entered, lit the candles,
and therewith kindled once more the flame of work in the awakened
Balzac.

This was the way in which Balzac worked for weeks and months at a stretch. He brooked no interruption until the task in hand was finished, and the intervals between the periods of utter absorption were always brief. One book followed upon another like a series of stitches in the vast fabric that was both his life's work and his shroud. He groaned in despair: "It is always the same. Night after night, and volume after volume! The structure I am trying to build is so tall and so wide. . . ." Often he would be assailed by the fear that he was missing life itself, and he rattled the chains that were of his own forging: "In a single month I have to do what others could not bring to completion in a whole year or more." But work had become for him a compulsive necessity and he was unable to stop: "When I work I forget my sufferings. Work is my salvation." Varied as his work was, that made no difference to its continuity: "When I am not writing I am thinking over my plans, and when I am not writing or thinking I have proofs to correct. That is what my life consists of." He lived with a chain round his ankle and it clanked even when he tried to escape. If he went on a journey he still had to write. When he was in love and travelled to see the woman on whom his passions were set, these passions were subordinated to a higher obligation. When he announced his forthcoming visit to Madame de Hanska or to the duchesse de Castries in Geneva, he might be burning with impatience and drunk with desire, but he warned his mistress in a letter that she would never be able to see him before five o'clock in the afternoon. Only after he had finished his relentless twelve to fifteen hours' work for the day could he devote himself to the lady of his choice. Work came before love. The *Comédie humaine* was more important than the world of reality.

When we think of Balzac's output during these twenty years, we can only marvel all the more if we take into account his private affairs and business transactions. Whereas Goethe or Voltaire always had two or three secretaries at his beck and call and even a Sainte-Beuve employed someone to do his spade-work for him, Balzac looked after his entire correspondence and conducted all business matters without any help whatsoever. With the exception of the last moving letter from his death-bed, when his fingers were unable to guide the pen and he could only add a postscript to a letter written by his wife—"I can no longer read or write"—

every page of his books, every line of his correspondence, was written by his own hand. He arranged his contracts and went through all the formalities in connection with the lawsuits in which he was involved without either an amanuensis, business agent or professional adviser. He took charge of the shopping for his household, gave orders in person to the tradespeople, and later on even looked after the financial affairs of Madame de Hanska and gave advice to his family. The degree to which he used up his energies verged on the pathological, but there were moments when he realised that such an unnatural expenditure of effort must have disastrous results: "Sometimes it seems to me as if my brain were on fire and as if I were fated to die on the ruins of my mind." When he allowed himself a rest after periods of overwork and strain it was always dangerously like a collapse: "I sleep eighteen hours a day, and during the other six hours I do nothing." His method of resting after an excess of work was itself a form of excess, and similarly when he was able to summon the strength to seek diversion. When he left his cell and sought the company of his fellow-men his mind was still in a state of excitement. After weeks of solitude during which he had hardly heard the sound of his own voice, he would monopolise the conversation as if from a pent-up urge to mock and laugh and bubble over with wit and comment. When he entered a shop he was still under the spell of the fictitious millions with which he had juggled in the stories that had poured from his brain, and he spent money as if it had no meaning for him, After weeks of frugal living he gormandised with reckless appetite; and when he travelled the horses could not be spurred on fast enough. All his actions retained something of the exuberant fantasy that is to be found in his novels and were instinct with a joyous vigour. He was like one of those bluff and hearty sailors of former days who had not seen land, slept in a bed, or spoken to a woman for months at a time and, when their ship reached port after surmounting the manifold dangers of the sea, would fling down a bulging purse upon the table, drink their fill and create an uproar from the sheer explosive joy of living. Or he might be compared to a racehorse that had been kept too long in its stable, and instead of starting off at a comfortable trot shot forward straight away like a rocket as soon as it breathed the intoxicating air of freedom and was able to give free play to its muscles. That was how Balzac behaved during the brief intervals of relief from his self-imposed ascetic discipline.

Yet the Gozlans, the Werdets, the whole tribe of journalistic gossip-mongers vented their cheap wit and jeered like the dwarfs of Lilliput at the giant who had been released from captivity and was stalking in their midst. They made a note of the little anecdotes that were going the rounds about his ridiculous dandyism and childish vanity, and they printed them assiduously in their papers so that every blockhead could feel he was cleverer than the great Balzac. None of them understood that in a man who worked as Balzac worked it would have been abnormal if he had behaved normally, if he had kept careful account of each franc and invested his savings in the four per cents., if after holding sway in the magic dream-world he controlled he had followed the fashionable conventions of the salons when he emerged into the world of actuality, if he had constrained his creative genius within the bounds of cool, diplomatic calculation. The witlings could only caricature the grotesque shadow which his gigantic figure cast on the wall as it passed by. His contemporaries knew nothing of his real nature, for, like a ghost allowed to roam a world to which it did not belong only until the inexorable striking of the clock called it back to the shades, Balzac had but a few brief hours in which to enjoy the breath of freedom. Then he was summoned back to his solitary retreat, to the world which he had himself created and which for him was the only real one.

CHAPTER IX

The Duchesse de Castries

 alzac's real form of existence was work, and he enjoyed with a secret pleasure and admiration the daemonic energy and creative will-power which enabled him to extract the maximum, and even more than the maximum, from his massive body and elastic mind. He cast his days and nights into the fiery furnace and declared proudly: "*Mes débauches sont mes travaux.*" Getting the utmost out of life was essential to his way of working.

Yet the most tyrannical will cannot entirely suppress the demands of a man's nature, which is bound to rebel against an unnatural way of life that seeks satisfaction in the imagination alone and tries to dull the edge of appetite by absorption in some specific task. At times—and ever more frequently as he grew older—Balzac was assailed by the grim foreboding that his best years were slipping away from him, that even the most sublime form of artistic creation could be no more than a surrogate for life itself. "I am attempting to concentrate my life in my brain," he admitted to Zulma Carraud, but this was something he could not completely achieve. The artist, who was also an epicure, groaned under the ascetic monotony of his daily round. The man demanded a more fiery form of expression than the pouring out of words on to unresponsive paper. The creator of character, who portrayed women in love with men, needed a woman he could love and by whom he would be loved.

How was such a woman to be found? Here again his work jealously barred his path. He had no time to seek a wife or a mistress. He could not look around at his leisure, and it is touching to see how over and over again he charged both his sister and Zulma Carraud to find him a suitable wife who would deliver him from his emotional stress and tortured longings.

His sudden celebrity brought a strange turn, for when he was already on the verge of despair at the seeming impossibility of ever finding the woman he wanted women began to seek him out. Women always have a preference for the writer who is concerned with their problems, and Balzac's predilection for his women characters, whom he depicted as the unhappy, misunderstood victims of man, the allowances he made for their failings, his sympathy with abandoned, outcast or ageing females, stirred the curiosity not only of the Parisiennes. From the remotest corners of provincial France, from Germany, Russia, and Poland, came letters to the author who had "plumbed the heights and the depths".

In general, Balzac was a negligent correspondent. He rarely answered letters, and one will seek in vain for intellectual discussions with the outstanding men of his time. But these letters from his women readers gave him pleasure while at the same time causing him a certain mental excitement. To his imaginative mind every communication of this kind implied the possibility of a novel to be experienced in real life, and in enthusiastic anticipation of spiritual communion he would address to women who were complete strangers to him confessions and outpourings of the heart that he denied even to his closest friends.

One day, on the 5th of October, 1831, there was forwarded to him at Saché, where he was staying with his friends the Margonnes, a letter which awakened his particular interest. We know from his novels how his imagination could be kindled by the most trifling details. In this case the quality of the notepaper, the handwriting, and the mode of expression inspired him with the presentiment that the writer, who did not sign her name but used an English pseudonym, must be a lady of high rank, possibly of the highest rank.

11

He at once allowed full play to his airy dreams. She must be young, beautiful, and unhappy, a woman who had gone through tragic experiences and was undoubtedly either a countess, a marquise or a duchess.

His curiosity—and perhaps also his snobbishness—gave him no rest. He straightway replied to his unknown correspondent in a letter six pages long. He knew nothing, as he said, of her age and circumstances, and he intended at first only to defend himself against the charge of frivolity she had brought against him after reading his *Physiologie du mariage*. But Balzac was incapable of keeping his enthusiasm within bounds. When he wanted to show his admiration it had to be expressed in terms of ecstasy, and when he opened his heart it was an orgy of confession. He confided to her that it was his intention to marry none but a widow, painted the ideal object of his desires in half-sentimental, half-passionate colours, and told her of his "most secret plans for the future". *La peau de chagrin*, he informed her, was to be the keystone of a monumental structure—the *Comédie humaine*—and he was "full of pride at having attempted it, even though I should fail in my intention."

The unknown recipient of this missive must have been astounded when she read this intimate self-revelation instead of the polite reply, or at most the page or two of literary argument, which she no doubt expected. She appears to have answered without delay, and a correspondence developed between them of which unfortunately little has survived. It led to a mutual desire for personal acquaintance. The unknown already knew something about Balzac, apart from what was common gossip, and his picture had appeared in a number of papers, but he knew nothing about her. His curiosity must have been stimulated to the pitch of almost uncontrollable impatience to find out whether she was indeed young and beautiful, whether she was one of those tragic souls that were yearning for consolation, whether she was merely a sentimental blue-stocking, the over-educated daughter of some prosperous bourgeois or (audacious hope!) in very truth a countess, a marquise or a duchess.

◦⟫∘⟪◦

It turned out a triumph for Balzac's psychological instinct. His unknown correspondent was a marquise, with eventual succession to the title of duchess. Unlike his former *amorosa*, the Duchesse d'Abrantès, who owed her fresh patent of nobility to the Corsican usurper, she was of the best and bluest blood to be found in the Faubourg Saint-Germain. The father of the Marquise, later Duchesse Henriette Marie de Castries, was the Duc de Maillé, formerly a Marshal of France, whose coat of arms could be traced back to the eleventh century, while her mother had been a Duchesse de Fitz-James, that is to say, one of the royal Stuarts. Her husband, the Marquis de Castries, was a grandson of the famous Marshal of the same name and the son of a Duchesse de Guines. Balzac's almost morbid craze for the aristocracy could hardly have been more completely satisfied than by a family tree with branches so impressively entwined on both sides. In age, too, she fulfilled his ideal to perfection. She was thirty-five, and could therefore be regarded as a *"femme de trente ans"*. In other respects she was the most Balzacian type of all, for she was a sentimental, unhappy, disappointed woman with a love story in her past that was no less celebrated in Parisian society than *La peau de chagrin* and had even been utilised by Stendhal in his first book, *Armance*.

Balzac had little difficulty in discovering the details of her romantic story. At the age of twenty-two, when she was one of the most beautiful young women in the French aristocracy, she had met the son of the all-powerful Austrian Chancellor Metternich. She fell passionately in love with the young man, who had inherited his father's looks and social charm, though not his robust health, and since the French *haute noblesse* still adhered to the enlightened philosophic tradition of the eighteenth century, her husband would have been prepared to connive at a love-affair, however passionate, if kept within discreet bounds. But with a sincerity of purpose which stirred the enthusiasm not only of Stendhal but of the whole of Parisian society, the two lovers scorned any compromise. Madame de Castries quitted her husband's house, Prince Victor Metternich abandoned his brilliant career, and with utter unconcern for the opinion of the world they determined to live only for each other and for their mutual love. So the romantic couple travelled in the most beautiful parts of Europe, and led a free, nomadic existence in Switzerland and Italy. Soon a son was born to them, the idolised pledge of their happiness, upon whom the Austrian Emperor later conferred the title of Baron von Aldenburg.

Such fortune, however, was too perfect to last. Catastrophe descended from a cloudless sky. While out hunting the Marquise had an unlucky fall from her horse and damaged her spine. Since then she had had to spend the greater part of the day reclining on a sofa or in bed, and it was not long before she was deprived even of her lover's tender care. In November, 1829, Victor Metternich died of consumption. This was a heavier blow than had been her accident in the hunting-field. Unable to remain longer amid the landscapes whose beauty she had seen only in the reflected glow of their love, she returned to Paris. She did not, however, resume her place in her husband's house or in the society whose conventions she had flaunted. She passed her days in complete retirement in her father's mansion, the Palais de Castellane, and denying herself to her former friends she sought the companionship only of books.

To carry on a correspondence with such a woman, to be addressed by her in friendly terms, could not but stir the heart of Balzac, for in every way she was the realisation of his boldest dreams. An aristocrat, a *femme de trente ans*, a *femme abandonnée*, had selected him, Balzac, the grandson of a peasant and the son of a quondam *petit bourgeois*, for such an honour! What a triumph over the Victor Hugos, the Dumas, the de Mussets, who had taken bourgeois women for their wives and actresses, writers or *cocottes* for their mistresses! And what an excess of triumph it would be if he should succeed in acquiring the right to boast of more than friendship, if after a petty aristocrat like Madame de Berny and a parvenue Duchess like Madame d'Abrantès he should become the lover or even the husband of a genuine duchess of the old French nobility, the successor of a Prince Metternich whose father he had succeeded in the case of the Duchesse d'Abrantès! With restless impatience he awaited the invitation that would permit him to pay a personal call on the illustrious unknown. At last, on the 26th of February, a letter arrived containing this "sign of confidence", and he replied at once that he hastened to accept her "generous offer" despite the risk he ran "of losing considerably on personal acquaintance".

He answered her letter so precipitately, in such a state of happiness and rapture, that he overlooked another which lay on his table unopened. It had arrived that day from Russia and was from a woman who signed herself "*L'Etrangère*".

It goes without saying that Balzac could not help falling in love with Madame de Castries even before he saw her. If she had turned out to be ugly or stupid, quarrelsome or spiteful, it would have made no difference to his feelings, for all his emotions, including love, were dominated by his will. Before he had completed his elaborate toilet, put on his new suit, and seated himself in his carriage for the drive to the Palais de Castellane he had firmly made up his mind to love this woman and to be loved by her in return. As he was to do later in the case of the woman whose letter he had left lying unopened on his table, he had fashioned the Marquise de Castries into the ideal figure to whom he intended to allot the rôle of heroine in his life-story.

The first chapters were indeed entirely in accord with his imaginative conception. Lying on a sofa in a drawing-room furnished with great taste and distinction there awaited him a young woman, though not too young, looking a little pale, a little tired, a woman who had loved, who knew all that love implied, and who needed solace in her loneliness. And wonderful to relate, this aristocrat whose intercourse hitherto had been with dukes and princes, and whose lover had been the slim, elegant son of the Austrian Chancellor, was not disappointed with the broad-shouldered, corpulent plebeian whom no sartorial art could endow with elegance or spruceness. With a look of animated interest in her eyes she listened gratefully to his lively conversation, for he was the first writer she had known, a being from another world, and despite her reserve she felt the understanding sympathy as well as the stimulating and exciting impetuosity with which he approached her. Two or three hours went by like magic as they talked, and for all her loyalty to her dead lover she could not resist a stirring of admiration for this remarkable man whom the fates had sent to her. For her it was the beginning of a friendship, for Balzac the beginning of a delirium. He wrote to her: "You have received me so kindly, the hours I have spent in your company were so delightful, that I am firmly convinced that in you alone shall I find happiness."

Their relations grew more and more cordial. During the following weeks and months Balzac's carriage drew up every evening before the Palais de Castellane and the two talked till after midnight. He escorted her to the theatre, read to her from his latest writings, asked her advice, and made her a present of the manuscripts of *La femme de trente ans*, *Le Colonel Chabert* and *Le Message*. The lonely woman, who had sorrowed so long for her lost lover, began in this intellectual friendship to experience something like happiness; but for Balzac friendship was not enough.

Balzac wanted more than intellectual communion, and his wooing grew tempestuous. He showed her plainly that she was the object of his desires, and he demanded more and more urgently the first and then the final pledges of her submission. Madame de Castries could not help feeling flattered, though perhaps unconsciously, at being loved by a man whose genius she admired and honoured, and she did not ward off his little intimacies with cold disdain. She may even have provoked him to them, though we cannot completely trust Balzac's description in his later novel of revenge, *La duchesse de Langeais*:

> This woman not only received me kindly, but also displayed for my benefit all the arts of her very considerable powers of coquetry. She desired to please me and exerted herself to the utmost to keep me in my state of intoxication and to spur me on. She did all she could to force a quiet and timorous lover to declare himself.

When, however, the situation began to reach the point of danger she parried his advances determinedly. Perhaps she wished to remain faithful to the father of her child, for whom she had surrendered her position in the social world; perhaps she felt inhibited by her physical infirmity; or possibly she really was in the last resort repelled by the commonplace element in Balzac's appearance. She may also, and not unjustly, have feared that his vanity would lead him to boast in public of his aristocratic liaison; so she allowed him no more than what in the *Duchesse de Langeais* he calls "the small, slow conquests with which timorous lovers have to be content", and stubbornly refused "to confirm the surrender of her heart by the surrender of her body". For the first time in his life he was compelled to admit that his will was not omnipotent. After months of the most insistent wooing, daily visits, and literary activity on behalf of the Royalist Party, in spite of the humbling to which his pride had been subjected, he was still only on terms of intellectual friendship with Madame de Castries, and not her lover.

Even the shrewdest of intellects is always the last to realise that it is behaving unworthily. Without having any clear knowledge of the facts, Balzac's friends were struck by a change in his bearing when he appeared in public. They observed with disquiet that he was growing dandified, that from the *Loge Infernale* of the Théâtre des Italiens he always ogled through his lorgnon towards a certain box, and that he was an assiduous guest in the Royalist drawing-rooms of the Ducs de Fitz-James and de Rauzan, where men of bourgeois origin, even though they might be great writers, painters, musicians or statesmen, were regarded as no more than lackeys. His friends in general inclined to consider such snobbish flights of extravagance as a threat to his prestige, but they grew positively alarmed when their Honoré de Balzac suddenly blossomed forth as a political writer in the ultra-reactionary journal *Le Renovateur*, where he toadied enthusiastically to feudal privilege and made a public genuflexion before the Duchesse de Berry. They were sufficiently acquainted with his character to know that he was not of the base type which sells itself for money, and their instinct told them that he was being led through these dark political by-ways by some hidden hand. Madame de Berny, from whom he had been careful to conceal all knowledge of his correspondence with the Marquise de Castries and his subsequent visits, was the first to warn him. Though she herself was inclined to favour the Royalist movement, both by family tradition and as a godchild of Louis XVI and Marie Antoinette, she viewed with distaste Balzac's sudden emergence as a propagandist in its cause and urged him not to become "the slave of these people". From her distant point of vantage, and with her experience of these aristocratic circles, she realised that they had no real respect for Balzac as a writer, but were merely exploiting his snobbishness:

They have always been an essentially ungrateful crew, and they are not going to change their ways just for your sake, my friend.

Even more blunt was the admonition addressed to him by Zulma Carraud when with deep shame and disappointment she read Balzac's hymn to the Duchesse de Berry, who was endeavouring at that juncture to secure the succession of her son, the grandson of Charles X, to the throne of France. She advised him to leave the protection of these interests to the people around the court and not to soil his reputation by mixing with them. At the risk of forfeiting his friendship, the most precious thing she possessed, she told him relentlessly that her very love for his genius inspired her with loathing for the servility which attached greater importance to a patent of nobility than to integrity of mind:

> You have attached yourself to the unbending and privileged aristocracy! Will you then never awaken from your illusions?

Neither of these two sincere friends knew whether it was chains of gold or chains of roses that kept him fettered to the somewhat rickety equipage of the Bourbons. They only felt that he was being coerced to surrender his independence and that he was being untrue to himself.

For nearly five months, from February to June, he danced attendance on the Marquise de Castries. Suddenly, at the beginning of June, he left Paris and went to stay with the Margonnes at Saché. Had his passion subsided? Had his self-confidence sunk to such a depth that he had raised the siege of the impregnable fortress? Was he weary of a relationship that despite all his efforts remained within the bounds of platonic friendship? Not at all. He was still under the spell of a passion born of ambition, though he had the insight to realise its hopelessness. With the candour of despair he at last confessed his situation to Zulma Carraud:

> I must now go to Aix and climb up to Savoy, running after someone who is perhaps making fun of me—one of those aristocratic ladies who are no doubt an abomination in your eyes, one of those faces of angelic beauty behind which one assumes there is a beautiful soul. She is a real duchess, very condescending, very amiable, sensitive, witty, *coquette*, completely different from anything I have ever seen before. A woman who withdraws from every attempt at closer contact, who asserts that she loves me, yet if she had her way would keep me under supervision in the depths of a Venetian palace, . . . a woman (you know that I confess everything to you!) who wants me to write exclusively

for her, one of those women whom one has to worship without reserve and on one's knees if they ask for it and whom it is such a pleasure to conquer—a woman such as one meets in one's dreams! . . . jealous of everything! Oh! It would be better for me if I were with you in Angoulême, near your powder factory, being sensible and having my peace of mind, listening to the windmills going round, cramming myself with truffles, laughing and gossiping in the company of you and your friends—instead of here where I am wasting my time and my life!

His temporary flight from Paris and Madame de Castries was not due, however, to the realisation that his love for her was doomed to frustration. The reason was far less romantic. One of those financial catastrophes that gathered round his head and broke with the regularity of summer storms had once more burst upon him. Balzac was the exact opposite of Midas. Everything he touched turned not to gold but to debts. When he fell in love, tried his hand at speculation or even went on a journey, the result was always financial catastrophe. Since his budget was permanently balanced on a razor edge, every minute stolen from his work represented an item on the debit side. The evenings he spent in the drawing-room of Madame de Castries or at the theatre were the equivalent of two unwritten novels, and the loss of this income was aggravated by a considerable increase in his expenses. His unhappy idea of going a-wooing in a manner befitting an aristocratic lover piled his debts to preposterous heights. His two carriage horses alone, with which he drove up to the Palais de Castellane, had already consumed over nine hundred francs worth of hay, while his domestic household of three servants, his tailoring bills, and his whole sumptuous way of life were a cumulative liability. It was no longer creditors who besieged the house in the rue de Cassini, but the *huissiers*, the bailiffs. There was only one thing that could save him, and that was a return to his writing, but in order to write he had to have peace of mind, so there was only one possibility left to him—flight. Flight from Paris, flight from love, flight from his creditors, flight to some place where he could not be found and could not be reached.

Whatever he might write was, of course, already sold beforehand. On the day before his journey he had signed two contracts and received an advance of fifteen hundred francs, which was to serve

him as pocket-money during the next few months. But fourteen
hundred had to be paid out just as he was on the verge of leaving
Paris, and when he mounted the stage-coach that took him to
Saché all he possessed was a sum total of one hundred and twenty
francs. At the house of his friends, the Margonnes, however, all his
wants were provided for and his expenses were nil. Throughout the
day and half the night he sat writing in his room, appearing only
for an hour or two at mealtimes. Yet sitting quietly at Saché did
not diminish the running costs of his household in Paris. He had to
find somebody who could put his affairs in order, reduce his
expenses, struggle with his creditors and pacify the tradesmen, and
the only person he knew who was capable of assuming such an
onerous burden was his mother. After having fought for years to
escape her tutelage, he was now compelled to take humble refuge
in her thrift and business acumen.

The capitulation of her arrogant and stubborn son was a triumph
for the old woman, who set about defending a lost position with
courageous energy. She reduced his household expenses, dismissed
the superfluous servants, fought with tradesmen and sequestrators,
and sold the tilbury together with the voracious horses. Sou by sou,
franc by franc, she sought to restore his shattered finances, but
even she soon stood helpless in the face of the quickening onrush
of creditors. The rent had not been paid and the landlord wanted
to distrain on the furniture. The baker alone presented a bill
amounting to seven hundred francs. It is difficult to conceive how a
bachelor could have got through so much bread. Every day further
bills of exchange and promissory notes, that had been floating
around from hand to hand on the Paris money market, fell due for
redemption, and in desperation she wrote letter after letter to her
son, who had long since sold the books that he still had to write
and could see no prospect of extracting another franc from either
publishers or editors until they were finished. Even if he were to
work twenty-four hours a day he would not be able to overtake
the debts incurred during the past few months. Salvation would not
come from literature; that was quite evident. He therefore placed
his hopes once more in his old remedy, a rich marriage, odd as this
may seem in one who was apparently already passionately in love.
With a remarkable co-ordination of heart and brain he had earlier
that year, while still in a romantic glow of desire for Madame de

Castries, paid serious court to a young girl named Mademoiselle de Trumilly, and it was probably not a mere coincidence that this fresh object of his affections had just come into a fortune on the death of her father. For reasons that history has not recorded his suit was rejected, and the wealthy orphan having scorned him, he decided to renew his search for a wealthy widow, thereby bringing final peace to his restless heart and ensuring the essential material conditions for tranquil work. In desperation he commissioned not only his mother, but even his old friend Madame de Berny, to explore the field and find him with all possible speed a widow with large means who would save him from the disgrace of a second bankruptcy. And a candidate with the necessary qualifications was actually discovered, a certain Baroness Deurbroucq, who, moreover, was an enthusiastic admirer of the writings of Honoré de Balzac. A little plot was hatched. During the summer this golden argosy was due to reach port, for the Baroness possessed an estate not far from Saché, and Balzac kept every weapon in his armoury of eloquence ready to capture the rich prize. In order to soften her defences before the final assault he sent her copies of his works with ardent dedications. She was staying at the time in her other château at Jarzé, and these gifts might perhaps increase her impatience to make the personal acquaintance of the interesting young author. Three times a week he abandoned his writing-table and walked from Saché to her neighbouring estate at Méré for the purpose of inquiring whether she had yet arrived.

Unfortunately the Baroness showed no inclination to leave her château at Jarzé, and she would presumably have been in even less of a hurry if she had had any inkling of Balzac's eagerness to fall in love with her income. She let him wait, while menacing letters were pouring in daily from Paris and his slender store of pocket-money was melting away. His hundred and twenty francs had dwindled to a few pieces of silver, and his sojourn at Saché could not be prolonged for more than another couple of weeks at the most without abusing the hospitality of his friends. If he left without seeing the Baroness his last hope of an unobtrusive meeting with her would be gone. He was at his wits' end:

When one has such worries over one's literary work, and all these business difficulties into the bargain, one would like best to put an end to one's life.

When we read the letters Balzac wrote during these days of
catastrophe, we are driven to the conclusion that no artist could
produce anything worth while under conditions which reduced his
mind to such a state of agitation and despair. But in the case of
Balzac logic was set at naught and the improbable was always to be
expected. The two worlds in which he lived, the real and the
imaginary, were hermetically sealed off from one another. As a
creative artist he was able to immure himself so effectively in the
world of his mind that the storms which raged round his external
existence were shut out. The visionary who sat at a little table
unfolding the destinies of a multitude of characters by the light of
his flickering candles had nothing in common with the other Honoré
de Balzac who was being sued for debt and having his furniture
seized by the bailiffs. He was not in the slightest degree affected by
the despairing moods of the Honoré de Balzac who lived and had
his being in the world of actuality. On the contrary, he was at his
best as an artist when things were at their worst. Worries and cares
were transmuted in some mysterious way into an intenser inward
concentration, and nothing is more true than his comment, "My
finest flashes of inspiration always came to me in my moments of
deepest anxiety and distress." It was only when he was harassed on
all sides and could see no way out that he threw himself into his
work as a hunted stag takes to the river. Only when his path in life
seemed to be barred did he find his real self, and never was this
innermost secret of his being revealed more clearly than during this
summer of storms and tempests. On the one hand he was writing
love-letters to the unresponsive Madame de Castries, making his
pilgrimage three times a week to see if the wealthy widow had yet
arrived, counting every day his dwindling store of ready money,
trying to renew his promissory notes as they fell due, pacifying
the publishers who had paid him for books that were not yet
written, and postponing by every device he could think of the
bankruptcy that appeared inevitable. On the other hand he was
writing his *Louis Lambert*, the most profound and thoughtful of all
his works, the ambitious novel with which he hoped to excel everything he had yet produced and prove his superiority to all his
contemporaries. It was to represent the renunciation of that which
had gone before, a farewell to the fashionable and romantic novelist
who was the darling of his feminine readers, and it was a proof of

his integrity that he applied himself to a work which had no prospect whatsoever of wide popularity at a time when the public demand for exciting love stories or society novels offered him an easy opportunity to win the material success he so urgently needed. While publishers and booksellers were eagerly awaiting his next book in the manner of Sir Walter Scott or Fenimore Cooper, he was devoting himself to a tragic tale of purely intellectual interest which should set his conception of an intellectual hero beside Byron's *Manfred* and Goethe's *Faust*.

This ambitious work, which has been appreciated by few people at its true value, was never carried to completion in the higher sense. In the figure of Louis Lambert, in which he mirrored his own youth with its ideas and aspirations, Balzac attempted to come to grips with an important problem. He wanted to show that a person of genius who applied himself to the deepening of his powers of concentration in complete asceticism would thereby render himself incapable of earthly existence, since a brain overburdened to fever point would in the long run be unable to stand the strain. The tragedy of obsession by an idea, on which Balzac has rung the changes a hundred times in his novels, is here transferred to the intellectual sphere, and it is a problem which verges on the pathological. The mysterious association between genius and madness is a theme with which Balzac was concerned long in advance of his generation.

In the early chapters, which depict in the figure of Louis Lambert the budding of his own genius, he succeeded in drawing a credible character to whom he transferred the authorship of his own crowning idea, the "*théorie de la volonté*", which was to throw a final light on the obscure relation between the pyschological and the physiological sides of man's nature. It is no exaggeration to place the conception of Louis Lambert, who likewise "craves the impossible" and is destroyed by his excessive urge to knowledge, on a par with Goethe's conception of Faust, with which Balzac consciously or unconsciously wanted to compete. There was, however, the essential difference that Goethe worked at his *Faust* for sixty years, while Balzac had to deliver the finished manuscript of his novel to Gosselin, the publisher, after six weeks. In order to provide it with some sort of plot that he could bring to a conclusion, he draped a tedious love-story round the marble torso of his hero. The philosophical theories were wound up in hasty improvisation, and one's half-hearted admiration is tinged with regret for the spoiling of a work which more than any other gives us the measure of its author's potentialities. As a work of art it has remained incomplete despite later emendations, but from the intellectual point of view it represents the highest peak of his ambition to deal with serious problems.

⊸⊃∘⊂⊷

At the end of July the manuscript was sent to the publisher in Paris. The six weeks at Saché had served their purpose, but his pecuniary position had not in the slightest degree improved. Madame de Deurbroucq had not yet arrived, and if he stayed any longer he would be abusing the hospitality of his friends. He was evidently ashamed to ask these generous people for a small loan and thus reveal his wretched situation, but luckily there was another place of refuge always open to him. He knew that the Carrauds would be happy to receive him, and as they were themselves as poor as church mice he would have no need to disguise his poverty and could confess the truth that he, the celebrated Honoré de Balzac, had not enough money in his pocket to have his shoes repaired. He could not even afford the stage-coach fare from Saché to Angoulême, and the one-time owner of a carriage and two fine horses went on foot in the scorching heat as far as Tours. Only from there did he take the diligence to his destination, where he arrived with a completely empty purse and proceeded immediately to borrow thirty francs from Zulma's husband.

His good friends the Carrauds, who had themselves passed through many vicissitudes, laughed with hearty sympathy when Balzac told them of his preposterous dilemma, and they gave him everything it was in their power to provide. He found a quiet room in which to work, a cheerful atmosphere, and kindly affection in the evening when he joined them for conversation. As always, a couple of hours with these open-hearted friends made him happier than the society of all his aristocratic acquaintances. His work went smoothly and within a short space of time he wrote *La femme abandonnée* and a number of stories for the *Contes drolatiques*, besides correcting the proofs of *Louis Lambert*. Everything would have been fine if only he had not been plagued nearly every morning with a fresh letter from his mother in Paris demanding money for the creditors who could no longer be held at bay. There seemed no way of procuring the thousands and tens of thousands of francs that were now urgently necessary, seeing that he had had to struggle with his pride before borrowing a miserable thirty francs from his impecunious friends. A dark hour had come for Balzac. During the two or three years of triumph he had boasted that he would pay back all his mother had lent him. Intoxicated with success and confident of his talent, he had lived as though money were of no importance. He had relied on his distinguished connections and trusted in the last resort to the safe harbour of a wealthy marriage. And now he was again, like the prodigal son, forced to creep home and humbly implore his family to help him. He, the darling of the Faubourg Saint-Germain, the famous writer and *cavaliere servente* of a lady of rank, had to fly to his mother like a helpless child and beg her to borrow ten thousand francs for him under her own guarantee to save him from public insolvency. His work and his honour were at stake.

The miracle was achieved. Madame Balzac succeeded in persuading an old friend, Madame Delanoix, to advance ten thousand francs to the penitent spendthrift. To be sure, this juicy morsel was not set before the hungry man before it had been thickly sprinkled with salt and pepper. He had to bow his head low beneath the yoke. The pardoned sinner promised to change his luxurious way of life forthwith, to give up his ruinous extravagances, to cultivate the bourgeois virtues of modesty and thrift, and to pay all his debts from now on with compound interest.

⌁

Balzac had been rescued by a miracle; but whenever there was a prospect of regulating his life on an ordered basis some deeper instinct within him, which needed chaos and the pressure of outward circumstance, responded with new disorder. He could only breathe air that was charged with fire. His sanguine temperament tended to forget the vexations to which he had been subjected, and obligations that did not demand immediate fulfilment simply did not exist so far as he was concerned. If he had thought the matter

over coolly, he would have been bound to admit to himself that his
financial situation had been in no way ameliorated. All that had
happened was that twenty or thirty small but pressing debts had
been consolidated into a single large one. Balzac, however, realised
only that the noose around his neck had been loosened, and as soon
as he was able to breathe once more he filled his lungs. So long as
he had been occupied with *Louis Lambert* and in the stranglehold
of a financial crisis he had ceased to think of Madame de Castries,
and in his heart he had given up the game as lost. With the weight
of debt temporarily lifted from his shoulders he was once again
tempted to venture a last throw. Madame de Castries had more
than once during the summer invited him to visit her at Aix in
Savoy and join her and her uncle, the Duc de Fitz-James, on a
journey in the autumn to Italy. His lack of funds had hitherto
prevented him even from considering such an enticing prospect,
but now that he again had a few louis d'or chinking in his purse the
temptation was more than he could resist. It seemed to him that
this invitation to the shores of the Lake of Annecy, to the landscape
of Jean-Jacques Rousseau, must be more than a mere courteous
gesture, and that such a delicate hint ought not to be disregarded.
Perhaps the unresponsive Marquise, whom he knew nevertheless
to be "as sensual as a thousand cats", had refused herself to him in
Paris only from fear of gossip. Would not the aristocrat of the
Faubourg Saint-Germain be prepared to satisfy a natural appetite
in a natural way amid the divine beauties of nature? If Lord
Byron, the author of *Manfred*, had been able to find happiness on
the shores of the Swiss lakes, why should it be denied in the same
environment to the author of *Louis Lambert*?

In the exuberant dreams of the artist there is always a watchful
instinct keeping guard. Three forms of vanity were struggling in
Balzac's soul—the conceit of snobbishness, the ambition to conquer
a woman who continually tempted him yet eluded his grasp, and
the desire to renounce a society coquette who was making a fool of
a man of his worth. For days on end he discussed with Zulma, the
one person to whom he could speak frankly, whether or not he
should make the journey to Aix. Every feminine instinct in Zulma,
who no doubt detested the woman on whom Balzac's affections
were fixed, must have urged her to dissuade him from paying this
visit to her aristocratic rival. She did not believe for a single

moment that Madame de Castries, despite her admiration for his literary genius, would allow herself to be compromised by a love affair with a plebeian. When, however, she saw with what burning impatience he waited for her to fortify him in the conviction that he ought to go, something in her heart gave her the strength to offer him the assurance he wanted. She did not wish to incur the suspicion that she had advised him against seizing a brilliant opportunity merely out of petty jealousy. Let him learn from experience! So at last she said what he was longing to hear, and the die was cast. On the 22nd of August he set off for Aix.

❦

All his life Balzac clung to the most primitive forms of superstition. He believed in amulets, always wore a lucky ring with mysterious oriental symbols, and before taking any important decision he would creep up five flights of stairs to consult a fortuneteller like any Parisian seamstress. He had faith in telepathy, secret promptings, and the warning power of instinct. If he had listened in this case to such inner admonitions he would have broken off his journey to Aix at the start, for it began with an accident. In the act of descending from the stage-coach while the horses were being changed, the animals drew on the shafts and he fell with his whole not inconsiderable weight against the iron step, cutting his leg to the bone. Another man would have cut short his journey and put himself in the hands of a doctor, for the wound was fairly serious, but impediments only had the effect of strengthening Balzac's determination, and after the application of a hasty bandage he travelled on as far as Lyons lying stretched out on the floor of the coach. From there he continued on his way to Aix, where he arrived leaning painfully on a stick and in the worst possible shape for the resumption of a passionate love-affair.

With touching solicitude Madame de Castries had booked for him a "*jolie petite chambre*" with a magnificent view of the lake and the mountains. It had the further advantage of being exceedingly cheap. It cost only two francs a day. He had never before been able to work in such comfort and tranquillity, but the forethought shown by Madame de Castries had also been a measure of prudence. The room occupied by Balzac was not in the same hotel as the

12

one at which she herself was staying, but a few streets away, so his evening visits could only be of a social nature and would not allow of more intimate contact.

It was only in the evening that he could see her. That had been his own stipulation, for his days were to be devoted to work, and the one concession he made at her request was to begin his stretch of twelve hours at six o'clock in the morning instead of at midnight as was his usual custom. He sat down to write shortly after dawn and did not move from his table until six o'clock in the evening. Eggs and milk were the only food he took, and they were brought to his room at a cost of fifteen sous a day. When the twelve hours were up his time belonged to Madame de Castries, but unfortunately she still refused to succumb to his blandishments. She was as amiable as could be imagined, driving him out to Lake Bourget and Chartreuse in her carriage while his leg was still unhealed, indulgently humouring him when he grew romantically enthusiastic, making him coffee according to his own recipe during the long evenings when they talked together, introducing him at the Casino to her elegant friends, and even permitting him to call her Marie instead of Henriette, a privilege accorded only to her closest friends. This was about all she did permit him, however. It was of no avail that he had sent her Louis Lambert's ardent love-letter in a form which was bound to make her realise that every word was addressed to herself. It was of no avail that he ordered half a dozen pairs of gloves, a pot of pomade, and a bottle of Portugal water to be sent post-haste from Paris. Sometimes there seemed a promise of submission in the way she tolerantly accepted or even provoked certain intimacies:

> All the joys of love were heralded in her bold, expressive glances, the caressing tone of her voice, the charm of her words. And she allowed him to discern that there was something of the noble courtesan in her. . . .

During a romantic stroll by the side of the lake she allowed him to snatch a willing or a stolen kiss, but whenever he demanded the final pledge of love, when the champion of the *femme de trente ans* and the *femme abandonnée* wanted to be rewarded in the coin of the *Contes drolatiques*, she again became the aloof aristocrat. The summer was drawing to a close, the leaves on the trees by the Lake of Annecy were turning brown and beginning to fall, and the new Saint-Preux had made no more progress with his Héloïse than he had done six months before in the cool, high-ceilinged salon of the Palais de Castellane.

❧⊙❧

The summer was drawing to a close, the strollers on the promenade were beginning to thin out, the distinguished visitors were preparing to depart. Madame de Castries was also about to pack, though not for the return to Paris. She intended first of all to make a trip to Italy with her uncle, and Balzac was invited to accompany them. He hesitated. He could not delude himself about the undignified figure he was cutting by his long and fruitless wooing, as can be seen from the despairing tone in which he wrote to Zulma Carraud: "Why did you let me go to Aix?" Furthermore, a journey to Italy would be expensive, and doubly so since the hours and days spent on the road would be hours and days lost to his work. On the other hand, it was a great temptation for an artist whose ideas were expanded by travel, as he once put it. He would see Rome and Naples, he would be in the company of a clever, elegant woman with whom he was in love, and he would travel in the carriage of a duke. Once more Balzac resisted his inner foreboding and yielded to temptation. At the beginning of October the three of them set out for Italy.

Geneva was the first halt on the journey south, and for Balzac it was also the last. On their arrival in that city there was a scene between him and Madame de Castries about which no details are known. He appears to have presented her with a kind of ultimatum, and this time she must have rebuffed him in a way that caused him deep offence. There can be no doubt that she wounded him cruelly in his most sensitive spot, either his manly or his human pride, for he rushed off at once, filled with dark rage and a sense of burning shame, resolved to revenge himself on the woman who had kept him for so many months in a fool's paradise. He probably already had in mind the idea of repaying her for his humiliation by drawing a merciless portrait of her in one of his novels, and in *La duchesse de Langeais*, which he at first called *Ne touchez pas la hache*, he later on made the whole of Paris privy to the affair. For the sake of appearances the two remained on outwardly friendly terms, and Balzac even allowed himself the chivalrous gesture of reading to her beforehand the novel in which, with a regrettable lack of good taste, he was about to give her picture to the world. She replied with the still nobler gesture of sanctioning the not very flattering portrait. She then took unto herself another literary father-confessor in the person of Sainte-Beuve, and Balzac declared resolutely:

> I said to myself that a life like mine cannot remain attached to a petticoat; I must boldly follow my destiny and lift my eyes to a higher level than a woman's apron-strings.

Like a child that dashes about madly in spite of all warnings and knocks itself against a stone, then flies back to the arms of its mother to be soothed and have its wounds looked after, Balzac went from Geneva straight to Madame de Berny at Nemours. His return to her was both a confession and a liquidation of the recent past. From the woman whom he had desired merely out of vanity and who had refused to give herself to him either from indifference or from cold calculation of what she would lose by doing so, he fled to the woman who had sacrificed everything for him and given him everything. Never did he feel more deeply what she had been to him and what she still was, the first woman he had ever loved. Now that she was only a friend who stretched out her hand to him in motherly sympathy, he realised more than ever before how much he owed to her, and in order to express his profound sense of gratitude he dedicated to her the book which throughout his life was the most dear to him of all his works, *Louis Lambert*. The inscription on the first page runs: *Et nunc et semper dilectae*—"To the woman I have chosen, now and forever."

CHAPTER X

Balzac discovers his Secret

If we were to believe Balzac's own words, we should be forced to conclude that his affair with Madame de Castries had been a tragedy that left indelible scars behind. "I detest Madame de Castries," he wrote in a tone of exalted emotion. "She has shattered my life without giving me a new one in its place."

And in another letter to an unknown correspondent he even declared: "The relationship between us, which in accordance with the wish of Madame de Castries remained within entirely irreproachable bounds, was one of the most severe strokes of ill-fortune I have ever suffered." We have to get used to such overdramatised statements in his letters. Undoubtedly his pride and vanity had been deeply hurt by the rebuff, but he was too firmly rooted in himself, too egocentric, for the yea or the nay of any woman to be capable of "shattering" his life. The affair with Madame de Castries was not a catastrophe, but only an episode, for the essential Balzac was by no means so despairing and embittered as he represented himself to be in his romantic outpourings to his unknown feminine correspondents. He never conceived the idea, as did his General Montriveau in *La duchesse de Langeais*, of branding the aristocratic coquette with a red-hot iron. He did not after the first shock foam with revenge, but continued to exchange friendly letters with her, paid her visits, and read to her the novel in which she was portrayed. That which appeared in the book as a tempestuous tragedy gradually flickered out in reality in an atmosphere of *"faibles relations de politesse"*. Balzac, it may be said with all due respect, never told the truth when he was drawing his own portrait. The hall-mark of his novels is their exuberance; he endeavoured to extract the maximum from every contact; and it would indeed be incongruous to expect that his creative imagination should ignore his own personal experiences and refrain from embroidering them.

The biographer of Balzac has to contend with the misleading evidence which Balzac himself supplies. He must not allow himself to be dazzled by exalted emotional outbursts into believing that the refusal of a lady in high society to grant what in France they call *"la bagatelle"* was the original cause of the heart trouble which eventually brought him to the grave. It did not "shatter" his life, for he was probably never more robust, energetic and industrious, more full of vitality than during the ensuing years. His books offer more trustworthy evidence than his letters. His literary output during the next three years alone would have been sufficient for a life's work and would have made him the greatest writer of his time. Yet even this he regarded merely as a beginning, as the preliminary to his real task of becoming the *"historien des moeurs du 19ième siècle"*.

His early successes had brought him the realisation that he had power within his grasp. He had got to know his own strength, and he felt that he could conquer the world with his pen as Napoleon had attempted to do with the sword. If, however, he had been concerned only with material success, as one might be led to think from reading his letters, if he had wanted merely to make money on a large scale, all he had to do was to provide the public with the kind of reading matter for which it was clamouring. The women in particular remained loyal to him : he could become the fêted hero of the salons, the idol of all the disappointed women of Paris, the darling of lonely females, the successful rival of his less ambitious colleagues Alexandre Dumas and Eugène Sue. But in the consciousness of his strength his soul was kindled with the flame of a higher purpose, and at the risk of losing his readers he was bold enough to deviate further and further from their tastes. He wanted to find out where his own limits lay, and the scope of his talent never ceased to surprise him even as his pen moved across the paper.

His writings during the years 1832 to 1836 are notable for their variety. Those who come to them for the first time must find it difficult to believe that the author of *Louis Lambert* and *Séraphita* also wrote the *Contes drolatiques*, and that he wrote them, moreover, simultaneously, jotting down a "droll story" on the same day that he corrected the proofs of his philosophic novel. Such a phenomenon can be explained only by his desire to test his own genius, to see how high and how low he could reach. Just as an architect, before finishing off the plan of his future structure, calculates and checks the dimensions and stresses, so Balzac worked out an estimate of his powers and laid the foundations on which the edifice of his divine *Comédie humaine* was to arise.

The *Contes drolatiques*, written in the style of Rabelais and in an archaic French of his own invention, are an essay in pure storytelling which enabled him to give free rein to his high spirits. They show no sign of effort, there was no necessity for deep thought or observation, and he could play with an idea to his heart's content. It is evident that Balzac thoroughly enjoyed writing in this light vein. The Gallic spirit in him and his earthy virility expressed themselves in an outpouring of carefree sensuality. It delighted him to have his fun with Mrs. Grundy, and of all his works these stories fit in best with the outward picture of the corpulent man with the ruddy cheeks and thick lips. The boisterous guffaw which sounded ill-bred in the salons is here distilled to bubbling mirth. We see Balzac writing at his ease, and if life had treated him less hardly, if it had allowed him to breathe more freely, then instead of the score and a half of droll tales we should have had the hundred which he promised in the prospectus addressed to his readers.

This was the lower limit of his genius, the tribute he paid to his temperament. Simultaneously, however, he was seeking the highest pitch to which he could rise in those works which he called "philosophical". Ambition spurred him on to prove that his "*succès de mouchoir*", the ability to bring tears to his readers' eyes, which he had demonstrated in his sentimental female characters, did not suffice him. Now that he understood himself he did not want to be misunderstood by others. Having reached maturity, and in full consciousness of his powers, he wanted to proclaim that to a novelist of his rank there had been assigned the task of elevating the novel into an exalted form of art by the treatment of the decisive problems which concern humanity, whether social, philosophic or religious. He wanted to contrast the people who obey the laws of society and conform to its conventions with those who step beyond the bounds observed by the ordinary man. It was his aim to portray the true leaders and the tragedy of all those who either raise themselves above the common herd and venture out into solitude or immure themselves in an illusion of their own creating. The epoch of his life which brought Balzac a personal defeat was the one in which he revealed the greatest audacity.

In these novels Balzac tried to depict men who imposed upon themselves the highest tasks, tasks which were in reality insoluble. He devoted his most strenuous efforts to the portrayal of men who came to grief through their excess of effort, men of genius who eventually lost touch with reality. Louis Lambert was his first attempt in this field, the figure of a philosopher who strove to solve the ultimate problems of life and ended in madness, and it was a theme on which he rang the changes in every conceivable form. In *Un chef d'oeuvre inconnu* he showed the fate of a painter who, in the illusory urge to achieve perfection, went beyond perfection. His excess of effort destroyed, so to speak, the material in which he worked, just as the ideas of Louis Lambert at last became unintelligible. The musician Cambara stepped beyond the limits of his art until he alone could hear the harmonies he created, just as Louis Lambert alone could understand his own ideas or Frenhofer his visions. The chemist Claes in the *Recherche de l'absolu* destroyed himself in his search for the primordial element. They were all seeking the absolute. They were all Icarus figures of the mind.

Side by side with these men of genius in art and science he set the

moral and religious genius in *Le médecin de campagne* and *Séraphita*.
The inspiration for the former novel he owed indirectly to his visit
to Madame de Castries. During an outing they had made together
to call upon the Contesse d'Agoult, he heard about a physician in
the neighbourhood, a certain Dr. Rommel, who had colonised a
derelict tract of land and restored an almost ruined peasantry by
his humanitarian activity. This story, combined with the magnificence of the landscape, made a deep impression on Balzac, and
the scenery linked with the name of Jean-Jacques Rousseau
inspired him, as it were, with the latter's reformatory zeal. In his
other works he was a critic of society, but here he wanted to adopt a
more positive rôle and outlined a plan by which the social problem
could be solved. He wished to show that a creative genius could
shape an immortal masterpiece not only out of sounds, colour or
ideas, but also out of the more brittle material of human society.

Even bolder, perhaps, was his attempt at characterisation in
"Séraphitus-Séraphita". Whereas Dr. Benassis withdrew from the
world in order to create a better one, Balzac wanted in this figure
to depict a man who succeeded in casting off all earthly trammels
and so completely sublimated his love-emotion into an *amor
intellectualis* that all sexual attributes disappeared. The practical
thinker, who in the person of Dr. Benassis provided the solution
to practical problems with an amazing breadth of knowledge, here
turned to the mystic sphere of Swedenborgian ideas. Neither *Le
médecin de campagne* nor *Séraphita* can be called successful in the
highest sense, and though Balzac was greatly mortified by their
failure it was not unjustified. They were written with too light a
touch, and it was out of character for a man with his strong sense
of reality to appear as a protagonist of religion. Above all, a work
which purports to supply the ultimate solution of eternal problems
must not be written in instalments as a newspaper serial and paid
for in advance. His philosophical novels were not on the highest
level as works of art, but only the result of his highest aspirations.
He understood and portrayed the quality of genius as only a man
of genius can, but his successful works are only those where he
depicts the artist as an artist. *Un chef d'oeuvre inconnu* is a supreme
and enduring masterpiece, but philosophy cannot be combined with
haste or religious feeling with impatience. His philosophical novels
only serve to show the astonishing development, the incredible

width of knowledge, the versatility and the scope of his mind, which was equal to every problem except the ultimate one of religion.

⊷⊙⊶

Between the story-teller and the thinker stood the observer of the pageant of life. His true métier was realism, and he found his balance in the novels where he is seen as the historian of his own times. His first great success had been *Le colonel Chabert*, and his second success during these years was *Eugénie Grandet*. He had discovered the law which from now on was to govern his work— the depiction of reality, but with a stronger dynamic because the cast was limited to a few characters. Before this he had tried to find the essential quality of the novel in the sphere of Romanticism, on the one hand in period stories, on the other by employing fantastic or mystic constituents. Now, however, he discovered that the con-temporary scene, if observed from the right angle, teemed with an equally vivid and abundant life, and that what mattered was not the theme or the setting but the inner dynamic. The same effect could be achieved in a more true and natural way if the author succeeded in charging his characters with sufficient tension and supplying the appropriate action. The dynamic resides not in the atmosphere or in the plot, but only in the characters themselves. There are no specific raw materials, for everything is raw material. Under the humble roof of the wine-grower Grandet the air could be as highly charged as in the cabin of a corsair in *Une femme de trente ans*. When the commonplace and rather simple-minded little Eugénie Grandet, under the threatening eye of her avaricious father, dropped an extra lump of sugar into the coffee-cup of her cousin Charles, with whom she was in love, she displayed no less courage than Napoleon did when he stormed across the bridge at Lodi brandishing a banner in his hand. The old miser, in his struggle to get the better of his brother's creditors, exhibited just as much craft, quick-wittedness, tenacity, and even genius as did Talley-rand at the Congress of Vienna. It is not the *milieu* which is impor-tant. The Pension Vauquer in *Père Goriot*, with its twelve young students, contained as much possibility of drama as Lavoisier's laboratory or Cuvier's study. Creation, therefore, demands the right kind of observation, concentration, and intensification, extracting the maximum, the revealing of passion, laying bare the weakness that is to be found in the strongest, bringing to the surface the forces that lie latent. *Eugénie Grandet* was the first step in this direction. The simple, pious girl's devotion was so heightened that it became almost religious, while old Grandet's greed and the loyalty of the ugly old domestic became endowed with a daemonic intensity. Père Goriot's love for the children became an obsession and drove him to action. Every character was rightly observed and his or her secret was known to the author, who only had to play them off one against the other, blend the different worlds, take good and evil as he found them, and accept cowardice, cunning, and baseness as natural forces without indulging in any sort of moral emphasis.

❦

Balzac had discovered the great secret. Everything was raw material. Reality was an inexhaustible mine. One only had to observe from the right angle and everybody became an actor in the human comedy. There was no distinction between high and low. One could choose everything, one *had* to choose everything. That was the decisive point for Balzac. An author who wished to portray the world could not afford to ignore any of its aspects. Every grade of the social hierarchy had to be represented, the artist as well as the lawyer and the physician, the wine-grower, the porter's wife, the general and the private, the duchess and the woman of the street, the water-carrier and the banker. All these spheres were interwoven. They all had their points of contact. Similarly, every type of character had to be brought on to the stage : the ambitious man and the avaricious one, the man of integrity and the intriguer, the thrifty man and the spendthrift—every variety of the species Man and every pattern of behaviour. There was no need to keep on inventing new characters, for by appropriate grouping the same figures could be repeated, one physician or perhaps two representing all physicians, one banker appearing as the exemplar of all bankers, in order to compress the vast wealth of material within the compass of a single novel. It became more and more clear to Balzac that if this abundance was to be kept within bounds he must prepare a plan of work that would occupy him for the rest of his life. He must not merely set his novels one beside the other, but he must dovetail them, becoming a *"Walter Scott plus un architecte"*. It would not be enough to produce *"peintures de la vie individuelle"*, since it was the linked associations which were the important thing.

Balzac had not yet quite realised the full scope of his conception of the *Comédie humaine,* and ten years were to pass before he had the plan clearly fixed in his mind. Of one thing he was sure, however. His completed work must not be a juxtaposition of individual volumes, but he must build it up in a series of steps. On the 26th of October, 1834, without being yet aware of the dimensions which his work was to assume, he outlined the scheme on which he placed his hopes:

By 1838 the three sections of the gigantic work will have been so far completed that one will at least be able to recognise the plan of the structure and arrive at some judgment of the conception as a whole.

In the "Studies of Manners" are to be depicted all the repercussions of social conditions. I want to portray every situation in life, every type of physiognomy, every kind of male and female character, every way of living, every profession, every social stratum, every French province, childhood, the prime of life and old age, politics, law, and war—nothing is to be omitted. When this has been done and the story of the human heart revealed thread by thread, social history displayed in all its branches, then the foundations will have been laid. I have no wish to describe episodes that have their springs in the imagination. My theme is that which actually happens everywhere.

Then comes the second stage—the "Philosophical Studies". The depiction of effects is to be followed by the description of causes. In the "Studies of Manners" I shall have shown the inter-play of emotion, life and its consequences. In the "Philosophical Studies" I shall speak of the origin of the emotions and of the motivating causes of life. I shall pose the question— "What are the operating forces, the conditions, without which neither society nor the life of the individual is possible?" And after I have dealt with society in this way, I shall examine it with a critical eye. In the "Studies of Manners" individuals will be depicted in types; in the "Philosophical Studies" the types will be depicted as individuals. It will always be life that I am portraying. . . .

And finally, after the effects and causes, will come the "Analytical Studies", a part of which will be the *Physiologie du mariage*; for after the effects and causes we must look for the principles. The manners provide the drama, the causes represent the *coulisse* and the stage-machinery. And finally the principles, in other words, the author of the play. In proportion, however, as the whole work gains height as though in a series of spirals, it narrows and becomes more concentrated. If I shall need twenty-four volumes for the "Studies of Manners", I shall require fifteen for the "Philosophical Studies" and only another nine for the "Analytical Studies". In this way I shall describe, criticise, and analyse man himself, society, and humanity without indulging in repetitions in a work which is to be a kind of *Arabian Nights* of the Occident.

When all this is completed . . . when I have written the last word—then either I shall have been right or I shall have been wrong. But after this literary achievement, after this portrayal of a whole system, I shall apply myself to the scientific aspect and write an *Essay on the Forces by which Man is motivated*. And on the base of this great edifice I shall have traced, as a childlike and humorous decoration, the vast arabesque of the *Hundred Droll Stories*.

With awed enthusiasm at the task he had undertaken, he cried: "This is my work, the abyss, the crater which yawns before me. This is the raw material that I intend to shape."

The realisation that he had a lifetime of work in front of him determined from now on Balzac's future course. In September 1833 he had written with supreme self-confidence:

I shall rule unchallenged in the intellectual life of Europe! Another two years of work and patience—then I shall stride on over the heads of all those who wanted to fetter my hands and hinder my advance! Under persecution and injustice my courage has grown hard as bronze.

Conscious of the work ahead of him and the public behind him, he was resolved to parley with no one. Nevermore would he accommodate himself to the wishes of publishers and newspaper editors. Petty annoyances and irritations no longer had any power over

him. He dictated his terms to the publishers, whom he had no
hesitation in changing if they did not completely meet his demands.
Even when his financial situation was desperate he renounced his
collaboration with the most influential reviews if they took liber-
ties with the contributions he sent them. And he contemptuously
turned his back on the journalists, who believed that they controlled public opinion. Let them slate this novel or that! They were
powerless to prevent the achievement of the comprehensive
structure, which was more important than its component parts.
Let them attack him, make fun of him in their witty *entrefilets*, and
ridicule him in their malicious anecdotes and caricatures! He would
take his revenge in his novels and show up the whole clique with
its power and its impotence. In the *Illusions perdues* he drew
with indelible lines on the wall of the century a picture of their
systematic corruption of public opinion, their chaffering with
reputations and spiritual values. Though his creditors might plague
him with demands for redemption of his promissory notes and
with lawsuits, though they might seize his furniture as security,
yet they could not remove a single stone or a single grain of earth
from the world that he was going to build. Nothing any longer had
the power to unsettle him now that the design was ready, for he
felt the strength within him to accomplish a work which he alone
had been bold enough to plan, and he alone possessed the genius
to bring to completion.

THE NOVEL OF BALZAC'S LIFE

CHAPTER XI

The Unknown

Balzac had no illusions about the immensity of the task that lay before him if he was to "take the lead in European literature, the place occupied hitherto by Byron, Scott, Goethe and Hoffmann". He had reckoned that he would live to be at least sixty. During the thirty years or so that remained to him, practically every day would have to be spent at his writing-table. There would be no margin for pleasure or personal comfort, and even when his debts were at last paid off and money was flowing in there would be no time left for enjoyment. He knew what the price involved in the way of renunciation, but he was not afraid because he took delight in his work. Yet in order to achieve his purpose he needed one more thing—a modicum of solid ground under his feet. Now that he had launched on an enterprise that demanded his whole strength and concentration, his longing for the primal essentials of life became more fervent and more impatient. He wanted a wife and a home, relief from the torments of the flesh, from harassment by debts, from struggling with publishers, from having to beg for advances on books which were not yet written. He wanted to be able to concentrate all his powers on the "monument that will endure longer on account of its

massive dimensions and the immense accumulation of material
than because of its structural beauty". In order to acquire the
peace of mind that would enable him to devote all his efforts to his
task, he had to find the wife and the fortune that had for so long
been the object of his search.

He was too clear-sighted not to realise that his plebeian appearance and manners contrasted unfavourably with the elegant
habitués of the salons. Mademoiselle de Trumilly had turned him
down. His experience with Madame de Castries had taught him
that even his most passionate advances did not make him seductive. He was partly too proud, partly too shy, to spend his time in
tedious courtship. Madame de Berny, despite her fifty-four years,
was understandably reluctant to choose her successor, while Zulma
Carraud had little opportunity in her provincial circle to find him
the wealthy aristocrat who alone would possess the necessary
qualifications. His hopes could be fulfilled only by a miracle. Since
he had neither the time, nor the courage, nor the opportunity to
look around for what he wanted, the woman he dreamed of would
have to come to him.

This was not logically to be expected, but in Balzac's life it was
the improbable that always happened. Without knowing him
personally, or perhaps just because they did not know him personally and cherished romantic notions about their favourite
writer, women did come to Balzac. Again and again he received
letters from his feminine readers, many of which have survived.
These readers were curious about him and sometimes not averse
from adventure. Madame de Castries was not the only woman
whose acquaintance he owed to the postman. There was a series of
affectionate women friends, of whom we mostly know only the
Christian names, who eventually followed up their letters with
personal visits, and one of them, as has already been pointed out,
had a child by him. Might not one of these letters one day lead to a
permanent love instead of a short-lived liaison? That is why Balzac
read these epistles from his feminine admirers with particular care.
They strengthened him in his feeling that he could mean a great
deal to a woman, and whenever the tone of a letter or any special
phrase awakened his curiosity he replied at considerable length.
When a communication of this sort reached him it was as though
a delicate and alluring fragrance suddenly pervaded his isolated,

closely curtained chamber. It brought home to him more vividly
than did any critique or other public appreciation that a vibration
emanated from him to which women were especially sensitive.

One day there lay on his table a voluminous letter in a feminine
hand which had taken some weeks to reach him. It had come from
Russia and was sealed with a crest bearing the words *Diis ignotis*
and signed *L'Etrangère*—the Unknown. It arrived, however, on an
inauspicious day, on that 28th of February, 1832, when Balzac
received his first invitation from Madame de Castries to call on her
at the Palais de Castellane. He therefore left it unopened, but it
was to have a decisive influence on the rest of his life.

This fateful letter had a strange story behind it, and Balzac himself could have invented no more theatrical or exotic beginning for
a romantic love-story. The scene was set in a country mansion in
Volhynia, one of those great, rambling manors of the nobility which
look all the more impressive because they are so completely
isolated. There was no town in the vicinity, not even a proper
village, only the low thatched huts of the serfs. Round about, as
far as the eye could see, stretched the vast, fertile fields and endless
forests of the Ukraine, all belonging to the rich Russo-Polish
Baron Wenceslav Hanski.

The noble manor which dominated the wretched dwellings of the
serfs was equipped with every luxury that Europe had to offer. It
contained valuable paintings, a well-stocked library, Oriental
carpets, silver plate from England, furniture from France, and
porcelain from China. The stables were filled with carriages, sledges,
and horses. Yet the whole host of serfs, indoor and outdoor servants,
grooms, cooks, and governesses could not protect Baron Hanski
and his wife, Evelina Hanska, from their most ferocious enemy,
from the boredom of their isolation. Baron Hanski, in the early
fifties and not very robust, differed from his neighbours in that he
was not a keen huntsman, a confirmed gambler, or a hard drinker.
The administration of his estates inspired him with little interest,
since in any case he did not know what to do with the millions he
had inherited. Even the ownership of thousands of "souls", as the
serfs were called in Tsarist Russia, gave no pleasure to his own

prosaic soul. His wife was even more bored than he was by the complete absence of any kind of stimulus or intellectual intercourse. As the Countess Rzewuska, she had once been a famous beauty, and in the house of her parents, who belonged to the highest Polish aristocracy, she had learned to regard cultured society as a necessity. She spoke French, English, and German, possessed literary tastes, and her interests were those of the Western world which, alas, was now so far off.

In Wierzchownia there was not a single person to be found far and wide who could satisfy her need for intellectual stimulus and friendly conversation. The owners of the neighbouring estates were uncultured and uninterested in the things of the mind, while the two impoverished relatives whom Madame de Hanska had taken into her home as companions, Severine and Denise Wyleczinska, had little to impart. The house was too spacious, and the solitude by which it was encompassed was even more spacious. For six months of the year it was enveloped in snow, in a pall of unrelieved white, and never a visitor came to the door. In the spring they made a journey to Kiev to dance at a ball, and once every three or four years they would perhaps go to Moscow or St. Petersburg. Otherwise the days passed bleak and empty. In eleven or twelve years of marriage Eva de Hanska had presented her husband, who was almost twenty-five years older than herself, with seven—or, according to another account, five—children, of whom all except one had died. The Baron was prematurely ageing, but she herself at the age of thirty was a well-built, attractive woman, though inclined to corpulence. Soon, however, she too would have grown old and life would have passed her by.

With the monotony of the enveloping snows in winter and the endless fields in summer, an equally boundless boredom brooded over the house. The sole event of the week to which its occupants could look forward with eagerness was the arrival of the post. There were still no railways in Russia, and once every seven days the sledge or coach brought its precious freight from the distant and almost legendary "West". And what an event it was! The Hanskis subscribed to foreign newspapers in so far as the censorship permitted, particularly the Parisian conservative *Quotidienne*, and to such literary reviews as existed in France. Furthermore, their bookseller sent them regularly all the new publications of any importance. Distance lent significance to the commonplace happenings of every day, and the newspapers which in Paris were scanned with a listless eye were here read through with absorbed interest from the first syllable to the last. Similarly with the books. No Paris journal criticised or discussed the latest publications in such detail as did this isolated household on the extreme edge of European civilisation. In the evening Madame de Hanska would sit with her two nieces and Mademoiselle Henriette Borel, her daughter's Swiss governess, exchanging views on the day's reading. Sometimes, though not very often, her husband or her brother, if he happened to be paying them a visit, would join the gathering, and they argued the pros and cons until every petty *fait divers* mentioned in the Parisian journals had been analysed with passionate absorption. Actors, writers, and politicians were spoken of with bated breath as if they were divine creatures with whom mere mortals could have no contact.

On one of these long winter evenings in 1831 the discussion had been particularly vehement. They had been arguing about a new writer who had recently achieved fame in France, a certain Honoré de Balzac. His name was on everybody's lips, and the women in particular were roused to either enthusiasm or wrath. He had written a magnificent book, *Scènes de la vie privée*, and never had any novelist looked so deeply into the feminine soul or manifested such sympathy with lonely, disillusioned women. What touching indulgence he showed for their faults and weaknesses! Yet there was the incredible paradox that a man of such delicate perceptions had at the same time published a book called *Physiologie du mariage*, which was filled with a detestable irony and cynicism! How could an author with such insight into the feminine temperament lower himself to such an extent as to make the whole sex the subject of mockery and scorn? And then there was his new novel, *La peau de chagrin*! A masterpiece, no doubt, but how could Balzac allow his charming young hero, who was loved by such a noble girl as Pauline, to abandon her for the sake of a cold, society coquette like the Countess Fédore? No! A genius like this Monsieur de Balzac ought to have a better opinion of women. He ought only to portray noble souls, as in the *Scènes de la vie privée*, and not waste his talent on people like the Countess Fédore, to say nothing of that frivolous bacchanalian orgy. What a pity that he could not remain

true to his better self! Somebody really ought to take him in hand
and try to keep him on the right path!

"Well!" suggested one of the ladies present. "Why should we
not do it ourselves? Let us write to Monsieur de Balzac!" The other
ladies were divided between laughter and horrified protests. No,
that was quite impossible! What would Monsieur de Hanski say if
his wife were to correspond with a strange gentleman in Paris? One
must not compromise one's reputation, for Monsieur de Balzac was
said to be a youngish man, and since he had been flippant enough
to write a *Physiologie du mariage* there was no placing any trust in
him. In any case, who could tell what a Frenchman of that kind
might not do when he received such a letter? All these speculations
and apprehensions, however, only served to make the adventure all
the more piquant, and they decided eventually to send him a joint
letter from them all. It would be an amusing idea if this mysterious
author, who idolised women and made fun of them in the same
breath, could himself be mystified for a change. So they would
concoct a letter between them, something very romantic and
sentimental, in high-flown language and liberally sprinkled with
honeyed words of admiration, a charade which he would have to
exert himself to puzzle out. It would not, of course, be signed by
Madame de Hanska or even be in her handwriting. Either her
brother or Mademoiselle Borel, the governess, could copy it out,
and in order to enhance Monsieur de Balzac's bewilderment and
tickle his curiosity even further, the letter would be sealed with the
motto *Diis ignotis*. He should imagine that he was esteemed by
"unknown gods" who wished to bring him to a realisation of his
true self, and not be made aware that his real admirer was a certain
terrestrial Madame de Hanska who already possessed a very
terrestrial husband.

Unfortunately the letter has not survived, and we can only
surmise its actual contents. There is another letter available,
however, which escaped destruction and was likewise written at
the time when the communications signed *L'Etrangère* were being
composed jointly by Madame de Hanska and her mirthful little
circle at Wierzchownia. Later on, when the correspondence entered
a more serious stage, she certainly refrained from effusions such as:
"From the moment I read your works I identified myself with you
and with your genius. Your soul stood before me in shining clarity.

I followed your progress step by step." Or: "In my eyes your genius
appears exalted—but it should be divine." Or: "There you have
my whole essential being in a few words. I admire your talent, I
honour your soul. I should like to be a sister to you."

This, however, must have been the key in which the first anonymous letter was written, for one can feel in every word how heartily
the conspirators must have applauded the successful concoction of
each inflated phrase, and perhaps the note of mystery was even
more effective when it reached its addressee. The hotchpotch of
sincere admiration, leg-pulling, and puckish humour could not have
fulfilled its purpose more completely, since Balzac was teased and
fascinated. Gushing letters from ladies were not an unusual
phenomenon, so far as he was concerned, but they had hitherto
emanated from Paris, or at the most distant, from one of the
French provinces. A letter from an admirer in the Ukraine was in
those days a far greater cause for astonishment than would be a
similar missive to-day from the South Sea Islands. Balzac realised
with swelling pride how far his name had been carried on the wings
of fame. Up till then he had been vaguely aware that his writings
were awakening some interest abroad, but he had not the faintest
inkling of the fact that even the great Goethe was discussing *La
peau de chagrin* with Eckermann at Weimar. And as in the case of
the first communication from Madame de Castries, he breathed in
the heady fragrance of aristocracy. Only an aristocrat in Russia
could write such perfect French, and only a wealthy personage
could afford the luxury of the heavy postage incurred in regularly
dispatching all the latest publications from Paris to the remote
wilds of the Ukraine. Balzac's imagination set to work. His unknown correspondent must be young, beautiful, and of noble birth.
Before long he was irrevocably convinced that she was a princess
at the very least, and in the first intoxication of flattered delight he
informed his intimate friends of the "*divine lettre de la princesse
russe ou polonaise*", which he showed to Zulma Carraud and
possibly to others as well.

Balzac never let a princess wait for an answer, but his anonymous admirer had given neither name nor address. Even much later
she assured him: "For you I am 'the Unknown', and I shall remain
so all my life. You shall never learn who I am. . . ." How, therefore, could he write to thank her? There seemed no way of getting

into touch. At last he hit upon an ingenious idea. A new and
enlarged edition of the *Scènes de la vie privée* was already in type
and one of the stories he had added, *L'expiation*, was not yet
dedicated to anybody. So he sent a note over to the printer
instructing him to reproduce the seal, with its motto *Diis ignotis*,
on the title-page in facsimile, and to put beneath it the date "28
February 1832". When she looked through the new volume, which
she would doubtless receive in due course from her bookseller, she
would realise with what delicate discretion he had chosen this way
of thanking her. He would reply to princely homage in a princely
fashion.

Unluckily Madame de Berny was still doing him the friendly
service of reading his proofs, and she apparently did not welcome
the intrusion of "unknown gods", or rather goddesses, in the career
of her protégé. At her express desire the "silent token of my innermost feelings" was deleted before the final printing, and the little
group of mischievous ladies at Wierzchownia remained unaware
of the fact that their mysterious missive had stirred Balzac's
exuberant imagination beyond anything they could have expected.

They had not, however, expected an answer. They had shot an
arrow into the air, but were not awaiting news of whether it had
pierced its target. For two or three weeks they relieved their boredom by speculating on the probable effect of their letter on Monsieur de Balzac, and they amused themselves with the invention
of further devices for stimulating his curiosity and rousing him to
a sense of his true vocation. Then they composed a second and
probably a third letter. One of their objects at least had been
achieved. They had discovered a new game to take the place of
l'hombre or whist or patience—writing letters to Monsieur de
Balzac.

It was an amusing game, but like all games it tended in the long
run to become wearisome unless the stakes were raised. Gradually
they began to wonder whether their letters, concocted with so much
art, cunning, and fanciful humour, had really reached their destination. Perhaps it might be possible to find out by some means or
other whether Monsieur de Balzac had felt annoyed or flattered. As

it happened, Madame de Hanska and her husband were planning a trip to western Europe in the spring, and perhaps the correspondence could be continued more easily from Switzerland, with the prospect of even receiving a reply from the famous author.

Curiosity, like necessity, is the mother of invention, and in November Madame de Hanska decided jointly with her confidantes to send a further anonymous letter. This is the first that has survived. After the usual effusive outpourings and assurances of spiritual communion a challenge was offered to destiny. Did Monsieur de Balzac wish to receive further letters from his unknown correspondent? Was he "prepared to enter into contact with the divine spark of eternal truth?" After a spate of emotional rhetoric she suggested to him that he should at any rate acknowledge receipt of the present communication. Since she was still unwilling to let him know either her name or her address, she proposed the at that time unusual method of inserting a personal announcement in a newspaper:

A word from you in the *Quotidienne* will assure me that you have received this letter and that I may write to you again with an easy mind. Please sign your communication *à l'E.* . . . *H.B.*

Madame de Hanska must have experienced a strange thrill when on the 8th of January, 1833, she opened the number of the *Quotidienne* dated the 9th of December and read in the advertising section:

Monsieur de B. has received the communication addressed to him. It is only to-day that he is in a position, with the help of this journal, to acknowledge it, and it is a source of regret to him that he does not know where he can send his answer. *à l'E.* . . . *H. de B.*

In the first startled surge of emotion she no doubt felt delighted that the great Balzac had expressed a wish to write to her. Her second feeling, however, must have been one of shame that he should have been led into taking seriously the deliberately exaggerated sentiments of the family circle at Wierzchownia. The situation had passed beyond its humorous stage and was growing dangerous. Her husband, a sober-minded country gentleman with a strict sense of honour, had been kept entirely in the dark about the joke which was being perpetrated by his wife, her two nieces, and the Swiss governess, and the joke had remained harmless so long as "the Unknown" was a pseudonym for the four ladies whose joint efforts had kept it going. If she were now to enter into a serious correspondence it would have to be behind her husband's back and without the knowledge of those who had hitherto been her accomplices.

Madame de Hanska was beset by doubts. She had a foreboding that she was about to embark upon an adventure which was incompatible either with the demands of her rank or with personal honesty. Yet there was a piquant satisfaction to be gained from the tasting of forbidden fruits, and it was difficult to resist the temptation of looking forward to a reply in the author's own hand. Nor was she insensible to the pleasurable prospect of being able to figure in her own imagination as the heroine of a Balzac novel.

For the moment she could not make up her mind and, as women will, she postponed the inevitable decision. She did, it is true, send Balzac an immediate reply, but the tone of this letter was different from that of its predecessors. Refraining from any further ebullitions of gushing admiration, she merely informed him that it was her intention in the near future to take a trip which would bring her nearer to the frontiers of France, and though she was desirous of continuing the correspondence, this would be feasible only if she could be assured that there was no risk of her being personally compromised by any act of indiscretion:

> I should like to receive an answer from you, but I have to be so careful, it is necessary to choose so many devious means, that I cannot yet venture to give a binding promise. On the other hand, I do not wish to remain in a state of uncertainty about my letters, and I beg you to let me know at the earliest opportunity what possibilities you may be able to envisage for an unimpeded correspondence between us. I trust entirely to your word of honour that you will make no attempt to discover the identity of the recipient of your communications, for I should be lost if it were to become known that I am writing to you.

This was in a completely different key. This was Madame de Hanska herself, and one can deduce for the first time something of her real character. She was a woman who kept a clear head even when about to launch into an adventure. If she were to take a false

step, she would do so with head proudly erect and in full command
of her wits.

✆

The new turn of events involved, in particular, a struggle with
her pride. Once Balzac had replied in the columns of the *Quotidienne*
a combination of curiosity, vanity, and the instinct to try a gamble
impelled her to exchange letters with him of a more personal
nature. But a letter from Paris was too rare an event at Wierzchownia for it to be able to reach her hands without attracting
attention. When the postman arrived the whole household was
agog with excitement and everyone who received a letter or parcel
of any kind was the envy of all the others. So there was no prospect
whatsoever of smuggling anything through without her husband
and her relatives being aware of it. She would have to let a third
party into the secret, somebody who would meet her wishes without question and was absolutely trustworthy. Fortunately there
was such a paragon near at hand in the person of her daughter's
governess, Henriette Borel, affectionately called Lirette, who came
from a pious middle-class family in Neuchâtel and had been in the
service of Madame de Hanska for some years. Living so far away
from her people and her friends, with no opportunity of meeting
men, her whole interests were devoted to her employers and their
daughter. It is practically certain that the first letters, composed
as a *plaisanterie* by the little circle to which she belonged, were in
her handwriting, and when Madame de Hanska decided to give the
correspondence a more personal touch without the cognisance of
her nieces nobody seemed more suitable than Lirette to act as an
intermediary. It would not occur to anyone that a letter from Paris
addressed to Henriette Borel could possibly be from Honoré de
Balzac, and there was little doubt that the pious, simple young
woman would agree to the subterfuge, since she could have no
inkling that she was doing her mistress more than an innocent
favour. She was, however, being led by her loyalty to Madame de
Hanska into committing at the very least an act of disloyalty
towards the Baron, and this conflict of duties, though she was not
aware of it at the time, appears to have deeply troubled her conscience later on when the relations between Madame de Hanska and

Balzac began to assume a "sinful" character. For the rest of her life she remained oppressed by a sense of guilt at having been a go-between in a deception which ended in adultery. A conflict of feelings seems to have developed at a fairly early stage, and she was never able to conquer a secret antipathy towards Balzac, who for his part immortalised her in *La cousine Bette*. When Monsieur de Hanski died her suppressed sense of guilt broke forth from its restraint, and immediately after the funeral she declared that she could no longer stay in the house. In order to do penance for having helped others to commit a mortal sin she took refuge in a convent.

It was Henriette's connivance that made a regular correspondence possible. Balzac was informed of the cover-address to which he was to write, and Madame de Hanska, fascinated by the dangerous game she was playing, waited with growing impatience to see whether he would reply.

⋙०⋘

Her astonishment can be imagined when not one but two letters arrived in quick succession. One of them (which opens the correspondence in so far as it has come down to us) was calculated both to thrill and to discomfort the châtelaine of Wierzchownia. Balzac had taken the gushing phrases perfectly seriously, in spite, as he said, of "the mistrust which my friends have constantly tried to arouse in me against certain communications which are similar to those I have had the honour to receive from you." He allowed himself "to be carried away by a feeling of confidence" and described to her the enthusiasm to which he had been stirred by her letter: "You were the subject of my most delightful dreams!" In a further passage, adopting and even excelling her own extravagant tone, he declared: "If you had been able to witness the effect which your letter had on me you would have perceived at once the gratitude of a man in love, the heartfelt trust, the pure affection which binds a son to his mother . . . the sincere respect felt by a young man for a woman and his delicious hopes of a long and ardent friendship."

Sentiments of this kind, which were expressed in Balzac's worst style and smacked of the romantic novelettes of his youth, were bound to go to the head of a lonely woman whose lot was cast in

the darkest depths of the Ukraine. It was really frightfully kind
and magnanimous of him to wish to dedicate one of his stories to
her, whom he had never met! Her first impulse was to reply with
equal candour. Unhappily, however, there was one disagreeable
circumstance which clouded her joy. Almost similtaneously
(whether a little later or a little earlier we cannot say, since this
letter has not survived) a second communication arrived from
Honoré de Balzac, and this too was in answer to her last letter, but
in an entirely different handwriting. Which, then, had been written
by Balzac and who had written the other? Or was, perhaps, neither
from Balzac? Was it possible that he could be trying to make a fool
of her by sending her letters made up by second and third parties
in the same way that her own earlier missives had been concocted
by a kind of drafting committee? Was he playing the same game
with her that she had been playing with him, or was he in earnest?
In her disquiet she compared the two letters again and again.
Finally she decided to write and ask him for an explanation of the
discrepancy in the handwriting and diction.

It was now Balzac's turn to feel embarrassed. Working under
pressure as he was, it had slipped his notice when he wrote to
Madame de Hanska that a reply had already been or was about to
be dispatched in his name. When the letters from his feminine
admirers became too numerous for him to cope with, he had found
a way of keeping these ladies in a good humour without encroaching upon his own valuable time. They were simply handed over to
Zulma Carraud, who answered them in his name. Zulma, to whose
nature jealousy was foreign, had plenty of leisure in the dull
provincial town where she lived, and she found it amusing to go
through these effusions and reply to them in Balzac's characteristic
style. It seems that the *"divine lettre de la princesse russe ou
polonaise"* had got mixed up with her work in hand, and she dealt
with it in the usual way as a matter of routine.

Balzac at once realised that he had committed a *gaffe*. Another
man would either have been at a loss or would have been honest
enough to admit the truth. But Balzac was never at a loss and he
never, or hardly ever, told "the Unknown" the truth about himself.

Right up to the end their correspondence remained as insincere as it had been when it started. To a novelist like Balzac improbabilities never presented a serious obstacle, so with a magnificently impudent somersault he overleapt the barriers of logic and bade her cast her doubts to the wind:

> You have asked me with a certain mistrust to explain my two different handwritings. The fact is that I have as many handwritings as there are days in the year. . . . This flexibility springs from a power of imagination which can conceive any idea whatsoever and yet remain as immaculate as a mirror which no reflection can sully.

He urged her to have faith in him and not entertain any apprehension that he might be jesting. The Balzac who was even then writing his priapic *Contes drolatiques* asked her to believe that he was "a poor child who had always been and always would be a victim of his own delicacy of feeling towards women". In accordance with this self-portrait he began shyly to confide in her and to speak of his "heart, which has hitherto known but one woman in the whole world". For a dozen pages and more he poured out similar vague confessions, discussed his literary style, and referred to his work, which compelled him "to renounce the love of women, though they are the only religion I have". He mentioned the loneliness of his life, and one cannot help admiring the cautious subtlety with which he struck a slightly amorous note:

> You, round whom I am fluttering as round a beloved illusion, you who are a pervading hope in all my dreams . . . you do not know what it means to a writer when he can enliven his solitude with such a sweet figure, whose form is rendered all the more charming by the elusive and indefinable quality of her being.

Before he had even learned her name or seen her picture he was assuring her in his third letter:

> I love you, my Unknown! And this singular circumstance is but the natural consequence of a life that has always been bleak and unhappy. . . . If there ever was a man whom such an adventure had to befall, I was that man.

One's first reaction to these premature outpourings is a sense of discomfort. There is a strained artificiality which leaves a bad taste in the mouth, and one cannot free oneself from the suspicion that

Balzac was deliberately working himself up into a state of romantic sentimentality that was far from his true feelings. So far as can be judged from the only example of Madame de Hanska's epistolary style that has survived, since after his death she prudently burned the letters she had written to him, these could have contained little other than rapturous adulation and an affectation of mawkish melancholy. Nor is there to be found in her letters to her brother a single line which offers any hint of an outstanding personality. Balzac himself has unconsciously thrown light on what would otherwise remain inexplicable: "I have to create passions for myself!" He wanted to make a love-story out of his own life, and when his first concept was ruined by the aloofness of Madame de Castries he tried another shot at random with his new admirer. He was instinctively acting in accordance with the temper of the age, for during the Romantic decades the reading public of Paris and in Europe generally expected its writers not only to write exciting novels but also to live them. In order to win his readers' hearts an author had himself to be the hero of a love-story which was unfolded against a background of high society and formed the topic of sensational gossip. Byron's adventures and his liaison with the Countess Guiccioli, Liszt's elopement with Madame d'Agoult, the relations of de Musset and Chopin with George Sand, Alfieri's association with the Countess Albany—these had stirred the public interest no less than their writings or their music; and Balzac, who was even more ambitious to succeed in society than he was to produce literary masterpieces, was anxious not to lag behind his colleagues. When, therefore, he laid bare his heart to his unknown "princess" and overwhelmed her with veiled declarations of love, instead of the mere polite letter of thanks that might have been expected, it was done out of no spirit of naivety, as he alleged, but with the fixed intention of building up a romantic liaison. He wanted to "créer" a passion.

His early letters to Madame de Hanska are comprehensible only if we regard them as the first chapters of a novel, for the continuation of which he relied not on inspiration but on the course of events. His unknown heroine, whose vague outline was to become more clearly delineated in the later chapters, was for the time being invested with glamour only by the magical effects of distance and high social rank. The hero was to be Balzac himself, but transposed

into a different key as a romantic youth yearning in vain for the
"pure" love which had hitherto been denied him by a cruel fate
that had sown his melancholy path with thorns.

If we follow line by line the self-portrait which Balzac drew for
Madame de Hanska, the following picture emerges. He lived alone
in the great city. In the whole wide world there was not a single
soul to whom he could confide his inmost thoughts. Whenever his
heart had been set upon anything the result had been only disillusionment and none of his dreams had been fulfilled. He had
been misunderstood by everybody and there was none to appreciate
his affectionate nature: "I am the victim of malicious calumny.
You can have no conception of the spiteful reports that are spread
concerning me, the slanders and the crazy charges." In Paris, in
the world outside, people only saw him through a distorting lens:
"One thing alone is certain—my solitude, my increasing labours,
and my sorrow." In his despair he had buried himself in his work
as "Empedocles flung himself into the crater where he hoped to
find peace." He was a "poor artist", despising money, scorning
fame, longing only for love as Parsifal longed for the Holy Grail:
"My sole passion, which has brought me nothing but disappointment, is woman. . . . I have observed women, studied them,
learned to know them and to love them tenderly. Yet the only
reward that has fallen to my lot is to have been understood by great
and noble hearts that are far away. I had to entrust my desires
and my dreams to my writings." No one wanted "the love that
dwells within my heart, the kind of love I crave, and which is
always misunderstood." And why was it misunderstood? " Doubtless because my love is too strong."

On another occasion he wrote:

I was prepared for the greatest sacrifices. I went so far as to
dream of enjoying but one full day of happiness a year with a
young woman who would appear in my eyes to be a creature
from fairyland. With this I should have been content and to such
a woman I should have remained faithful. But here I am, growing older, already thirty-five years of age, wearing myself out
in work that demands more and more effort, with my best years
already consumed, and in reality I have achieved nothing.

In order to accelerate the pace of his novel, Balzac adapted his
elastic emotions to what he deduced to be the moral and intellectual

qualities of Madame de Hanska, who would presumably make little response to the advances of a Casanova. What she would expect from an artist would doubtless be purity of mind and a sense of piety. His yearning for a woman's love must therefore be tinged with melancholy. He must put on a little Byronic make-up in the way of romantic despair. After this well-thought-out preliminary skirmishing, however, in which he presented a touching picture of sincerity, purity of mind, trustworthiness, solitude, and innocence, he went over in swift crescendo to the attack. With his mastery of technique he knew that if a novel is to provide the excitement intended by its author, it must swing into its stride from the very first chapter. In his opening letter the heroine had only been "the subject of my most delightful dreams", in the second he was "caressing" her "like a dream-picture", in the third he was already saying, "I love you, my Unknown!" In the fourth he loved her "more deeply, even without having seen you" and was convinced that at long last he had encountered the ideal woman of his dreams: "If you knew with what passion I turn to you, for whom I have so long yearned, of what devotion I feel myself capable!" After two more letters she had become the heart "in which for the first time I have found comfort"—which can only be described as base ingratitude towards Madame de Berny and Zulma Carraud. He addressed her as his "dear and pure love", as his "treasure" and "beloved angel". She had become the one and only mistress of his fate, though he did not yet know what she looked like or even how old she was:

> If you ask me to do so I will snap my pen in two to-morrow and in future no other woman will hear my voice. I shall request your indulgence only for my *dilecta*, who is like a mother to me. She is already fifty-eight, and you who are so young cannot be jealous of her! Oh, accept all the feeling I have to offer you and guard my emotions like a treasure! Take charge of my dreams and make my longings come true!

She alone had made him realise the miracle of love, she alone who had been "the first to succeed in filling the emptiness of a heart that was ready to despair of love". By the time he had learned her Christian name he was dedicating himself to her body and soul for all eternity:

14

You alone can make me happy. Eva, I lie before you on my bended knees, my life and my heart belong to you. Slay me at one blow, but do not permit me to suffer! I love you with the wh. le strength of my soul. Do not allow my beautiful hopes to be frustrated!

If one asks how it was possible for Balzac to put such rapturous utterances on paper, utterances which not only appear to us insincere but must have repelled any normal sensible woman, the only feasible explanation is that he was working up a romantic love-story, and as always happened when he was trying to be sentimental, he fell into an ecstasy of false feeling. Having idealised his heroine he was compelled, in order to harmonise the picture, to present an idealised portrait of his hero as well, namely himself. On closer study of his letters one cannot fail to be struck by the fact that his tender desire for love was emphasised in more and more colourful and fiery tones in proportion as the prospect of personal contact came nearer. His calculations turned out to be correct. His apparently frank self-revelation and ardent assurances titillated Madame de Hanska's desire to know more about the man who could write to her in such passionate terms. After having solemnly announced her irrevocable determination to remain nameless and inaccessible, she allowed the veil of strict anonymity to flutter a little in the wafting breeze of her curiosity. Monsieur de Hanski suddenly found himself being urged by his wife to take her on a trip to western Europe, and Balzac, in a fit of indiscretion that was unusual with him, wrote mockingly to his sister: "Don't you think it's a pretty piece of work to have torn a husband from the Ukraine and made him travel fifteen hundred miles in order to oblige a lover, who now only needs to journey a mere four hundred miles, the monster?"

At the beginning of the year 1833 a whole caravan set out from Wierzchownia. The de Hanskis travelled after the manner of the Russian nobility, in their own equipage, with numerous servants and followed by a vast amount of luggage. The indispensable Lirette accompanied them, ostensibly to look after their daughter Anna, but in reality to continue her good offices as a secret means of communication.

The first lengthy halt was made at Vienna, evidently at the desire of Monsieur de Hanski, who had passed his early years in the

Austrian capital and possessed many,friends there; but the choice
of Neuchâtel as a summer resort was doubtless due to his wife,
since it was near enough to the French frontier to be within fairly
easy reach if Balzac really wanted to meet her. Monsieur de
Hanski was presumably persuaded to agree on the ground that
Lirette's parents lived at Neuchâtel and she ought to be afforded
the opportunity of spending some time in their company after
having been exiled in the Ukraine so long. In any case, he raised no
objection, and in July they arrived in Neuchâtel, where they rented
the Villa André for a few months.

Balzac was secretly advised to put up at the Hôtel du Faubourg,
which was in close proximity to the Villa André, and there to await
further instructions. He was delighted and counted the minutes
that must pass before life itself penned the crucial chapter that
was now to follow upon the romantic prelude of his own creation—
the first corporeal meeting of two souls that had been destined for
one another by Providence. There was just time to send off a
hasty letter:

> Oh, my unknown Beloved, do not distrust me, do not believe
> anything bad of me; I am a more wanton child than you
> probably imagine, but I am also as pure as a child and I love
> as only a child can love!''

He declared his readiness to travel under an assumed name, so as
to avoid all suspicion, and it was arranged that in the first place he
should stay at Neuchâtel for only a few days, returning later in
October for a whole month. One thing remained to be done before
his departure. Neither Zulma Carraud nor the still jealous Madame
de Berny must be allowed to learn the real reason for his sudden
journey to Switzerland. They had to be put on the wrong scent, and
Balzac was never at a loss for an explanation. He told them that he
had to go to Besançon in order to procure a special kind of paper
for the printing of his next novel. Then he flung himself into the
coach, and after four nights of bone-shaking travel he arrived at
Neuchâtel on the 25th of September in such a state of exhaustion
that instead of putting up at the Hôtel du Faubourg, as arranged,
he inadvertently booked a room at the Hôtel du Faucon. Awaiting
him was a letter with instructions to appear on the promenade on
the following day, the 26th of September, between the hours of one

and four. He had just enough strength left to indite another hasty note announcing his arrival and imploring her: "For Heaven's sake let me know your real name!" He had sworn to love her for ever and to die for her, but he did not know what she looked like and was aware only that her Christian name was Eva.

⋙∘⋘

The curtain was about to go up on the most exciting scene in Balzac's love-story—the contact of two pure spirits. His dream princess must now remove her veil and reveal herself as an earthly being. On the promenade at Neuchâtel, famed throughout the world for its beauty, their eyes would seek one another and at last would meet. What would happen then? Would his hopes be dashed when he found that the aristocratic figure of his dreams was in reality a woman of very ordinary appearance? What would be her feelings when the ethereal author whom she had pictured as pale and slender, with eyes in which languishing melancholy alternated with fiery passion, turned out to be a ruddy-cheeked, corpulent gentleman who looked more like a wine-merchant from Touraine than a literary knight who had entered the lists on behalf of the misunderstood women of the world? Would each flee from the sight of the other, or would they find one another sympathetic? What would be their first sign of recognition or the first words that passed their lips?

Alas! Posterity possesses no record of this important episode in the novel of Balzac's life. There are a few legends, one of which states that he had already caught a glimpse of her at a window of the Villa André and been overwhelmed at her resemblance to the creature of his prophetic vision. Another pretends that she recognised him at once from his pictures and walked up to him without the slightest hesitation. According to a third, she was unable to conceal her first shock of disappointment at his commonplace appearance. These, however, are all later interpolations to which little credence can be attached, and nothing is known for certain except that at their first clandestine rendezvous some ingenious scheme must have been hatched out whereby they could meet on a formal footing, so that she might be able to introduce him to her unsuspecting husband as a social acquaintance. At any rate, on

that self-same evening Balzac was presented with all due solemnity
to the de Hanski family, and instead of proceeding without delay
to the hoped-for practical demonstration of his passion for his
"beloved angel" he found himself confined to the rôle of entertaining Monsieur de Hanski and the latter's niece.

Monsieur de Hanski was a man of few words and a little eccentric, but he was also a man of culture with a profound respect for
literary and social achievements. It pleased him greatly to be
afforded the opportunity of meeting such a celebrated author, and
he fell under the spell of Balzac's sparkling conversation. It could
never have occurred to him that there might be any reason for
jealousy, since he had not the faintest suspicion of the possibility
that his wife, née Countess Rzewuska, might be the recipient of
ardent love-letters from a bourgeois writer of such unprepossessing
appearance and *embonpoint*. On the contrary, he was most cordial,
invited Balzac to come again, and they took walks together. Such
warmth of hospitality was, however, most inconvenient to the
impatient lover, who had not endured four days and nights in a
rattling coach merely for the pleasure of regaling the de Hanski
family with literary anecdotes. He was on tenterhooks until he
could draw down his "polar star" from the heavens and fold her in
his arms.

Only on two or three occasions did Madame de Hanska manage
to elude the eyes of her household and spend a short hour in
Balzac's company. As he wrote wrathfully to his sister: "Her
confounded husband has not left us alone for a single second during
these five days. He oscillates continually between his wife's skirts
and my waistcoat." Doubtless the pious Henriette Borel did her
share in keeping them apart. All they succeeded in achieving was
a fleeting tête-à-tête in the shadows of the promenade at some
secluded spot on the lakeside. Yet to his surprise—he confessed to
her later, "I was afraid that you might find me unattractive!"—
he gained a minor success in the preliminary skirmishing. In her
remote Ukrainian fastness she had never come across anything like
this fiery specimen of humanity, and she was able to appease her
conscience by persuading herself that such a sensitive soul must not
be upset by a display of cruelty on her part, so she allowed him to
make love to her and even to steal a kiss in the shade of a spreading
oak. This early pledge of affection was warranted to encourage an

even less optimistic wooer than Balzac in his hopes of greater
favours to come.

❖❖◦❖

In a rapture of delight he travelled back to Paris. Four further
days and nights spent restlessly as an outside passenger herded
with a number of equally stout companions on the uncomfortable
top-deck of the stage-coach failed to damp his ardour. These were
petty discomforts compared with the triumphant issue of his
journey to Switzerland. All his expectations had been exceeded.
His hitherto unknown correspondent could not have fitted more
perfectly into his scheme of things if he had invented her himself
as the heroine of one of his own novels. Unlike his former partners
in love, she had not yet reached middle age. As revenge for the
deception he had played on her she had tried to make him believe
that she was only twenty-seven, and though this was certainly not
true, yet she could not be more than thirty-two and she was a fine
figure of a woman to boot, *un bel pezzo di carne*, as the Italians
would say, an appetising morsel. If Balzac, with his aptitude for
artistic exaggeration, describes her as a *"chef d'oeuvre de beauté"*,
that need not surprise us. A portrait by the Viennese miniaturist
Daffinger confirms the features which found favour in Balzac's
sight: "the most beautiful black hair in the world, an exquisite skin
with a delicate brownish tint, a charming little hand, the eyes
languishing and revealing a voluptuous brilliance when opened to
the full". Otherwise Daffinger's doubtless somewhat flattering
picture discloses a threatening tendency to amplitude, with a
double chin, plump arms, rather thickset figure, and small, dark
eyes with the veiled look in them which one finds in very short-
sighted people. The face offers no clear indication of character,
though there is more than a hint of secret depths. It was not,
however, her physical charms alone which had so captivated
Balzac. He had found a real *grande dame*, cultivated, well-read,
with a knowledge of languages, intelligent, and with polished
manners that mightily impressed the plebeian in him. She was
descended from one of the most distinguished families of the Polish
nobility, and one of her great-great aunts had been Anna Leczinska,
a Queen of France, so the lips on which he had been permitted to

imprint a furtive kiss were privileged—or so at least he persuaded himself—to address the French monarch as *"mon cousin"*. Yet even this was not the final miracle. The diadem he was about to set upon his brow was of pure gold encrusted with precious gems. Madame de Hanska's husband, to be sure, was not a prince or even a count, as he had fondly imagined, but he possessed another important merit—the highest of all in Balzac's estimation. He was immensely rich. He owned in actuality the millions which Balzac could only scatter fictitiously in the pages of his novels. He owned them in the form of good Russian securities, of fields and forests, estates and serfs, and his wife—or rather, his widow—would inherit them in due course. So Balzac discovered that Monsieur de Hanski too was endowed with a number of admirable and endearing qualities. In the first place, he was about twenty-five years older than his wife. Secondly, she was not passionately attached to him. Thirdly, his state of health left much to be desired. Since his days of poverty in rue Lesdiguières Balzac had never ceased to dream of being one day enabled to put his affairs in order through some lucky stroke of fate, which would magically transform his life of toil, worry, and humiliation into one of wealth, luxury, and the leisure to write as he wished. Now this prospect was brought within the bounds of possibility thanks to a fantastic adventure with a woman who, moreover, attracted him physically and was herself not disappointed in him. From that moment he devoted all his patience, tenacity, and energy to the task of winning her. The time had come for Madame de Berny, whom he had once "chosen now and forever", to retire into the background. His "polar star" was to shine in unrivalled splendour—"the beloved, the only woman that the world holds for me."

CHAPTER XII

Geneva

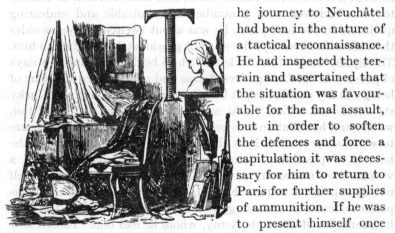

The journey to Neuchâtel had been in the nature of a tactical reconnaissance. He had inspected the terrain and ascertained that the situation was favourable for the final assault, but in order to soften the defences and force a capitulation it was necessary for him to return to Paris for further supplies of ammunition. If he was to present himself once more in the rôle of lover, as the wooer of a pampered woman and the esteemed friend of her wealthy husband, he must live in adequate style, put up at a decent hotel, and cut a good figure. He knew what was at stake. This adventure which had begun so promisingly held the prospect of great material and social advantages, and he redoubled his efforts to attain his goal. It was no exaggeration when he wrote: "Some of my friends here are very perplexed at the furious determination I am now displaying." He was still crushed by a weight of debt that he could not shake off, but once more he succeeded in gaining a breathing space by the discovery of a publisher, a widow named Béchet, who was prepared to pay him twenty-seven thousand francs for the twelve volumes of his *Etudes de moeurs au* 19*ième siècle*, which were in part to be a new edition of the *Scènes de la vie privée* together with the *Scènes de la vie de province* and the *Scènes de la vie parisienne*. He was again receiving advance payment for work that was still to be done, but at any rate it was an excellent contract for those days and he exclaimed joyfully: "It will have its echo in our world of grudging envy and stupidity. It will rouse the choler of all those who so presumptuously believed that they could walk in my shadow." He was now in a position to satisfy at least his most importunate creditors, though he was still in debt to his mother and Madame de Berny; and though his jubilation was somewhat premature, since a fortnight later he was again reporting: "On Thursday I have to pay out five thousand francs and I literally do not possess a single sou," yet this did not worry him. He was used, as he said, to "these little jousts", and he knew that he could earn plenty more by two or three months of hard work. His forthcoming visit to Geneva would probably determine his fate for some time to come, and perhaps for the rest of his life: "So now it is a matter of getting down to work, day and night. I must win my fortnight of happiness in Geneva —these are the words that appear constantly before my eyes as if they were engraved on the inside of my forehead. They have given me courage such as I have never known before in my life."

This time Balzac was not exaggerating. Rarely had he worked more intensively and to better effect than under the intoxicating inspiration of his anticipated happiness. He was spurred on by the thought that he was working not merely for a publisher's fee which would afford him a momentary respite, but for his final delivery from all the financial troubles by which he was beset, and the books he wrote during these months fully confirm the faith he expressed in his ability to give of his best:

> I believe that at this thought the blood streams into my heart and ideas press into my brain. My whole being feels that it is being raised to a higher pitch. Animated by this hope I shall undoubtedly create the finest work of which I am capable.

Balzac was trying to excel his previous achievement not only quantitatively, but also artistically and morally. From his talks with Madame de Hanska and from her letters he had inferred that she was rather perturbed at the "frivolity" of such works as the *Physiologie du mariage*, and he feared that his attempt to pass

himself off as a pure-minded and romantic lover might be frustrated
by the recent publication of the *Contes drolatiques*. He wanted to
prove that he was capable of greater and more noble feelings and
that his mind was filled with humane and even religious ideals. His
Médecin de campagne, too serious a book for his normal public, was
to testify to the fact that his lighter stories had only been thrown
off in his more irresponsible moods, whereas his best energies were
being devoted to a genuine idealism. At the same time he completed
Eugénie Grandet, one of his imperishable masterpieces. Thus he had
two further unimpeachable witnesses to his genius as an artist and
his character as a man.

While he was so boldly and vigorously preparing the way for the
decisive scene in the novel of his own life, he did not neglect to
strike the iron while it was still hot. He had no intention of allowing it to cool off, and every week he wrote ardent missives to his
"dear *épouse d'amour*" in which the more intimate *tu* had long
since been substituted for the formal *vous*. He assured her that "a
new and delightful existence" had begun for him, and that she was
the only woman he could love in this world. He adored everything
about her, "your accent and your lips that speak of goodness and
of bliss". He was shaken at the realisation of the completeness with
which his life belonged to her—"There is no other woman in the
whole world; there is only you." He represented himself from the
outset as a "poor slave" subject to her will, a *moujik* who dared to
gaze up at his exalted mistress. He surrendered himself to her,
fettered hand and foot, to deal with as she would. If one were to
believe his protestations, there had never been since the beginning
of creation any man who felt such boundless love for a woman.
Every week he launched his incendiary bombs against the distant
fortress: "Each day I find you more attractive. Each day you take
up more room in my heart. You must never betray this great love
I feel for you." In order to disperse her suspicions as to his immoral
leanings—to his horror he learned that she had procured a copy of
the *Contes drolatiques*—he assured her: "You do not realise the
virgin purity of my love." And he confessed: "For three years my
life has been as chaste as that of a young girl." This was all the
more surprising in view of the fact that he had just proudly confided to his sister the news of his having become the father of an
illegitimate child.

While he was thus bringing up his heavy guns to break down his beloved's outer defences, he was at the same time skilfully boring his way into her husband's good graces by a process of underground sapping. In addition to the more intimate letters which were for her eyes alone, he wrote others couched in more aloof terms, with the polite *vous* and *Madame*, which were clearly intended for the delectation of Monsieur de Hanski. Their purpose was to impress him with Monsieur de Balzac's particular affection for the whole family, including the daughter, the niece, the governess, and Monsieur de Hanski himself, and to emphasise that the celebrated author's sole object in coming to Geneva was that he might afford himself the pleasure of spending a few weeks in the company of such a charming household. As a special mark of friendship he sent Monsieur de Hanski, who collected autographs, a manuscript of Rossini and begged him with touching modesty for permission to present his wife with the manuscript of *Eugénie Grandet*. He omitted to inform Monsieur de Hanski that he intended to inscribe in pencil on the back of the title-page the date on which he proposed to arrive in Geneva. The unsuspecting husband had no idea that both his wife and the pious Swiss governess were collaborating behind his back in the autobiographical novel on which Monsieur de Balzac was so busily and cunningly engaged.

By December all his preparations had been completed. *Eugénie Grandet*, for the publication of which he had been waiting, turned out a triumphant success that confounded the most spiteful of his critics and supplemented his resources for the journey to an extent that exceeded his expectations. It was in a cheerful frame of mind that he registered on Christmas Day, 1833, at the Hôtel de l'Arc in Geneva, where he was welcomed by a first greeting in the shape of a valuable ring enclosing in a hidden capsule a lock of the black hair which he had so admired. This was a pledge that promised more to come, and for the rest of his life he wore it like a talisman.

Balzac's sojourn in Geneva lasted forty-four days, and twelve hours of each day were devoted to his work. When announcing his imminent arrival, in rapturous terms which included an assurance of the joy with which he looked forward to the blissful hours to be spent in the proximity of his beloved angel, he did not forget to inform her that his time-table would keep him tied to his desk from twelve midnight until twelve noon every day. Even in Paradise he could allow himself no respite. His afternoons and evenings would be available for demonstrations of the affection he felt for Madame de Hanska and her family respectively. The rest of the time was reserved for a very different emotion—the desire for revenge. He had brought with him to Geneva the manuscript of *La duchesse de Langeais*, which described his abortive adventure with Madame de Castries, in order to complete it in the city where he had experienced the final rebuff, and it was not without deliberate intent that he chose this occasion for doing so. He doubtless relied upon the psychological pressure that he would thereby be able to exert on Madame de Hanska. If he read this manuscript to her evening after evening, she would realise an author's power to avenge himself on a woman who trifled with his affections and refused to grant him the final pledge of love. She would be bound, either consciously or unconsciously, to feel apprehensive lest she herself should be exposed with equal ruthlessness to the purgatory of public scorn. The more one studies Balzac's letters, the more clearly does one recognise the skill with which he played his cards. While on the one hand he let her see the threat implicit in his malicious treatment of Madame de Castries, so that she might know how implacably he could behave towards a woman who was herself implacable, on the other hand he showed her by the naive enthusiasm with which he spoke of Madame de Berny how grateful he could feel to a woman who had surrendered to him body and soul. Both the malice and the enthusiasm were touched-up for Madame de Hanska's edification, but of this she was not aware. Little as we know of what happened at their furtive meetings, it is quite certain that Balzac's mind was set on one absorbing purpose, to persuade his angel to "descend from heaven to earth" and yield him that which Madame de Castries in this self-same city of Geneva had stubbornly refused to yield.

It is evident from Balzac's letters and entreaties that Madame de Hanska put up a determined defence. It is to be gathered that her final doubts as to his discretion had not yet been dispelled. Biographers and students of psychology have rather foolishly argued the point whether she was ever really "in love" with Balzac, as if the emotion of love were something that could be clearly and unambiguously defined, without being subject to fluctuations or inhibitions. Even though, as her later life bears witness, she was of a strongly sensual nature, her passions were by no means uncontrolled by her reason. They were constantly kept in check by regard for her reputation and social position. Those dark, short-sighted eyes of hers could see clearly enough the path she was treading, the marble brow on which Balzac lavished his praise was capable of keeping her thoughts cool, and from the outset she was concerned to avoid being compromised by an adventure in which she was becoming more deeply involved than she had intended. In this she was at odds with Balzac, who impatiently urged her to make the final decision. She never overcame a duality of feeling towards him, since in different spheres both her emotions and her judgment were different. While not ignoring his weaknesses, she admired him as a writer and recognised the uniqueness of his genius at a time when the critics of Paris were lumping him together with Alexandre Dumas and other contemporary novelists; but with the same clarity of vision she saw through the absurd exaggerations of his ecstatic method of courtship. Her ear grew more and more alert to his little insincerities and opportunistic prevarications, and though as a woman she was unable to resist his erotic impulsiveness, her aristocratic instincts were offended by his uncouth manners, his lack of taste, and his plebeian self-assertiveness. All the soothing syrup in which he steeped his letters could not completely drowse her senses. She drank in eagerly the strange and overpowering fragrance of his blandishments, which pandered to her vanity and curiosity, but she did not allow it to go too far to her head. A letter she wrote to her brother during these days at Neuchâtel shows how lucidly she was able to review her relations with Balzac:

I have at last made the acquaintance of Balzac, and you will ask whether my blind predilection for him, as you call it, has survived our meeting or whether I have been cured. You will remember how you always predicted that he would eat with his knife and blow his nose on his table-napkin. Well, he has not exactly committed the second of these crimes, but he really has been guilty of the first. It was, of course, embarrassing to watch him do this, and on various occasions when he made mistakes which we should describe as the result of being "badly brought up" I tried to correct him, just as I would teach Anna the right thing to do in similar circumstances. But all this is merely superficial. The man himself possesses something that is more important than good manners or bad. The genius of his temperament electrifies you and lifts you up to the highest realms of the spirit. It carries you away from your earthly self. He makes you understand what has been lacking hitherto in your life. I suppose you will again tell me that I am being "*exaltée*", but I assure you that is by no means the case. My admiration for him certainly does not render me blind to his faults—of which he has not a few. But he loves me, and I feel that this love is the most precious thing I have ever possessed. If we had to part to-day, the effect he has had on my life would be that of a torch whose light will never cease to shine before my dazzled eyes—my poor eyes which sometimes grow so weary when I think of all the paltriness and pettiness of the world and of the people by whom I am surrounded.

These lines have a ring of sincerity which is absent from Balzac's letters. She could not resist a feeling of pride at being loved by a man of his genius, and she was ambitious enough to realise that her correspondence with him made her the custodian of documents that would be of interest to posterity and would invest her, the wife of a landowner in the Ukraine, with historical significance. Fundamentally her mental and emotional attitude bore a remarkable analogy to that of Madame de Castries, who had likewise found happiness and pride in being wooed and idolised by the celebrated writer, while remaining cool-headed enough to prevent herself from being carried away by passion. She too drew back as he grew more importunate: "Let us love! Do not refuse me that which means everything!" She must have felt that she was acting dishonourably in paying clandestine visits to Balzac at his hotel, and certain boastings or gossiping on his part may have reinforced her doubts of his discretion, for he vowed that her surrender would only increase his love and gratitude:

You will see that your acquiescence will only render my love more deep and strong. . . . How can I put it into words? I am intoxicated by the slightest waft of fragrance that comes from you, and if I had possessed you a thousand times you would see me only the more drunk with love.

Thus the weeks went by. From midnight to noon he sat at his desk and drew his vengeful portrait of the Duchesse de Langeais who declined to grant her lover the final favour. Then he put down his pen and in the afternoon resumed his attempt to break the resistance of this other woman who would not submit to his will.

At last fortune beckoned. After four weeks of obstinate refusal his angel descended from heaven to earth and the room in the Hôtel de l'Arc was the witness to their adulterous love: "All yesterday evening I was saying to myself: 'She is mine!' Oh, the angels in Paradise are not so happy as I was yesterday."

Balzac had set out to experience a romantic novel in real life, and he had succeeded. With a masterly sense of technique he had brought it to its climax, showing that the improbable was in fact probable and turning illusion into reality. A woman he had never seen had materialised as the handsome, wealthy young aristocrat of his dreams and, after having offered himself as her lover before they had even met, he had at last attained his desire. His life was as full of unexpected excitements and exotic situations as any story in his *Comédie humaine*.

Yet this was only a first culminating point. The lovers had embraced and sworn eternal fidelity, but what was to be the sequel? Would Madame de Hanska now follow him to Paris, abandoning the ageing husband whom she did not love? Would she demand a divorce, so that she might honourably spend the rest of her life at the side of Honoré de Balzac, exchanging her estate in the Ukraine and untold wealth for the right to bear his name? Would Balzac invent some fantastic continuation of the adventure that had been so fantastically begun?

In this, as in all other matters, Balzac combined fantasy with realism. He had been guided from the start by the maxim *une femme et une fortune*, and the chief stimulus to his ardour had been the fact that Madame de Hanska possessed both a patent of nobility *and* a fortune. Nor did she for a single moment entertain the idea of settling down in a modest establishment in Paris where her principal occupation would be opening the door to Balzac's creditors. Instead of the romantic sequel of an elopement, a divorce, and a duel, their plunge into sin was followed by a pact which was almost business-like in its cool calculation. The lovers promised to inform one another daily of their feelings and the happenings in their lives, and they exchanged caskets in which the letters they were to write could be preserved until . . . well, until Monsieur de Hanski should be so amiable as to refrain from being any longer an obstacle to their union. Meanwhile they would consider ways and means of meeting occasionally in an inconspicuous manner that would cause no damage to Madame de Hanska's reputation or give rise, God forbid, to scandalous gossip. Their love would be sanctified in the eternal bond of matrimony as soon as her husband's demise made her the undisputed owner of Wierzchownia and the inheritress of his millions.

To sentimental natures these vows may appear somewhat cold-blooded after the extravagant display of emotion by which they had been preceded. But Balzac saw nothing wrong in them. The peevish old invalid could not last much longer than another year or two anyway, so he thought, and his unshakable optimism told him that where one miracle had happened two were not impossible. So he shook hands heartily with the cuckolded husband, thanked him for his hospitality and a number of valuable presents, and the de Hanski family went off with their retinue and their baggage on a trip to Italy for the continuation of their holiday, while Balzac returned to Paris for the resumption of his work.

CHAPTER XIII

Farewell in Vienna

y a tactical stroke of genius Balzac succeeded in concealing the things that he really wanted to keep secret behind an apparently naive pleasure in talking about himself. When he bragged of his enormous fees, it was mainly so that people should not suspect the extent to which he had fallen into debt. When he adorned his coat with gold buttons and kept his own carriage, it helped to hide the fact that he was unable to pay his baker's bill. When he attempted to convince Gautier and George Sand that an author must lead a life of monastic chastity, his object was to silence any prying curiosity about the women who paid him clandestine visits. At a time when other men of letters publicised their affairs and did their best to keep their readers informed during every stage of their amorous adventures, Balzac maintained the utmost discretion. From the moment of his meeting with Madame de Hanska he preserved complete silence even to his closest friends, who for ten whole years had no inkling of her existence. Apart from the letter written to his sister in his first intoxication of delight at the prospect of the visit to Neuchâtel, he never mentioned her name to a soul. All her letters were kept in the casket she had given him, the key of which never left his person, while the dedication of *Séraphita* was couched in general terms of emotional lyricism that might have been addressed to any one of the numerous dukes, counts, and foreign aristocrats both male and female to whom he dedicated his stories.

Madame de Berny, in particular, had to be kept in the dark about this woman, who from now on was to be the recipient of his confessions, the custodian of his manuscripts, and his eventual liberator from servitude. Shortly after his return from Geneva he visited his former *dilecta*. He wanted to spare her the knowledge that he had chosen (to use his own term) a *predilecta*, to indulge her illusion until the last moment that she was the sole confidante of his secrets, for her health had rapidly deteriorated and the doctors left no room for doubt in Balzac's mind that she had not much longer to live. It appeared almost incomprehensible to him that this frail old woman had but recently been his mistress:

> Even if she should recover her health—as I hope she will—it would always be painful to me to watch the melancholy decline into old age. It is as if nature had avenged itself suddenly, and at one stroke, for this woman's prolonged resistance to the laws of life and of time.

This paling of the moon as the sun rose above the horizon was like a symbol. At the moment when Balzac decided that another woman was to be everything to him, the life of the one who had given him her all began to ebb.

There was perhaps a latent feeling of guilt in his visit to Madame de Berny immediately after his return from Geneva. He was about to leave her, but he wanted to keep from her the knowledge that in his heart he had already done so. His weeks of tense excitement were succeeded by a brief lull. Sitting at her side, he could once more think over the past, the tortuous, thorny paths along which she had guided him. But the road had taken a new turn, and with renewed vigour Balzac threw himself into his work, intent on attaining his twin goals of wealth and immortality.

Whether it was his recent triumph at Geneva, the determination to prove to Madame de Hanska that she had given herself to a man who was worthy of her trust, or simply the need to earn enough money during the coming months for the defrayal of his expenses in following his "*épouse d'amour*" once more on her journey across Europe before she vanished into the twilit regions of the Ukraine, Balzac almost excelled his previous efforts in the way of literary output after his return to Paris. Some of his best work was produced during this period, but the doctors were shaking their heads and warning him to spare his strength. He himself was apprehensive at times lest he should have a breakdown: "I am beginning to tremble. I am afraid that I may be overwhelmed by fatigue and exhaustion before I have completed the structure on which I am engaged." Yet he continued to produce book after book. And what books they were! "Never has my imagination moved in so many different spheres." He finished *La duchesse de Langeais*, wrote *La recherche de l'absolu* in "a hundred nights" between June and September, began on *Séraphita* in October, started *Père Goriot* in November and concluded it in forty days, turned out *Un drame au bord de la mer*, *La fille aux yeux d'or*, *Melmoth réconcilié*, and further sections of *La femme de trente ans* in December and the following months, and sketched out in his mind the plan of *César Birotteau* and *Le lys dans la vallée*. Incredible as this may sound, yet it was not the sum total of his output during these months. He was at the same time recasting some of his earlier novels, collaborating in a play with Jules Sandeau, composing his *Lettres aux écrivains français du* 19*ième siècle*, arguing with publishers and dispatching with punctual fidelity five hundred pages of letters and diaries to his "*épouse d'amour*".

⋙∘⋘

While this Sisyphus of French literature was thus rolling his rock up the hill, Madame de Hanska was enjoying her *dolce far niente* in Italy. She wandered with her numerous retinue from one expensive hotel to the next, took her daily walks, had her portrait painted, ransacked the shops, and revelled in the artistic delights which Venice, Florence, and Naples had to offer a woman of cultured mind who had never hitherto stepped beyond the threshold of Russia. She possessed in abundance everything that Balzac lacked—money, leisure, and the entertainment in which these enabled her to indulge—and there is no indication whatsoever in their correspondence that she was moved by the slightest desire to interrupt her holiday and rush back to the arms of her lover. It is difficult to resist the suspicion that Madame de Hanska was less interested in Balzac himself than in his letters. They were a tribute which she appears to have insisted on receiving regularly as her due, whereas despite the fact that she had plenty of time on her hands, her own replies—as he so frequently complained—were few and far between. Throughout the whole twelve months or so of travel she expected a letter from him at each stopping-place, and the *moujik* did not fail to write faithfully and obediently in accordance with the demands of his imperious mistress.

The form and temper of his letters had, however, to be altered to suit the circumstances. It was no longer possible to conduct their correspondence in secret, as in the days of Wierzchownia, Neuchâtel, and Geneva, either because of the watch kept by the Italian censorship on letters addressed *poste restante* or because the arrival of too many communications from Paris for the Swiss governess was bound to attract the attention even of the most unsuspicious husband. Balzac was compelled therefore to write openly to Madame de Hanska in a style which her husband too could be allowed to read. The intimate *tu* was replaced by the formal *vous*, and the "*épouse d'amour*" became *Madame*, who was always politely requested to convey his affectionate greetings to "the Grand Marshal of the Ukraine", to her daughter Anna, to Mademoiselle Borel, and to the rest of the household. There were no asseverations of eternal love and no further references to himself —one notes this with a sigh of relief—as her devoted "slave". He wrote as though he had found in her during his sojourn at Geneva only a lady with literary interests and an infallible critical insight which had won his respectful esteem, so that he felt compelled to report to her all the details of his life. During the weeks he had spent in their company he had become so attached to the whole family that he could not resist the temptation to continue chatting with them in this way through the post.

Nevertheless, his letters contained a code which was intelligible only to Madame de Hanska. When he confessed his passionate fondness for the Swiss landscape she knew quite well what was the real object of his nostalgia. The enticing but dangerous game went on. Balzac was concerned not merely to hoodwink Monsieur de

Hanski into believing that this friendship with his wife was of a purely literary and intellectual nature. He was also anxious to assure Madame de Hanska that she remained his one and only love, to whom he was immutably faithful even when she was so far away. It seems that when they entered into their remarkable pact concerning their relations with one another while her husband was still alive, either she had demanded or he, with his accustomed audacity, had promised that after the incident at Geneva he would return to his former alleged state of chastity. At any rate, each succeeding letter outbid the previous ones in protestations of the loneliness and seclusion in which he was spending not only his days but also his nights. Again and again he spoke of the "monastic life" he was leading, and declared: "Never was solitude more complete than mine", or "I am as solitary as a rock set in the middle of the ocean. My unending work is to no man's taste". Another time he wrote: "Here I sit, as completely alone as any woman in all the yearning of her love could wish me to be."

Unfortunately, Madame de Hanska appears to have given little credence to his assurances. She was shrewd enough to have realised in Geneva how unlike he was to the romantic portrait he had drawn of himself in his early letters, and having no doubt caught him out a dozen times in untruths she could have had no illusions about the extent to which he was prepared to allow his imagination to colour reality. Their intimate meetings in his room at the Hôtel de l'Arc may have proved to her that he was not the shy, inexperienced ascetic, unversed in the arts of love, that he had pretended; and in any case she seems to have organised a fairly efficient intelligence service behind his back. Not perhaps entirely without an ulterior motive, she had furnished him on his departure from Geneva with introductions to the Russian and Polish aristocracy in Paris, and the Potockis or the Kisselews must have sent her reports which raised doubts in her mind as to whether he was in fact passing his days and nights in inexorable devotion to his work and sorrow for his sick friend, Madame de Berny. Balzac was too well known in Paris not to be noticed when he appeared at the theatre twice a week, invariably in the company of some equally celebrated society beauty. Nor could it have remained hidden from her that her "poor galley-slave", in addition to his house in the rue Cassini, had rented another lodging in the rue des Batailles. She must have hinted to him—since she destroyed her letters we cannot know for certain—that she was not so simple as to allow herself to be duped, for Balzac found himself hard pressed to explain. He assured her—expatiating, for her husband's edification, on the theme of friendship, but she could read between the lines—that inconstancy and infidelity were alien to his nature. In case incriminating evidence should reach her ears he skilfully tried to prepare his brief beforehand by a brilliant turning of the tables: "There are women who plume themselves on being of some consequence in my life and boast that they pay me visits." It was all lies, calumny, and exaggeration. It was true that he had taken refuge in music, but only because of his profound loneliness: "Sighing for the poetry I lack and which you know so well." (She would think of the aria in *Figaro* and understand what he meant!) No, this had nothing to do with worldly pleasures, with a desire to mingle in society: "Listening to music! That means loving the object of one's affections only the more deeply. It means thinking voluptuously of one's secret longings, gazing into the eyes whose fire one loves and hearing the beloved voice."

Yet still she did not trust him, in spite of—or perhaps because of—the resourceful way in which he placed everything in a plausible light. Her relations with Balzac depended upon her being able to have implicit confidence in him, since she feared nothing more than indiscretion on his part, and she began to display a certain reserve which made him uneasy. The trip to Italy came to an end in the summer, when the de Hanskis moved on to Vienna, where they intended to pass the winter months. In the following spring Monsieur de Hanski would be carrying his wife back to that confounded estate of his on the borders of civilisation, and Balzac's polar star, his one shining ray of hope, would for ever be beyond his reach. It was therefore essential that he should see her again if the bond between them was to be strengthened. She had given herself to him in an unguarded moment, and unless her affection could be quickened by a renewal of personal contact there was a danger of his losing her. So he must go to Vienna. A pretext was easily found. All his friends, including Monsieur de Hanski, were informed that a visit to the battlefields of Aspern and Wagram was necessary in order that he might put the finishing touches to his novel *La bataille*, which he had been planning for some years. But the

autumn slipped past, winter drew towards its close, and spring
succeeded to winter. Balzac remained in Paris, thwarted by the
obstacle which always stood in his way and was always the same
whichever shape it took. He either had to finish a novel, or collect
a fee of which he was in urgent need, or pay off a small debt in order
that he might incur a larger one. Meanwhile, with a view to stoking
the fires that had already burnt rather low, he sent off letter after
letter containing assurances of an early reunion. It was his hope
that the fresh breeze of his presence in Vienna would soon fan
the flames to their former glow.

◈⊃०⊂◈

An unfortunate accident nearly put an end for ever to the prospect of reunion. The de Hanski household had arrived in Vienna at
the end of July, and since the arrangements for the conducting of
his secret correspondence had functioned without a hitch during
their previous stay in that city, Balzac thought that after so many
months of restraint he might venture to send Madame de Hanska
poste restante a letter, couched in ardent terms, that was not destined
for her husband's eyes. This time there was no formal use of *vous*
and *Madame*, there were no friendly greetings to the "Grand
Marshal" or to Mademoiselle Séverine and Henriette Borel, but
only glowing torrents of affection for Madame de Hanska herself:

> Oh, my angel, my love, my life, my happiness, my treasure, my
> dearest—how dreadful this enforced reserve has been! What joy
> it is to be able to write to you now from heart to heart!

This impetuous opening was followed by the glad announcement
that he proposed to leave Paris shortly for the purpose of paying a
visit to the de Hanskis at Baden near Vienna:

> I shall hasten to you like the wind, though I cannot possibly
> give an exact date in advance, since the journey will demand
> titanic exertions on my part. But I love you with superhuman
> force.

After "six months of longing, of pent-up love" he wanted at last

> to kiss the divine brow, touch the beloved hair of which I have
> worn a lock so carefully next to my heart.

Three days together with her would give him "life and strength for a thousand years".

Unfortunately this letter to his "*chère blanche Minette*", perhaps together with another of an equally intimate nature, fell into the hands of Monsieur de Hanski, and there appears to have been a violent scene. Though we do not know what the immediate consequences were, Balzac, who had meanwhile had to postpone his departure owing to financial difficulties, was compelled to take up his pen for the purpose of explaining to the outraged husband what had induced him to indite such an unambiguous declaration of love for Madame de Hanska. In view of the clear facts of the case, this was no easy task. The inventive genius of a Balzac was, however, not to be deterred by a problem of this nature. With the same effrontery that he had shown in persuading Madame de Hanska that he had different handwritings to correspond with his varying moods, he cheerfully served up an equally glib tale for the appeasement of her cuckolded husband. Madame de Hanska, he declared, "the purest of beings, an utter child, the most serious, mocking, clever, holy, and philosophical person I know," had laughingly said to him one evening that "she would like to see what a real loveletter looks like." He had thereupon replied in the same vein, "Well, it's something like a letter by de Monteran to Marie de Verneuil," meaning in the style of the two chief characters of his novel *Les Chouans*. They had joked about it innocently at the time, and later on Madame de Hanska had written to him from Trieste to remind him. "Have you forgotten about Marie de Verneuil?" she asked. This had recalled to his memory the fact that he had promised to show her a copy of a model love-letter, and he had sent two missives of this kind to Vienna—both of which had apparently occasioned Monsieur de Hanski no less surprise than indignation when they fell into his hands.

To expect that any intelligent man would believe such an explanation was equivalent to telling him in so many words that he thought him a fool. Balzac's next move, however, was far more dexterous. He asserted that immediately on receipt of the first letter—that is to say, before Monsieur de Hanski had discovered the compromising evidence—Madame de Hanska had sent him an indignant reply. "You cannot imagine," he wrote, "how dumbfounded I was at the success of my stupid joke. She answered the first of these humorous letters with frigid disdain—and I had already posted the second one!''

Instead of candidly admitting to the deceived husband that he had been going behind his back or begging him to excuse an unfortunate misunderstanding, he requested Monsieur de Hanski as one gentleman to another—and this was really a brilliant move—to take his part and help him to allay the wrath of the chaste and guileless Madame de Hanska. The very fact that she had forgotten their joke about the letters to Marie de Verneuil proved—according to Balzac's peculiar logic—that she regarded the reading of a love-letter, even of one shown to her jestingly as a model, as highly improper:

> Madame de Hanska's indulgence would provide a noble demonstration of the foolishness of my conduct. It would show what a saint she is, and that would be my consolation.

He further entreated Monsieur de Hanski ("if I have not already forfeited your friendship") to be good enough to pass on to his wife the third volume of the *Etudes de moeurs* together with its accompanying manuscript. If, however, either of them should consider it unfitting to accept further tokens of friendship from the unworthy jester, "then please burn both the book and the manuscript". Even if Madame de Hanska were to grant him a complete pardon, he would never be able to forgive himself for having hurt or offended but for a single moment such a noble soul:

> It will doubtless be my fate never to see you again, but I should like to assure you how deeply I would regret that. I do not possess so many really affectionate friends that I could afford to lose one of them without shedding a tear.

This was a clear hint to Monsieur de Hanski that the right and proper thing for him to do would be to beg Balzac to remain in correspondence with his wife and to insist that their mutual friendship must continue undimmed.

Was Monsieur de Hanski really so naive as to believe this fantastic story? Or did he take the situation philosophically in the knowledge that in a few months his wife and her lover would be a thousand miles apart? Perhaps Madame de Hanska, reluctant to renounce her rôle as Balzac's "immortal beloved", persuaded him to yield. All we know for certain is that they both acted as if they entered into the spirit of the joke, that Monsieur de Hanski wrote Balzac a conciliatory letter and that Madame de Hanska generously pardoned the sinner, for a month later we find him replying:

> I resume our correspondence with all the respect due to Your Beauty (with a capital B, as in Your Highness, Your Grace, Your Mightiness, Your Holiness, Your Excellence, Your Majesty —*Your Beauty* comprises all of these).

Having eaten humble pie until he was forgiven, he was taken into favour once more and allowed to continue amusing his exalted friends with the petty details of his insignificant existence. His noble patroness and her husband even accorded him their gracious permission to come to Vienna and pay his dutiful respects before they returned to their estate in the Ukraine.

⬥⊃◦⊂⬥

The "misunderstanding" having been formally cleared up, it was to be expected that Balzac would set forth without further delay on his journey to Vienna. But the winter passed by, April had arrived, and his departure from Paris was still delayed by fresh obstacles, or rather by the one great obstacle. Balzac was out of funds. He had finished *Père Goriot*, three other novels, and a series of short stories, reaping his greatest literary success hitherto and considerable monetary rewards for his work, but whatever his industrious right hand managed to accumulate was recklessly squandered by his extravagant left. His new lodging and its furnishings, which according to his letters to Madame de Hanska were intended not for himself but for Jules Sandeau, had only been partly paid for. The revenues from *Père Goriot* and other recent books were swallowed up in advance by jewellers, tailors, and upholsterers. His calculation that he could earn a month of freedom by five months of intensive work had once again been falsified, and he had to admit: "I feel deeply humiliated at being as cruelly fettered to my debts as a serf is to the soil. I am not the master of my own movements, but am rooted to the spot where I stand."

It was now Madame de Hanska's turn to be importunate. Her husband was insisting that it was time for them to return home, and it was evidently only with the greatest difficulty that she had succeeded under a variety of pretexts in persuading him to remain in Vienna until the spring. April had been the final date to which he would agree, but relying on Balzac's promise to come as soon as he had finished *Séraphita*, she extorted a further postponement of their departure. If he had not arrived by May it would be out of the question to wait any longer. Whatever further reasons he might adduce for his delay, that would be the end.

Balzac realised that this was the crucial moment. Since his prospective union with Madame de Hanska after the demise of her husband seemed to him the last chance he would ever have of consolidating his fortunes, no stake was too high to risk. *Séraphita*, though already paid for, was still unfinished, but the last chapters could be written in Vienna. He had no money, but that did not worry him now. The whole of his silver plate in the rue de Cassini was sent to the pawnshop, further advances exacted from publishers and editors, and his signature appended to another I.O.U. or two. On the 9th of May he left Paris and arrived in Vienna on the 16th.

Balzac's journey to Vienna has added considerably to our knowledge of the qualities that go to make up the temperament of the man of genius, for there can hardly be a more perfect example of the folly to which even the most rational mind can descend. A strong light casts a deep shadow, and a childish weakness that would pass unnoticed in a normal person, or would be met with a sympathetic smile, cannot but appear grotesque in the case of a man like Balzac whose knowledge of the world and its ways can only be compared with that of Shakespeare. Even his most embittered critics had by now recognised his genius, the announcement of a forthcoming novel was sufficient to bring hosts of subscribers, and homage was paid to his fame from every corner of the world. Yet though he was fully aware of the immortal position he had achieved, he was consumed by the puerile ambition to impress people with something that he did not and never could possess. He was the grandson of a peasant and wanted to be regarded as an aristocrat. He was head over ears in debt and wanted to be thought wealthy. He knew from Madame de Hanska that Viennese society was impatiently awaiting his arrival, and he was seized by the unhappy aspiration to meet these nobles and plutocrats as if he were one of themselves, though their attitude to Beethoven had shown that nothing on earth impressed them more than the independent spirit of a sovereign genius. The Esterhazys, the Schwarzenbergs, the Lubomirskys, and the Lichtensteins must not be allowed to think that a personage like Monsieur de Balzac was to be classed with the poor, worn-out hacks of the literary world. So he fitted himself out in what he imagined was the height of elegance, while in effect stamping himself as a parvenu, with his "stick that is the talk of Paris, a divine lorgnon specially ordered for me by my alchemists from the optician of the Observatory, and gold buttons on my blue coat that were chased by the hand of a fairy." Instead of travelling like other mortals in a common stage-coach, he ordered a special carriage, had the coat of arms of the d'Entragues family painted on it, hired a liveried footman, and even gave himself out on the journey as a marquis. For this luxury alone he paid five thousand francs, though to his annoyance nobody remarked upon it during his stay in Vienna. The whole five weeks of his trip, two of which were spent in his expensive carriage and half the remainder at his writing-table in the hotel, cost him fifteen thousand francs.

Since the de Hanskis were staying in the smart diplomats' quarter of Vienna, they had booked a room for Balzac in the nearby Hotel zur goldenen Birne. It was a curious choice, for in this same room Charles Tyrian, the secretary of Count Rasumowski and secret husband of the latter's sister-in-law, the Countess Lulu Türheim, had shortly before shot himself with a pistol he held in his right hand, while his left clasped one of Balzac's novels. Almost before he crossed the threshold it was borne home to him how idolised he was by the Viennese, and that it would have made no difference even if he had arrived without a liveried servant and someone else's coat of arms painted on the door of his carriage. The treatment to which he had been subjected in the Faubourg Saint-Germain and at the hands of spiteful colleagues in Paris was now atoned for. The most distinguished members of the Austrian aristocracy vied with one another in inviting him to their palaces. Prince Metternich, the most powerful statesman in Europe, asked him to his house and during a long talk told him an anecdote which Balzac used later as the basis of his play *Paméla Giraud*.

Unfortunately he was unable to accept all the invitations that came pouring in, manna as they were to his appetite for noble names, because Madame de Hanska requisitioned him for her own social circle, though she would lend him occasionally to her closest friends of the Polish aristocracy, such as the Lubomirskys or the Lanskoronskis. He met no writers or scholars apart from the Orientalist Baron Hammer-Purgstall, who presented him with an eastern talisman that he superstitiously preserved for the rest of his life, and a minor dramatist named Baron von Zedlitz, who was shaken to the core when he found that the celebrated Balzac confined his conversation entirely to the absorbing topic of literary fees and money in general.

Balzac was in the seventh heaven. In this foreign city he was enjoying to the full the fruits of his literary renown, and those who paid homage to his name were themselves the bearers of names which sprang to his lips with a feeling of reverence. Amid such temptations to relax it was difficult even for him not to tear himself from his writing-table, where he sat in the forenoon completing such an esoteric, world-renouncing work as the religio-mystic *Séraphita*. He corrected a few proofs, visited the battle-fields of Aspern and Esslingen to make notes for his novel *La bataille*, and passed much of his time dancing attendance on Madame de Hanska, though it seems that Vienna offered fewer opportunities for amorous dalliance than had Neuchâtel or Geneva. After the episode of the intercepted letter she had to be very careful and Balzac's very fame proved a more effective guardian of virtue than any duenna. Shortly before he left Vienna he wrote to her gloomily:

There is not an hour, not a single minute that we can call our own. These hindrances put me in such a fever that the best thing I can do is to hasten my departure.

His departure was, to be sure, hastened by a more material reason than the fever induced by an unsatisfied thirst for Madame de Hanska's embraces, namely his inability to settle his accounts. Though he had drawn a bill on his publisher Werdet without the formality of obtaining the latter's sanction beforehand, his resources were daily dwindling, and when he said good-bye to Madame de Hanska on the 4th of June he had to borrow a ducat from her in order to tip the servant who had waited on him at his hotel.

He rushed back to Paris at the same furious speed with which he had made the outward journey, and arrived a week later. Seven years were to pass before he saw Madame de Hanska again. The first volume of his love-story, with its moments of tense excitement, had come to a close. As so often happened in the case of his other stories, he postponed its continuation to a later date in order to apply himself in the meantime to more urgent and tempting projects.

SPLENDOUR AND MISERY OF
BALZAC THE NOVELIST

CHAPTER XIV

A Year of Disasters

ature sometimes presents the peculiar phenomenon of two or three different storms driving up from opposite points of the compass and gathering over one particular spot, where they break with the accumulated fury of their combined and concentrated forces. This was the way in which disaster overtook Balzac when he returned from Vienna. His days of carefree relaxation had to be paid for in the form of an increased weight of anxiety.

The first worry that beset him was a renewal of his old trouble with his family. His sister, Madame de Surville, had fallen ill, her husband was in financial difficulties, and his younger brother Henri, a ne'er-do-well who had been sent overseas to get him out of the way, had come back from India without a penny in his pocket and accompanied by a wife fifteen years older than himself. Balzac's mother treated him to a display of nerves. Honoré, the great and powerful Honoré, must find his brother a job, and it was about time he thought of paying back the money he owed her! This was at a time when the newspapers were maliciously informing their readers that he had disappeared from Paris because he was unable to meet his obligations.

Whenever his mother made demands on him or loaded him with reproaches it had been his habit to fly to his maternal friend

Madame de Berny for consolation. But now it was his turn to comfort her. She was seriously ill, the weak heart from which she suffered having been aggravated by shock at the death of one of her sons and the mental derangement of one of her daughters, and she was in no condition to help him with her advice. Even the kindly service of reading his proofs had to be given up, since it was beyond her strength; and Balzac, not knowing which way to turn, had himself to assume the rôle of comforter.

This time his situation was more than usually disastrous. He not only owed money all round, which was the normal state of affairs with him, but he was badly in arrears with his work. Since it was his custom to insist on payment in advance for books which he agreed to supply at a given future date, everything he wrote was already mortgaged before he had set his pen to paper. His friends had warned him in vain against this ill-advised system, and Zulma Carraud in particular urged him repeatedly to dispense with a few luxurious but superfluous trifles and trinkets rather than degrade his genius by over-hasty production. Yet he stuck to his practice. His literary credit was the only kind of credit he possessed, and he enjoyed the feeling of power it gave him when he compelled his publishers to buy a pig in a poke. He sold them novels of which he had written nothing but the title, and perhaps he needed the coercion of having to finish a book by a fixed date before he could whip himself up to the pitch of industry which enabled him to extract the maximum from his hand and brain.

Before leaving for Vienna he had rounded up every penny he could in the way of advances. Not only had he sold the rights of republication of his old sensational novels written under the pseudonym of Saint-Aubin, but he had also disposed of a new book. *Les mémoires d'une jeune mariée*, to the *Revue des deux mondes*, This still remained to be written, and Buloz was waiting for the concluding chapters of *Séraphita*, which he had begun to publish in instalments months before. Balzac was not worrying much about *Séraphita*, which he expected to be able to finish in eight days, or rather nights, at the Hotel zur goldenen Birne in Vienna, and even *Les mémoires d'une jeune mariée* would not take, according to his calculations, more than a fortnight. On his return to Paris, therefore, the way would be clear for the contracting of fresh mortgages on further books.

For the first time, however, he found himself unable to keep to his time-table. His calendar made no allowances for holidays, and in Vienna he had succumbed to social temptations which played havoc with his plans. His time had been spent in the salons of the Austrian and Polish aristocracy, or in agreeable drives with Madame de Hanska, and the nights that should have seen him occupied at his writing-table had been given up to the pleasures of conversation. Buloz was forced to interrupt the publication of the unfinished *Séraphita*, though his subscribers did not take this too much amiss, since they did not find its Swedenborgian mysticism and exalted style particularly entertaining. A far more serious matter was that Balzac had not yet written a single line of *Les mémoires d'une jeune mariée*, in which he had lost interest owing to the fact that during his journey to Vienna an idea for another novel had occurred to him—*Le lys dans la vallée*. Travel always stimulated his inspiration. He offered Buloz this new work in lieu of the one already promised and sent him the first instalment while he was still in Vienna.

Buloz agreed, and the first instalment of *Le lys dans la vallée* was duly printed, but he thought himself entitled to recoup himself in another way for Balzac's remissness with regard to *Séraphita*. For some time there had been appearing in St. Petersburg a *Revue Etrangère* which had adopted a policy of offering its Russian readers the latest productions of French literature simultaneously with, and even occasionally prior to, their publication in Paris. Buloz arranged that this journal was to have the right to print contributions which their authors had sent to the *Revue des deux Mondes* and the *Revue de Paris*, and for this purpose he sold it the proof-sheets. Balzac was the most popular French author in Russia at the time, and Buloz had no scruple in selling the proofs of *Le lys dans la vallée* to the Russian review. Balzac owed him money anyway, and was not likely to pick a quarrel.

Hardly, however, had Balzac learned of this transaction on his return to Paris than he sprang at Buloz' throat like a wounded lion. To his honour it must be said that it was not so much the money side of the question which roused his ire as the fact that he felt his artistic integrity to have been outraged. Buloz had sent the first proofs to St. Petersburg, and the *Revue Etrangère* printed this version verbatim without Balzac being consulted, though his invariable method was to regard the first galleys merely as a rough draft. He always demanded half a dozen or more revises from the *Revue des deux Mondes* before finally passing his work for press. His wrath can therefore be imagined when he received a copy of the *Revue Étrangère* containing the first chapters of his new novel in their first raw shape with all the technical defects and clumsy turns of phrase which he would never have allowed to be submitted to the public eye. He justifiably felt that Buloz had taken advantage of his absence to impose upon him, and he at once resolved to break off relations with the culprit who had violated his artistic conscience and to bring an action against the *Revue des deux Mondes*.

❧◦❧

When Balzac's friends heard of his intention they were horrified. Buloz controlled the two most powerful reviews in France and his influence was enormous. He could make or mar an author's reputation, and four-fifths of the writers and journalists in Paris were directly or indirectly dependent on him. Moreover, he could bring pressure to bear on the editors of the great newspapers, so that if it came to an open conflict Balzac would not find a single journal or even a colleague prepared to offer testimony on his behalf or to help him in any other way. Apart from his lack of popularity with his fellow-writers, they would not have the courage to stand up against Buloz, who could, so his friends warned Balzac, damage his prestige in a hundred ways, expose him to ridicule in the public press, intimidate his publishers, and even influence the booksellers. So a lawsuit was out of the question. Even if he were to win his case he would, in fact, have lost it from the start. It was impossible for any man to fight an anonymous power whose tentacles stretched underground in every direction, and particularly so when he stood completely alone.

When his artistic integrity was at stake, however, Balzac was not to be deterred. His sojourn in Vienna had reinforced his self-confidence and helped him to realise the extent to which spite and envy had masked his true stature in his own country. He was conscious of his strength, and setbacks or humiliations only made him more determined to triumph. He had never deigned to reply to individual attacks, which left him unconcerned, but he derived a kind of pleasure from the thought of challenging the whole mob of Parisian journalism with its corruption and treacherous malice, of standing at bay against a yapping horde. Every attempt at mediation was implacably rejected and he brought his action against Buloz, who retorted with a counter-action for non-fulfilment of contractual obligations. The dispute overflowed, of course, from the courts to the newspapers and the literary world generally. Buloz left no stone unturned. In the *Revue de Paris* he printed the most savage calumnies about Balzac, not sparing his private life, jeering at him for having usurped a title of nobility, disclosing his authorship of and collaboration in the hack productions of his early years, gleefully revealing the extent to which he was in debt, and deriding his character. The whole of Buloz' literary militia was summoned to arms. One writer after another was induced to declare that it was common usage for an editor to sell an author's contributions, without further payment, to foreign journals. Since the *Revue de Paris* and the *Revue des deux Mondes* helped to provide their bread and butter, they all nodded their heads in agreement when Buloz cracked the whip. Instead of standing in a spirit of fraternal comradeship at the side of their colleague, men like Alexandre Dumas, Eugène Sue, Gozlan, Jules Janin, and a dozen others bore witness against Balzac. Victor Hugo, as noble as ever, and George Sand alone refused to lick Buloz' boots.

When the case came up for judgment Balzac won a moral victory. The court's verdict, important for the whole literary profession, was to the effect that an author could not be compelled to indemnify a publisher or editor if he was unable to deliver a promised work owing to the fact that he lacked either the inclination or the capacity to complete it. Balzac was ordered merely to repay the advances he had received from Buloz. It was a victory, but a Pyrrhic victory. He had lost weeks of valuable time in dealing with lawyers, appearing at court, and indulging in polemics. The whole journalistic rabble of Paris was at his heels, and even the strongest man can be worn out in a constant struggle with a host of enemies.

❧

From this experience in the courts Balzac drew a moral lesson. He was made to realise how right he had been in causing his

fictitious heroes, his Vautrins, de Marseils, Rastignacs, and Rubem-
prés, to act according to the ruthless maxim: "Acquire power, then
people will pay heed to you!" Acquire power, no matter what kind
of power, power through wealth, power through political influence, power through military triumphs, power through terror,
power through connections, power through women, but whatever
you do, acquire power! Keep your weapons polished, otherwise you
are lost! It is not sufficient to be independent. You must learn to
make others dependent on you. Only when people feel that they
can be attacked in their weakest spot, in their vanity or their
cowardice, only when they are afraid of you, can you show them
that you are the master.

Hitherto Balzac had believed that his own power lay in the
loyalty of his readers. But these were scattered over all the countries of the earth, they were not organised or subject to discipline,
they did not inspire his opponents with fear, but only with envy.
They were unable to help him in his struggle against a clique of
hacks and parasites who moulded and swayed public opinion in
Paris. Yet he was the most widely read of all French writers, and
he felt that the time had come to free himself from dependence on
the reviews. If he could himself obtain control of an organ of public
opinion, he would be able to cut the ground away from beneath the
feet of those who had cast him out from their critical strongholds
and, entrenched behind their money-bags, were covering him with
derision.

Since 1834 there had existed in Paris a small journal called *La
Chronique de Paris*, which appeared twice a week and was not very
much in the public eye. The fact that its tendency was ultra-
clerical and legitimist did not worry Balzac. Nor was he at all
perturbed by its precarious financial condition and meagre circula-
tion. He was confident that a paper to which Honoré de Balzac was
a regular contributor, and in which he allowed his novels to be
published, would be set on its feet without more ado. Apart from
this it would be a useful stepping-stone to the political arena.
Despite his previous failures in the world of politics Balzac was
still dreaming of entering Parliament, becoming a peer of France,
and holding a ministerial portfolio. He was still lured by the
prospect of political power, power visible and tangible, with all its
excitements and tempestuous storms.

The shares of the *Chronique de Paris* were intrinsically almost worthless, and Balzac managed to float some sort of company in which he had a majority holding. The complicated transaction involved his assuming also the heavy responsibility of providing funds for the journal's continued publication, but this he did with his usual optimism. As soon as the contract was signed he threw himself into his new task for all he was worth. An editorial staff of talented young men was soon assembled, of whom the only one to remain a lasting friend was Théophile Gautier. As secretaries he engaged two young aristocrats, the Marquis de Belloy and the Comte de Grammont, trusting more to his snobbish instinct than to his critical insight. Secretaries and editorial assistants were of minor importance, however, when the conduct of affairs was in the hands of a Balzac, who could write enough for a dozen men. At the first set off, while he was still interested in his new activity, he turned out nearly the whole contents of the paper himself. Every conceivable kind of contribution flowed from his pen, a hotch-potch of political, literary, and polemical articles being garnished with a series of his best short stories. For the first number under his own editorship, which appeared in January, 1836, he wrote *La messe de l'athée* in a single night. This was followed by *L'interdiction, Le cabinet des antiques, Facino Cane, Ecce homo,* and *Le martyre ignoré.* At all hours of the day he would storm into the editorial offices to find out what was happening, to spur on his staff, and to make suggestions. Pricked by the desire for power and perhaps also for revenge on the other reviews, whose prestige he hoped to lower as that of his own journal increased, he launched an expensive publicity campaign. On the 10th, 14th, 17th, 22nd, 24th, and 27th of January he gave a series of dinner-parties in the rue Cassini, on a luxurious scale and with wine flowing in streams, to which he invited the most influential of his literary colleagues. His last two quarters' rent had not yet been paid and his landlord was compelled to call in the bailiffs to help him collect the 473 francs 70 centimes that Balzac owed him.

This sumptuous hospitality was an investment on which he expected to be repaid a hundredfold. Paris was curious about his paper, and four weeks after the issue of the first number he sounded one of his premature fanfares of victory in a rapturous letter to Madame de Hanska:

The *Chronique de Paris* leaves me no time for anything else. I sleep only five hours a day, but if your affairs and those of Monsieur de Hanski may be said to be going well, I can say of myself that my project is beginning to thrive magnificently. Subscriptions are flowing in to a fabulous extent, and in a single month my shares in the paper have acquired a capital value of ninety thousand francs.

The valuation of his holding in the *Chronique de Paris* at ninety thousand francs applied only to their quotation on the stock exchange of his own private hopes, an institution which was notoriously unreliable. In his dreams Balzac saw Paris at his feet, and he fully expected that Buloz would before long come creeping into his presence in an attitude of humble supplication, ready to lay a hundred thousand francs on his table in return for a promise to abandon the *Chronique de Paris* and to resume his contributions to the older reviews. Soon the writers who had but recently been making him the butt of their spiteful wit would be attempting to curry favour with the editor of the most influential journal in France. Ministers and deputies would find themselves obliged to adopt the policy of Monsieur de Balzac as their own.

Unfortunately, the hosts of readers who were falling over one another in their eagerness to pay their subscriptions were merely a figment of Balzac's exuberant imagination. The figures in the balance-sheet were on a more modest scale, and the other shareholders, who possessed less genius than Balzac but a sounder business instinct, quietly got rid of their holdings and left him to dispose of his own shares at a fraction of the price he had paid for them. When he realised that his new venture was falling flat he began to lose interest. His editorial work bored him, his appearances at the office grew less and less frequent, his contributions became more and more scanty, and before the year was over the enterprise had met the fate of all Balzac's material enterprises— total collapse and an increased weight of debt. Six to eight months of frantic industry had only added another forty thousand francs to his burden. He would have done better to take a holiday and travel round the world. Like Antaeus, he derived fresh strength from contact with his own mother earth, but when he went outside his own sphere his genius and clear-sighted intelligence failed him so that dwarfs dared to mock his giant efforts. His bold pronouncement: "In 1836 I shall be rich!" was followed by the admission: "In 1836 I got no further ahead than I had been in 1829."

◦⟫◦⟨◦

The lawsuit against Buloz and the failure of the *Chronique de Paris* were only two exhibition pieces in this year's collection of disasters. Almost every day brought its unwelcome episode. Balzac's disputes with publishers were not confined to Buloz. The *"excellente Madame Béchet"* suddenly changed to an *"odieuse Madame Béchet"* when her former employee Werdet set up in business for himself and lured Balzac away from her. She relentlessly demanded delivery of the volumes still in arrear. Werdet, on the other hand, was not possessed of sufficient capital to finance Balzac, and in order to obtain a breathing-space the latter prepared to publish a new edition of the *Contes drolatiques* on his own account, forgetting the old proverb that a burned child dreads the fire. His previous publishing ventures had already landed him in bankruptcy. Nevertheless he bought paper on credit, found a printer to produce the new edition on credit, and the sheets were all ready for binding. Then a fire broke out in the warehouse where they were stored and three thousand five hundred francs went up literally in smoke.

Balzac was now at his wits' end for a way to stave off his creditors. He barricaded his door in the rue Cassini and had his most valuable furniture and books moved by night into a new apartment in the rue des Batailles which he had rented under the name of "the Widow Durand" before his departure for Vienna. As in the rue Cassini, he enjoyed here the amenity of a secret staircase as a means of escape in case a bailiff or any other unwelcome visitor should succeed in penetrating to the front door. It was, however, by no means a simple matter to reach the front door of "the Widow Durand". With the naive pleasure he derived from enveloping his everyday existence in a cloak of romantic mystification, he invented a system of passwords which were continually changed. Nobody could hope to pierce the triple ramparts of Balzac's fortress unless he had been entrusted with the "Open, Sesame!" that would make the gates fly open. The porter, so we are told by Théophile Gautier, had to be addressed, for example, on a certain

day, with the words: "The plums are ripe." Cerberus then admitted
the visitor across the threshold. This, however, was merely the first
step. Balzac's trusty servant was waiting at the bottom of the
stairs, and he had to be told: "I'm bringing lace from Belgium."
The visitor was then allowed as far as the door of the apartment,
where his assurance that "Madame Bertrand is enjoying the best
of health" was the final key to the inner sanctum of the mysterious
widow.

Every ingenious device to which the heroes of his novels resorted
was tried out by Balzac himself. Bills of exchange were passed
on to third and fourth parties, legal artifices employed to obtain
the adjournment of court hearings, and the acceptance of writs
avoided by rendering himself inaccessible through the post. Like
his Lapalferine, who was a master of the art, he adopted a hundred
devious ways of holding his creditors at bay, aided by his intimate
knowledge of the laws, his inventive skill, and his unscrupulous
effrontery. His bills were floating around among the publishers and
money-lenders, and there was not a bailiff in Paris who had not a
notice of distraint to serve on Monsieur de Balzac, but not one of
them managed to meet him face to face.

From a feeling of pride, and perhaps also from a sense of mischief,
Balzac deliberately added to the number of those who were trying
to track him down by openly flouting the laws of the country. In
accordance with a recent decree every citizen was liable to undergo
a term of militia service in the National Guard, but this was an
obligation which Balzac refused to recognise. As a legitimist he
regarded the bourgeois king, Louis Philippe, as a usurper who had
no right to give him orders. In any case, his time was too valuable
and he thought it beneath his dignity to stand about with a musket
on his shoulder pretending to be a soldier while the printing presses
were hungry for his manuscripts. There is little doubt that by
friendly arrangement ways and means could have been discovered
whereby a citizen of Balzac's physical and literary magnitude
might be relieved of these patriotic duties, but he would tolerate
no compromise. He did not even reply to the orders he received
calling him up for service. Three times he was summoned to explain
his failure to report, and each time he ignored the instruction. At
last the disciplinary board of the National Guard condemned him
to eight days' imprisonment, which made him laugh till his sides

shook. The impertinence of ordering the Field Marshal of European letters to be thrown into gaol for declining to shoulder a musket! All right, let them try! It amused him to play a cat-and-mouse game with the police who had been instructed to arrest the refractory military absentee. They could arrest him if they wanted to, but first they would have to find him! The gold-braided blockheads would learn that they needed a little more grey matter in their skulls before they could hope to outwit a man of his calibre.

For the next few weeks Balzac disappeared from view. At all hours of the day the minions of the law forced their way into the house in the rue Cassini, but without success. Monsieur de Balzac was invariably away on a journey and had left no address—though on the same evening he might emerge in a box at the *Italiens* or even appear in the forenoon at the office of one of his publishers to collect a fee. It amused him enormously to learn from his servant how often the moustachioed policemen had called to inquire after him, and it was even greater fun to stand behind a concealed door and listen to the louts scratching their heads in bewilderment at their inability to discover his whereabouts. This was something that would help him to infuse a little gusto into his next novel. It provided excellent inspiration for his description of the struggle waged by Vautrin and Paccard against Corentin, Peyrade, and the other bloodhounds of the law. One morning, however, on the 27th of April, King Louis Philippe was able to celebrate a victory. A police inspector and two detectives, who had been lying in wait for hours, pushed their way in behind him as he entered his apartment in the rue Cassini, and thirty minutes later the notorious green van carried him away to the lock-up, the Hôtel de Bazincour, popularly known as the Hôtel des Haricots. It is some indication of the small place Balzac held in the public esteem of his own countrymen that he had to serve his full term in gaol. His aristocratic acquaintances abroad, the ambassadors who had invited him to their receptions, Prince Metternich, who had honoured him with a private interview—these were of no help to him in Paris, where from the 27th of April until the 4th of May the law exacted its due without according him any special privileges whatsoever. He had to sit in a vast hall amidst a horde of bawling culprits, from the lowest class of society, who were all amusing themselves in their various ways. They were mostly workmen who

had refused to sacrifice the two days that they were required to
serve in the National Guard because their wives and children would
go hungry owing to the loss of their wages for that period. The only
concession Balzac managed to extract was the provision of a table
and a chair, and that was all he needed. Amid the pandemonium
around him he was able to concentrate on the correction of his
proofs as imperturbably as if he were sitting in the silence and
solitude of his study. His good humour was no whit diminished, as
can be seen from his cheerful description in a letter to Madame de
Hanska. Far from feeling humiliated at his imprisonment, it tickled
his sound Gallic sense of the farcical. It may even be said that
he rather enjoyed the sensation of being sheltered by the State
from the importunities of publishers and bailiffs. He was inured
to less tolerable restrictions on his liberty than confinement in
the Hôtel des Haricots. For Balzac freedom meant having to
resume the struggle for survival day after day and night after
night.

For six months he manfully withstood the blows of fate, though
he would groan occasionally: "I am literally killing myself," or:
"My head is hanging down like that of a tired nag." It was during
this period that even his iron constitution received its first warning
that he was overdoing things. He was overcome by an attack of
dizziness, and his doctor urged him to have more consideration for
his health. Balzac followed his advice to go away for two or three
months in the country and rest, though he ignored the second half
of the prescription. He went to stay with his friends, the Margonnes, in his native Touraine, but he did not rest as Dr. Nacquart
had ordered. On the contrary, he worked as frantically as ever. He
had repeatedly to learn the lesson that rescue from his desperate
situation could come not from speculation, from business enterprises, or from a wealthy marriage, but only from devoting himself
to his real vocation, for which he had been destined from the womb.
The artist possesses a remedy which no physician can prescribe
for other patients. He alone can throw off his worries by giving
them artistic expression. He can transmute the bitterness of experience into the moving portrayal of human character, and fashion the
constraint of outward circumstance into creative freedom.

When Balzac went to stay at Saché he was certainly being constrained by the force of outward circumstance. The Widow Béchet

had married again, and her new husband was a keen man of
business who knew no mercy in matters which touched his pocket.
Under his influence she obtained a court order instructing Balzac
to deliver the two outstanding volumes of his *Etudes de moeurs*
within twenty-four days or to pay a fine of fifty francs for every
day's delay. So Balzac decided to "let this woman have her
volumes in twenty days" and rid himself of his obligation to her.
He saw that there were two things he had to do: "I must fulfil my
last contract, but apart from that I must produce a first-class
book." He achieved both his objectives. Some of his best work was
written when he was most beset by material difficulties. In eight
days he conceived the idea of the *Illusions perdues* and wrote the
whole of the first part:

> I exerted all my strength and wrote for fifteen hours a day. I rose
> with the sun and worked until it was time for lunch, without
> taking anything except black coffee.

This book, produced in a race to avoid a fine, is one of his pivotal
works. It was as if Balzac had fiercely lashed himself into revealing
the depths of his soul, parading before him for inspection his most
secret desires and the most menacing of the dangers that threatened
him. Though it is apparently a picture of contemporary life, with
a breadth and realism such as had hitherto had no parallel in
French literature, the *Illusions perdues* was a determined attempt
on the part of Balzac to come to grips with himself. In two separate
characters he showed on the one hand what a writer can achieve
if he remains steadfastly true to himself and his art, and on the
other what happens if he yields to the temptation to acquire a swift
and unworthy fame. Lucien de Rubempré symbolised the spiritual
peril in which Balzac stood, while Daniel d'Arthez represented his
innermost ideal. He realised the duality of his own nature. He knew
that he possessed an inviolable artistic conscience that strove to
give of the best that lay within him, rejecting every compromise
and prepared to stand alone against society. But he also knew the
other side of his character, his love of the fleshpots, his extravagance, his snobbery, his inability to resist his little vanities and the
allurements of the luxurious life. So in order to steel himself and to
bring before his eyes the jeopardy to which an artist is exposed
when he betrays his art for the sake of transient success, he depicted

as a warning to himself a writer who failed to stand firm and,
having once succumbed to temptation, was unable to regain his
footing. Lucien de Rubempré, whose real name is Chardon, but who
like Balzac has adopted a noble title to which he has no right,
arrives in Paris as a young idealist with a volume of poems in his
pocket—the equivalent of Balzac's *Cromwell*—in the expectation
of being able to make his way by force of talent alone. Chance
brings him into the circle of the *Cénacle*, a group of poor young
students living in the attics of the Latin Quarter who, thanks to
their sacrificing devotion to their preconceived mission, represent
the future élite of France. They are the friends of Louis Lambert.
D'Arthez is the writer among them, Bianchon the physician, and
Michel Chrestien the philosopher. They all scorn ephemeral success
for the sake of the future achievement to which they have con-
secrated themselves. Through Daniel d'Arthez, in whose strength of
character and proud patience Balzac portrayed his own better self,
Lucien de Rubempré is introduced into the circle of these sincere
and idealistic young men, but instead of remaining loyal to the
noble intellectual integrity to which they are sworn he gives way
to the temptation of trying to impress the hereditary nobility of the
Faubourg Saint-Germain. He wants swift success, money, admiration, the favours of women, political power, and since poetry cannot be minted so speedily into such valuable coin he sells his pen
to the newspapers. He prostitutes his talent, as Balzac had once
done, turning out hack-work, joining forces with the manufacturers
of literature, helping to form public opinion, becoming a journalistic pimp; and while he does succeed in making a name for himself
as one of the innumerable bubbles in the literary morass of the day,
he is in reality all the time sinking lower and lower. With the cruel
realisation that had come from years of journalistic servitude, and
the deep bitterness of his experiences at the hands of a spiteful
clique fresh in his mind, Balzac unmasked the whole system by
which public opinion was organised, the world of literature and the
theatre with its internal decay, where men hung together yet would
stab one another in the back when opportunity offered. And though
he only intended to present a segment of the Parisian society of his
time, it developed into a complete picture of the age and one that is
valid for all ages. It is a book that is infused with a sense of pride
and indignation, a summons to hold aloof from impatience and

greed, to remain strong and to draw ever greater strength from the renewal of resistance. Always when the clouds were blackest Balzac found his true courage, and when the turmoil of his life was at its height he produced his finest and most personal works.

CHAPTER XV

The Contessa Guidoboni-Visconti

his year of catastrophe, with its lawsuits, distraints, insolvencies, days in gaol, and other hardships, was duly recorded in Balzac's letters to Madame de Hanska with an almost masochistic pleasure and at times passionate rhetoric. One cannot help suspecting that the very detail with which he filled his bulletins as he discoursed, week after week, on his worries and setbacks, his loneliness and his melancholy, was intended as a screen to conceal other facts that he wished to keep from the cognisance of his correspondent in the far-away Ukraine. There is nothing more misleading than Balzac's description of himself as an ascetic living only for his work, who spent his few leisure hours in the collapse of utter exhaustion. His character becomes comprehensible only if we realise that his unfathomable self-confidence rendered him indifferent to what are commonly known as the trials of fate. There was something in him, perhaps the essential part of him, which was unconcerned with the disasters that overtook his outward existence, merely noting the phenomena with tense curiosity, like a man on dry land watching a devastating storm at sea. The fact that the bailiffs had been knocking at his door that morning never prevented him from visiting a jeweller's in the afternoon to purchase on credit some trinket for which he could have no possible use. In this very year of 1836, when the tally of his debts had already mounted to a

hundred and forty thousand francs and he literally had to borrow
the price of his lunch from his tailor or his doctor, he bought
another stick to go with his famous *"canne de Monsieur de Balzac"*,
this time of rhinoceros horn and costing six hundred francs—as
well as a gold penknife for a hundred and ninety francs, a purse for
a hundred and ten, and a chain for four hundred and twenty. All
these were things that a shopkeeper might have expected to sell to
a cocotte who had just wheedled a nabob into unloosening his
purse-strings rather than to a *"forçat de travail"* who was determined to adhere to his ascetic way of life. Some secret counter-
force within him was striving to preserve a constant equilibrium.
The deeper he plunged into debt, the more he tried to maintain the
illusion of luxury by indulgence in expensive and effeminate trifles.
The more hard pressed he was by outward circumstance, the more
buoyant he became. The more firmly he was compelled to keep his
feet on the treadmill, the keener he grew to enjoy what life had to
offer. Unless we understand this antithesis in his character, his
behaviour seems merely foolish. It was, in point of fact, a means by
which his volcanic temperament succeeded in discharging the
pent-up forces that had to find an explosive outlet.

Because 1836 was the year in which he experienced his most
serious crises, it was therefore also a year of scorching sun and
refreshing showers, a special vintage year of luxury and sensuous
satisfaction for Balzac. His astonishing effrontery in conjuring out
of sight facts that he did not want to reveal is seen at its best in
a comparison of the life he was actually leading with the autobiographical details which he communicated to Madame de
Hanska. He told her, for example, that in order to have a safe
refuge from his creditors he had rented a "garret" where he could
pass his solitary days and nights as a weary, grey-haired old hermit, and would not be discovered by his closest friends or even by
his family. It was not a garret that he had rented, but a most
luxurious dwelling which he spared no cost in fitting up. Though he
possessed ample furniture in the rue Cassini for four rooms, he
bought everything afresh from the expensive upholsterer Moreau in
the Boulevard des Capucines. Even Auguste, his servant, was
decked out with a new livery, all in blue except the waistcoat, which
was red, and this alone would have cost him three hundred and
sixty-eight francs if he had paid for it. The crowning achievement

17

in the furnishing of his alleged hermitage was the boudoir, which
would not have been scorned by the Lady of the Camelias. He was
so pleased with this accumulation of valuable upholstery and bric-
à-brac, with its carefully chosen contrasts in sensuous colouring,
that he gave a full description of it in *La fille aux yeux d'or*:

One half of the boudoir formed a gentle, gracious curve, in contrast to the other half which was quite square and had in the
centre a shining marble mantelpiece in white and gold. One
entered through a side door concealed by a portière of rich
tapestry and facing a window. The horseshoe was adorned with a
real Turkish divan, that is to say, a mattress placed on the floor,
but a mattress as wide as a bed, with a perimeter of fifty feet,
in white cashmere set off by rosettes of black and flame-red silk
arranged in diamond patterns. The back of this vast couch was
raised several inches above the numerous cushions which enriched it further by the tasteful manner in which they had been
embellished. The boudoir was hung with a red material upon
which had been laid Indian muslin that was fluted like a Corinth-
ian column with alternate concave and convex strips, ending
above and below in a band of flame-red material with a design of
black arabesques. Behind the muslin the flame-red colour looked
pink, an amorous tint that was repeated in the window curtains,
which were of Indian muslin lined with pink taffeta and orna-
mented with fringes of flame-red mingled with black. Six
brackets of silver-gilt, each holding two candles, were attached
to the hangings at equal intervals to illumine the divan. The
ceiling, from the centre of which hung a chandelier in dull silver-
gilt, was of dazzling white, and the cornice was gilded. The
carpet was like an oriental shawl, with designs reminiscent of
Persian poetry, that had been worked by the hands of slaves.
The furniture was upholstered in white cashmere, set off by
black and flame-red ornamentation. The clock, the candelabra,
all were of white and gold marble. The only table in the room
was covered with a cashmere cloth. Elegant flower-stands were
filled with roses of all kinds, blooms of white or red.

Unlike Richard Wagner, who had a similar taste for voluptuous
silk and cashmere furnishings, Balzac did not need them as a means
of providing the right atmosphere for artistic inspiration, which he
could find anywhere. The purpose he had in view was of a more
tangible nature. When he showed his *"fameux canapé blanc"* to his
friend Fontaney, he forgot for a moment his usual discretion and

admitted with a laugh: "I had it made when I was on the point of
having a lady in high society. You see, she needed a handsome piece
of furniture, because that was what she was accustomed to. When
she found herself on the divan she wasn't at all displeased."

Even if Fontanney had not carefully noted this remark in his
diary, we could have inferred the purpose to which he intended to
put his new apartment from the way in which it was fitted up.
Whenever Balzac began to equip himself afresh it was a sign that he
had fallen in love again. Whenever he furnished a new apartment
it was because he was preparing to receive a mistress. His emotions,
like his worries, could be gauged by the size of his bills. When he
was wooing Madame de Castries he had acquired a carriage and
groom, and it was for her that he had bought his first sofa. The
bedroom in the rue des Marais had been adorned for Madame de
Berny. In order to visit Madame de Hanska in Vienna he had
hired a special equipage. In this year of contrasting fortunes, when
he was still swearing eternal fidelity to his "*épouse d'amour*" in
Wierzchownia and describing to her in letter after letter the torments of his life of chastity, he had fallen in love more violently
than ever. His love-letters to Madame de Hanska, which so deeply
stirred a whole generation with their touching and ardent eloquence, were written in the intervals between his hours of dalliance
with another woman.

Balzac's new mistress, who played an important part in his life
that he took great pains to conceal, had made his acquaintance
indirectly through Madame de Hanska herself. Before his departure
from Geneva she had given him an introduction to Countess
Apponyi, the wife of the Austrian Ambassador in Paris, and he lost
no time in calling at the embassy. At a big reception there one
evening in 1835 his interest was attracted by a tall, blonde, buxom
woman about thirty years of age and of striking beauty. She
appeared completely at ease as she moved through the throng with
a sensuous air and accepted the admiration and flattering compli-
ments of the male guests. Balzac's emotions were affected less by a
handsome face and figure than by the aristocratic name attached
to them, and when he learned that she was the Contessa Guidoboni-

Visconti this was sufficient to kindle his ardour. The Viscontis were Dukes of Milan, while the Guidobonis were one of the first noble families of Italy. Urged by an instinct he could not repress and forgetting his vows of undying loyalty to the distant châtelaine of Wierzchownia, who was then in Vienna, Balzac took steps to be presented to the beautiful Contessa.

The lovely stranger had not been born a countess nor, as a matter of fact, was she Italian. Her original name had been Sarah Lowell and she had been born near London, the offspring of an eccentric English family in which suicides and explosive outbursts of passion were of epidemic occurrence. Her mother, equally celebrated for her beauty, put an end to her life when she felt that she was beginning to age, and one of her brothers did the same. Another brother came to grief through drink, while her younger sister suffered from religious mania. As the only normal member of this highly-strung family the Contessa confined her passions to the erotic sphere, and with typical English calm she appears to have yielded to any adventure by which she was tempted without inhibitions, but also without any particular demonstration of excitement. The fact that she possessed a husband in the person of Count Emilio Guidoboni-Visconti was not a matter to cause any disturbance of her peace of mind on these occasions, nor was she troubled by exhibitions of jealousy on his part. He was a quiet, modest man, whom she must have picked up and married on one of her trips through Europe.

Emilio Guidoboni-Visconti was not without his own passionate interests in life, though they had no connection with those of his wife. His real love was for music, and he was a character worthy of being immortalised in a story by Hoffmann. Though he was a descendant of the great *condottieri*, his greatest pleasure was to sit in a theatre orchestra among the professional musicians and play the violin. At Versailles, where he had a house in the Avenue de Neuilly in addition to his palaces in Paris and Vienna, he would slink out every evening and take his place in the orchestra pit, and wherever he went he humbly requested the favour of being allowed to scrape away at the local theatre. In the daytime he amused himself by playing at being a chemist. He would mix all sorts of ingredients, pour the result into bottles, and attach neat labels. Society bored him. He liked to keep in the background, so he was no bother at all to his wife's lovers. He was affable to every one of them, since they enabled him to devote his energies all the more uninterruptedly to his beloved music.

Balzac was lucky. After Monsieur de Berny and Monsieur de Hanski he had now found a third husband who, partly from a sense of chivalry and partly from indifference, raised no objection to his wife receiving the flattering attentions of a famous author. He set out with his usual impetuosity to attain his goal, spending all his leisure hours with the Guidoboni-Viscontis, driving out to Versailles, sharing their box at the Italiens, until in April we find him reporting, not of course to Madame de Hanska but to Zulma Carraud: "For some days I have been under the spell of a very encroaching personality and I do not know how to escape from it, for I am helpless to resist anything that pleases me."

The Contessa, for her part, was hesitant about accepting the "encroachments" of Balzac. She had just dismissed her latest lover, Prince Koslowski, through whose instrumentality she had been able to present her music-loving husband with a son, but she could not make up her mind whether Count Lionel de Bonval, one of the great lions of Parisian society, or Balzac was to be his immediate successor. So far as Balzac was concerned, he had his other iron to keep hot. Madame de Hanska in Vienna was being kept informed of his sudden partiality for music by her compatriots in the French capital, and she was aware that at the opera he had exchanged the innocuous box of Olympe Pélissier, mistress of Rossini, for that of the Viscontis. Since she had cast herself for the principal feminine rôle in Balzac's life, she reproached him for his unfaithfulness and insincerity. It seems that in the pact they had made together she had laid down that any recreation he might need was to be sought only among "*les filles*", where there would be no question of spiritual relationship and she would therefore have no cause for pangs of jealousy. She knew him well enough to be certain that a Contessa Guidoboni-Visconti would be the recipient of similar letters to those he was writing to her, and she intended to assert her monopoly. Finally Balzac had no alternative, since he did not want to relinquish his bird in the hand, but to set off for Vienna on that expensive and fantastic journey in order to assure her once more that she alone occupied a niche in his heart. After that he went to Saché to work off his arrears, and in August, 1835, he again entered the lists to compete with Lionel de Bonval for the favours of the beautiful Contessa. Victory fell to his arms, and he became her lover. If that suspiciously well-informed book by an anonymous writer, *Balzac mis à nu*, is to be believed, he was also in all probability the father of Lionel Richard Guidoboni-Visconti, born on the 29th of May, 1836—one of his three illegitimate children, who inherited neither the name nor the genius of their sire.

Although she was his mistress and indefatigable friend and helper for five years, the Contessa Guidoboni-Visconti has not received her due meed of attention from any of Balzac's biographers. She herself was responsible for this neglect, since it is frequently not a person's achievements and influence but his or her capacity for self-advertisement which is the decisive factor in the acquirement of fame. She never sought posthumous literary celebrity, and her figure has therefore been completely overshadowed by that of the incomparably more vain, ambitious, and assiduous Madame de Hanska, who had made up her mind as to the position she intended to occupy almost from the outset. Balzac would not have been true to himself if he had not written passionate letters to the Contessa as well, but she neither numbered them nor preserved them in a special casket for future publication. Either from pure unconcern or from a sovereign pride which made her regard with distaste the prospect of having her name bandied about after they were both dead and gone, she made no attempt to assist future literary historians to enshrine her in their pages, but she devoted herself all the more wholeheartedly and frankly to Balzac's well-being while he was alive. That was why her relations with him were free from the painful sense of strain which is so noticeable on closer examination in the case of Madame de Hanska. Even during the period of their alleged great passion the latter was constantly concerned for her position in society and the place that would be allotted to her in literary history. For twenty years she was continually plagued by apprehension lest she should be compromised by her relations with Balzac. She wanted to retain her place of honour in his career without herself communicating any real warmth. She was prepared neither to renounce her husband and his millions nor to risk a single jot or tittle of her immaculate reputation, and even when at last she was free she was reluctant to take the plunge into marriage with a man who was her social inferior. The cautious calculation and petty-mindedness of her attitude are unmistakable, and even her single surrender at Geneva gives the impression of having been a hesitant succumbing to curiosity which was swiftly repented rather than a deliberate and unselfish yielding of herself to the man she loved.

Compared with this exhibition of insincerity, jealous nagging, and cool scheming, the seemingly immoral Contessa appears as the acme of generosity and a woman of sterling, independent character. Once she had decided to give herself to Balzac, she did so without reserve, as we can see from her portrait in *Le lys dans la vallée*, and it was a matter of complete indifference to her whether the whole of Paris knew about it or not. She appeared with him in her box at the opera, took him into her house when he was seeking refuge from his creditors, and when he built himself a home in the country she occupied the cottage next door.

She made no pretence to her husband of being a faithful wife, and just as she would have tolerated no jealousy on his part, so she in turn did not torment Balzac with narrow-minded jealousies and petty spying. She left him his liberty and laughed at his adventures with other women. Since she told him no lies herself, she did not compel him to lie to her, as he so constantly had to do when writing to Wierzchownia. Though not a tenth part as rich as the de Hanskis, she helped him a dozen times over his financial difficulties in one way or another. As a true friend she always displayed, in her relations with him, the intrepid candour and freedom which were only possible in a woman who refused to submit to the strict conventions of the social or moral order and obeyed only the dictates of her own will.

Such a disregard of public opinion made it impossible, of course, for Balzac to conceal his relations with the Contessa from Madame de Hanska. Even if he had been successful in denying that the passionate love-scenes of Lady Dudley in *Le lys dans la vallée* had been written under the immediate inspiration of his first ecstatic trysts with the Contessa, he could not prevent her Russian and Polish friends in Paris from reporting the known facts of the situation, with such embroidery as might occur to their fertile imaginations. From the distant Ukraine came a shower of *"lettres pleines de doutes et reproches"*, but Balzac stuck to his guns and insisted that it was only a platonic friendship. In order to fortify Madame de Hanska's belief in his honesty, he artfully sang the praises of this *"amitié qui me console de bien des chagrins"* and assured her:

> Madame de Visconti, of whom you speak, is one of the most amiable of women, and of an infinite and exquisite kindness. She has a delicate, elegant beauty, and helps me to bear my existence. She is gentle yet steadfast, unshakable and implacable in her ideas and her dislikes. She has a self-reliant manner. She is not well-off, or rather her fortune and that of the Count are not in accord with their resplendent name. . . .

He concluded this eulogy, however, with the melancholy sigh: "Unfortunately, I see her only very rarely."

Perhaps he did not, at the bottom of his heart, care very much if she disbelieved him, for the brilliance of his "polar star" was beginning to pale now that it had receded so far away and Monsieur de Hanski's health, moreover, was proving so much more robust than had been expected. The Contessa was near at hand, young, handsome, and sensual. He could see her whenever he wished, and she never disturbed his peace of mind. So during the next few years he shared his life with her, while at the same time providing Madame de Hanska with imaginary biographical details for preservation in her casket and the ultimate delectation of posterity.

It was Madame de Hanska's ambition to be Balzac's guide and adviser as the woman who possessed a deeper understanding of him than anyone else, and her literary judgment was no doubt far superior to that of the Contessa. But the Contessa had a better understanding of his human needs. She realised how tired and harassed he was, and that it was essential for him to have some form of diversion, so in her warm sympathy she arranged for him the one thing that could refresh his creative powers, namely a visit to Italy. This was what he had longed for ever since the sudden interruption of the journey he had commenced in the company of Madame de Castries, and the Contessa managed matters so that it would not cost him anything.

Count Guidoboni-Visconti had inherited from his mother a sum
of money which he had difficulty in collecting, and since he
possessed no aptitude for dealing with affairs of business he had
practically given up hope of recovering the amounts due to him.
The Contessa now suggested that Balzac, their mutual friend, of
whose energy and business instinct he was well aware, should be
authorised to go to Italy as his agent. To this the good-natured
Count agreed, a power of attorney was drawn up by his notary,
and in July Balzac, no doubt with his travelling expenses in his
pocket, set off in a post-chaise on his long-dreamed-of journey to
the *"pays de l'amour"*.

This was not the only way in which the Contessa displayed her
generous heart. It is understandable that she did not accompany
Balzac on his trip to the south, for it was little more than a month
since she had given birth to the son who was in all probability the
pledge of their love, but it is rather surprising that she raised no
objection to his being accompanied by a good-looking youth with
short, black hair whose name was Marcel and who was completely
unknown to Balzac's other friends. The only one who might have
been able to give any information about this youth was the tailor
Buisson, to whom a few days previously Balzac had brought a
dark young woman with the request that he should fit her out with
a gentleman's costume and a grey frock-coat. The new clothes
fitted the young lady admirably, though not so admirably that a
keen eye would not be able to discover the curved outlines of the
weaker sex. Instead of seeking adventures in the *"pays de l'amour"*
Balzac was taking his adventure with him.

As in the case of nearly all his women friends, he owed his first
meeting with this new mistress to his correspondence with his
reading public. Again like most of his women friends, she was
married and had a complaisant husband. Madame Caroline Marbouty found things boring in Limoges as the wife of a high official
at the Court of Justice, and like all the other disappointed wives in
France she wrote to Balzac. This was in 1833, when the advocate
of the rights of misunderstood women was too busy to answer. She
therefore looked round for a substitute elsewhere, and gazing down
the alphabetical list of authors, where *Ba* was followed by *Be*, she
hit upon Sainte-Beuve—as also, strange to say, did Madame de
Castries. Sainte-Beuve was more forthcoming. He invited her to

come to Paris, and she accepted his invitation. The dry and pompous Sainte-Beuve, however, did not appeal to this fiery young woman, in spite of the fact that he addressed a stirring sonnet to her charms, and she preferred to try her luck again with Balzac. Since his success with Madame de Hanska, Balzac had begun to appreciate women who were younger than himself, and he did not, like Joseph, reject the advances of this insistent Potiphar's wife. The initial interview was extended to three nights in the boudoir of the rue des Batailles, and she accorded so well with his taste and appetite that he proposed a joint trip to Touraine. Madame Marbouty was unable to comply with this suggestion for a variety of reasons, but after his return from Saché he renewed his invitation, this time for a journey to Italy at his other lady friend's expense. She agreed enthusiastically to accompany him in the disguise of a page, for a journey to the land of romance had itself to be invested with a romantic thrill.

One of Balzac's friends in Paris happened by chance to witness this comedy of disguise. Jules Sandeau, who had come to the rue Cassini to see him off, suddenly saw a young lady with cropped hair drive up in a cab and, showing an evident familiarity with the topography of the place, hurriedly mount the stairs that led to Balzac's bedroom. He was still smiling to himself at his friend's new acquisition when, a few minutes later, an elegant young man emerged from the bedroom wearing a grey frock-coat and carrying a riding-whip and a small trunk. The trunk, which contained sufficient linen for a week and a supply of feminine clothing in case of emergency, was taken down the self-same staircase and stowed in the waiting post-chaise. Behind the young man came Balzac, who took the seat beside him with a look of naive happiness at the success of his prank, and a minute later the coach rolled away in the direction of Italy.

It was a delightful start, and in accordance with Balzac's expectations the most amusing episodes occurred during the journey. The monks of the Grande Chartreuse were not deceived by the well-filled frock-coat and taut breeches of the young Marcel, and refused admission to their monastery. The nymph avenged herself by taking a bath in a nearby stream. The author of the *Contes drolatiques* found ample occasion for mirth, and after a swift, perilous drive across Mont Cenis the two of them arrived safely at Turin.

Here, one would have thought, the time had come to end the masquerade, or at the very least it was to be expected that they would have put up at a small inn off the beaten track where there was less chance of attracting attention. But Balzac liked to carry everything to extremes, and he drove up to the principal hotel in the city, the Hôtel de l'Europe, facing the royal palace, where he ordered two adjoining rooms for himself and his companion. Of course the *Gazetta Piemontese* announced the famous author's arrival on the following day, and the whole of Turin society was agog to see Balzac and his celebrated stick, which was acquiring a European celebrity equal to that of his novels. The most distinguished families sent their footmen to leave invitations, everybody wanted to meet him, and some friendly noblemen even arranged for him to have the use of horses from the royal mews.

Balzac accepted the invitations of the Piedmontese aristocracy with alacrity, but the devil of mischief persuaded him to take his companion with him, still in her masculine disguise. This led to fresh complications, for it was soon bruited abroad that young Marcel, like his namesake in Meyerbeer's opera *The Huguenots*, was really a woman, and since no one conceived it possible that Balzac could have the colossal impertinence to introduce some unknown bedmate into the salons of the Piedmontese nobility it was not long before a curious rumour went the rounds. It was known that his famous colleague George Sand wore her hair short, smoked cigars, preferred trousers to a skirt, and changed her lovers more frequently than her handkerchiefs. She had recently been to Italy with Alfred de Musset, so it was quite possible that she was repeating the journey with Honoré de Balzac. So poor Madame Marbouty suddenly found herself surrounded on all sides by a throng of ladies and gentlemen who were anxious to discuss literature with her, to listen to her witty sayings, and if possible obtain an autograph of George Sand.

The situation was growing too embarrassing even for a jester of Balzac's calibre, and he needed all his presence of mind to extricate himself from the tangle in which he had become involved. He confided to the Marquis Félix de St. Thomas the truth about the masquerade, but took care to give it a moral twist in palliation of his conduct: "She entrusted herself to me because she knows I am possessed body and soul by such an absorbing passion that I hardly know other women exist in the world." In any case, he realised that the time had come to put an end to his little joke before it flared up into a scandal. After settling the business affairs of his friends the Viscontis with a fair amount of success, he left Turin in some haste and set off on the return journey to Paris.

The last place where they stopped for more than one night was Geneva, the city which had already been the scene of two decisive episodes in his life. It was here that he had received his final rebuff from Madame de Castries and overcome the last, lingering reluctance of Madame de Hanska. Now he had returned in the company of Madame Marbouty. If we were to believe his letters to Madame de Hanska, he did nothing in Geneva except indulge in sweet memories of the past and think with tears in his eyes of her who was now so far away. The truth was less romantic, but much more amusing. In contrast to the impatience with which he normally used to urge the postillions to whip up their horses so that he might arrive the sooner at his destination, this time he spent ten days on the journey from Geneva to Paris, putting up in a different town each night. There is no reason to assume that these nights were devoted exclusively to sentimental and melancholy brooding on the distance which separated him from his inaccessible polar star.

⊰⊱

On the 21st of August he was back in Paris and the weeks of enchantment were over. On the door of his apartment were pasted the notices left by the bailiffs and his table was piled high with unpaid bills. Before he had been in the house an hour he learned that his publisher, Werdet, was on the verge of bankruptcy. In all this he found no cause either for surprise or perturbation. He knew from grim experience that every breath of freedom which he allowed himself only strengthened the stranglehold of fate. Among the heap of letters, however, was one with a black border. Alexandre de Berny wrote to say that his mother had died on the 27th of July. We know from Balzac's own letters how deeply he was shaken by this news. For many months he had been prepared to hear that the end had come, and shortly before his departure for Italy he had visited her for the last time, but found her too weak to take pleasure in the way he had expressed his gratitude to her by portraying the figure of Madame de Mortsauf in *Le lys dans la vallée*. Yet he must have been overwhelmed by a feeling of shame and grief that he had been gallivanting in Italy with the insignificant Caroline Marbouty while she lay on her deathbed. Perhaps he had been laughing and jesting in the salons of Turin while she, who had been the first to offer him her love, a love more sincere than that of any other woman in his life, was being lowered into the tomb. During the next day or two he left Paris and went to see her grave. Some deep instinct told him that an epoch of his life had closed and that in the grave of Laure de Berny he had buried his own youth.

CHAPTER XVI

The Second Italian Journey

he death of Madame de Berny was a turning-point in Balzac's life. She was no longer there to protect and encourage him, and in spite of his mistress in the Ukraine and his mistress in Paris, he felt more alone than ever. A new sensation began to take hold of him, one that had hitherto been foreign to his self-reliant and optimistic nature, an unfathomable apprehension of what the future might bring; apprehension lest his strength might not last out until he had completed the vast work he had undertaken, lest he might fail too soon, and lest in the meantime he should let the reality of life slip by. He asked himself what he had made out of his life and what he was yet to make out of it. He looked into the mirror and saw grey hairs, a whole streak of grey hair in his thinning mane, the result of his harassed struggle to cope with his arrears of work and the daily worries by which he was beset. His puffy cheeks and sallow complexion, his double chin and flabby body, these were due to endless nights of writing behind curtained windows, to weeks and months without fresh air or exercise. This was the way he had lived for seventeen years, day after day, week after week, month after month, covering hundreds of thousands of sheets of paper, correcting hundreds of thousands of galley proofs, turning out book after book. And what had he achieved? Very little. Or at least, very little for him. The *Comédie humaine* was planned on a scale as vast and spacious as a French cathedral, yet he had erected no more than a few pillars. He had not even begun to set the overarching roof or the towers that were to reach up to the sky. Would he ever be able to finish it? Would the years during which he had abused and exhausted his strength exact their penalty? There had already been warning indications that the machine was beginning to run down: sudden attacks of vertigo, fits of tiredness followed by a death-like sleep, and stomach cramps due to over-indulgence in strong black coffee. Was it not time to call a halt, to rest and enjoy life instead of obeying the inexorable dictate to "*créer, toujours créer*"? Who had thanked him for his frantic self-sacrifice, his fanatical renunciation, except the woman who now lay in her grave? What had his work brought him? A certain fame, in fact, very considerable fame, but also hatred, spite, and grievous experiences. The one thing it had not brought him was the most important of all, the one he longed for most, his freedom. Seven years ago he had started afresh with a load of debt amounting to a hundred thousand francs, and he had worked like ten men. Yet thirty novels had not sufficed to clear the slate. His debts had almost doubled, though he had written thirty novels which had been translated into every language in Europe and touched the hearts of hundreds of thousands of readers. He was still tied to the will of publishers and editors, still compelled to climb up five flights of stairs to visit the dens of sordid money-lenders, still forced to tremble like a thief at the thought of the bailiffs who came to execute the sentence of the law. What was the point of working himself to death if it did not enable him to secure his independence? At the age of thirty-seven he realised that he had arranged his life on a false plan, since he had sacrificed it to a task which had disappointed and betrayed his most earnest hopes.

An inner voice now exhorted him to live differently. It urged him to be content no longer merely with accepting the sentimental admiration of women from afar, but to seek the enjoyment of their soft, sensuous bodies; to quit his writing-table and travel, refreshing his eye with new scenes and intoxicating his weary spirit with stimulating pleasures; to break his chains and cast them behind him, breathing the relaxing air of idleness after his feverish striving towards a pre-established goal. He was growing prematurely old, every day brought its further quota of vexations, and he wanted to escape. So at the age of thirty-seven Balzac was seized by a far wilder and more presumptuous craving for life than he had been ten or even twenty years before. His success with Madame de Hanska seems to have awakened the erotic side of him, for amorous adventures followed swiftly upon one another's heels and he gained the favours of more women in a single year than he had previously done in a decade. Apart from the Contessa and Caroline Marbouty there was a young aristocrat from Brittany, Hélène de Valette, and an unknown "Louise" after whom he angled in his usual way by entering into correspondence with her. He also became an habitué at certain sumptuous supper-parties at which the most distinguished of the Paris cocottes, models for his Torpille and Aquilina, demonstrated their arts and gave freely of their charms. Now that the first warning shadow of a cold hand had lightly touched his heart, it was no longer work and the desire for fame that absorbed his being. The longing for freedom, the appetite for enjoyment, the impulse to take life easily burst forth from him in full measure.

It is to the lasting credit of the Contessa that she appreciated Balzac's need and did not seek to keep her lover chained to her side. For a second time she made it possible for him to undertake a journey to Italy, and on the same pretext as before. The bailiffs had grown tired of trying to track him down in the rue Cassini and they succeeded at last in discovering his secret apartment in the rue des Batailles, so he was forced to take refuge in a residential hotel in the rue de Provence. Even there, however, he was not safe, and the Contessa could see how weary he was of the never-ending struggle. She neither plagued him with jealousy nor irritated him with censure. He was incorrigible and she gave him something more valuable than good advice, namely the chance to spend two or three months free from worry. Once more the Count was persuaded to engage Balzac as his business agent, and on the 12th of February, 1837, he crossed the Alps, this time alone, for he had long since become bored with the rather importunate Madame Marbouty. Théophile Gautier, who was to have accompanied him, had to change his plans at the last moment.

His journey through Ticino and the loveliest scenery in Europe dissipated his cares, and they vanished into the blue sky. Balzac had a genius for receiving and retaining impressions, but he also had a genius for forgetting. All his worries had slipped from his shoulders by the time he alighted at the Hotel della Bella Venezia in Milan, for he had become another person. He was no longer that Monsieur Honoré de Balzac whom the French courts had condemned to pay so many thousands of francs here and so many thousands of francs there, but the celebrated author whose arrival was respectfully reported in the newspapers and whom two hours later the whole city was agog to see. The Countess Maffei took him driving in her carriage, he attended the Scala Opera in the box of Prince Portia and his sister the Countess Sanseverino, he received invitations from the Princess Belgiojoso and the Marquise Trivulsio; in fact, all the bearers of the most resounding names in Italian history paid homage to the name of Balzac. The officers of the Austrian army spoilt him no less. The Governor asked him to dinner, the General in command of the troops offered his services, and the foremost sculptor in Milan, Puttinati, requested the honour of being allowed to make a statuette of him, which Balzac then presented not to Madame de Hanska but to the Contessa Guidoboni-Visconti. The young Prince Portia showered him with gifts and hastened to anticipate every wish. Balzac's pride and happiness can be imagined at being asked to write his signature in the albums of princes and princesses instead of, as in Paris, under I.O.Us.

His reception by the Italian writers was somewhat cooler, since they felt a little slighted by the exaggerated attention paid to a foreigner, and Balzac was too absorbed in his new-found aristocratic acquaintances to have much time left for his professional colleagues. A meeting with Manzoni was not very fruitful. Balzac had not read the *Promessi Sposi*, so he talked only about himself.

Preoccupied though he was with sightseeing and festivities, he did not forget the mission which had brought him to Italy, and as he was an excellent business man so long as it was not his own affairs with which he was concerned, he succeeded in settling the outstanding questions connected with Count Visconti's legacy. Everything seemed to be going so well for him this time that at the conclusion of the transactions he even found a visit to Venice on

18

his programme, the city he had wanted to see first in the company
of Madame de Castries and then with Madame de Hanska, and
which provided the setting for his *Facino Cane*.

His first day there was disappointing. Rain, snow, and mist
took all the colour out of Venice. But the first day on which the sun
shone stirred his excited appreciation of its beauty. He went everywhere and saw everything: the museums, the churches, the palaces
and the theatres. In a few fleeting days he absorbed its atmosphere,
its history, its way of living, the very soul of the city. Though he
was there only nine days in all, half of which were spent on business
matters and in paying visits, none of the innumerable novelists or
travellers who have given descriptions of Venice—neither Byron,
nor Goethe, nor Stendhal, nor d'Annunzio—has pictured it with
such illuminating insight as Balzac has done in his short story
Massimilla Doni, which includes one of the most perfect pieces of
musical interpretation in the whole of literature. It is almost incon-
ceivable how in such a short space of time, and knowing no more
than a few scraps of the language, his eye could have seized the
essentials so unerringly as to enable him to sublimate and personify
in such a masterly way the noble, sensuous spirit of Italy. Again
and again we are made to realise that to Balzac seeing a thing meant
piercing to the heart of it, appreciating the substance in a flash,
by a kind of magical process.

These nine days in Venice were the climax of his Italian journey.
When he returned to Milan he was not received so warmly as on his
previous visit. With his usual light-hearted loquacity he had been
tempted by his good spirits and innocent trust in his hearers to talk
a little too freely in public about his debts and the money he was
able to make by his writing. This was a bad habit of his which had
irritated his friends in Vienna and now proved equally distasteful
to the Venetians, but even more painful to them was the fact that
he spoke rather condescendingly of Lamartine and Manzoni.
Unfortunately for Balzac there happened to be present some minor
writers suffering from a feeling of exasperation, and one of them
found nothing better to do than to send a report of his disparaging
comments on Manzoni to a Milan newspaper, where this ill repayment of the hospitality he had received roused considerable wrath.
Balzac did well not to prolong his second stay in Milan, but this
first misfortune was soon followed by another. At Genoa, where he

went with a view to travelling through the Riviera and on to Nice, he was held back in quarantine on account of a threatening epidemic. This was apparently only a petty inconvenience, but it gave rise later on to a far greater vexation. For some reason which we do not know he changed his plans and, instead of continuing his journey to Paris, travelled back to Leghorn and Florence. It was not until the 3rd of May, after an absence of nearly three months, that he saw Paris again. For the first time since he launched out on a career of authorship he had not written a single line or corrected a single proof for a period of nearly three months. He had only lived, learned, and enjoyed himself.

◆◼◦◼◆

His mood can have been none too cheerful as the stage-coach approached the outskirts of Paris, for he was aware of what awaited him after these blissful months of *dolce far niente*. It was not only that a pile of unpaid accounts would be lying on his table, that his tilbury and other accessible possessions had been seized in distraint, that the editors were still expecting delivery of *La maison Nucingen* and *La femme supérieure*, for which payment had been made in advance, or that the fifty thousand francs agreed upon by his new publisher, Bohain, before he set out on his journey had already gone up in smoke. Things were far worse. When Werdet went bankrupt the bills of exchange which Balzac had drawn so liberally were repudiated and his creditors had obtained a warrant for his arrest. If he were caught he would be flung into a debtors' prison.

His first concern, therefore, was to avoid being caught. He now had three apartments—in the rue Cassini, which was still rented in his own name and from which he had succeeded in rescuing his furniture, in the rue des Batailles, allegedly occupied by the "Veuve Durand" or a mythical "Dr. Méget", and his lodging in the rue de Provence. But his creditors had seen through all his dodges and neither secret pass-words nor false reports were of any further avail. Despite his multiplicity of abodes he no longer had a safe roof over his head, and he would willingly have exchanged the celebrity he had so enjoyed in Italy for an oblivion that would secure him from those who were on his track. There was danger even in staying with the Carrauds at Frapesle, where a room was always held at his disposal, since his arrival would be bruited abroad before he had alighted from the coach.

In his dilemma he turned to the young Comte de Belloy, who had been his secretary on the editorial staff of the *Chronique de Paris*, and begged him for "a room, complete secrecy, bread and water, together with a salad, a pound of mutton, a bottle of ink and a bed." He no longer craved silken hangings, damask sofas, or gold pen-knives, but only a table to write on and a bed in which to sleep. The hands of the clock had been turned back seventeen years, to the days when he was living in his old garret in the rue Lesdiguières.

For some reason or other de Belloy was unable to offer him the shelter for which he asked, and once more it was the Contessa Guidoboni-Visconti who came to his rescue. Caring nothing for the gossip of friends and acquaintances, she took her lover into her own house in the Avenue des Champs Elysées, where he was enjoined to remain in the strictest seclusion. He was not allowed to venture into the street or to show himself to visitors, and the only glimpse permitted him of the advent of spring in Paris was from a place of concealment behind the window-curtains. Monastic retirement had no terrors for Balzac, however, especially when nothing but a door separated him from the bed-chamber of his voluptuous mistress. He settled down enthusiastically to his arrears of work, and in the short space of two months completed *La maison Nucingen* and *La femme supérieure*, wrote the final episodes of the *Contes drolatiques*, and sketched out the short story *Gambara*.

He would probably have continued to work on here in the best of spirits if one day the *huissiers* had not knocked on the door even of this sacred retreat. As always, it was a Delilah who betrayed the whereabouts of Samson. One of the Contessa's rivals, possibly Caroline Marbouty, whom Balzac had not invited to accompany him on his second Italian journey, had revealed his place of refuge to the police, and now the servants of the law were standing in the Contessa's salon and presenting him with the grim alternatives of either settling his debts on the spot or accompanying them to a debtors' gaol. Once more the Contessa's generosity stood the test, and though she was by no means a wealthy woman she paid the *huissiers* what they demanded and they took their departure.

To Balzac's annoyance it soon became common property that the Contessa had purchased her lover's freedom. From the *Gazette des Tribunaux* the awkward facts trickled into the newspapers, and Balzac, who was still playing the senseless game of pretending to the distant Madame de Hanska that he was leading an unhappy, solitary existence, had to write to her and provide an explanation:

> These fellows, whose task it is to seek out debtors and fling them into prison, managed to find me thanks to an act of treachery, and to my grief I found myself in the position of having compromised the people who had so generously offered me refuge. In order to avoid going to gaol I had to find without delay the money I owed to Werdet, and in consequence I have been placed under an obligation to my friends who lent it to me.

He carefully omitted to reveal to his jealous correspondent the name of the lady who had been his salvation. In the relations between the Contessa and Balzac it was always she alone who gave proof of courage and magnanimity.

Whenever Balzac reached the end of his resources and did not know which way to turn, it was invariably a woman who came to his help. He was now relieved, at least, of his most pressing difficulties, his *dettes criardes*, and could emerge from his hiding-place with head erect. His room at the Margonnes in his beloved Touraine was waiting for him, and he could work there with the assurance that no one would attempt to trespass on his privacy and that his board and lodging would cost him nothing. Once again his reply to the vexations which life held for him was a literary masterpiece. In the great bourgeois epic of *César Birotteau* he related the story of a man who had fallen into debt from a simple credulity of mind which caused him to become involved in disastrous speculations. Every tormenting and humiliating experience that Balzac had himself suffered during the past months and years was reproduced in this picture of a world which no French writer had ever before explored. The desperate attempts to borrow money, the unreliability of friends, the inexorable demands of creditors, the diabolical retribution exacted from the financial dabbler who does not devote himself body and soul to the acquirement of wealth, the machinations of lawyers and the artifices of the law—all these concomitants

of a petty bankruptcy constitute a tragedy, the tragedy of a man
in modest circumstances, which provides a fitting counterpart to
the great and often grandiose novels of the *Comédie humaine*. Once
more Balzac had succeeded by a process of artistic sublimation in
mastering the anxieties by which his spirit was harassed.

In the autumn he returned to Paris refreshed in mind and body.

CHAPTER XVII

The Sardinian Silver Mines

 and 1837 were years of strain for Balzac, when one disaster followed swiftly upon the heels of another. By normal hazards, if anything in Balzac's life could be judged by normal standards, the year 1838 should have brought the ultimate turning-point. In the previous summer the Contessa had settled the most pressing of his debts and *César Birotteau* had earned him a fee larger than any he had yet received. Twenty thousand francs in cash for the serial rights alone was an enormous sum at a time when money was worth far more than it is to-day and income-tax was unknown. His writings were in such great demand that with his incomparable capacity for work and inexhaustible supply of raw material he could easily have made sixty to a hundred thousand francs a year. While maintaining a comfortable standard of living, and without exerting himself unduly, he could have worked off his debts in two years. Now that his novels were growing more and more lucrative every year, with the great collected edition in active preparation and his literary fame firmly rooted throughout the Continent, circumstances had never been more favourable for placing his chaotic fortunes upon an ordered basis. His life, however, seemed to be governed by some guiding principle. Whenever the skies began to turn blue an apparently sheer wantonness, which nevertheless sprang from the deepest motive forces of his nature, summoned up

fresh storm-clouds. When his barque was already in sight of port he always reversed the helm and drove back into the teeth of the gale. In the year 1838, when his affairs were beginning to straighten out, he once more reduced order to chaos by two extravagantly foolish ideas.

It was typical of all Balzac's follies that at the start they were perfectly sensible. His speculations were founded on sound observation and were the result of correct and precise calculations. His printing-works and type-foundry, as his successors sufficiently proved, were undertakings capable of producing a profit. The *Chronique de Paris*, with its brilliant editorial staff, could have become the leading journal in France. The factor that spoilt his business enterprises, and sometimes his novels, was the passionate impatience which led him to begin on the largest possible scale and prevented him from maintaining the just and sober proportions that would have resulted from mature deliberation. The grandiose heightening which was a primordial feature of his genius as a novelist had fateful effects when it was exercised in a sphere which demands the exact weighing-up even of trivial items.

The first of Balzac's new projects sprang from the logical desire of the artist to provide himself with a place where he could work in peace. For years he had been tantalised by the dream by which all creative minds are lured, that of a secluded cottage somewhere amid green fields where intruders cannot disturb their tranquil absorption in the things of the spirit, a Villa Délices like that of Voltaire, a Montmorency like that of Jean-Jacques Rousseau, or a Vaucluse like that of Petrarch. Paris had been a wonderful background during his years of development, so long as he could live there in obscurity and observe its activity while himself remaining unobserved. Now that he had himself become the object of other people's curiosity, when every detail of his private life was retailed to the newspapers, while journalists and creditors were tearing his front-door bell from one another's hands, he felt the restriction on his personal freedom and the injury that was being done to his capacity for artistic concentration. So why should he continue to live in Paris? The time had long since passed when he had to beard editors and publishers in their own offices. The Kings of France were able to govern their realm from Blois or Versailles, so why should not Balzac rule the press and the public from some idyllic spot off the main track, chosen by himself? He was, in any case, tired of spending the summer with the Margonnes or the Carrauds or other hospitable friends. At the age of thirty-eight Balzac wanted to have his own modest little house, such as any peasant or small *rentier* could enjoy. Years before he had cherished the intention of acquiring a cottage called *La Grenadière* in Touraine, where he could work without having to give up his apartment in Paris, but he had never been able to find the necessary funds. Now he decided to be more economical—his most foolhardy ventures always began with attempts to reduce his budget—and he abandoned the thought of having two places of residence. Why keep on an apartment in Paris when he had a house in the country? Would it not be better and cheaper to look for a cottage in some rural beauty-spot in the environs of the capital, where he could live permanently free from the exhausting claims that the metropolis made upon his energies, yet near enough to journey in at any time either for business or for pleasure?

He had not to seek very far before he found the right spot. A man of his amazing memory had no difficulty in recalling throughout his life every hill and every house on which his eye had rested with interest but for a single moment. During his innumerable journeys to Versailles, first to visit the Duchesse d'Abrantès and later the Contessa, the valley of Sèvres and Ville-d'Avray had become firmly fixed in his memory, and it was here that he hoped to find again "all the freshness, the shade, the fragrance, and the verdure of a Swiss vale". How wonderful it would be, when he rose wearily from work, to stand upon the hills of Sèvres and let his eyes roam across the broad landscape and the winding silvery ribbon of the Seine, with only vineyards, gardens, and fields about him, yet near to Paris, the Paris he had sworn to conquer! Here he could build himself a little house and furnish it with the barest necessities, an inexpensive little house that would fit him like a glove, a house where he could write in peace and be relieved once and for all from the anxiety of not knowing how to pay his quarter's rent.

With his accustomed swift decision he set about acquiring a "humble cottage", as he put it to Madame de Hanska, in this "remote hamlet". In September, 1837, a contract was signed with a married couple named Valet, and Balzac became the owner of a piece of ground measuring about nine thousand square feet, together with a small dwelling and outhouses, the cost of purchase being four thousand five hundred francs. By Balzac's standards this was a very modest speculation, and from the purely business point of view it was a prudent transaction. To a man earning between fifty and eighty thousand francs a year the acquisition of such an excellently situated plot of land for four thousand five hundred francs was something he could well afford. In three or four weeks he could make enough to cover the outlay and thereby fulfil the dream of years.

In all Balzac's money dealings, however, he was spurred on by that urge which forces the gambler to double and quadruple his stake. Hardly had he entered into possession of his plot of ground when his unpretentious plan assumed larger dimensions. In some way or other he had learned that the projected railway to Versailles would pass through the station at Sèvres just below his little estate, and with accurate intuition he told himself that the fields bordering on this railway station were bound very soon to rise in value. The obvious thing to do was to buy more land, and this he did, but so eagerly that he lost all sense of proportion. The peasants and other owners did not take long to discover that in his inordinate impatience he was prepared to pay any price they asked. His dream of a small cottage was forgotten, the prospect of orchards, plantations, and a magnificent park rose up before his mind's eye, and in a few weeks he had become the possessor of some forty thousand square feet at a cost of eighteen thousand francs, without having taken the precaution of having the land surveyed by experts, or even troubling to examine it more closely himself.

Balzac never regarded expenditure as money actually laid out so long as it was still in the form of a debt. He revelled in the early delights of ownership, and before his new house was built he refused to worry about how he was to pay for it. What was his pen for, anyway, that magic instrument which could so swiftly turn blank paper into thousand-franc notes? Moreover, the fruit-trees which he intended to plant on the still virgin soil would alone bring in a fortune. Suppose he were to lay down a pineapple plantation? Nobody in France had yet hit upon the idea of growing pineapples in glasshouses instead of shipping them from distant parts. If it was set about in the right way, so he confided to his friend Théophile Gautier, he could make a profit of a hundred thousand francs, or

three times as much as his new house would cost him. As a matter
of fact, it would cost him nothing at all, since he had persuaded the
Viscontis to join him in this brilliant venture. While he was building his new house they were going to fit up the old cottage for their
own use, and would pay him a suitable rent. So what was there to
worry about?

Balzac had no anxieties, except that caused by his impatient
desire to move into his new house as soon as it was possible to erect
it. A whole army of workmen appeared on the scene. Masons,
joiners, carpenters, gardeners, painters, and locksmiths all set to
work at once. A wall was hastily built to support the foundations,
the earth was dug out where the chalet was to stand, paths were
laid down and gravelled, forty apple-trees and eighty pear-trees
were planted, trellises were set up on which further fruit trees were
to be trained, and overnight the vicinity of the "remote hamlet"
was transformed by an atmosphere of tumult such as Balzac needed
to stimulate his mind and emotions. Week after week he panted up
the hill to spur on the workmen. No matter what the cost, everything must be ready by the spring of 1838, and if he could he would
even have forced the fruit trees to yield their harvest by the same
prescribed date instead of waiting till the autumn.

This went on week after week until they had reached the depths
of winter. The walls rose higher and higher, and as they rose so the
costs mounted. Gradually Balzac began to be assailed by a slight
feeling of perturbation. The fee he had received for *César Birotteau*
had been sunk in the ground, the publishers had been sucked dry
and no further advances were to be expected from that quarter,
while he was unable to get on with his own work owing to the
impatience with which he was looking forward to moving into his
new home. In accordance with the maxim he had himself propounded, his new enthusiasm was drawing off the energies hitherto
available for the old one. As formerly in the case of his printing
venture, a modest enterprise had assumed proportions which
exceeded his strength. Just as on that occasion he had acquired a
type-foundry, as if to outbid one piece of folly by a greater one, so
he now bent his mind towards a further speculation which was to
rescue him from the difficulties in which he had become involved
through his investment in real estate. An additional indebtedness
of a hundred thousand francs could not be wiped out by small

economies or even by his literary labours, but only by the acquisition of a vast sum at one stroke. Some way must be found of
gaining a *"fortune rapide"*, and this Balzac thought he had discovered. Before the leaves appeared on the trees he suddenly
vanished without a trace. Nobody in Paris knew where he had
gone, and all he himself revealed of his plan was in the form of the
vague declaration, "I shall be free, with no more worries and no
material cares. I am going to be rich!"

This story of how he proposed to become a millionaire by one
swift coup sounds so incredible, that if it were incorporated into a
novel it would be condemned as a poor invention wholly lacking in
psychological plausibility. It was a piece of extravagant folly of
truly Balzacian dimensions, and if it were not fully documented in
every detail no biographer would have the courage to recount it as
an example of the aberration of a genius. Yet again and again we
find in Balzac's career the paradoxical phenomenon, repeated with
uncanny precision, that the brain which was able to pierce unerringly
to the heart of every situation in the fictitious world of its own
creation functioned in the world of reality with a naïve and childlike
credulity. So long as he was portraying a Grandet or a Nucingen his
sense of logic and insight into psychology were unparalleled, but he
was easy prey for any clumsy sharper and his purse-strings could
be loosened for any tempting scheme more swiftly than those of the
most confirmed lottery addict. He refused to learn from experience
how to face the very situation of which he showed himself such a
sovereign master in his novels, and this simultaneous lucidity and
blindness in one and the same brain were never more clearly demonstrated than in the episode of Balzac's hunt for hidden treasure.

In the summer of 1836 he had taken this theme as the subject of
one of his most brilliant short stories, *Facino Cane*. In this literary
gem he described how among three musicians at a wedding he had
been particularly struck by the clarinet player, a blind old man of
eighty with a majestic head, whom he intuitively felt to have been
the victim of some mysterious fate. Drawing him into conversation
he learned from the old clarinet player, who was stimulated by a
glass or two of wine, that he was the last descendant of the princely
family of Cane, that he had once been a senator in Venice, and that
he had spent years in prison. On breaking through the prison walls
during his attempt to escape he had come upon the secret treasure-

vault of the procurators, where the republic's vast stores of gold and silver lay heaped up. He alone knew how to find the place again, but he had grown blind owing to his years of incarceration and was unable to take advantage of his discovery. He still remembered the exact spot, and if anyone was prepared to undertake the journey with him to Venice, they would both become the richest men in the world. Seizing his companion, that is to say, Balzac, by the arm, he conjured him to go with him to Italy.

All those within earshot laughed at the foolish old man. The other musicians had heard his story before and neither of them believed it. Nor did Balzac, who had no intention of accompanying Facino Cane to Venice and paying his expenses. He rejected the fantastic proposal and left the old man to die in an asylum for the blind, without making any attempt to seek out his legacy. In this fictitious story Balzac describes himself as acting no less rationally than any other sensible person would have done, but how differently he behaved scarcely a year later when the imaginary episode was translated into reality!

On the way back after his second Italian journey in April, 1937, Balzac had the misfortune to be quarantined at the hospital in Genoa. Being held in quarantine is a very tedious business. It is like being in a prison without walls. One is free and yet not free; one cannot work or go for a stroll, and the only diversion available is to sit and talk with one's fortuitous companions in adversity. Among those with whom Balzac struck up an acquaintance on this occasion was a merchant named Giuseppe Pezzi, who told him quite casually, and certainly without the slightest intention of trying to dupe him or to entice him into a venturesome speculation, of the treasures which could still be brought to light in his native land. In Sardinia, for example, the old silver mines had been abandoned because the opinion was held that they had been completely worked out by the Romans. As a matter of fact, the Romans, with their undeveloped technique, had been able to extract only a small proportion of the silver from the lead ore, and the great slag-heaps they had left there, under the impression that they were entirely valueless, contained a high percentage of silver which could be smelted out by modern refining processes. Anyone who took the trouble to acquire the concession, which could no doubt be bought for a song, would very soon become a wealthy man.

Thus the worthy Signor Pezzi chatted to his neighbour at table, and what he said was true. The metallurgists of to-day can extract a far higher percentage of precious metal from mixed ores than was possible in earlier centuries, and numerous mines which their owners ceased to exploit a couple of thousand years ago are now being worked at a profit. Signor Pezzi, however, did not realise that he was throwing a spark into a powder-barrel. Balzac, with his capacity for seeing things immediately in plastic form, was already visualising the gleaming white silver as it separated from the grey slag, piling up and becoming minted into coins, hundreds of thousands and millions of minted coins, and the very thought intoxicated him. It was like giving a child a glass of brandy. He urged the unsuspecting Pezzi to have the residues examined at once by expert chemists. There would be no difficulty in raising the necessary capital for such a sound investment, and by securing for themselves a major share they would both become rich, enormously rich, fantastically rich. The worthy Signor Pezzi, dumbfounded by the passionate enthusiasm of this unknown gentleman from Paris, grew somewhat more reserved, but he promised Balzac to look into the matter and to send him specimens of the ore.

From that moment Balzac was obsessed by the illusion that his salvation would come from the silver mines of Sardinia and that they would not only defray the cost of his new house, *Les Jardies*, but also enable him to settle his outstanding debts and make him at last into a free man. In his fictitious story of *Facino Cane* he had regarded the old man with his story of hidden treasure as a babbling fool, and now he himself had become the dupe of the same idea. As soon as he had dashed off the last pages of *César Birotteau*, which would not take long—and meanwhile Signor Pezzi would have sent him the specimen ores for which he had asked—he would fling himself with all his energies into the task of raising capital and providing the technical experts for his great new business venture.

But weeks went by and the weeks lengthened into months. *César Birotteau* had been finished long since and Signor Pezzi had not yet forwarded the promised specimens to Paris. Balzac grew uneasy. He had himself been responsible by his guileless enthusiasm for drawing the Italian blockhead's attention to the riches that were lying fallow in Sardinia, and now the scoundrel was doubtless trying to secure the concession and to exclude him from any participation in it. There was only one thing to do. He must catch up with him and investigate the situation for himself on the spot. Unfortunately the few hundred francs of initial capital that he required for the journey were lacking, and he did not know where they were to be obtained. He could have gone to his friends the Rothschilds, or to some other great financial house, and have submitted his plan to them, but naive as he was, and one must even say as stupid as ever, where his own business affairs were concerned, he believed that Signor Pezzi had confided the tremendous secret to him alone and if he offered a hint of it to a third party the idea would be stolen from him by the wealthy capitalists in the same way that David Séchard had been swindled of his formula for the manufacture of cheap paper in the *Illusions perdues*. Commandant Carraud was the only person in whom he would place his trust, for he imagined that superannuated officer, who sometimes amused himself with trifling experiments to pass the time, to be a great chemical expert in possession of "a secret process by which he can separate gold and silver from any other elements with which they may be alloyed—and at very little cost". The good-natured Commandant found the idea worth considering, but was not prepared either to accompany Balzac to Sardinia or to invest money in the project. So Balzac was reduced to borrowing part of his travelling expenses from his mother, who was always ready to take money from her stocking for a promising speculation. The remainder was provided by Dr. Nacquart and his tailor, and in the middle of March, 1838, he set off for Sardinia to take possession of the silver mines.

It is obvious that this fantastic journey was bound to end in a ridiculous fiasco. Even if the plan had had any prospect of success —and there was nothing wrong with Balzac's original intuition— how could an author who had never seen a mine in his life judge in a visit of two or three days whether these old workings were likely to yield a profit or not? He took no technical equipment with him, and even if he had done so he would have had no notion of how to use it. He had not discussed the matter with a real expert; and his knowledge of Italian was insufficient to enable him to make himself understood. Owing to his unwillingness to confide in anyone he carried no letters of introduction, he had no money with which to obtain the information he required, he did not know to what authorities he would have to apply in order to acquire the concession he was seeking, and even if he had been in possession of this knowledge he was unfamiliar with the business routine. Above all, he lacked the necessary capital. It is true that he declared, "All I need is a specimen of the stuff." But where was the "stuff" to be found and what was it? Was it in the slag-heaps, now overgrown with vegetation, or did it consist of the ore in mines that had long since been disused and choked-up? An experienced mining engineer would have needed months to establish the facts. Balzac relied on nothing but his intuition.

In any case, it was impossible for Balzac to spend months over the task, since for him time was money, and as he had no money he had to hurry. He started off at his usual *tempo*, spending five sleepless days and night on the coach-box between Paris and Marseilles, and his funds were so short that he lived on ten sous' worth of milk a day. Hard facts, however, proved unwilling to adapt themselves to his need for haste. In Marseilles he learned that there was no ship likely to sail for Sardinia within any measurable space of time. The only way to get there was by a roundabout route via Corsica, where he might perhaps be able to find a small boat that would take him across. This was the first blow to his hopes, and he went on to Toulon with his ardour considerably cooled after having written in a melancholy strain to Zulma: "In a few days I shall unhappily be one illusion the poorer. That is what always happens. Just when one is about to reach the culmination one begins to lose faith." After an unusually stormy voyage he arrived at Ajaccio in the throes of severe sea-sickness. Then came a new trial of patience. He was forced to remain in quarantine for five days because of an alleged outbreak of cholera at Marseilles, and at the end of these five days he had to waste more time trying to find a boatman who was ready to sail across to Sardinia. Too agitated and upset to work during his days of waiting, he plodded around Ajaccio, visited Napoleon's birthplace, and cursed Giuseppe Pezzi, who had lured him into undertaking this ridiculous journey. At last, on the 2nd of April, he was able to make the crossing in the barque of a coral-diver, with no other nourishment than the fish they caught on the way. In Alghiero came another test of endurance, five further days of quarantine to keep him on tenterhooks. Finally, on the 12th of April, he was allowed to land on the shores of the island which so jealously guarded the millions he expected to pocket. A whole month had gone by and he had not yet glimpsed a single grain of silver.

Now for the mines! They were less than twenty miles away, but since the days of the Romans all the roads had disappeared. There were neither roads nor coaches in Sardinia, whose inhabitants, so Balzac wrote, were no more civilised than the Polynesians or the Huns. The people went about half-naked and in rags, the houses contained no stoves, there were neither hotels nor inns. So Balzac, who had not mounted a horse for years, was compelled to entrust his corpulence to the tender mercies of a rocking saddle until at length he reached Nurra, where his hopes were finally and utterly shattered. It was no longer of any consequence whether the mines could be rendered profitable or not, for he had arrived too late. Giuseppe Pezzi, inspired by Balzac's enthusiasm, had employed the eighteen months that had elapsed since their meeting to some purpose. He had not, it is true, written an immortal novel or built himself a house with a pineapple plantation, but he had besieged the various relevant authorities until he had obtained the issue of a royal decree giving him the right to exploit the abandoned slag-heaps. So Balzac's journey had been quite unnecessary. Like Napoleon after Waterloo, his only desire now was to hasten back to Paris, to his "beloved Inferno", as speedily as possible. The fare, however, exceeded his means, and he had to travel to Genoa and then on to Milan in order to borrow his fare to Paris on the credit of the Viscontis. This time his sojourn in Milan was a melancholy affair, with no splendid receptions or visits to aristocratic acquaintances. Weary, downcast, but with his energies unimpaired, the eternal bankrupt arrived back in Paris in the month of June.

On balance he had lost three months' work and spent money uselessly in the attempt to acquire more. He had risked his health and exposed himself to nervous strain for the sake of an absurd adventure, or rather for an adventure that was absurd so far as he was concerned. For with tragic irony, as in the case of all his other projects, his calculations in the first place had been correct and his intuition had not deceived him. The Sardinian silver mines brought wealth to others. In two or three decades they were in full swing and growing more and more profitable. In 1851 they provided work for 616 men, nine years later they were employing 2,038, nine years

19

after that 9,171, and the company known as the *Minas d'Argentiera* was garnering the millions of which Balzac had dreamed. His flair was always right ; but it helped him only as an artist and merely led him astray when he sought to step beyond his proper sphere. When he transmuted his imaginative gift into literary production it brought him not only monetary rewards, but imperishable fame; when he tried to transform his illusions into money he only succeeded in adding to his debts and multiplying his labours.

Before his departure from Paris he had written to Zulma the prophetic words: "It is not the journey I am afraid of, but the return if my plan should come to grief." He knew that he would find unpaid bills, threatening lawsuits, and work without end, as he always did when he got back home, and this time Pelion would be piled on Ossa. One thing alone inspired him with the courage to face the fulfilment of these dark forebodings—the prospect of being able to take refuge in his new house, where he could make up for the time lost on his trip to Sardinia. But here again disappointment awaited him. Nothing was ready. The ground was "as bare as the palm of one's hand", the house still unroofed, and he could not settle down to write at *Les Jardies* because the architects, the masons, and the navvies who were excavating the soil had dallied over their work. He had once more forgotten that not everybody could keep up with his own *tempo*. With his accustomed impatience he began to drive them on, and before the last plank was on the roof he moved in, defying the orders of his doctor, who told him that it would be injurious to his health if he lived in a newly built house that had not had time to dry out. His furniture had not yet been transferred from the rue des Batailles and there was the noise of hammering and sawing the whole day long, for the old cottage was being reconstructed from top to bottom for occupation by the Contessa. The paths were still being gravelled and asphalted, while the retaining walls were being erected with a haste that was to prove disastrous. Yet amid all the chaos Balzac enjoyed the sensation of living on his own estate, and in premature enthusiasm he described his new home:

My house lies on the slope of the mount or hill of Saint-Cloud, which borders half-way up on the King's park towards the south. To westward the view embraces the whole of Ville-d'Avray, and to the south I look down upon the Ville-d'Avray road, which stretches along the hills to where the park of Versailles begins. To eastward my eyes can roam beyond Sèvres and take in a vast horizon behind which lies Paris. The haze of the metropolis veils the edge of the famous slopes of Meudon and Bellevue. In the distance lie the plain of Montrouge and the road which runs from Orleans to Tours. It is a landscape of rare grandeur and alluring contrasts! In the immediate proximity of my property lies the railway station on the line from Paris to Versailles, the embankment of which runs through the valley of Ville-d'Avray, without, however, restricting my view in any way. Thus I can travel in ten minutes, and at the price of ten sous, from *Les Jardies* to the Madeleine in the heart of Paris! From the rue des Batailles, from Chaillot, or from the rue Cassini it cost me at least forty sous and took an hour. Taking this convenient situation into account it can never be said that the purchase of *Les Jardies* has been a foolish move on my part, since the price of the property is bound to go up enormously. The whole estate comprises an acre of land, bounded by a terrace one hundred and fifty feet long to the south and surrounded by walls. Nothing has yet been planted, but in the autumn we shall make a veritable Garden of Eden out of this little corner of the earth, with flowers, shrubs, and fragrant odours. In Paris or its environs anything is to be had for money, so I shall buy twenty-year-old magnolia trees, sixteen-year-old limes, twelve-year-old poplars, birches, and so on, which can be transported with clods of earth round the roots. I shall also have vines, which are brought in baskets, and will produce grapes this year. Yes, civilisation is a wonderful thing! It is true that to-day the ground is as bare as the palm of one's hand, but by May there will be an amazing transformation. I must acquire another two acres of land in the vicinity for kitchen gardens, fruit trees, and so on, for which I need thirty thousand francs, but this sum I propose to earn during the winter.

The house is steep and narrow like the perch in a parrot's cage, three stories high with one main room on each floor. On the ground-floor are my dining-room and salon, on the first-floor my bedroom and dressing-room, on the second-floor my study, where I am writing this letter to you in the middle of the night. A staircase almost like a ladder leads from one storey to the next. Right round the house runs a covered gallery, along which one can walk, reaching up to the first floor and supported on brick pilasters. The whole of this little pavilion, which has an Italian air about it, is painted in brick-colour, the corners are of hewn stone, and the annex containing the well of the staircase is red. There is just room for me in this house of mine. Sixty paces to the rear, in the direction of the park of Saint-Cloud, is an out-building with kitchen, servants' quarters and larder, etc., on the ground floor, together with stable, coachhouse, harness room, bath, wooden shed, etc. On the first-floor there is a large apart-ment which might, if necessary, be let, and on the second-floor there are bedrooms for the servants and a guest-room for friends. I have a spring of water at my disposal which is as good as the celebrated spring of Ville-d'Avray, since it is fed from the same underground pool, and my property is surrounded on all sides by pleasant walks. None of the rooms is furnished as yet, but I shall gradually transfer all my possessions from Paris. . . . Here I shall remain until I have made my fortune. I already find it so much to my liking that I believe I shall one day settle down here to end my days in peace as soon as I have enough money on which to retire. Then I shall bid farewell to all my aspirations and ambitious plans, without beating of drums and without fanfares.

This was Balzac's description of his new home. His friends and visitors have given a different account, and in their reports we can discern without exception the difficulty they had in suppressing a desire to laugh. Even those with whom he was most intimate, and who wished him nothing but well, were hard put to it to remain completely serious when he expatiated with his usual persuasive and exuberant eloquence on the splendours of his estate. The little house, which anticipated in a remarkable way the architectural ideas of Le Corbusier and his school, bore an odd resemblance to an empty birdcage. In the garden, which Balzac had transformed in his dreams into a paradise, a few scattered fruit trees raised their meagre branches to the sky, and not a single blade of grass had yet pushed its way through the clayey soil. October arrived and then November, and a noisy swarm of workmen were still busily engaged about the grounds, since not a day passed without Balzac thinking out some further embellishment. He was either planning to erect glasshouses for his pineapples, which he intended to sell at a dizzy profit in Paris, or to plant Tokay grapes which would produce a wine of hitherto unknown fieriness, or to put up a stone gate with the name of his house, *Les Jardies*, engraved on it in mighty letters, from which a green arcade would lead to the front door. At the same time he was supervising the fitting up of the neighbouring cottage for the Contessa, who after a short interval followed her lover to the allegedly quiet hillside on which he had built his country retreat. None of the bills had yet been paid and there was nothing growing in this Garden of Eden except the interest on the mortgages. Then the series of catastrophes began.

In his enthusiasm at the beautiful view, and absorbed as he was in his vision of blossoming orchards and arbours covered with lusty vines, he had omitted to engage an expert to survey the ground, which consisted of soft, slippery clay. One morning he was awakened by a thunderous reverberation that brought him rushing to the window. The sky was clear, without a trace of menacing cloud as far as the eye could reach. It was not the crash of thunder that had roused him from sleep, but the collapse of his expensive retaining wall. Balzac was in despair and wrote to Zulma:

> To you, sister of my soul, I can confide my innermost secrets. Here I am, sitting in the midst of the most wretched misery. The walls of *Les Jardies* have given way. It is the architect's fault, because he did not lay proper foundations; but though he is to blame it all falls back on me. The man doesn't possess a sou, though I paid him eight thousand francs on account.

The walls round Balzac's estate were indispensable to him. They were a symbol of his isolation from the world and confirmed his consciousness of owning the ground he stood on. So the workmen had to be recalled to erect them anew, but after a few more days and a few more rainy nights he was again awakened by the rumble of thunder. The soft ground had once more given way and once more the walls had collapsed. This time the situation was aggravated, for the stony avalanche had rolled down over the fields of a neighbour, who complained vociferously and threatened to bring an action. *Qui terre a, guerre a.* He who owns land has a war on his hands. This is the theme of Balzac's novel *Les paysans*, and as in the case of the *Illusions perdues* he had the same intimate personal experience of the subject about which he was writing. He had, moreover, to suffer the malicious glee of the whole of Paris. Every newspaper printed anecdotes, more or less veracious, about Balzac's house. It was even said that he had forgotten to put in a staircase. Those who went out to view the scene came back and

reported with great delight how they had had to clamber over the
rubble at the risk of their lives, and their stories proliferated far
more luxuriantly than did the trees and flowers in Balzac's garden.
He retired into stricter seclusion and ceased to invite guests to visit
him, but to no avail. His old friends the bailiffs and other minions of
the law were not deterred by the rocky approach from climbing the
hill and providing him with a little more room in his cramped
dwelling by the removal of his most valuable articles of furniture.
In his rural retreat, where he had looked forward to devoting himself to his work and the beauties of the landscape, the old game
began again. Whenever it was reported from his look-out post that
a suspicious stranger had been spied in the vicinity, he moved his
valuables over to the Contessa's cottage. When the coast was clear
once more and the disappointed *huissier* had departed after finding the "parrot's cage" unfurnished except for a writing-table, an
iron bedstead, and a few worthless sticks, Balzac's treasures were
cheerfully returned to their accustomed place.

For some months he succeeded by this means in putting a spoke
in his creditors' wheel. It was a proceeding in which he took a naive
pleasure, his attempts to outwit them being the only amusement he
managed to extract from the lifelong struggle. Eventually, however, he found himself up against a real Gobseck, who had perhaps
learned from Balzac's own novels how to get the better of fraudu-
lent debtors. To the joy of all the scandal-mongers of Paris he
brought an action not against Balzac or even against his mistress,
but against the innocent cuckold, Count Guidoboni-Visconti. The
Count was charged with

> having, on the one hand, brought part of the chattels of Mon-
> sieur de Balzac into a place of concealment, and having, on the
> other hand, been concerned in the removal of the aforesaid
> chattels from the property known as *Les Jardies*. Furthermore,
> he has of his own deliberate intent been a party to the act of
> depriving the creditors of Monsieur de Balzac of objects of con-
> siderable value which represented the security for their claims,
> thereby causing them loss which he must make good.

This was the end of Balzac's dream. His "humble cottage" had
cost him a hundred thousand francs, which was more than he would
have had to pay for a house in the Champs Elysées. The Contessa had
also had enough. Her relations with Balzac could no longer stand

the strain of his continual financial embarrassments, and she shook the dust of *Les Jardies* from her shoes. Balzac did not know which way to turn, yet he could not reconcile himself to the entire abandonment of his illusion. In an effort to cling to his vain ambition to be a landed proprietor, he tried the subterfuge of a fictitious sale at the price of fifteen thousand francs in the hope of being able to return in triumph later on, but this too was unsuccessful. Once more he was compelled to search for a new place of refuge and his choice fell upon a house in the rue Basse, Passy. This is the only one of his numerous dwelling-places which has survived, and which we can still visit to-day and honour as "*la maison de Balzac*".

CHAPTER XVIII

Speculations in the Theatre

"Everything has changed for the worse—both my work and my debts." In this pithy sentence Balzac summed up the situation in which he found himself at the age of forty. The three years he spent at *Les Jardies* were absorbed in a desperate but fruitless endeavour to meet the commitments in which his new building venture had involved him. Never had he worked more feverishly, yet he had to admit in the end that even five novels a year would not suffice to cancel his six-figure indebtedness. It was in vain that he drew from their pigeon-holes all the works he had once begun and left unfinished. He even botched together a collection of Napoleon's maxims for a worthy master craftsman who was anxious to obtain the Legion of Honour, presenting us with a pathetic picture of Balzac at the height of his fame lending his pen anonymously to satisfy a stranger's petty vanity and earn a small fee. Sums such as he required could not be earned in a normal way. A miraculous windfall was needed, and since the mines of Sardinia had refused to yield up their silver to him he turned to another source from which he hoped to derive adequate quantities of the precious metal, namely, the theatre.

It was only under extreme constraint and very much against his will that Balzac forced himself to write for the stage. He was quite well aware that it was his mission to complete the cycle of the *Comédie humaine* and that he had no business turning out comedies. His instinct warned him that his gifts could never find their full expression in dramatic form. His novels are characterised by the gradual chemical transmutations of character and its relation to its *milieu*, not by the dramatic representation of striking scenes. When he wrote it was like a torrent pouring from his pen : he needed the amplitude of space, and it is not merely fortuitous that every attempt to adapt his novels for the stage has proved a failure. The artificial limits of a stage setting make his characters appear unnatural, since there is no scope for the delicate play of nuance or the logic of imperceptible change.

Yet by an effort of concentrated will-power, and with the expenditure of all the energy that lay within him, it is probable that Balzac's genius could have acquired the same mastery of dramatic technique as he revealed in the novel. Such concentration and single-minded devotion to the theatre had no part in his plan. His whilom dream of becoming a new Racine or Corneille had long since vanished into limbo. For the moment he regarded the theatre merely as a means of making easy money. It was a cool and deliberate calculation to which he attached no more artistic value than he had to his scheme for growing pineapples or his dabbling in railway shares. With calm cynicism he had written to Zulma Carraud before setting off on his journey to Sardinia: "If I should fail in my present undertaking I shall throw myself body and soul into the theatre." It was nothing more for him than a "last resort" from which he hoped for a "more lucrative yield" than he could obtain from his books. He had worked out the possibility of a successful play bringing him in anything from one hundred to two hundred thousand francs, and though of course there was no guarantee of his being able to reap such a harvest at the first attempt, if he turned out a dozen or more pieces a year it could be reckoned as a mathematical certainty that in the long run he could not help drawing a winner.

This cold-blooded way of computing the hazards is evidence enough of the lack of seriousness with which Balzac set out to conquer the theatre. It was his intention to fling his plays on to the stage with the easy gesture of a man throwing down a *louis d'or* on to the roulette table. It was not merit but chance that would decide the issue. His plan of action was simple and unambiguous. The first and most important step, the one that would make the most strenuous demand upon his eloquence and ingenuity, was to find a theatrical manager with whom he could conclude the most favourable contract and who was prepared to pay him the largest advance. Once this was accomplished there would remain only the trifling matter of delivering the completed drama on the stipulated date—mere child's-play compared with the Herculean task of extracting a suitable advance from a reluctant manager. Balzac had no lack of ideas, and in the drawers of his writing-table there still lay a dozen or so of his youthful efforts. He would have to employ a "ghost" to do a little literary hackwork for him, some young fellow who would do the job cheaply. All that would be necessary would be to expound the plot to his collaborator and then spend a night or two injecting the requisite *brio* and applying the requisite polish. Thus, without devoting more than three or four days to each play, he could turn out a score or so comfortably in a year with his left hand, while his right was engaged in the work that really mattered —the writing of novels that were as ardently conceived as they were carefully planned.

Balzac took so light-hearted a view of the requirements of the theatre, despite the huge royalties he expected to enjoy, that he did not even take the trouble to look for a collaborator who was versed in the technique of the stage. He took the first available drudge that crossed his path, a down-at-heel Bohemian named Charles Lassailly, who had never had any connection with the theatre and whose talent remained concealed from even the most benevolent critics. No one knows where he picked up this poor little neurotic, who looked like a walking caricature, with his dolorous visage, enormous nose, and a bushy mane that flowed down over his shoulders with a romantic, melancholy air. He may have met him in the street or in a café. At any rate, he did not stop to inquire into his qualifications, but dragged his bewildered victim without more ado to stay with him at *Les Jardies*, so determined was he to begin that very day on the composition of a tragedy. The sequel was a piece of buffoonery such as even Balzac never surpassed.

The wretched Lassailly had not the faintest notion what Balzac wanted of him as he accompanied his persuasive companion out to Ville-d'Avray. His mind was completely blank of ideas so far as the theatre was concerned, nor had he any conception of the way in which to set about the writing of a play. Though Balzac bombarded him on the way with a constant drum-fire of plans and projects, however, his first step on reaching home was to provide his future collaborator with a hearty meal. Balzac's normal dinner-hour was five o'clock. The table was amply spread, and the melancholy guest was plied with wines such as he had never tasted before in his life. He expanded visibly under the warmth of this reception, and by the end of the repast he may actually have been in a condition to offer his host inspiring advice, but to his surprise Balzac rose from the table at six o'clock and ordered him to go to bed.

Lassailly, whose day only began when the sun had set and who had probably never gone to bed at six o'clock since his childhood, did not dare to protest. He allowed himself to be conducted to his room, meekly undressed, got between the sheets and, thanks to the wine of which he had partaken so copiously, was soon sleeping soundly.

When his slumbers were at their deepest, at the hour of midnight, he was shaken rudely by the shoulder and started up in alarm to see Balzac standing at his bedside like a ghost, dressed in his white robe. He was commanded to get up forthwith, since it was time to start work.

Poor Lassailly, unaccustomed to Balzac's reversal of night and day, collected his wits with a sigh. He had not the courage to oppose his will to that of his new master, who had provided him with a seat at his board, and until six o'clock in the morning, sleepy-eyed as he was and with his mind in confusion, he sat listening to Balzac's exposition of the play he was commissioned to write. Then Balzac permitted him to go back to bed. During the day, while Balzac was working on his current novel, Lassailly was to draft the first scenes, and at night he was to submit the text for joint revision.

When midnight came round again Lassailly was in a state of trepidation. While waiting for this ludicrous hour to approach he had slept badly, and his work had of course suffered even more than his slumbers. The lamentable draft which he brought to the conference table was rejected at the nocturnal session and he was given fresh directives. For another two or three days he racked his exhausted brain. Balzac's good food no longer had any savour for the wretched slave: from six o'clock until midnight he lay awake dreading the ensuing discussion, and one night, when Balzac came to rouse him, he found him gone. On the table was a letter:

> I am obliged to renounce the work which you have been so extremely kind as to entrust to me. I have passed the night without being able to think of anything worthy of being put to paper in fulfilment of the dramatic demands of your plan. I have not dared to tell you this in person, but it is useless for me to continue eating your bread. I am, however, in despair that my sterility of mind should thus have frustrated the willing hope I had cherished of being able to extract myself from my present difficulties by an unexpected stroke of good fortune. . . .

This desertion was so sudden that Balzac had no time to look round for another collaborator, and in order to collect the advance payment of six thousand francs which had been promised him by the Théâtre de la Renaissance he had to finish the play himself. While he was working on the last act of *La première demoiselle* or, as it was to be called later, *L'école de ménage,* no less than twenty compositors were engaged in setting up the first act in type so that he could get his contract signed as quickly as possible. In a few days he was ready to hand over the finished article. But now he discovered that his fame as a novelist carried no weight with theatrical managers, whose minds were dominated by their box-office returns. The director of the Théâtre de la Renaissance flatly refused to accept his play, and another of Balzac's dreams of easy money was dispersed by the cold breath of reality. He had merely added a further chapter to the story of his own *illusions perdues.*

Another man would have felt humiliated, or at least would have had his enthusiasm damped, but Balzac's failures only had the effect of causing him to redouble his efforts. Had not the same thing happened in the case of his novels? Did they not rebuff him at first and do their best to discourage him? His superstitious nature even saw in this initial setback a guarantee of future success. He had written to the Contessa: "My career in the theatre will follow the same course as my literary career has done. My first work will be rejected." So he must try again! He must see what could be done in the way of a fresh contract!

In view of Balzac's incorrigible method of dramatising conversation and calling the result a play, there was little prospect that his new drama would be any better, but his new contract certainly was very much better. Drawing the logical conclusions from his first experience, he determined not to expose himself again to the humiliation of having his play rejected, and Harel, the director of the Théâtre Porte Saint-Martin, agreed to accept and produce it even before he had seen the script. By a lucky chance Balzac had learned that Harel was urgently in need of a play that would draw the public, and that he was in a hurry, so he proposed a dramatisation of his Vautrin. Harel kindled with enthusiasm. Thanks to *Père Goriot* and the *Illusions perdues*, Vautrin had become such a popular figure that his appearance on the stage, particularly if the rôle were taken by Frédéric Lemaître, was bound to create a sensation. The contract was duly signed and each of the two parties hugged to himself the illusion that the money would soon come rolling in.

This time Balzac took more pains. In order to keep an eye on Harel he left *Les Jardies* for a few weeks and went to live at the house of his tailor, Buisson, in the rue de Richelieu, which was only a few minutes away from the theatre. It was his intention to be present at all the rehearsals of his new play and to prepare the way for the great triumph that was to come. He began to work on the press, inaugurated a vast publicity campaign, and discussed their parts with the actors. Every day he could be seen in his working coat and wide, badly-cut trousers, hatless and with the leather tongues hanging out of his shoes, panting across to the theatre to talk over some specially effective scene with the cast or to reserve seats at the box-office for his various acquaintances, for he insisted from the very start that the whole social and intellectual *élite* of Paris must attend the first performance. Amid all this hurly-burly there was one trifling matter that appears to have slipped his mind. He had forgotten to write the play. The manager had been given a general synopsis of the plot, each of the actors had been instructed in his part, everything was ready for the first rehearsal, but Harel was still waiting for the book and the actors for their scripts. In twenty-four hours, promised Balzac, their needs would be supplied; all was ready and to-morrow rehearsals could begin.

Théophile Gautier, one of his few contemporaries whose accounts are not suspect on the score of exaggeration, has described for us the way in which Balzac proceeded to put into effect his promise to produce a five-act play in the space of twenty-four hours. He invited four or five reliable friends, whom he had selected for his operational staff, to assemble for an urgent conference at his lodging in the house of Monsieur Buisson. Théophile Gautier was the last to appear, and he was greeted with a cheerful laugh by his white-garbed host, who had been pacing impatiently up and down the room like a caged lion:

Ah, here you are, Théo! You lazy fellow! Late as ever, sleepy-head! Get a move on now! You ought to have been here an hour ago. I've got to read a five-act play to Harel to-morrow morning.

There then followed the entertaining spectacle which Gautier has recounted in his *Portraits*:

"So you want to ask my opinion?" I inquired, settling down comfortably in an armchair to listen to a lengthy reading.

Balzac guessed my thoughts from my attitude of ease, and replied with an air of innocence: "The play isn't written yet."

"The deuce!" I exclaimed. "Then the reading will have to be postponed for six weeks."

"Oh no! We are going to polish it off at once and collect the cash. I have a pressing obligation to meet and can't wait."

"But you can't turn out a play by to-morrow! There isn't even time to have it copied."

"This is how I am going to do it. You will write one act, Ourliac another, Laurent-Jan will compose the third act, de Belloy the fourth, I myself will be responsible for the fifth, and to-morrow at midday I shall read the whole play to Harel as arranged. Each act of a drama doesn't contain more than four or five hundred lines and one can turn out five hundred lines of dialogue in a day and a night."

"Let me have the subject, give me an idea of the way you want the plot to develop, describe the characters as concisely as you can, and I will set to work," I replied with a certain bewilderment.

"Oh!" he cried, with magnificent disdain and a superb air of being overwhelmed by such a request. "If I've got to tell you the plot we shall never be finished in time!"

It had not occurred to me that I was being indiscreet in asking what the play was about, but Balzac regarded it as mere idle curiosity.

With great difficulty I managed to extract from him a brief indication of the theme, and then sat down to draft out a scenario, of which no more than a few words survived in the final version. As can well be imagined, the play was *not* read to Harel on the following day. I do not know how the other collaborators got on, but the only one who had a serious finger in the pie was Laurent-Jan, to whom the play is dedicated.

After this prologue one can figure out for oneself what the play was like. It is hardly probable that the French stage in the past hundred years had ever seen such a miserable piece of patchwork as Balzac's *Vautrin*, which Harel had advertised in advance as a masterpiece. Despite the fact that its hopeful author had bought up half the seats in the theatre, the first three acts were received in icy and even embarrassed silence. His real friends experienced the same feeling of discomfort at seeing his name linked with such an appalling exhibition of ineptitude as we ourselves do to-day when we find this ridiculous aberration of a great literary genius printed in the collected edition of his works. During the fourth act the storm broke. For the appearance of Vautrin as a Mexican general Frédéric Lemaître had chosen a wig which resembled suspiciously the style of hairdressing affected by Louis Philippe, and some Royalists in the audience began to whistle their disapproval, while the Prince d'Orléans ostentatiously left his box. The performance ended in a scene of wild disorder.

On the following day the King banned the play from the stage. To forestall Balzac's protests the Ministry of Fine Arts privately offered him the sum of five thousand francs as compensation, but he proudly rejected it so that he might at least salvage some sort of moral triumph from the wreck. Yet even a catastrophe of these dimensions could not teach him to mend his ways. He tried his luck four more times. *Les ressources de Quinola* and *Paméla Giraud*, though both these plays were of slightly better quality, were likewise failures, and so was *La marâtre*. *Le faiseur*, the only play that was not entirely unworthy of his genius, was not produced till after his death. He thought sadly of the wise advice given him by the witty poet Heine, whom he met one day on the boulevard before the first and only performance of *Vautrin*. Heine recommended him to confine himself to the writing of novels: "You must be careful! A man who is used to serving his sentence at Brest cannot get accustomed to Toulon. Stick to the gaol you know."

The building of *Les Jardies*, the Sardinian silver mines, and the fabrication of stage-plays were three great manifestations of folly that prove Balzac to have been no less simple and incorrigible in mundane matters at the age of forty than he had been ten and twenty years before. His extravagances had, in truth, taken on more fantastic proportions. He seemed to have become possessed of an even more impulsive urge to buffoonery. Yet it is not fitting that we, who can see him in the perspective afforded by the intervening years, should follow his disrespectful contemporaries in stressing his tendency to blind exuberance at the expense of the essential lucidity of mind which enabled him to produce his creative work. During the years when the newspapers were revelling in spicy anecdotes about his schemes and misadventures at *Les Jardies*, when critics, journalists, and public were gloating over his failures in the theatre, he continued to work unwearyingly at the *Comédie humaine*. His attempt to establish his own journal, his speculation in real estate, his involvement in harassing lawsuits did not prevent him from devoting his brain and his pen with unshakable tenacity to a world which to him was very real. While the workmen were hammering away and the walls round his house were collapsing, he completed the grandiose second part of *Les illusions perdues* and worked simultaneously on the continuation of his *Splendeurs et misères des courtisanes* as well as on *Le cabinet des antiques* and the ambitiously planned but not wholly successful novel *Béatrix*. He wrote two such perfect works as the political novel *Une ténébreuse affaire* and the realistic *La rabouilleuse*; *Les mémoires de deux jeunes mariés*; the musical short story, a masterpiece of its kind, *Massimilla Doni*; *La fausse maîtresse*; *Ursule Mirouet*; *Z. Marcas*; *Pierrette*; *Une fille d'Eve*; *Le secret de la princesse de Cadignan*; *La muse du département*; *Le martyre calviniste*; and *Pierre Grassou*. In addition he published a dozen essays, prepared preliminary sketches for *Le curé de village*, and drafted fragments of *Petites misères de la vie conjugale*. Once again during four stormy years his literary output would have sufficed both in volume and value for the lifelong achievement of any other writer. No hint of the external confusion in which his life was steeped succeeded in penetrating his creative waking dream. No sign of his much-derided temperamental eccentricities is to be found in the writings which, while he was engaged upon them, absorbed him to the exclusion of everything else. Many of them surpass all his previous stories in the compactness of their style, the subduing of the slovenly verbosity in which he was otherwise wont to indulge. It is as if his secret bitterness at the disappointments and failures which had fallen to his lot had slowly absorbed and neutralised the mawkish sentimentality that in his earlier writings betrayed the artificially romantic taste of the age. The more he progressed in the hard school of life the more realistic did his work become. With increasingly keen and mistrustful insight he penetrated to the heart of the social organism, and his understanding of the interwoven elements which hold society together grew more and more prophetic. At the age of forty Balzac was closer to the world of to-day than he had been at thirty. The ten years between had brought him a hundred years nearer.

Titanic as his literary achievements were during this period, they by no means exhausted his resilient energy. Immersed in his work though he was, yet he looked out into the world from behind his drawn curtains with watchful eyes and was tempted more than once to try his strength against the stubborn facts with which he would there be faced. In Paris a few writers had at last made an attempt to unite for the purpose of protecting their professional interests and had founded an impotent little association, the *Société des Gens de Lettres*, whose members occasionally gathered round a table and passed resolutions which they were too indolent to follow up, and which were in consequence allowed to collect the dust in the file-cupboards of the Ministries. Balzac was the first to realise that writers, if they were really united and conscious of their mission, could represent a power in the land, and with his usual impetuosity he sought to transform this feeble organisation into an effective weapon for the preservation of the rights of authorship.

Balzac was at his best when he was inspired by wrath, and he had good personal grounds for being wrathful. Every book he wrote was

20

pirated in Belgium before the print was dry, and the Belgian publishers, who never offered him a sou out of their profits, flooded
every foreign country in Europe with editions which they could sell
more cheaply than the authorised ones, since there were no author's
fees to pay, and they were turned out in the most slovenly manner.
Balzac did not pursue the matter as a personal grievance, however.
He was concerned with the honour and status of his profession, and
he drafted a *Code littéraire de la Société des Gens de Lettres* which, in
the republic of letters, is a document of historical importance on a
par with the Declaration of Human Rights in the Republic of
France and the Declaration of Independence in the United States
of America. He delivered lectures at Rouen and tried repeatedly to
organise his fellow-authors for joint action, but his efforts were
doomed to failure. The opposition and petty wrangling with which
he had to contend proved too strong for him, and he withdrew from
an association that was not big enough for his ideas or active
enough for his forceful temperament.

His ability to influence his generation was tested again in his
championship of the notary Peytel, and again it was found wanting.
An obscure notary named Peytel had been condemned to the
guillotine for the murder of his wife and his manservant, and in all
probability he had been justly sentenced. After having passed
through continual financial difficulties Peytel, who had formerly
been a journalist, eventually married a squinting but well-to-do
creole woman whose previous life was the subject of unpleasant
rumours. The manservant in her parents' home was said to have
been her lover and she brought him with her when she married
Peytel. One night both she and this man were murdered on their
way back from a neighbouring village. Peytel, who was submitted
to a keen interrogation, was forced to confess that he had killed
the manservant, and for this alone he might have got off lightly.
But the jury were unanimously of the opinion that he had taken
advantage of the favourable opportunity only in order to rid
himself of his wife, so that he might inherit her fortune.

Balzac had been well acquainted with Peytel some years previously, when they were colleagues on the journal *Le Voleur*, and he
was interested in the case from its psychological aspect. Perhaps
he was also tempted by the thought of continuing the tradition
established by Voltaire in the Calas affair, a tradition which was

later to be carried on so magnificently by Zola in the Dreyfus case —the French writer as the champion of the rights of the citizen, the defender of the innocently accused. Pushing his work to one side, he travelled with Gavarni to Belley for an interview with the condemned man and his easily kindled imagination soon convinced him that Peytel had fired the fatal shots in self-defence, hitting the woman by accident as she fled in the darkness. He immediately sat down and drew up a memorial for the Court of Appeal, a masterpiece of juridical acumen and forensic logic. Unfortunately the Court of Appeal declined to take cognisance of any document submitted from an unofficial source and considered only the plea of nullity put in by the defending attorney. This too was rejected, as was the petition for mercy presented to the King. Balzac, who had spared neither time, money, nor energy on behalf of a man whom he regarded as innocent, once more suffered defeat and Peytel was executed.

He was to receive yet a further warning to stick to his last. Four years had been sufficient to erase from his mind the catastrophe of the *Chronique de Paris* and the money he had lost in the venture. In the long run he was unable to suppress his keen desire to speak directly to his compatriots, to proclaim to them his literary, social, and political ideas. He knew that the editors and publishers of the Paris journals would not allow him to write freely. He had offended them by his independent attitude, and any attempt to put forward his views in the organs which they controlled would either be passed over in silence or mutilated beyond recognition. If he were not to be suffocated by his surfeit of ideas it was essential that he should provide himself from time to time with his own mouthpiece.

This time he called it *La Revue Parisienne*, and he was convinced that it would be successful since he intended to write practically the whole of the contents himself. Paris and the world could not refuse to listen when Honoré de Balzac, the only free, independent thinker and politician in France, commented on affairs week by week, when Honoré de Balzac in person reviewed all the new and important books and plays, when Honoré de Balzac, the first novelist in Europe, published his stories in his own journal. That was the only road to success. Nothing must be left to others. He took upon himself the work of five men, not only combining the functions of editor and editorial staff, but even looking after the financial side. He read the proofs, negotiated with the printers, spurred on the compositors, supervised the distribution, sweated up and downstairs from morning till night between the composing-room and his office, or sat in his shirtsleeves at a dirty table amid a hubbub of noise busily engaged in dashing off an article while at the same time issuing orders to his underlings. For three months he worked in this way, writing enough to fill three or four normal volumes, but soon he was again one illusion the poorer. Neither Paris nor the outside world manifested any particular curiosity as to what Honoré de Balzac thought of the political situation, while his literary, philosophical, and social views were received with nonchalance. After three months he quitted the editorial chair and once more there was nothing to show for a vast expenditure of effort.

❖⊃∘⊂❖

Yet his exertions had not been entirely fruitless. If the *Revue Parisienne* had printed nothing during its short existence but Balzac's essay on Stendhal's *La chartreuse de Parme*, it would have deserved its niche in the annals of French literature. Never were Balzac's essential generosity and amazing artistic insight more superbly revealed than in this enthusiastically laudatory notice of a completely unknown book by a completely unknown author. World literature has few instances to offer of such an intuitive feeling of comradeship. In order to estimate at its true value the magnanimous spontaneity with which Balzac freely and of his own will awarded the palm to his greatest rival in the field of the novel and, many decades in advance of his age, tried to win for him the recognition which he merited, we must compare the relative standing of the two men in the eyes of their contemporaries. Balzac's fame had long since spread from one end of Europe to the other, while Stendhal was still so utterly disregarded that when he died his obituaries, in so far as any appeared at all, referred to him as "Stenhal" and his real name was given as "Bayle". He was never included in the ranks of French writers. The journals filled their pages with praise or criticism of such authors as Alphonse Carr, Jules Janin, Sandeau, Paul de Kock, and other industrious scribblers whose works are now forgotten, but in their time sold in tens of

thousands of copies. The sum total of the sales of Stendhal's
L'amour amounted to twenty-two copies, so that he himself mock-
ingly dubbed it "a sacred book" since nobody dared to touch it.
Le rouge et le noir did not reach a second edition during his lifetime.

The professional critics ignored him. When *Le rouge et le noir* was
first published Sainte-Beuve did not think it worth a notice, and
when he gave it one later on he was rather disdainful. "His characters," he said, "are not alive; they are ingeniously constructed
automata." The *Gazette de France* commented, "Monsieur de
Stendhal is not a fool, though he writes foolish books." Goethe's
praise in his conversations with Eckermann did not attract attention until long after Stendhal's death. Balzac, however, realised
even from the early volumes the particular quality of Stendhal's
intelligence and his mastery of psychology, and he utilised every
opportunity that came his way to pay reverence to a man who only
wrote books for his own amusement and published them without
entertaining ambitious hopes for their success. In the *Comédie
humaine* he mentioned the crystallisation process in love which
Stendhal was the first to describe, and referred to the latter's
Italian travel-books. Stendhal was too modest to approach his famous
colleague on the basis of these friendly indications. He did not even
send him his new publications, but fortunately his loyal friend
Raymond Colomb drew Balzac's attention to them, begging him at
the same time to espouse the cause of this author whom the critics
had failed to appreciate. Balzac replied at once, on the 20th of
March, 1839:

> I had already read in the *Constitutionnel* an extract from *La
> chartreuse* which caused me to commit the sin of being envious.
> Yes, I was assailed by a fit of jealousy on reading that superb
> and accurate account of a battle such as I had dreamed of for
> my *Scènes de la vie militaire*, the most difficult thing I have ever
> undertaken. I was ravished, chagrined, enchanted, driven to
> despair by the morsel. . . . You may count on me to tell you
> sincerely what I think of it. The fragment has roused my expecta-
> tions and is going to make me exacting in my demands. . . .

A smaller mind would have been vexed at finding that the chief
scene in his forthcoming novel, the description of a Napoleonic
battle, had already been portrayed with consummate skill by
another writer. For ten years Balzac had been turning over in his

thoughts the plan of *La bataille*. Instead of the traditional heroic and sentimental picture, he wanted to present a realistic account that would be true to historical fact, authentic in its details, and imbued with the spirit of actuality. Now he was too late, for Stendhal had anticipated him. An artist whose mind is stored with riches and whose inventive genius is inexhaustible can afford to be generous. With a hundred themes still to be worked out and embodied in books, Balzac was not upset because one of his contemporaries had produced a masterpiece that he himself had set his heart on writing. He therefore did not stint his praise of *La chartreuse de Parme*, which he called "*le chef-d'oeuvre de la littérature à idée*":

> This great work could have been conceived and executed only by a man of fifty in all the vigour of his years and the maturity of his talents.

His masterly analysis of the inward action, with its recognition of Stendhal's profound understanding of the Italian spirit in all its forms and variants, has not been surpassed by any critic who has written on the subject since.

Stendhal was astonished and startled when Balzac's essay broke in upon his solitude at Civitavecchia, where he was employed as consul. At first he could not believe his eyes. Hitherto his work had met with nothing but paltry comment, but this was the voice of a man whom he respected. Balzac was greeting him as a fellow-author of his own rank, and the letter Stendhal wrote in acknowledgment betrayed a sense of bewilderment that he tried in vain to subdue. He began:

> I received a great surprise yesterday evening, Monsieur. I do not think anyone has ever before had his work discussed in such a way in the pages of a review, and moreover by the best judge in the matter. You have had compassion on an orphan who had been cast out into the streets.

And he expressed his gratitude for " an astonishing article such as no writer has ever received from another." With an artistic insight equalling that of Balzac himself, he accepted the fraternal hand that was held out to him. He knew that they were both writing for a later age than their own:

When we are dead we shall exchange rôles with these others. So long as we are alive they possess absolute power over our mortal bodies, but after that they will be wrapped for ever in oblivion.

Thanks to some mysterious affinity of substance, mind was calling to mind, and above the noise and turmoil of the ephemeral literature of the day these two immortals looked one another tranquilly in the eye, assured in their own hearts that they stood apart. Rarely had Balzac's intuition been more superbly demonstrated than when, from the thousands of books that were being published, he chose one of the most disregarded of them all for special praise. Yet his championship of Stendhal awakened no echo among his contemporaries. It was ignored by the literary pundits of the day as his argument in defence of Peytel had been rejected by the legal courts of appeal. His flaming plea was made in vain, in so far as any great moral deed, whether crowned with success or not, can ever be said to have been performed in vain.

In vain! In vain! Too often had Balzac uttered these words to himself, and all too often had he experienced their truth. At the age of forty-two his restless brain had produced a hundred books and created some two thousand characters, among them many that will remain imperishable. He had constructed a whole world out of his own mind, but the world in which he lived had given him nothing in return. At the age of forty-two he was poorer than ever before. In the rue Lesdiguières he had at least been rich in illusions, but now even these had been dispersed and his labours had brought him nothing but debts. He had built himself a house and it had been taken from him in distraint. He had founded reviews and they had defied his efforts to keep them afloat. His business ventures had failed ; his attempt to launch into politics had been frustrated by unsympathetic electors; his candidature for the Academy had been rejected. Everything he had undertaken had been in vain, or appeared to have been in vain. Would his physical resistance, his over-excited brain and unduly strained heart, be equal in the long run to the almost intolerable burden? Would he still possess the strength to complete the *Comédie humaine*? Would he again be able to afford a period of rest, when like other people he could travel

and be free from care? For the first time in his life Balzac was
assailed by momentary fits of discouragement, and he seriously
entertained the idea of quitting Paris, France, and Europe. He
thought of settling in Brazil, where there was an Emperor called
Dom Pedro who might rescue him and offer him a home. He procured books about Brazil, turned the matter over in his mind, and
dreamt of the future. Things could not continue as they had done,
of that he felt convinced. Some miracle would occur to relieve him
of his fruitless labours. He would be freed overnight from his life
of servitude, delivered from a strain that had become more than he
could endure.

Yet was it possible that such a miracle could eventuate at the
eleventh hour? Balzac hardly dared any longer to hope for it. Then
one morning, on the 5th of January, 1842, when he had risen from
the writing-table at which he had spent the night, his servant
brought in his letters. Among these was one in a hand which had
long been familiar to him, but this time the paper was black-edged
and the seal was of the same mournful colour. He tore the letter
open and learned that Monsieur de Hanski was dead. The woman
who had plighted her troth to him, and to whom he had vowed
eternal love, was now a widow and had succeeded to her husband's
millions. His half-forgotten dream had suddenly been fulfilled.
Incipit vita nuova. A new life was about to begin, a happy life,
peaceful and free from care. Balzac's last illusion had again taken
shape, the last one of all, in which he was to spend the rest of his
life and in which he was to die.

THE AUTHOR OF THE
"COMÉDIE HUMAINE"

CHAPTER XIX

The Wooing of Madame de Hanska

he letter which Balzac received on the 5th of January, 1842, represented the last great turning-point in his life. The past was suddenly transformed into the present and dominated the future. From that moment his whole powerful will was concentrated on one single aim. His relations with Madame de Hanska, already waning, must be renewed, their secret engagement must be consummated in marriage, promise must become fulfilment.

The achievement of this goal would require more than ordinary effort, for during the years that had gone by since their last meeting their association had gradually been transferred to a more formal footing. Their correspondence had grown more and more cool and insincere, for it was not possible in the long run to violate the laws of Nature. They had not seen one another for seven long years. On account of his financial embarrassments, and perhaps too because of his relations with the Contessa, Balzac had been unable to undertake the journey to Wierzchownia, while Madame de Hanska either could not or would not persuade her husband to travel once more to western Europe, where she would have had the opportunity of meeting her quondam lover.

Since love needs proximity if it is to endure, just as a flame is kept alive by the invigorating quality of oxygen, passion died away between them. Balzac tried to maintain the old ecstatic tone in his letters, but nobody realised more clearly than Madame de Hanska that this was merely an affected warmth. Her kinsmen and acquaintances in Paris did not omit to inform her that the Contessa Guidoboni-Visconti was living next door to him at *Les Jardies*. The escapade with Madame Marbouty had been the subject of comment which had reached as far as the Ukraine. And it is not surprising if Madame de Hanska was irritated by Balzac's insincerities, or if she found it difficult to swallow the despairing lament and assurances of eternal faithfulness with which he sought to conjure away the suspicions that were only too evidently confirmed by facts known to every gossip in Paris. A tart tone crept into their correspondence. Madame de Hanska could apparently no longer conceal the chagrin she felt at being expected to believe the stories he told her of his ascetic life, and she must have expressed her doubts as to his veracity in fairly unambiguous language, for Balzac, with his nerves on edge, sent her a letter in which he too did not mince his words. He could no longer brook being superciliously rebuked for his "extravagant follies" by a woman who was leading a life of ease at her husband's side and, though she might have been bored, did not know the meaning of worry. In his wrath he stormed at her:

> I beg you never to interfere, either with praise or censure, in the affairs of people who feel the waters meeting over their heads and are trying to rise to the surface! Rich people will never be capable of understanding the difficulties of those less fortunate.

He wrote even more vehemently on one occasion when she had spoken of his "frivolous nature":

> In what way am I frivolous? Is it because during the past twelve years I have been devoting myself without respite to the completion of an immense literary task? Is it because for ten years there has been no room in my heart for more than one love? Is it because for the past twelve years I have been toiling day and night to pay off an enormous debt with which my mother's insensate and deliberate design has burdened me? Is it because despite so much misery I have neither smothered myself, nor blown out my brains, nor flung myself into the river? Is it

because I work without intermission and try, in a variety of ingenious ways, to shorten the period of penal servitude to which I am condemned? Please explain! Is it because I shun society, because I keep to myself, in order that I may concentrate on my one passion, on my work and the paying off of my debts? . . . Frivolous nature, indeed! Really, you are behaving like a *bon bourgeois* might have done if he saw Napoleon turning to right and left and in every direction to examine the field on which he was going to give battle, and then commented: "This fellow can't stay in one spot! He has no *idée fixe*!"

This correspondence between two lovers who had not met for seven years, and had become used to their own separate ways of living, had ceased to have any rhyme or reason. Madame de Hanska had a growing daughter whom she was able to make the recipient of her confidences. She no longer needed the outlet which she had found in her letters to Balzac, and in her assured, restricted existence she had no secrets to communicate. Balzac, for his part, had wearied of the long term of waiting and was beginning to forget the vow that was apparently destined to remain unfulfilled. In 1839 he had written to Zulma Carraud asking her to bear him in mind if she should happen to come across a woman with a couple of hundred thousand francs, or even a mere hundred thousand, "provided that her dowry can be applied to the settling of my affairs". He had ceased to dream of a fairy princess since it had become evident that Monsieur de Hanski was in no hurry to abandon his millions. He was prepared to withdraw his gaze from his unattainable polar star and to marry any woman who would pay off his debts, cut an adequate figure as the wife of Balzac, and look after his household at *Les Jardies*. At the age of forty the realist had given up his extravagant flights of imagination in the marital sphere and had returned to the old formula of his earlier years, "*une femme et une fortune*".

The correspondence with Madame de Hanska might well have come to a close at this point. It could have died away to a mere trickle, as in the case of Zulma Carraud, with whom Balzac likewise had a feeling of discomfort because of her demand for greater honesty. Yet neither Balzac nor Madame de Hanska wanted to break off their relations with one another. Her pride in the humble devotion of the greatest novelist of the day had become almost the most important thing in her life, and she had no reason to abandon voluntarily a correspondence which pandered so satisfyingly to her vanity. Balzac, on the other hand, could not dispense with the habit of self-portrayal which had by now become second nature to him. He needed somebody to whom he could pour out his troubles, describe his work, and total up his debts; and just as she was covertly planning to preserve the letters he wrote to her, so he enjoyed the thought that they were being preserved in some secret place. So they continued to write to one another, though more sparingly as time went on. Occasionally he would complain of the "*rareté de vos envois*" or the "*intervalle entre vos lettres*", and she would reproach him for not writing often enough. But in the latter case he would let fly. How could she allow herself to make comparisons between his share in the correspondence and hers! She had nothing to do all day, she lived "*dans une solitude profonde et sans beaucoup de travaux*", while he was always pressed for time and had to work for fifteen hours a day writing and correcting proofs. Every page he wrote to her had to be wrung from the hours he would otherwise have spent either in doing work for which he was paid or in snatching much-needed sleep. He had no scruple in letting her know that whenever she, who was rolling in money, received a longer letter from her impoverished lover, it represented for him a loss of hundreds of francs that he might have earned by writing the same quantity of words for an editor or a publisher. It was not asking too much of her, therefore, if he expected a letter every fortnight. Her reply to this appears to have been in the form of a declaration that she would only write to him when he wrote to her, that she would return letter for letter, and he thundered:

Ah! So at last I discover how extremely petty you are, and that proves to me that you are a creature of this world! Ah! So you stopped writing to me because my letters to you were infrequent! Well, they were infrequent because I did not always have the money for postage, though I did not want to tell you this. Yes, I had sunk as deep as that, and even deeper. It is very horrible and very dismal, but it is true, like the Ukraine where you are living. Yes, there have been days when I proudly devoured a roll as I walked along the boulevards.

These little skirmishes grew sharper and the intervals between their letters increased until at last, just before the arrival of the fateful black-bordered missive with its black seal, a whole three months went by without Balzac putting pen to paper. One can feel that they had begun to jar on one another's nerves. They were indulging in mutual recriminations on the score of coldness, indolence or dishonesty, and each was charging the other with responsibility for the gradual ebbing of a harmonious correspondence which had started off *fortissimo* and *prestissimo* and was now losing its *appassionato*.

⋘∘⋙

Neither of them was really at fault. The blame lay with the peculiarly unnatural relationship into which they had entered from the start. They had expected to be separated only for short periods at a time until their union became permanent, an eventuality which they regarded as not far distant; and when they plighted their troth in this strange way while her husband was still alive, Madame de Hanska imposed the condition that Balzac should remain faithful to her. The only concession she allowed him was that he might seek satisfaction for his physical desires from the ladies whose profession it was to cater for such needs. Monsieur de Hanski, however, lived for another eight years, and Madame de Hanska's jealousy, which was at bottom nothing more than offended pride, became a source of exasperation to her distant lover.

Come, come, [he wrote to her without any subterfuge after having long pretended that he was keeping to his promise] a man isn't a woman, is he? You do not think a man can remain without a woman from 1834 to 1843, do you? You are sufficiently informed, medically speaking, to know that he would degenerate into impotence and imbecility. You said, "prostitutes". I might have got into a state like that of G.'s friend in Rome. You must weigh the dominating need for distraction felt by people of imagination who have to work all the time, their wretchedness, their weariness, and so on, against the few reasons you have for finding fault with me and the cruel manner in which these faults have been punished—then you will not talk of the past except to lament the fact that we have been separated.

His plain speaking had no effect. Though she had been able to convince herself personally of his full-blooded virility, she was unable to forgive his escapades with other women. After all, he was not a professional lady-killer and he had proved to the whole world the seriousness with which he was devoting himself to a vast intellectual task, yet she reproached him with inconstancy and frivolity of character. Living as she was in comfort and prosperity at her husband's side, with no thought herself of making the slightest sacrifice, she insisted that the harassed Balzac should live as chastely as a monk and as frugally as a clerk, allowing himself no relaxation or small luxuries, writing all night and half the day, and waiting, waiting, until perhaps—but only perhaps—after the death of Monsieur de Hanski she decided to reward him for his renunciation and perseverance. Undoubtedly she had some cause for complaint, but he should have insisted on his right to lead his own life free from her domineering attempts to control his actions. Instead of this, he concealed the essentials, pretended that he was quite other than he was, and told clumsy lies about his relations with the Contessa and other women like a schoolboy fearful of a thrashing. For some inscrutable reason he was unable to adopt a courageous attitude towards her imperious demands on his loyalty and to confront this aristocratic female despot of the Russian provinces with the dignified mien of an artist who was sure of himself. Yet amid all his little subterfuges and deviations from the truth he was being perfectly honest when he assured her time and again that, far from seeking adventures, his one longing was to escape from the hazardous conditions under which he was living into the peace and stability that had hitherto been denied him. He had begun to grow a trifle weary of the eternal struggle, and after twenty years of incessant buffeting by storms he wanted nothing better than to sail into more tranquil waters. He had had enough of adventures, of women for whom he could only find time between the completing of one book and the beginning of another, with the added inconveniences of secret rendezvous and the presence of a more or less complaisant husband in the background. As long ago as September, 1838, he had written to Zulma Carraud, to whom he never dared to lie, in accents of undoubted sincerity:

> I swear to you that I have sent all my hopes packing, all my extravagances, all my ambitions! I want to lead the life of a parson, a simple, peaceful existence. A woman of thirty with three or four hundred thousand francs, provided she is of agree-

able disposition and comely appearance, would find me ready to marry her if she were willing to have me. She would pay off my debts and in five years she would be recouped by my earnings.

This was the rôle he had contemplated for Madame de Hanska, but with the passage of time he found it intolerable to base all his expectations on a woman who was living a thousand miles away and who was perhaps no longer the adored mistress he had known six or seven years ago. His polar star was too distant to illumine his life. Imperceptibly his *épouse d'amour* reverted once more to the *Etrangère* to whom he had confided his secret dreams, and even the process of pouring out his confessions had lost its charm, for it had degenerated into a routine to which he applied himself at intervals almost with nonchalance. In September, 1841, three months before the receipt of the fateful letter, he wrote to her for what might have been the last time. He no longer believed in the illusion of becoming the husband of Madame de Hanska. His dream of love and riches was over and could be relegated to the limbo of his other *illusions perdues*.

⟨⟩∘⟨⟩

When he tore open the black-bordered letter and read that Monsieur de Hanski had passed away on the 10th of November, 1841, the blood rushed from his heart and he was so overcome that his hands trembled. The unthinkable, or rather that of which he had no longer dared to think, had happened. The woman to whom he had pledged eternal love was free. She was a widow, and a widow, moreover, abundantly supplied with all the wealth of which he had ever dreamed, the ideal wife for him, aristocratic, still young, intelligent, acceptable to the outer world as the spouse of Honoré de Balzac, a woman who would pay off his debts, enable him to devote his energies to the work that really mattered, foster his genius, enhance his reputation, and satisfy his senses. He had once loved this woman and she had loved him, and in the electrifying moment when he knew that she was free his passion flared up again from the glimmering ashes. The sheet of paper which he held in his trembling hand had changed his life. Everything for which he had hoped and longed had suddenly taken shape, the shape of Madame de Hanska, and he realised that there was only one thing left for

him to do. The woman whom he had once carried off her feet must
be conquered once more, and this time for ever.

The deep emotion by which he was stirred can be felt in the letter
he sent to her in reply. It was an honest and manly letter, in which
he made no hypocritical attempt to console the widow for her loss.
He knew that she had loved her husband little or not at all, and he
employed no artificial phrases to praise the dead man's merits or
pretend that he was overwhelmed with grief at his decease. He
confined himself to refuting any possible imputation that, much as
he had desired her, there could have been any room in his heart for
the wish to see her widowed:

> So far as I am concerned, dear adored one, though this occur-
> rence brings within my reach that which I have desired so
> ardently for nearly ten years, I can do myself the justice before
> you and before God of declaring that I have never cherished any
> other thought in my heart than that of complete submission, and
> that even in the most cruel moments of my life I have never
> sullied my soul by harbouring evil wishes. One cannot prevent
> oneself from indulging in occasional involuntary flights of fancy.
> I have often said to myself: "How buoyant my life would be
> with her!" One cannot preserve one's faith, keep up one's spirits,
> or maintain one's inner integrity without hope.

One thing alone caused him to rejoice at this turn of events, the fact
that he could now write to her "with open heart", and he assured
her that he had in no way changed. Since Neuchâtel she had never
ceased to remain the be-all and end-all of his existence, and he
implored her: "Write and tell me that your life will henceforth
belong wholly to me, that now we shall be happy with no possible
cloud to cast its shadow."

Letter followed swiftly upon letter. The engagement into which
he had entered so many years ago had been transformed into
reality overnight. What could now stand in the way of their final
union? Everything suddenly appeared to him in a different light,
even himself. Twelve months before he had been depicting himself
in melancholy tones as a white-haired old man, weary, addicted to
unwelcome corpulence, unable to collect his thoughts, afflicted with
congestion of the blood and tending to apoplexy. Now he painted
his personality in the most attractive colours to his future bride.
His snowy locks had darkened again and his weariness was gone:

There are only a few white hairs here and there, and owing to my studious way of life I am well preserved, apart from my *embonpoint*, which is inevitable in view of my sedentary occupation. I do not think I have changed since Vienna, and my heart is so young that it has kept me young in body despite the monastic austerity of my existence. I still have fifteen years of youth, more or less, left to me, just as you have, my dear one, and at this moment I would willingly give ten years of my old age to hasten the hour when we shall see one another again.

His rapid imagination was already working out the whole future course of his life. For her daughter he advised her to find, as soon as possible, "a hard-headed, capable husband", above all one who was "rich enough to permit you to meet your commitments in the way of a dowry by the payment of a lump sum". Then she would be as free from material encumbrances as she was legally and morally, and they would be able to live together as he had always dreamed of doing, happier than they had ever dared to imagine they could be. There was no need to waste a single further day. He would settle his affairs in Paris forthwith and go to Dresden, where he would be nearer to the object of his boundless love. He was ready, readier than he had ever been, he loved her as he had never loved her before, and it is evident from his letters that he had never looked forward to anything with such glowing impatience as he did now to the single word from her lips that would bid him come to her.

Her answer reached him on the 21st of February, six weeks after he had first learned the news. We do not know its exact text, since she destroyed it, together with her other letters, but we do know that it contained a harsh rejection of his wooing, a blunt refusal of his plea to be allowed to hasten to her side. He had regarded it as a matter of course that she would give her consent, but with a "glacial calm" she cancelled the vows they had made to one another and gave him back the freedom he did not want. "*Vous êtes libre*", she wrote with incisive clarity, and apparently went on to elaborate in detail the reasons for her decision. She no longer trusted him, since for seven years he had never yielded to the desire to see her, though he had had no difficulty in finding both the time and the money to make a number of journeys to Italy, where, moreover, he had not been unaccompanied. He had thus, and no doubt on other occasions too, violated the terms of their mutual pledge, and all was over. She intended to devote the rest of her life to her daughter, whom she would never leave. "If my poor child were taken from me, I should die." To judge from Balzac's despairing reply, her letter must have been sharp-edged as an axe, bringing his hopes crashing to the ground with one hard blow that struck to their very roots.

Was Madame de Hanska's "No!" final and deliberate or was it only her way of putting him to the test, a feint dictated by her pride and vanity to make him woo her all the more ardently? It is a critical question, all the harder to answer since it touches the core of the whole complicated relationship between them and involves, with all the delicate psychological appreciation that the circumstances demand, an examination of the problem of her own attitude to Balzac. It is not a matter of choosing between two apparently simple alternatives—did she love him or did she not? Such a way of dealing with the question would merely avoid the issue and would be unjust to an association which was dominated, both outwardly and inwardly, by inhibitions and contradictions. Passionate love in a woman is characterised by a boundless capacity for surrender. In this sense Madame de Hanska was incapable of passion—or at least of a passion for Balzac. Imbued with a sense of aristocratic pride, domineering, self-reliant, capricious, and intolerant as she was, she demanded his love as a tribute which she could magnanimously accept or contemptuously reject. Her own readiness to surrender was curbed, as can be seen from the letters, by the constant exercise of restraint. She regarded him from the very start as her social inferior, and her submission implied a stepping down to his level. Balzac, for his part, accepted the inferior status which she assigned to him. When he called himself her *moujik*, or her serf, he was unconsciously confirming the masochistic note in his own attitude. His relations with women generally were marked by a lack of manly self-assertion, and he placed himself completely under Madame de Hanska's yoke. It is frequently painful to observe in his letters the continual gesture of going down on his bended knees, the rhapsodic adoration, the total abnegation of personal dignity. It is distressing to see one of the greatest geniuses of all time humbly bowing his head for seven years to kiss her shoe, lowering himself to the dust before a woman who was, after all, a very mediocre member of the Russian provincial aristocracy ; and if anything is warranted to arouse one's mistrust of Madame de Hanska's character and the tact which her advocates are so wont to praise, it is not only the fact that she tolerated and encouraged Balzac's servile submission, but the suspicion that she even perhaps exacted it. A woman who had really perceived the greatness of Balzac could not have helped being embarrassed at the unseemly bearing he had seen fit to adopt, and she would have raised him from his knees to look her straight in the eye. She would have been prepared, if occasion called for it, to subordinate her will to his. There can be no doubt that Madame de Hanska was not capable of love on this level. It pleased her and gratified her pride to be the object of his adoration, and in a certain measure her feeling towards him was that of love, but—and this was the crucial factor—always with more than a tincture of condescension. It was she who descended from her pedestal and granted her favours with an air of magnanimity. "*Le bon Balzac*" or "*Le pauvre Balzac*"—this was the strain in which she referred to him in her letters to her daughter, and it tells us all we require to know. She was clever enough to recognise his worth, she was feminine enough and sensual enough to enjoy his tempestuous virility, she felt a deep sympathy for him despite her realisation of his weaknesses and his unreliability, but at bottom it was only herself she loved. She was excited by the adventure of which she had become the heroine, by the glowing, romantic idolisation which cast a glamour over her otherwise commonplace existence, but her cool intelligence was not equal to making the same heady response to his exuberant wooing. A woman so imbued with caste-prejudice could not soften to the point of flinging her inhibitions to the wind and giving herself without restraint. The only genuine love she ever displayed was for her daughter. Even during the years when she and Balzac lived as man and wife, he was never her most intimate confidant. It was always her stupid little daughter in whom alone she reposed her trust, while Balzac remained the plebeian intruder to whom the last citadel of her heart was firmly denied.

Yet while her husband was alive she had accepted Balzac as her lover and gone as far as she could without ruining her marriage and compromising her good name in society. The acid test of her real feelings came when the death of Monsieur de Hanski left her free to

decide between the two forms of aristocracy, that of rank and
wealth or that of genius and fame. She had always looked forward
with apprehension to the moment when she would be faced with the
necessity of making this decision, and even though her letters to
her brother (the originals of which are not yet available for inspection) cannot be regarded in every detail as wholly trustworthy,
there is one which effectively describes her state of mind in relation
to the problem:

> I am glad at times that I am not compelled to decide whether or
> not to marry the man whom you seem to be afraid of having as a
> future brother-in-law. Yet I know that I love him, and perhaps
> more than you imagine. His letters are the great event in my
> life of solitude. I await them impatiently, I want to read in their
> pages all the admiration with which they are filled, and I am
> proud of being something which no woman has ever been to
> him before. For he is a genius, one of the greatest that France
> has produced; and when I remember this, every other considera-
> tion disappears and is merged in the pride which suffuses my
> soul at the thought of having won his love, though I am so un-
> worthy of him. Yet when we are alone together I cannot avoid
> noticing certain incongruities and suffering from the thought
> that others too may observe them and draw their own conclu-
> sions. At such moments I would like to cry aloud my love and
> my pride, and reproach those who are unable to see what is so
> evident to me. I prefer not to think what my position would be
> if Monsieur de Hanski were to die. I hope that I shall know how
> to do my duty as I have always tried to do, in the way taught to
> us by our father, but perhaps I am glad in the depths of my soul
> that I am not called upon to make up my mind, while being
> able to forget at certain moments everything in the world except
> the single fact that this great man is prepared to sacrifice all for
> me, who have so little to offer him in return.

Their joint pledge, on which Balzac rested all his hopes, was for her
a source of constant disquiet.

It was, therefore, only natural that her first impulse should be
to postpone the inevitable decision still further and to refuse to
permit her impetuous lover, of whose passionate powers of persuasion she was afraid, to hasten to her side. Her freedom of action
was by no means so unrestricted as Balzac, far away in Paris,

fondly imagined, for her husband's death had been followed by an unwelcome increase in the attentions of her family. Her uncles and aunts on the neighbouring estates, as well as her nieces living in the house and her relatives in St. Petersburg and Paris, were all aware of her romantic attachment to Monsieur de Balzac, and they were united in their apprehension lest the handsome property of Wierzchownia, together with the millions which she had now inherited, should fall into the hands of an adventurer, a French writer who had turned the widow's head with his sentimental phrases. One of her relatives immediately brought an action to contest Monsieur de Hanski's will, according to which he had held the property jointly with his wife. The case was taken to Kiev, where judgment went against Madame de Hanska, and she had to travel to St. Petersburg to lodge an appeal with the supreme court and to petition the Tsar. Meanwhile she was beset on all sides by her other kinsmen and kinswomen, who did their best by malicious gossip and calumnies to turn her against Balzac. The most zealous of these was her notorious Aunt Rosalie, whom Balzac and all other Frenchmen had good reason to hate. During the French Revolution her mother had been guillotined as a spy; she had made acquaintance as a child with the Conciergerie, where those condemned to death under the Terror had been confined; and the thought that her niece might marry the son of a member of the red Commune lent a spiteful vehemence to her continual exhortations and other attempts to bring her influence to bear. Even if Madame de Hanska had really been desirous of letting Balzac come to Russia, she was not in a position to follow her own wishes in the matter. She would have damaged her case in the courts, her situation generally would have been worsened, and she would probably have exposed herself to the ridicule of society if the corpulent gentleman with the ill-bred manners and childish extravagances had suddenly made his appearance among the aristocratic circles of St. Petersburg and she had had to introduce him to her haughty family. So she had no choice but to decline his offer. The fact that she clothed her refusal in such harsh and cutting terms may, perhaps, have been her way of testing the sincerity and endurance of his attachment.

Her letter struck Balzac like a thunderbolt. He had already made preparations for his journey to Dresden. He had gratuitously advised Madame de Hanska on the best way in which she could safeguard the property for her daughter, while herself enjoying the interest on it. He had allowed his imagination to run riot in writing to her of their forthcoming marriage, of the travels they would undertake together, and of the mansions in which they would live. Now came this letter with its clear, incisive "You are free", its blunt and uncompromising "No!"

Balzac, however, was not in a mood to accept no for an answer. He was accustomed to opposition, which only served to enhance his powers of attack. Every week, almost every day, he wrote her urgent, imploring letters, conjuring her to believe his protestations of constancy, overwhelming her with a hurricane of endearing assurances. The outbursts of ecstatic passion that had once characterised his letters to Neuchâtel and Geneva erupted once more after having so long been muted: "You cannot know how strong my attachment to you has been. I was attached to you for all human ends—love, friendship, ambition, success, pride, vanity, memory, pleasure, certitude—and by the faith in you which I set above all created good." He declared that everything he had written since they first met had been intended for her alone. His thoughts had been only of her, who had always been *"celle au nom de qui tout s'est accompli"*.

He was ready, he said, to make every concession. Their pledge need not be fulfilled to-morrow or the day after to-morrow, but would she set a date, any date, a specific day or even a specific year, to which he could look forward for the consummation of his hopes?

Alas! my beloved angel, it is no great thing that I have asked of my Eva. I only wanted you to say: "In eighteen months, in two years, we shall be happy." I only wanted you to say "we" and to fix the term of my waiting.

He entreated her to offer him a gleam of hope, the promise that he would find with her the peace he sought, otherwise he could not carry on: "After fifteen years of constant toil I can no longer sustain this struggle all alone. *Créer, toujours créer!* God created only for six days and rested on the seventh."

The mere thought of their ultimate union went to his head like wine:

Oh, my dear one, to live at last heart to heart, each for the other with nothing to fetter us! There are moments when the thought makes me foolish, and I ask myself how these seventeen months have gone by, with me here and you so far away! How vast is the power of money! What a sad spectacle it is to see the most beautiful sentiments depending on it! To see oneself chained, nailed down in Passy when one's heart is five hundred leagues away! There are days when I abandon myself to dreams. I imagine to myself that all the difficulties have been smoothed out, that the wisdom, discretion, the skill of "the Queen" have triumphed, that a word has come from her bidding me: "Come!" And I pretend to myself that I am on my way. On such days my friends do not recognise me. They ask me what is the matter. . . . I reply: "My troubles are about to end. I have hope." And they say: "He is mad."

Hardly had he received the news that she had moved to St. Petersburg to arrange about her appeal when he began to work out how many days the journey from Paris would take and how much it would cost him. Four hundred francs from Havre to St. Petersburg and another four hundred for the return. Two hundred francs from Havre to Paris. He hastily invented the most absurd pretexts to give his journey the appearance of necessity. He declared that he ought to have gone to the Russian capital long before to prepare for the setting up of a French theatre. Then he spoke of a shipping company that his brother-in-law wanted to establish with a view to building ships at a very low cost, and of the commission he had received to submit the proposition to the relevant authorities in St. Petersburg. All at once he discovered—perhaps with an eye to the Russian censorship when his letters were opened and read— that he had an affection for the Tsar, because the latter was the only genuine autocrat among all the sovereigns of Europe, and he announced that he felt "no aversion whatsoever to becoming a Russian subject".

So it went on, letter after letter, a veritable drum-fire of impatience and impetuosity. February, March, April, May, the whole summer and the whole winter long, until spring and summer came round once more and he had still not received the sanction for which he was waiting. A year and a half had passed since the death of Monsieur de Hanski and his widow had not yet sent the signal for which Balzac was longing—"*Viens!*" Then at last, in July, it arrived. Exactly a decade after their first meeting, in July, 1843, he reached St. Petersburg from Dunkirk, and his first steps were towards the Kutaisov house, where Madame de Hanska was staying. There was symbolic significance in the fact that it was situated in a street called *Grande Millione*.

CHAPTER XX

The " Comédie humaine "

t the age of forty-three Balzac realised that his only hope of achieving the tranquillity in which it would be possible to complete the great task he had undertaken lay in the reconquest of Madame de Hanska. He staked everything on this one throw, and during the eighteen months that she allowed him to cool his heels before granting him permission to join her at St. Petersburg he made desperate efforts to enhance his prestige as a wooer in the eyes of her disapproving family. No degree of literary fame would suffice to wipe out the slur of his bourgeois origin. They were too arrogant a crew for that. The *de* he had inserted in front of his name did not blind them to the fact that he was the grandson of a peasant. Their attitude towards him would always be one of supercilious condescension. But supposing he were to be elected to the Chamber, to acquire political influence, to have his self-made title of nobility confirmed by the King, who might even possibly confer upon him a more imposing designation? Or supposing he were to become a member of the Académie Française? Such a distinction would endow him with a dignity which would put it entirely out of the question for anyone to attempt to make him the object of personal ridicule. As an academician, moreover, he would draw a stipend of two thousand francs a year, and if he were to be appointed to the commission that was working on the Dictionary, an office from which he could not be removed once he was appointed, his emoluments would be six thousand. He would wear the famous dress-coat

decorated with palms, so that even a Madame de Hanska, *née*
Rzewuska, would have no need to be ashamed of having contracted
a *mésalliance*.

In order to achieve social equality with Madame de Hanska he
explored both these avenues to success. In each case he found the
steps too slippery. Since he did not own the minimum amount of
capital requisite for the entry of his name in the electoral list, his
ambition to enter the Chamber was frustrated. Nor was he more
successful in his candidature for the Academy. His claim to a seat
among the forty immortals could not be seriously disputed, but a
variety of pretexts could easily be found for the purpose of squeezing him out. It was said that his financial situation was too confused and a seat under the sacred dome could not be granted to a
man for whom the bailiffs and usurers would always be lying in
wait outside the door. His frequent absences from Paris were also
alleged as a reason for his ineligibility. The most honest statement
came from one of his bitter enemies, whose jealousy was revealed
in the words: "Monsieur de Balzac is too large for our armchairs."
With the exception of Victor Hugo and Lamartine he would have
reduced them all to insignificance.

There still remained the theatre as a means of settling his more
urgent difficulties, and he hurriedly wrote a couple of plays of which
the first, *Paméla Giraud*, was accepted for production at the
Vaudeville. Four-fifths of it had been cobbled together by two of
his "ghosts". The other, *Les ressources de Quinola*, was put on meanwhile at the *Odéon*, and Balzac made up his mind to engineer a
resounding success which should wipe out the memory of his dismal
failure with *Vautrin*.

As usual he concentrated his efforts in the wrong direction.
Rehearsals began before the fifth act was completed, which so
incensed the principal actress, the celebrated Madame d'Orvalli,
that she threw up her part. Balzac's chief concern was to turn the
première into the most brilliant spectacle that Paris had ever
witnessed. Everybody in Paris with a name or a reputation was to
be present on the first night. Admission was to be sternly denied to
any hostile intruders who might disturb the favourable atmosphere
by cat-calls or hissing. He therefore arranged with the director of
the theatre that no tickets should be issued for the first performance until he himself had personally approved of the prospective

recipient, and he spent the time which could more profitably have been devoted to the improving of his play in hanging about the box-office.

His plan of action had been worked out on the grand scale. The stage boxes were to be occupied by ambassadors and cabinet ministers, the stalls by Knights of St. Louis and peers, the first balcony by members of parliament and state officials, the second by prominent men in the world of finance, and the third by wealthy members of the *bourgeoisie*. The auditorium was to be plentifully sprinkled with handsome women sitting where they would attract most attention, and artists were commissioned to immortalise a scene which would be unparalleled in the annals of the capital.

Balzac's initial calculation was right—as it always was. Rumours of the forthcoming spectacle created a sensation in Paris, the box-office was besieged, and inflated prices were offered for tickets. Balzac, however, always stretched the bow too far, with the result that it invariably snapped in his hands. Instead of accepting the offers of two and three times the normal cost of the tickets, he tried to heighten public interest still further by spreading the story that the theatre was sold out. He expected that people would be consoled for their inability to be present at the *première* and would buy seats for later performances. But when the evening of the 19th of March, 1842, arrived and the doors were thrown open to receive the brilliant audience, three-quarters of the seats were empty owing to Balzac's mistaken tactics, and those who had come to admire one another had their spirits damped from the very start. Lireux, the director of the theatre, sent at the last moment for a horde of *claqueurs* and tickets were rapidly handed our gratis to anybody who wanted to see the show, but it was all in vain. It was too late to avoid fiasco. The more tragically the play on the stage developed, the more hilarious did the audience become. The subsequent performances attracted only those members of the public who wanted to take part in a rowdy scene. There was trumpeting, whistling, and the singing of an improvised chorus:

> *"C'est Monsieur Balzac*
> *Qu'a fait tout ce mic-mac."*

Balzac himself did not receive a single call before the curtain on the first night, and in any case he was so exhausted by his efforts to fill

the theatre with an audience of his own choosing that at the end of
the play he was found asleep in his box. His castle in the air had
sunk down through the trap-door, and another of Fate's hard blows
drove him back to his true destiny. When he complained to Madame
de Hanska that if *Les ressources de Quinola* should turn out a
failure he would have to write another four novels, we cannot
share his lament, for the stories he produced between 1841 and
1843 are among the most powerful to which he ever put his pen.
If his wretched melodramas had been successful we should probably
have lost them.

In the novels of this period of his greatest maturity he gradually
discarded the taste for fashionable society which sometimes marred
his earlier work. He had learned to see through it, and the salons
of the Faubourg St. Germain lost their lure for him more and more.
It was no longer the vanities and petty ambitions of the great or
the great ambitions of the petty marquises and countesses that
stimulated his creative genius, but the absorbing passions of
ordinary men and women. The more bitter Balzac grew from
experience and disappointment, the closer he drew to truth. The
mawkish sentimentality that tinged the best of his youthful
writings, as a spot of oil will stain a valuable garment, was in process
of evaporating. As his perspective grew larger the focus became
more accurate. In *Une ténébreuse affaire* he cast a searching light
behind the scenes of Napoleonic politics. In *La rabouilleuse* he
revealed a boldness of perception in sexual matters such as none of
his contemporaries had equalled. The problem of perversion and
sexual bondage has never been approached so audaciously as in the
character of old Doctor Rouget, the septuagenarian who brought
up a thirteen-year-old girl to be his mistress, and in that of his son
who became her willing sacrifice. And what a tremendous figure he
created in Philippe Bridau, no less an amoralist than Vautrin, but
unmelodramatic, and starkly true to life! During these three years,
furthermore, he completed the great fresco of the *Illusions perdues*,
produced the lightly written *Ursule Mirouet*, the spiritualistic
artificialities of which detract from its sincerity, but with superbly
credible character-drawing, and enriched his achievement with *La*

fausse maîtresse, Mémoires de deux jeunes mariés, Albert Savarus,
Un début dans la vie, Honorine, La muse du département, and a
dozen fragments.

Now that Balzac was seriously thinking of tidying up his affairs,
the time had come to survey the almost immeasurable abundance
of his writings. Despite the pressure from his creditors he had
always kept one final resource untapped. He had cautiously kept
intact and in reserve his sole right to issue the collected edition of
his works. However sorely beset he may have been, he had invariably refrained from disposing of a copyright for more than a limited
number of editions. Lavish and thoughtless as he was in other
respects, he had refused to part with his most valuable property
until the moment had come when he could display to his friends and
his enemies the whole proud scope and extent of his imperishable
creation.

Now that he was wooing the widow of the plutocratic Monsieur
de Hanski, the moment had arrived when he could demonstrate his
own wealth to the world. Scarcely had he announced his readiness
to issue a collected edition when no less than three publishers
joined forces for the purpose of financing the important undertaking, which was to be added to year by year. The contract, which
was signed on the 14th of April, 1842, granted the publishing firms
of Dubochet, Furne and Hetzel

> the right to prepare at their discretion and for such time of
> publication as shall appear to them suitable two or three editions
> of the works published by him up to the present time, or which
> may be published during the validity of the present contract, the
> first edition consisting of three thousand copies. This edition will
> be produced in octavo size and will contain . . . about twenty
> volumes, more or less, according to the requirements of the
> completed work.

Balzac received fifteen thousand francs as advance payment,
further royalties to be calculated at the rate of fifty centimes per
volume after the sale of forty thousand volumes had been effected.
He was thus sure of a permanent source of income which was bound
to increase as the years went on. The only restrictive clause in his
contract was one that he accepted willingly. If the cost of proof
corrections should exceed five francs a folio he would have to
defray the extra expenditure out of his own pocket; and since

he could never resist the temptation to polish his style so long as the printer was prepared to send him further proofs, his bill for corrections amounted to five thousand, two hundred and twenty-four francs, twenty-five centimes. The publishers did not like the title "Collected Works", which was too commonplace to attract the public's attention, and they asked him to find a name which would emphasise the unity of the whole series of volumes, with their recurring characters and the microcosm of society in its heights and depths.

Balzac agreed. Ten years before, when he had helped Félix Davin to prepare an introduction to a collection of his novels, he had realised that his aim was directed towards a complete conspectus of human society in which each book represented one stage of the structure. The problem was to find a title that would express the comprehensive scope of the work. He dallied with various suggestions until finally a lucky chance came to his aid. De Belloy, his friend and former editorial secretary, had just returned from Italy, where he had been studying Italian literature and had read the *Divina Commedia* in the original text. This gave birth to the idea of presenting the collected stories as a worldly comedy in contrast to Dante's divine comedy, the sociological structure in contrast to the theological one. *Eureka!* What title could be more fitting than *La comédie humaine*!

Balzac was enthusiastic and the publishers were equally pleased. They requested him, however, to provide an introduction to the collected edition that would explain to the public why he had chosen this new title, which his readers might otherwise be inclined to regard as somewhat pretentious. Balzac was reluctant to do this, since there was more lucrative work awaiting his pen, and suggested that Félix Davin's old preface to the *Etudes de moeurs au 19me siècle* would sufficiently enlighten his readers as to his aims and intentions. Nine-tenths of it had been written by himself. Then he proposed the name of George Sand, who was well-disposed towards him and might be kind enough to contribute the new introduction on which the publishers insisted. Finally he was persuaded, very much against his will, by a tactful letter from Hetzel, who exhorted him not to repudiate his own child and offered some really useful indications as to how the preface might be composed. "Make it as modest and objective as you can. That is the only way you can show your just pride in having achieved what you have achieved. Speak quite calmly. Imagine that you are an old man looking at yourself down the vista of the years, speak like one of your own characters, and you will produce something of indispensable value. So get down to work, *mon gros père*, and forgive a humble publisher for having talked to Your Greatness in this way. You know that I have done so with the best intentions."

So Balzac sat down and wrote the celebrated preface to the *Comédie humaine*. It is, indeed, more tranquilly objective than we would normally have expected from him. With practical sagacity he had recognised that Hetzel's advice was eminently sensible, and he succeeded in finding the golden mean between the grandeur of his theme and the personal modesty which he had been recommended to exercise. When he confessed to Madame de Hanska that these sixteen pages of introduction had cost him more effort than a whole novel, he was probably not exaggerating. He expounded in it a system of human society which he compared with the systems of Geoffroy St. Hilaire and Buffon. Just as in Nature the various species of animals develop into more specialised creatures according to their environment, so do human beings under the influence of their social environment. If one wishes to write a "History of the Human Heart" containing some three to four thousand characters, each stratum of society, each of its forms and passions, must be represented in at least one character, and the artist's creative power must be devoted to linking the individual figures and episodes in such a way that they "constitute a complete story, of which each chapter is a novel and each novel an epoch".

In view of the infinite variety of human nature, the artist needs only to observe, and here Balzac develops the core of his theme. "Chance is the greatest of all novelists. In order to be creative one only has to study it. French society is the real historian, and I have merely tried to guide its pen. By taking an inventory of its virtues and vices, selecting the most important of social occurrences, and forming types by the combination of several similarly constituted characters, I have perhaps managed to write the history of morals which so many historians have forgotten to do." It was his endeavour to produce for the France of the nineteenth century a work such as had, unfortunately, not been bequeathed to posterity by Rome, Athens, Memphis, Persia or India. He wanted to portray

22

the society of his century and at the same time reveal its secret motive causes. Here Balzac openly proclaimed that the novelist's task is one of realism, but he expressly added that though the novel has no meaning if it does not adhere to truth in every detail, it must at the same time unconsciously voice the demand for a better world. In broad outline he unfolded his plan:

> The *Scenes from Private Life* depict childhood and youth, with the false steps to which they are prone. The *Scenes from Provincial Life* show the age of passion, calculation, self-interest, and ambition. The *Scenes from Parisian Life* portray finally the various tastes and vices, with all the unbridled forms of behaviour which are characteristic of the manners and morals of capital cities—for it is there that good and evil meet and have their strongest repercussions. . . .
>
> After having described the life of society in these three sections, I was still confronted with the task of showing the kind of existence led by those who are subject to exceptional conditions, in whom the interests of all or several merge, and who stand, so to speak, outside the law. This led me to write the *Scenes from Political Life*. And after completing this vast picture of society, was I not obliged to reveal it functioning in the most violent of its aspects—when it steps out of itself for the purpose either of defence or conquest? This I have done in the *Scenes from Military Life*, that part of my work which is still least complete. I have, however, left room for it in this edition, so that it may be included when the time is ripe. Finally, the *Scenes from Rural Life*, which will come at the end of my long labours, if I may so call the social drama which is here presented. In this part will be found the purest of my characters and the application of the great principles of order, politics and morals.

Balzac concluded his preface by sounding a mighty chord:

> The immeasurable scope of a plan which embraces not only a history and criticism of society, but also an analysis of its evils and an exposition of its principles, justifies me, so I believe, in giving my work the title under which it now appears, *La comédie humaine*. Is it too presumptuous? Is it indeed justified? When the whole work has been completed the public will decide.

Posterity has announced its verdict. The title was not presumptuous, even though the work as we have it to-day has remained a torso. Death struck down Balzac's hand while he was still engaged in shaping it into the perfect whole which he had intended. In accordance with his habit of drawing bills to be met at a later date, he outstripped the actual facts when he spoke of "three to four thousand characters". The *Comédie humaine* contains only—one hesitates to use the word "only"—some two thousand characters. The others, however, were already in process of creation within the recesses of Balzac's inexhaustible brain, as is evident from a list prepared in 1845 in which he enumerated by name the novels published up to that date together with those which still remained to be written. We read it to-day with a melancholy equal to that which we feel on perusing a list of the lost dramas of Sophocles or the pictures that we shall never see of Leonardo da Vinci. Of the hundred and forty-four titles mentioned, no less than fifty have remained mere names, but the plan is sufficient to show the supreme architectonic skill with which he had already worked out in his mind to the last detail his vast structural design of the multifarious forms of human society.

The first novel was to have been called *Les enfants*, while the second and third would have had as their milieu a girls' and a boys' boarding-school respectively. A separate volume was to be devoted to the theatre, and Balzac intended to reveal what went on behind the scenes in diplomacy, the Government offices, the academic world, and the political parties. In more than twelve novels, of which only *Les Chouans* saw the light of day, he proposed to depict the French army's Iliad during the Napoleonic era—the campaign in Egypt, the battles of Aspern and Wagram, the retreat from Moscow, the Battle of the Nations at Leipzig, the fighting in France, and even the hulks in which French prisoners of war were confined. The peasant, the judge, and the inventor were each to have their separate volumes, and these descriptive studies were to be supplemented by explanatory and analytical essays—a *Pathology of Social Life*, an *Anatomy of the Teaching Body*, and a *Philosophical and Political Dialogue on the Perfection of the Nineteenth Century*.

There can be no doubt that he would have produced these works if he had lived. With a visionary power such as he possessed,

anything which was present to his imagination invariably took
shape and form. The only thing he lacked to complete his plan was
time, and of that he never had enough in his short, crowded life.

Balzac must have been imbued with a feeling of tranquil pride
when he thus announced to the world the publication of his life-
work. For the first time he had revealed the goal towards which he
was moving and drawn a line of demarcation between himself and
his contemporaries, none of whom had had the courage or the
pretension even to conceive of such a tremendous task. He had
achieved four-fifths of what he had planned. A few years more and
the structure would be complete. With the issue of the final volume
of the *Comédie humaine*, and with his affairs in order, he would be
free to apply his energies to an ambition which had hitherto always
eluded him. He would be able to rest, to live, to enjoy, and to be
happy.

CHAPTER XXI

Warning Signs

Balzac had hoped that Madame de Hanska was only waiting for her year of widowhood to be over before fulfilling the pledge they had made together, but month after month went by before she yielded to his urgent pleading and allowed him to join her in St. Petersburg. She was in a difficult situation. Balzac was too well known to be able to travel to Russia without his presence attracting attention. Since the days of the Empress Catherine no French writer of world fame had sojourned in the city on the Neva, and his arrival was bound to create something of a sensation. All eyes would be upon him, and the same would apply to her too, since she was a member of high society and was even received by the Tsar, so there was no way of avoiding gossip. Balzac's visits while her husband was alive could be interpreted as social calls upon the family. A journey to see his widow, however, would be looked upon as an official confirmation of their engagement, and even if Madame de Hanska had been as anxious for marriage as he was, which was far from being the case, she was by no means free to pursue her own inclinations. According to the laws then prevailing in Russia marriage to a foreigner required the sanction of the Tsar. Property could not be transferred abroad without special permission. She was, therefore, not at liberty to dispose of her wealth in any way she might wish, as Balzac innocently imagined and as would have been possible in any other country but Russia. To employ a modern expression, her money was in the form of "block roubles" which could not be taken across the frontier unless resort was had to illegal methods. The opposition of her family did not make things any easier. Her Aunt Rosalie in particular ignored the genius in Balzac and saw only an impoverished foreigner with a dissolute reputation who was out fortune-hunting and doing his best to turn the head of a rich widow. She might—we do not know—have summoned up the resolution to overcome the resistance of her aristocratic relatives, but she had to think of her unmarried daughter, on whom she doted. If she contracted a *mésalliance*, Russian society would turn its back on both her and her daughter, whose prospects of marriage would suffer accordingly.

So it was not, as has so often falsely been said, either ill-will or aloofness that led her to keep Balzac waiting so long. It was, on the contrary, an act of courage to permit him to make the journey to St. Petersburg at all, since at the very least it afforded an indication of their intentions. Balzac realised quite well that he could not make her change her mind by letters alone and that he must speak to her personally if she were to be overwhelmed by his powers of persuasion, as she had once been in Geneva. He sold every manuscript that could be turned into money, as well as an unwritten play or two, and on the 17th of July, after an unpleasant sea-voyage, he disembarked in the Russian capital.

❧◦❧

It must have been a strange reunion in the elegant salon of the Kutaisov palace when Balzac and Madame de Hanska met again after eight years. He had not changed much. He had grown a little stouter and there were a few grey streaks in his hair, but his manner was as eager and forceful as ever. Imaginative natures possess the secret of eternal youth. In the life of a woman, however, eight years are a long time. Even in the miniature which Daffinger had painted of her in Vienna, and which was certainly intended to be flattering, she looked matronly. If Balzac's letters are to be believed she appeared to him younger and more beautiful than ever, and he acted as if his sensual desire for her had grown more tempestuous after their long parting. Perhaps she had hoped that when he saw her in the flesh, instead of as he had pictured her to himself during the long years between, he would desist from his purpose, but this was by no means what happened. He urged her to marry him, all his plans had been made, and he even carried in his pocket the necessary documents which would authorise the consul to perform the ceremony.

She continued to put him off. She did not, it seems, give him a point-blank refusal, but informed him that marriage was out of the question so long as her daughter had not yet found a husband. This meant, at any rate, that there was a definite date to which he could look forward. Another year, or two years, at the utmost. Jacob had served seven years for Rachel, and another seven years after that. Balzac had already waited his seven years for the demise of Monsieur de Hanski. Now there was to be a second period of waiting, until the daughter was safely settled.

There are few records of Balzac's stay at St. Petersburg. During the summer the nobility lived on their estates in the country, and the capital was empty. He appears to have seen very little and does not even mention the Hermitage and its pictures. Presumably his mind contained room for nothing but the one single purpose that had brought him to Russia, and when he left, this time returning to Paris by the overland route via Berlin, he had at least a promise in his pocket.

⊷⊶∘⊷⊶

He was back in Paris by November, and as usual plunged straight into a whirlpool. Four months had been lost in his constant race with time, and things had not gone well in his absence. His mother, who had been looking after his affairs, "continues to torment me like a veritable Shylock". His play *Paméla Giraud* had been produced on the stage while he was away, and he had relied upon it not only to cover his expenses in Russia, but to enable him to enjoy a period of leisure on his return. He was still *en route* for home when he learned of its failure. Though not so banal as *Vautrin* and less meretricious than *Les ressources de Quinola*, the critics could not forget the grudge they bore him for his attacks on the corruption of the Paris press, and they assailed it so vigorously that the piece had to be taken off. The fates seemed leagued against him. His shares in the Northern Railway, to speculate in which he

had obtained money from some unknown source, had fallen on the
Stock Exchange, and his worries were not lessened by the difficulties connected with the liquidation of his property at *Les Jardies*.
Once more he was faced with total financial collapse and had to pay
for his brief respite with nights of labour.

His misfortune, however, was our fortune. His failure in the
theatre forced him to return to the novel, and further volumes of
the *Comédie humaine* followed in rapid sequence, beginning with
revised editions of *Scènes de la vie privée* and *Scènes de la vie parisienne*. He negotiated for the serial publication of *Les paysans*, on
which he had been working for years and which was to be one of his
most important books, but there was always a risk when he delayed
too long in completing any of his plans. He had already calculated
that at sixty centimes a line, the highest rate he had yet received, he
would draw fourteen thousand francs from the sale of the serial
rights to *La Presse* and a further twelve thousand from the book
rights. *La Presse* had printed the preliminary announcements, and
he had written a number of chapters, when suddenly he had a
breakdown. The spring had been overwound. Even Balzac's
strength had its limits, and his vitality could no longer meet the
inexhaustible demands he had made on it.

⋙∘⋘

The undermining of his health had begun slowly. The trunk still
presented an appearance of gigantic strength and bore fruit in
abundance; its foliage was renewed every year; but the worm was
already gnawing at its core. Complaints of waning vigour revealed
the change that was taking place, as in April, 1844:

> I have sunk into a phase of irresistible, comforting sleep. My
> physical powers refuse to obey my will. They demand a rest. They
> no longer react to coffee. I have poured down streams of it in
> order to finish *Modeste Mignon*, but with no more effect than if I
> had been drinking water. I wake up at three o'clock and fall
> asleep again. I breakfast at eight, am overcome once more with
> a desire to sleep, and doze off.

His facial muscles would spasmodically contract, he was afflicted
with swellings, headaches, and nervous twitching of the eyes, and

he began to doubt whether he would possess the strength to write the second part of *Les paysans*:

> I have entered upon a stage of dreadful nervous suffering, of a malady of the stomach caused by the excessive addiction to coffee. I have to take a complete rest. These unprecedented, ghastly pains have been tormenting me for three days. At the first attack I thought it was only a passing affliction. . . . Oh! I am indescribably weary. This morning I worked out the sum total of what I have produced during the past two years —four volumes of the *Comédie humaine*. In twenty days or so from now I shall no longer be good for anything except to get into a stage-coach and go away from here.

And later he wrote:

> Here I am, exhausted like Jacob after he had wrestled with the angel. There are six volumes and more still to be written. The whole of France has its eyes and ears turned towards this forthcoming work. From the reports of the booksellers' travelling agents and the letters I receive there can be no doubt of this fact. *La Presse* has acquired another five thousand subscribers. The public is waiting for me—and I feel like an empty sack.

It was not merely a matter of physical fatigue. His mind too was worn out. "*Avoir du repos*", to be able to rest, that was his urgent need. He felt that only Madame de Hanska could bring him salvation: "There are moments when one veritably loses one's reason owing to one's expectations being screwed to such a pitch, and that is the condition to which I have been reduced. My whole life has been so concentrated on the achievement of this goal that I feel inwardly shattered." He could take little interest in what he was writing, for his thoughts were far away. Instead of shaping the destinies of his characters he was dreaming of the way he would shape his own life:

> In 1846 we shall possess one of the most delightful houses in Paris and I shall no longer be a single sou in debt. My work on the *Comédie humaine* will earn me in time half a million francs, not counting the further royalties I shall realise on it, which will amount to about as much again. Therefore, my beautiful lady, I shall be an excellent matrimonial match, with a million francs and more to my name if I live long enough. If, as you put it, I shall not be marrying a poor girl when I marry you, neither will you be marrying a poor youth. We shall be a charming old

couple, but when two people are in love that doesn't matter. . . .
Only it will be wretched for whichever of us outlives the other!
Life will be bitter for the survivor.

To return, however, to the year 1844. A gleam of hope had lit up
the horizon. Madame de Hanska had made up her mind to quit her
Ukrainian wilderness and move to Dresden. In July her daughter
Anna had become engaged to a wealthy young nobleman named
George Mniszech, and the optimistic Balzac assumed that the last
obstacle was now removed. The time had come for Jacob to bring
home his bride. But he was to suffer a further disappointment.
Madame de Hanska adhered to her resolve to spend the winter in
Dresden with her daughter and her future son-in-law, but Balzac's
requests to be allowed to visit her there were in vain. Whether she
was still afraid of the Russian compatriots or kinsmen whom she
might meet in the German city, whether she had acquired a distaste
for his physical presence, or whether she was anxious to postpone
their marriage beyond the date that he regarded as fixed—this is a
matter for speculation. At any rate, she refused to let him join her.
and the only token of her confidence that she deigned to convey
to him was to entrust him with a mission which caused him considerable inconvenience.

She sent him her companion, her children's former Swiss governess, Henriette Borel, the "Lirette" of their early correspondence,
Henriette had suddenly announced her intention of leaving the de
Hanski household and entering a convent. It was an astonishing
decision for a Swiss Calvinist, and there was evidently some obscure
motive behind it. The death of Monsieur de Hanski had apparently
come as a severe shock to her, either because she felt particularly
attached to him in some way or because she experienced pangs of
conscience on account of the part she had taken in bringing about
his wife's act of adultery. Whatever the cause, the relations
between her and Madame de Hanska had become strained and had
developed on her part into a secret hostility. This is indicated in
Balzac's *Cousine Bette*, in which he used her to some extent for a
model. Madame de Hanska no longer needed her services and the
unwelcome task of helping the hysterical, elderly spinster to carry

out her purpose was assigned to Balzac. He treated her with consideration, for he felt under an obligation to her, and Madame de Hanska had requested him to see that all the necessary steps were taken to arrange for her reception into the Roman Catholic Church. He wasted precious time visiting important ecclesiastics and monastic authorities, and eventually his efforts were crowned with success. He attended the ceremony of taking the veil, and his accessory in the opening chapters of the novel *L'Etrangère* disappeared behind the convent walls.

❦

At last, in the spring of 1845, he received intelligence that Madame de Hanska wished to see him. Flinging his manuscripts into a drawer, with complete unconcern about the thousands of readers who were waiting for the continuation of the serials on which he was engaged, or the editors whose wrath at his unreliability would be increased by the knowledge that they had paid him his fee in advance, he abandoned everything and made for Dresden. His own life's story was more important than the stories he was inventing for the delectation of others. He left his mother to struggle with his creditors and the editor, Girardin, to pacify his readers. He had had enough of work and wanted to live, just as other people were able to do.

There are no letters to tell us of Balzac's thoughts and experiences in Dresden, but they must have been happy, carefree days for him. He got on excellently with the young Count Mniszech and with Anna. Mniszech was not particularly clever or adroit. He was, in fact, rather silly, and his chief passion was collecting insects, but he was good-tempered and, like the pleasure-loving Anna, always ready to join in a laugh. It can well be imagined that Balzac was a godsend to them in their boredom. He enjoyed with them the lighter side of life, and in remembrance of a comedy he had once seen in Paris he dubbed his little circle the *"Saltimbanques"*, the buffoons. They wandered round Europe like a company of comedians, except that instead of having an audience to entertain they let the world entertain them.

For they did not remain in Dresden, but travelled together to Kannstadt, Karlsruhe, and Strasbourg. He even persuaded Madame de Hanska to visit Paris, though she had to do so incognito, since it was forbidden territory for Russian subjects, whom the Tsar would not permit to sojourn on the revolutionary soil of France. Balzac, however, was a master in the art of overcoming obstacles of this kind. Madame de Hanska received a travel permit in the guise of his sister, while Anna appeared as Eugénie, his niece. In Paris he rented a small house for them in the rue Basse and took a hearty delight in showing them the attractions of the capital. He was an incomparable guide and shared their pleasure in seeing Paris with fresh eyes. In August they all moved on to Fontainebleau, to Orleans and to Bourges. He conducted them round Tours, his native town, and from there they went to Rotterdam, the Hague, Antwerp, and Brussels, where a halt was made while Balzac returned for a short spell to Paris. In September he hastened to join them again at Baden-Baden, where they stayed for a fortnight. Then they started off on a trip to Italy. In October they were at Marseilles *en route* for Naples.

All this time he did not do a stroke of work. He did not even write letters. Friends, publishers, and editors were forgotten. All that mattered was that he was with the woman he intended to marry and that he was free. Even the *Comédie humaine* was of no consequence. With his tremendous capacity for receiving and communicating impressions he must have enjoyed himself enormously. After years of ceaseless creative activity, when he had given of himself without stint, he was replenishing his spirit and renewing his strength. He was happy and therefore he was silent. As an artist he created only when circumstances forced him to do so.

His debts and the other obligations to which he was committed during this interlude are veiled in obscurity. So far as can be ascertained (and no one has ever succeeded in finding his way through the labyrinthine maze of Balzac's financial affairs) it is improbable that his expenses were defrayed out of his own pocket. There seems already to have been some arrangement between them for sharing their possessions. Madame de Hanska had not yet made up her mind to marry him, but she was willing to link her life and destiny with his for a year or two without prejudice to her ultimate decision. She found it wonderful to be able to travel around in this carefree way with Balzac, her daughter, and her future son-in-law. Perhaps all she was afraid of was to be alone with him.

CHAPTER XXII

Balzac the Collector

If the letters which Balzac wrote during 1845 and 1846 were submitted to someone who had never heard of him and was asked for his opinion as to their author's profession and inclinations, he would reply with considerable confidence that they had been written by an antique dealer or a picture collector. Possible alternative suggestions would be a speculator in real estate or a house-agent. It would never occur to him that they had been penned by a novelist. Balzac was far less absorbed in the completion of the *Comédie humaine* than in thoughts of the house he was going to build for his prospective bride out of her prospective inheritance and the fruits of his own labours.

This time too he put the cart before the horse, or, rather, he put the empty cart in front of the spot where the horse was going to stand. In 1845 he owned neither a house nor a site on which to erect one, and he certainly had not got the money to acquire a plot of land suitable for the mansion he had in mind. Yet he applied himself eagerly to furnishing his castle in the air. He was seized by a mania for collecting bric-à-brac. The home to which he was going to bring his bride must be a treasure-house, a picture-gallery, and a museum rolled into one, and he set to work to rival the Louvre, the Hermitage, the Uffizi, and the royal palaces of Europe. He wanted Holbeins, Raphaels, Van Dycks, Rembrandts, and

335

Watteaus to hang on his walls, precious carpets for the floor of his salon, antique furniture and dainty porcelain. He dreamed of all the wonders that sprang from Aladdin's lamp.

It was naturally something of a problem to amass a valuable collection of works of art without an adequate supply of capital, but Balzac's solution was very simple. He bought up all the miscellaneous junk that caught his eye in the second-hand shops and then announced his discovery of an old master or a marvellous piece of ancient craftsmanship. The bent for speculation that he had inherited from his mother found an outlet in the hunt for antiques, and in every town he came to he went rummaging round in search of bargains. He seemed to be in the grip of an obsession he could not control. At one place he would buy pictures and at another he would buy frames, sometimes he would become the proud owner of a number of vases, at others it would be candelabra. From Germany, Italy, and Holland crates arrived with treasures for his future abode. Not having the slightest notion of the real value of his purchases, he was at the mercy of any tyro in the trade, but he acted as if he were in a trance. His mind was dominated by the conviction that he was going to make vast profits, and his letters to Madame de Hanska were a succession of bulletins keeping her abreast of his latest finds.

Madame de Hanska herself was not exactly a thrifty-minded woman. Both she and her daughter went in for an orgy of shopping, and the jewellers of the rue de la Paix did well out of them. She was fond in particular of expensive articles for the toilet-table, inlaid in gold, but though she reckoned in large sums she did not count the cost. It appears that she had placed about a hundred thousand francs at Balzac's disposal—which they called the "*trésor Loup-loup*" after the nickname for him which they used in their correspondence—in order that he might buy and furnish a house, and his basic idea was, as usual, reasonable. He wanted to acquire good antique pieces, and if he had been content to wait until favourable opportunities occurred to pick up bargains he could not only have obtained a handsome house for the money, but could have furnished it with a good deal of comfort and even luxury. He could not wait, however, and once he had begun to buy things he could not leave off. From an occasional purchaser he developed with startling rapidity into a collector with a passion for speculative buying.

Throughout his life there was always a very fine line of demarcation between cool reasoning and foolish extravagance. Madame de
Hanska grew uneasy and warned him to be cautious, but he proved
to her with a wealth of detailed calculation how shrewdly he was
going about his task and how economically he was expending the
money she had placed at his disposal.

The reader of his letters will find that his constant and ingenious
efforts at self-deception tend to become wearisome, but there is a
certain amusement to be derived from following up one of his
transactions and seeing how he proposed to make a profit on it.
For instance, he bought an old china dinner service for nine people
and announced triumphantly: "I got it for three hundred francs.
Dumas gave four thousand for a similar set. It is worth at least
six thousand." Eventually he had to admit that what he had
thought was Chinese porcelain had been manufactured in Holland:

It is no more Chinese than I am.

And he added sadly:

Believe me, collecting bric-à-brac is a science.

This did not deter him from continuing to pursue this difficult
science with a light heart. On one day alone, the 15th of February,
1846, he picked up one bargain after another:

For three whole hours I wandered around and made purchases.
First: a yellow cup (for five francs; it is worth at least ten: a
marvellous piece of craftsmanship). Secondly: a cup in blue
Sèvres, Empire style, which had been offered to Talma; with an
incredible wealth of colouring and a bouquet of flowers that must
alone have cost twenty-five ducats (I got it for a mere twenty
francs). Thirdly: six armchairs of truly royal workmanship. I
shall keep four of them and have the other two made into a
settee. The gilding is superb! They will almost be enough to
furnish the small salon (for two hundred and forty francs).

On the same day he found in the course of his wanderings:

Two Sèvres vases—they must have cost between five and six
hundred francs (don't whisper a word to anyone! I got them for
thirty-five!) It is the biggest bargain I have ever struck. People
do not know their Paris. With time and patience there is nothing
you cannot find here, and cheap to boot. When you see the royal
cup of yellow porcelain that I picked up for five francs you will
refuse to believe me.

At the same time he was negotiating for a chandelier:

> It once belonged to the German Emperor and weighs two hundred pounds. It is of solid brass, and the metal alone is worth two francs, twenty centimes a kilogram. I shall get the chandelier for the bare cost of the metal—four hundred and fifty francs.

So it was really not costing him anything. In fact, the whole house would be furnished in this way:

> You will live like a queen, surrounded by all the princely splendour the arts can provide, amid the greatest possible wealth and elegance, and moreover we shall still retain the capital value.

He was convinced that he could find cheaper bargains than anyone else:

> I want you to realise what a good manager and business-man your Loup-loup is. I am ransacking every corner of Paris. The really good things are doubling in price every day.

Occasionally he made a blunder which even he could not help admitting:

> I have discovered a miniature of Madame de Sévigné, painted at the time of Louis XIV, for a hundred francs. Would you like it? It is a masterpiece.

On the following day he acknowledged his error: "The miniature is really dreadful." Luckily, however, he had already drawn another prize out of the bag:

> I have found a portrait of your great-aunt, Marie Lescinska, Queen of France, an extraordinarily good likeness by Coypel, or at any rate by one of his pupils. I said to myself: "We've got to have that, Loup-loup!" I bought it for no more than the value of the frame.

A week later he knew that it was not a Coypel, but "only" a Lancret. Fortunately he could sell the frame to a dealer for eighty francs, and the whole thing had only cost him a hundred and thirty. Sometimes one wonders whether he was not a little crazy when one finds him writing in this strain: "The little landscape is a Ruysdael. Miville envies me my Natoire and the Holbein I picked up for three hundred and fifty francs." This was at a time when in *Le cousin Pons* he was discussing the great value of Holbein's pictures, each of which was worth so and so many thousand francs, and it seems incredible that he should never once have asked himself why the picture-dealers should be so foolish as to let him purchase one for so paltry a sum. He does not appear to have considered the problem in this light, but went blithely on his way dreaming and snapping up neglected treasures. There was a fantastic opportunity waiting for him at every street-corner. "Paris is literally paved with bargains like these!"

The reverse of the medal was revealed when Balzac's possessions were sold by auction at the Hôtel Drouot after his wife's death. Nothing was said about Holbeins and Ruysdaels, and nowhere to-day is there to be found a painting of any noteworthy significance marked "from the Balzac Collection". The prices attained for his most prized specimens were ludicrous. He did not live to see this sequel; but apart from his experience with *Les Jardies*, which cost him a hundred thousand francs and had to be disposed of for fifteen thousand, there was at least one episode which ought to have taught him how much easier it is to buy than to sell.

On the 21st of December, 1843, he saw in an antique-shop a writing-table and an old chest which were probably typical Italian products such as could be found by the score. With the magic intuition that enabled him to recognise an ordinary-looking clock in a heap of bric-à-brac as having once "belonged to Queen Henrietta of England", he asserted without hesitation:

> They are superb pieces from a palace—the escritoire and chest which were made for Maria de Medici in Florence. They bear her coat-of-arms and are of solid ebony inlaid with mother-of-pearl, with a richness and delicacy of design that would have sent the late Monsieur Sommerard into raptures. I was quite nonplussed. They ought really to be in the Louvre.

This was a characteristic example of the way in which Balzac's intuition was indissolubly bound up with his zest for speculation. His enthusiasm was mingled with the desire to make a profit, though his first instinct was an æsthetic one, not untinged with patriotism:

> These mementoes of a queen who was the patron of Rubens must be rescued from the hands of the bourgeois! I shall write an article of twenty pages about them.

23

In the same breath he added: "From the speculative point of view there is a profit of a thousand francs to be made." On the following day he acquired the two pieces of furniture for thirteen hundred and fifty francs, and his pleasure was enhanced by a further flash of insight:

I have made a wonderful historical discovery and shall ascertain the exact details this very morning. It is only the chest which belonged to Maria de Medici. The escritoire bears the coat-of-arms of Concini or of the Duc d'Epernon, but it also has the two letters "M" in a charmingly intertwined border! This proves that there was an intimate relationship between Maria de Medici and one or other of her favourites. She presented him with her chest and also had an escritoire made for him. The Marshal d'Ancre—though he cut a ridiculous figure as a Marshal—had it inlaid with cannon and other military emblems in mother-of-pearl.

The only grain of truth in this rigmarole was that Concini, who later became the Marshal d'Ancre, did in fact enjoy the favours of the Queen. All the rest was a figment of Balzac's imagination, but it at once increased the value of his find and he was not at a loss for a prospective purchaser: "The chest alone is worth four thousand francs. I shall sell it to the King for the *Musée de Sommerard*, but I intend to keep the escritoire." The profit, of course, would be invested in further purchases:

If I can get three thousand francs from Louis Philippe for the chest, I shall be very pleased. I shall have made a profit of sixteen hundred and fifty francs, which will provide me with a small fund to continue my explorations of the world of bric-à-brac and add to our treasures.

Madame de Hanska was dubious about the wisdom of these transactions and she admonished him for his "furniture craze", to which he replied:

I have given instructions that one of the two celebrated pieces is to be sold at the price I paid for both of them. I shall therefore be obtaining the other for nothing and shall have something in hand to pay for a candelabrum.

As a shrewd man of business, he made use of the advertising powers of the press:

In the near future you will probably see from the newspapers that my discovery has caused a sensation!

On the 11th of February there appeared in the *Messager* a notice composed by Balzac himself:

> One of our most famous authors, who is a great connoisseur of antiques, has by chance brought to light a piece of furniture of supreme historical interest. The article in question is a chest that once adorned the bed-chamber of Maria de Medici. This piece of furniture, one of the most superb works of art that it is possible to conceive, is of solid ebony. . . .

The King does not appear to have been impressed by the choice specimen that had once belonged to an illustrious Queen of France. Finally a few dealers, lured by the advertisement in the newspaper, came to look at it. Balzac was in the seventh heaven:

> A purchaser has arrived. He is willing to give ten thousand francs for the two Florentine pieces, which he proposes to pass on to the Crown for twenty thousand. He has promised Dufour, the dealer, a thousand francs commission. But I intend to let only the chest go. People are rushing from all sides, even antique dealers, and they are unanimous in their enthusiasm.

The enthusiasm of the throng of admirers, to say nothing of the prospective purchaser, seems to have abated, and when March went by without a sale being effected anyone else would have been persuaded that his intuition had been at fault. Not so Balzac. On the contrary, he raised the price:

> The piece that I propose to retain is here now in my apartment. It is beyond all praise. It is too marvellous and sublime to be described in words. I do not, by the way, intend to keep either piece indefinitely. Our best-known antique dealer estimates that this one is worth sixty thousand francs. The cabinet-maker who renovated the escritoire says that the workmanship alone is worth twenty-five thousand. He is of the opinion that it must have taken at least three years to make. The inlaid arabesques are such as a Raphael would not be ashamed to acknowledge. I will see whether the Duke of Sunderland in London, or a Lord, or some Robert Peel or other will be willing to offer me three thousand pounds sterling for it. I would let it go at that price, which would be enough to pay off my debts. Until then, however, I shall keep it in my rooms.

Another month passed and there was no sign of an offer from the English peerage. Balzac was not discouraged. With indomitable perseverance he had hatched out a new plan. He would have an engraving made of the two pieces of furniture for reproduction in the *Musée des Familles*. The magazine would pay him five hundred francs for the right of publication, and he could set this off against the price he had paid for the chest and the escritoire.

Spring gave way to summer and summer yielded to autumn. The *Musée des Familles* did not print the engraving and no further prospective purchasers appeared on the horizon. In October there came a ray of hope: "Great news! Rothschild is interested in my Florentine furniture and is going to pay me a visit, doubtless with a view to inspecting the two pieces. I shall ask forty thousand francs." Having been unable, in spite of his advertising effort, to find a buyer even after the lapse of twelve months, a mere polite gesture from the famous banker was enough to make him raise the price again. No more was heard of Rothschild's alleged visit, but instead we find him talking about the Duke of Devonshire and sighing: "Oh, if only something should come of it! It would be a happy turn of events!" But nothing came of this either. He made a last attempt in the following year with the King of Holland, and in desperation he named the utterly ludicrous price of seventy thousand francs. He even mobilised his friend Théophile Gautier to help him carry out the deal:

> I need Gautier to write an article on my two pieces of Florentine furniture. We have only a week in which to prepare the repro-ductions, proofs of which I shall send to the King of Holland. It will make a stir!

The stir did not materialise. He never managed to dispose of the chest or the escritoire, and he was spared from knowing how little was received for them when they were finally auctioned at the Hôtel Drouot.

Furniture and china, crates and chests, accumulated and were not easy to preserve from the clutches of keen-eyed creditors. It was time to think of procuring a house, which could be placed beyond their grasp by registering it in the name of Madame de Hanska. Balzac again started off in a comparatively modest way, for they were to lead an *"existence excessivement simple"* in Paris, though even so their expenses would be at least forty thousand francs a year. It could not be done more cheaply, he declared, since Victor Hugo spent twenty thousand and "lives like a rat".

Buying a house, so far as Balzac was concerned, did not mean merely acquiring a place in which to dwell. It had also to be a good stroke of business:

> The idea of owning a house has been in my mind these three years, and it sprang mainly from economic considerations. That the purchase of a house should be a profitable transaction is, after all, a very natural thought.

So he looked round, and whenever he saw anything suitable he invented some way of recouping part of the cost. There was a house in Passy priced at a hundred thousand francs. He worked out that this in reality would only amount to sixty thousand:

> They are going to build a new road in Passy in order to avoid the hill, and it will pass about twelve feet below the height on which the house stands. The authorities will have to buy part of the ground from us and we can obtain, so I have been informed, ten thousand francs as compensation. Apart from that we could sell some of the land in the rue Franklin for thirty thousand francs.

In December he inspected building sites at Mousseaux: "We could undoubtedly double our capital." Then he discovered a house in the rue Montparnasse: "It would fit us like a glove." There was only one trifling consideration to be taken into account: "It will have to be partly pulled down." The interior would have to be completely remodelled and that would involve an outlay of a hundred and twenty thousand francs. However, the cost could be recovered very easily by the simple process of buying other sites which could be resold at a profit. It was a return to the system of his earlier years, when he bought a printing business to keep his publishing firm on its feet and a type foundry to save his printing business from collapse.

In the spring his eyes roamed towards the countryside, where they would not only be able to live for nothing, but could bide their time in peace and quiet until land values rose in price. They merely had to wait and money would fall into their laps. Life was so simple!

> A vineyard in Vouvray will bring us in enough to live on and cost no more than twenty to twenty-five thousand francs.

Yet it was silly to buy a vineyard in Vouvray when they could have a château in Touraine complete with vineyards, fruit-trees, terraces, and a magnificent view over the Loire. It is true that this would appear to cost between two and three hundred thousand francs, but Balzac had worked it out very exactly and discovered that it would really cost them nothing at all:

> You will leap for joy at what I am going to tell you! Moncontour is up for sale! A dream I have cherished for thirty years has been fulfilled, or at any rate might be fulfilled.

Eighty thousand francs at most would have to be paid down in cash, but part of the ground could be sold in single lots:

> The vineyards on the estate alone—according to the most accurate calculation based on the average yield over ten years— will bring in a guaranteed rate of interest of five per cent. on the capital. If we wish to dispose of ten acres of these vineyards they will easily realise from forty to fifty thousand francs. In this way we can cover the whole cost of purchase.

He concluded this letter with a lyrical flourish:

> Do you remember Moncontour, the pretty château with its two little towers mirrored in the Loire? It overlooks the whole of Touraine. . . .

A former school-friend began negotiations on his behalf, but even this project was apparently on too small a scale. Balzac vigorously defended the thesis that the larger the property the cheaper the price:

> The small estates are absurdly expensive, since there are so many people with moderate fortunes. To do a really big stroke of business you have to choose a really large property.

So what about the château of Saint-Gratien? It belonged to Monsieur de Custine, who had ruined himself over it—just as Balzac himself had done over *Les Jardies*:

> Saint-Gratien cost him three hundred thousand francs, but he told me that he is prepared to sell it to the first comer for a hundred and fifty thousand. . . . In the end he will have to give it away.

Monsieur de Custine, however, was no Balzac, and it seems that he was not willing to give his château away, after all. So Balzac had to continue his search and in the autumn of 1846 he at last found the home he was looking for. It was the *Pavillon Beaujon* in the rue Fortunée, an eighteenth-century house that had once belonged to a wealthy *fermier générale*, a farmer of the state taxes, before the Revolution. To this new abode he transferred his sumptuous furniture, his precious china, his Holbeins and Ruysdaels, and his brass chandelier. It was to become the *Musée Balzac*, his own private Louvre, a monument to his skill in creating masterpieces of art out of nothing. But when Gautier later on inspected the house and cried out in astonishment that Balzac must have become a millionaire in a very short space of time, he replied sadly: "No, my friend, I am poorer than ever I was. None of this splendour belongs to me. I am merely the porter and caretaker of this mansion."

For he did not take up residence immediately in the *Pavillon Beaujon*. For the time being, as a precaution against his creditors, he remained in his modest apartment at Passy, where he kept his writing-table, and it is this simple house, not the *Pavillon Beaujon,* with its carpets, bronzes, and candelabra, which is for us the true *Musée Balzac*. It is an incontrovertible law of human existence that even the greatest men of genius desire to be admired for qualities that weigh lightly in the balance compared with their genuine achievement. In Balzac the collector we have an outstanding example of this strange law.

FULFILMENT AND FINALE

CHAPTER XXIII

Last Novels

uring these two or three restless years Balzac lost, temporarily at least, his primordial power to concentrate on his creative work to the exclusion of everything else. He had become a collector, not only literally but in a more sublimated sense of the word. He was accumulating not merely the solid comforts and luxuries with which he purposed to furnish his new home, but also experiences such as life had hitherto denied him—long hours of leisure, tranquil walks with the woman on whom his heart was set, and nights of love in an exotic land undisturbed by the menace of a husband in the background. The creative process had taken a new turn. Absorption in the development of a fictitious situation had given place to the search for a happy ending to the story of his own life.

The effect can be seen in his writings. In the years immediately preceding this interlude he had produced a magnificent political novel like *Une ténébreuse affaire*, with its living picture of state intrigue, *La rabouilleuse*, with its modern insight into sexual problems, and the concluding part of *Les illusions perdues*. These outstanding works were followed by *Splendeurs et misères des courtisanes*, in which the world of literature was linked with that of finance. The figure of Vautrin returned to the scene and the themes of his earlier novels were combined as if in a great panorama. Despite occasional slips into sensationalism and encroachments on the sphere of the detective story, it was in this novel more than in any other that he succeeded in embedding the spirit of Paris and Parisian society. Yet he was unable to finish *Les paysans*, which was an attempt to treat the important sociological problem of the struggle between town and country. This antithesis, which in Paris was seen as an affair of the markets and the stock exchange or as a theme in literature, retained in the country its original primitive form. It was not a matter of invisible or intangible values, but of the soil itself, of every single strip of ground. Balzac had been working at this novel for years and he felt that it was destined to be of decisive significance within the framework of the *Comédie humaine*. He returned to it again and again, even tried to commit himself to its completion by publishing the first part; but he had to break off. He applied his pen to less weighty subjects. The novel *Béatrix*, of which only the earlier chapters have any literary value, was provided with a sentimental ending lacking in any truth to life, and he turned out trifles like *Misères de la vie conjugale*, which was a rehash of his old *Physiologie du mariage*, though spiced with considerable wit and charm. The short story *Modeste Mignon*, for which Madame de Hanska (to whom he dedicated it) supplied the theme, might have been written by one of his imitators. There is no sign in it of the lion's claws. He said himself once that it takes an artist some time to get his hand in again after having abandoned his workshop for any length of time. Balzac had neglected his work too long while searching for houses and rummaging in antique shops. In his letters at this time there were pages and pages without a single reference either to the books on which he was engaged or to his literary plans for the future.

⚬⟚⟚⚬

He was well aware of the change in him. He knew that he had lost both his craftsman's skill and his joy in work since allowing himself to indulge in the "indolent surrender to life itself", and in January, 1846, he wrote to Madame de Hanska, who was then in Naples: "My mind is inactive. . . . I find everything boring and distasteful." He was no longer perturbed at not being able to make any headway with *Les Paysans* or *Les petits bourgeois*. He was writing merely with a view to liquidating his debts, and frequently one has the feeling that he had ceased to be interested in the artistic aspect. In March he suddenly abandoned everything and hastened off to Rome.

On his return to Paris he again wrote letter after letter to Madame de Hanska with the usual asseverations that now he would "have to work enormously". He was once more possessed by the belief that if he wrote day and night for three months, "without pause, or at the most an interruption of a fortnight during which we can get married", he must inevitably succeed in paying off what remained of his debts—now a mere sixty thousand francs. There is still no mention of artistic inspiration. Finally, however, on the 1st of June, he informed her: "During the last four days I have been seized by a consuming activity. . . ." and on the 12th he reported: "I am working at the plan of *Les paysans* and, besides that, on a short story." On the 14th he was able to announce the conception of two new works:

> I am going to write the following. First, *L'histoire des parents pauvres*, consisting of *Le bonhomme Pons*, which will take up three or four folios of the *Comédie humaine*, and *La cousine Bette*, which will amount to sixteen folios. Secondly, *Les méfaits d'un procureur du roi*.

The short story of which he had spoken two days before had now become two stories, but these were to assume a breadth and depth of which he was even then unaware. He still thought of them as short stories, not as novels, and he was considering them in terms of length, which meant that he was concerned simply with the fee he would receive for them. All at once, however, his old ambition was rekindled. As he worked at the drafts he realised their potentialities and the joy in creative achievement came back to him. On the 16th of June he indicated the scope of his task:

> The demand made upon me at this moment is that I should write two or three works of the first importance which will overthrow the false gods of that bastard literature and demonstrate that I am younger, fresher, and greater than ever I have been. *Le vieux musicien* is the "poor relation" who is crushed by misfortune, the man with a pure heart. *La cousine Bette* is the female "poor relation" who is also pursued by unhappiness. She spends her life in the mansions of three or four different families and takes her revenge for all her sufferings.

After all his babble about money matters, speculation in real estate, railway shares, and porcelain dinner-services it is pleasant to see the reawakening will to create works of art. It is true that he clung to his disastrous system of negotiating with the publishers about his prospective fee before he had had time to see how long the book was going to be, but once this was done he flung himself into his work. He returned to his old routine of turning night into day, and there is a reference in one of his letters to the fact that he found the diversions and excitements of daily life, particularly the arrival of consignments from the antique dealers, an irritating disturbance:

> I wish that all these crates were unpacked and finished with. The beautiful things that I am waiting to see, my anxiety to know in what condition they will arrive, all this has a very vivid effect on me, especially in my present excitable condition, exhausted as I am by the fever of inspiration and the inability to sleep. I hope to have finished *Le vieux musicien* by Monday if I rise at half-past one every morning, as I did to-day. As you see, I have gone back to my old hours of work again.

The novel was written with a rapidity remarkable even for Balzac, and on the 20th of June we find him commenting in a way that was rare with him:

> I am very satisfied with *Le vieux musicien.*

Then again we only hear that one of the pictures had been delivered in a scratched condition or that one of the bronzes he had bought had turned out to be a fake, together with references to his debts and his tailors. On the 28th of June he gave vent to a cry of exultation such as had not been heard from him for years:

> My beloved heart! I have just finished the volume that I intend to call *Le parasite*, for that is the final title of the manuscript which I have hitherto referred to as *Le bonhomme Pons*, *Le vieux musicien*, etc. It is, for me at least, one of those works of the first rank which are of the utmost simplicity and include within their span the whole of the human heart. It is as great as *Le curé de Tours*, even more lucid and no less heart-rending. I am filled with enthusiasm and will send you the proofs immediately.
>
> I am now going to set to work on *La cousine Bette*, a grim and formidable novel, since the chief character will be a compound of

traits taken from my mother, Madame Desbordes-Valmore, and your Aunt Rosalie. It will relate the history of a whole series of families.

His angry feelings towards his mother and the fate of Lirette, the witness to his early illicit love for Madame de Hanska, were reflected in *La cousine Bette*. While he was engaged on this novel he was simultaneously occupied with correcting the proofs of *Le cousin Pons*, which meant, in accordance with his usual custom, practically re-writing it. The impatience of the artist merged with that of the business-man, and instead of rendering praise to Heaven which had endowed him with the genius to create a masterpiece within such a short space of time he groaned at the slowness of his progress:

It is already the 15th of July, alas! . . . I shall finish *Les parents pauvres* in the sweat of my brow. It will bring me in about ten thousand francs, including its publication in book form.

It was impossible to keep to the date he had fixed, and by the end of August the book was still not finished, though on the 12th of that month alone he wrote no less than twenty-four pages. Scarcely had he put finis to the manuscript when the arduous labours of proof-correction began, and the state of complete physical exhaustion to which he was reduced horrified his doctor, as Balzac himself has recorded:

Neither he nor any of his medical colleagues had conceived that it was possible to submit one's brain to such immoderate exertion. He told me that the result will be injurious, repeating the statement with a gloomy air. He implored me at least to interrupt for a time these "cerebral excesses", as he put it, and was horrified at the strain to which I had exposed myself in writing *La cousine Bette*, which took me no more than six weeks. He said: "It is bound to end in a catastrophe." I do, as a matter of fact, feel that something has gone wrong with me. I have to search for words in conversation, and sometimes it demands a great effort. It is really time that I took a rest.

In September, while still engaged in revising the proofs, he went to Wiesbaden, to refresh himself in the society of Madame de Hanska. He was entitled to a rest, for during that summer he had written his greatest masterpiece. The two novels *Le cousin Pons* and *La cousine Bette*, which sprang from his original conception of *Les parents pauvres*, are his outstanding achievement. In the prime of life he had reached the summit of his art. Never had his insight been more penetrating, his craftsmanship more assured, his treatment more ruthless. He had written these two books after a long interval of repose, and there was no trace in them of the false idealism and mawkish sentimentality which marred some of his earlier works. They reflected the bitterness of actual experience, a real knowledge of the world. The scales had fallen from his eyes and he was no longer impressed by the outward appearance of success or by manifestations of luxury and elegance. In *Le père Goriot* and *Les illusions perdues* he had already shown something of the power to portray disillusionment that we see in Shakespeare's *King Lear*, but his last two novels have all the trenchancy of *Coriolanus*. Balzac was at his greatest when he stood above his age, creating absolute values and unconcerned with any desire to meet the taste of his contemporaries. The fact that the scene both of *Le cousin Pons* and *La cousine Bette* is set in Paris during the first half of the nineteenth century is of no essential importance. It might be transferred to the France, the England, the Germany or the United States of the present day, to any country and to any age, since Balzac is here concerned with elemental passions. His gallery of characters obsessed by a fixed idea was enriched by the erotomaniac Baron Hulot and the collector Pons. After the rather theatrical courtesan Torpille in his *Splendeurs et misères des courtisanes*, the fallen young woman *par excellence*, who reminds us a little too closely of the Lady of the Camelias and was served up to suit the taste of the Parisians, he drew a picture of the born harlot, Madame Marneffe, the bourgeois wife who sells herself to every comer. As a foil he created the incomparable Cousine Bette, a Lirette transferred to a daemonic plane, the ageing spinster who derives no healthy enjoyment from life and can only envy others, taking a warped and evil pleasure in acting as a go-between in clandestine love-affairs. The tragedy of the "poor relation" is seen in Cousin Pons, who is only tolerated so long as he still retains something of his former lustre, and the motive power of greed in the housekeeper Cibaut. We are shown the cunning rogues whose one desire is to make money and who cheat those who are innocent and pure of heart. The dramatic intensity of these last novels makes

the figure of Vautrin in the earlier books appear almost melodramatic by contrast. Their realism, genuineness of feeling, and
analysis of primitive passions have never been surpassed in French
literature.

∘⥹∘⥻∘

It was a magnificent farewell to his art, by which we can measure
the heights that the *Comédie humaine* would have touched if Balzac
had been granted ten or even five more years of mature achievement. In *Les paysans* he would have revealed the ultimate antithesis between town and country, the peasant as he really was, in
the same way that he had revealed Paris as it really was—not the
perfumed landscape of a Jean-Jacques Rousseau inhabited by
simple children of Nature. In *La bataille* and the other stories of
military life he would have depicted war in all its stark brutality,
in contrast to the panegyric of Napoleon he had offered in *Le
médecin de campagne*. In *Une ténébreuse affaire* he had progressed
far beyond the legendary conception of history, and if the fates
had been kinder he would have completed his pictures of the world
of the theatre, of the academies, of diplomacy, and of politics. The
list he drew up in 1845 contained the titles of fifty books he did not
live to write. In the theatre, where he had followed bad models and
found himself bogged in the morass of melodrama, he was on the
verge of setting foot on solid ground. *Le faiseur*, later called *Mercadet*, a comedy in which a debtor triumphs over his creditors, was
his first independent work in this field and after his death it reaped
the success which had been denied to all his other plays. His
powers were concentrated to their highest pitch and it is clear that
in the drama, as in the novel, he was conscious of the debt he owed
to his genius. Both physically and spiritually, however, he had to
call a halt. He felt the need of rest once more, complete and healing
rest, that would take him far away, as far away as possible. It was a
right that he had well earned, and he left Paris to journey—across
a quarter of the earth's surface, as he phrased it—to the distant
Ukraine, to Wierzchownia, to Madame de Hanska.

CHAPTER XXIV

Balzac in the Ukraine

n the autumn of 1846 it had seemed for a moment as if Balzac was at last about to enter into the haven of rest for which he craved. The pretext under which Madame de Hanska had so long evaded the issue no longer held good. She had insisted that she could not think of marriage until her beloved daughter was safely wedded, and the nuptials of Anna and Count Mniszech had been celebrated on the 13th of October in Wiesbaden. Balzac himself was present and his heart was again filled with hope. With admirable forethought he had provided himself with the personal documents necessary for the civil ceremony, pretending that he required them in connection with the award of the Legion of Honour, and he had made extensive preparations for his wedding to take place secretly at Metz, where neither he nor Madame de Hanska would be likely to have acquaintances. The mayor of Metz, with whom he was in touch, had been won over to the plan, and the civil ceremony, which was valid only in France, was to be performed at the town hall under cover of darkness and with as little publicity as possible. Two witnesses, the son of his physician, Dr. Nacquart, and another friend, were to come specially from Paris, while Madame de Hanska was to remain on German soil at Saarbrücken until the appointed day, arriving at Metz only in the evening. The religious ceremony would take place later in Germany. Either the Bishop of Metz or the priest at Passy would give his sanction, and they could then be married in church by a priest at Wiesbaden.

This complicated procedure was apparently essential to prevent knowledge of their wedding reaching the ears of the authorities in Russia. Balzac pressed for her immediate consent:

> I am waiting for your next communicatión, and I tell you that every hour of the day I live only in you. That is now true in a dual sense.

Circumstances had emphasised the need for urgency, for the pleasant prenuptial weeks they had spent in one another's society in Italy had not been without consequences. Madame de Hanska, though she was now forty-five years of age, was expecting a child. Balzac, with the premature optimism that was so characteristic of his temperament, was sure that it was going to be a boy, and had already decided to call him Victor Honoré.

Madame de Hanska, however, was still unable to make up her mind. She could not overcome her reluctance to part from her daughter, and instead of proceeding with her own marriage she preferred to accompany the young couple on their honeymoon. So Balzac had to put back in his portfolio the documents he had gone to so much trouble to acquire, abandon his artfully contrived plan for a secret wedding, and return to Paris, where the proof-sheets of *Le cousin Pons* and *La cousine Bette* were awaiting correction. Whatever one's views may be on the disputed question whether or not Madame de Hanska was really in love with Balzac, there can be no doubt about the fact that whenever she had to decide between him and her daughter, it was always her daughter who won the day. Neither Anna's marriage nor her own, when she eventually took the decisive step, affected in the slightest degree the particularly intimate relations that existed between the two women. They both treated husband or lover with a certain nonchalance and even disdain.

In the following February Madame de Hanska took it in her head to go to Paris, and Balzac had to journey to Vorbach to escort her. When she required his company he had to obey. His work could wait. Casting everything aside, he always hastened to join her wherever she might be. She only had to beckon and he would rush to Switzerland, Italy or Austria, spending days and nights in a rattling stage-coach and impatiently counting the minutes until he would see her again.

What happened during her second sojourn in Paris is wrapped in mystery. Her child was either still-born or died soon after birth. For obvious reasons very little has come to light on the matter. It was a girl, and with a father's blunt naivety Balzac wrote that this had mitigated his grief: "I was so anxious to have a Victor Honoré. A Victor would not have abandoned his mother. We should have had him with us for twenty-five years, which is the time we may expect to have together, you and I." But Madame de Hanska was still not prepared to take the plunge. She found continual excuses for further postponement, until we are induced to believe that her reluctance to enter into an irrevocable union only increased as her knowledge of him grew more intimate. This time she declared that it was essential for her to return to Wierzchownia to put her affairs in order, and he obediently accompanied her back to Vorbach before settling down once more at his writing-table in Paris.

He hoped to follow her with little delay. He only had *Les paysans* to finish, in addition to writing a play that would enable him to pay off a debt of fifteen thousand francs that he owed to his old friends the Viscontis, but the breakdown in his health intervened. His doctors warned him against overwork, he felt unsure of himself, and his publishers and editors were growing restless. Girardin, the editor of *La Presse*, had twice begun to print instalments of *Les paysans* in his journal, trusting to Balzac's capacity for work, which was famous all over Paris. Balzac had never left a publisher or editor completely in the lurch, for if the worst came to the worst he had always supplied something to take the place of the promised contribution. The point had been reached when Girardin insisted on having the complete manuscript in his hands before he would agree to begin a third attempt at printing the novel, and for the first time in his life Balzac had to capitulate. For the first time in his life he had to lay down his pen and utter the words: "I cannot!" To mask this defeat in his own eyes he managed in some way or other to find the money to repay the advance he had received from Girardin. It was the ransom for his freedom, freedom to escape to Wierzchownia, whence he would bring back his bride to their new home. This was now his sole obsession, and for its sake he made peace with his mother, whom in his heart he detested. Nothing was too harsh for him to say about her in his letters, but this old woman of seventy was the only person on whom he could rely to keep guard over his precious property while he was away, just as he had put her in charge when he had to flee from his apartment in the rue Cassini. She was a ruthless manager, and whenever he needed anyone whom he could really trust he had recourse to his old mother. The instructions he left her were very odd and read almost like an excerpt from a work of fiction. From time to time, he said, she was to frighten the servants by telling them that Monsieur de Balzac was expected back in two or three days. This was to be done every week: "It will help to keep them lively." She was to keep a watchful eye on the "*petite maison*", in which all his treasures were stored, for, as he wrote to his sister:

> Madame de Hanska is very concerned about the house, which contains so many riches. These are the result of six years of saving. There might be a robbery or some other misfortune.

To his mother he remarked with satisfaction:

> Neither of the servants is able to read or write. You are the only one who knows my handwriting and my signature.

At such moments he realised that he had nobody else but this old woman on whom he could implicitly rely. Having placed everything in her charge, he set out on his long journey to the Ukraine.

⊷⊶

A journey to Wierzchownia was in those days something of an adventure.

> I have traversed a quarter of the earth's surface [he wrote]. If I had gone twice as far I should have found myself on the other side of the Himalayas.

The normal time of travel was at least a fortnight, but Balzac went through without stopping and arrived in little more than a week. His appearance was unexpected, for the letter in which he had announced his coming did not reach Wierzchownia for another ten days.

His first impression was one of rapture. His enthusiasm was always easily kindled, but nothing went to his head more than the outward signs of wealth. There could be no doubt about the wealth of the mistress of Wierzchownia. He was now seeing with his own eyes the princely magnificence in which his friends lived. The house with its vast suites of rooms seemed to him on a par with the Louvre. The estate was no ordinary estate, but almost as large as a French *département*. He admired the rich, heavy earth of the Ukraine, on which the grain grew without the need for manure, the extensive forests belonging to the de Hanskis, and the hordes of servants. The reactionary in Balzac noted with complacency that the latter

> literally throw themselves on their stomachs when they come into one's presence, beat the ground three times with their foreheads, and kiss one's feet. It is only in the East that they really know the meaning of subservience. It is only there that the word "power" has any genuine significance.

He observed the superabundance of silver and porcelain, and felt that these people, surrounded by every luxury, had no cares of any kind. Their ancestors had once owned regions half as large as France. Count Mniszech still had no less than forty thousand "souls", as the serfs were called, on his estates, but if he were to attempt to cultivate the whole of his domain he would need ten times the number. Life for the aristocratic landowner was as extravagant as Nature itself. This was a scale of living which was in accordance with Balzac's dreams, and at the de Hanski manor in Wierzchownia he felt at home.

⟞⊙⟝

For the first time in his life he had no need to think of money. Everything was provided for him—board, lodging, servants, horses, carriages and books. There were no creditors to disturb his tranquillity and very few letters were forwarded. Yet a man cannot slough off his own skin, and Balzac could not help thinking in terms of money. As a composer transmutes an emotion or a mood into music, so Balzac made everything he saw into the basis of a financial calculation. He remained the incorrigible speculator.

Before he had even arrived at Wierzchownia, while still travelling
through the forests on the estate, he gazed at the magnificent trees
with an eye to the profit that their owner might reap. His previous
failures to make a large fortune at one stroke were forgotten and
he immediately submitted to Count Mniszech a plan for exploiting
the inexhaustible stocks of timber and turning them into cash. A
railway was being built on the frontiers, and in a short time this
would link Russia with France. With impatient pencil Balzac drew
on a piece of paper a line connecting the forests of Wierzchownia
with the sawmills of France:

> There is a demand in France at the present moment for enormous
> quantities of oak to make railway sleepers, but we haven't got
> the oak. I know that oak has almost doubled in price, both for
> building purposes and for cabinet-making.

Then he began to work out the profit and loss. The freight from
Brody to Cracow would have to be considered. From Cracow the
railway already ran as far as Paris, though with a number of
interruptions, since the River Elbe had not yet been adequately
bridged at Magdeburg or the Rhine at Cologne. The Ukrainian
sleepers would therefore have to be ferried across these two rivers.
"The transport of sixty thousand balks will be no trifling matter,"
and it would add very considerably to the cost, but they would
endeavour to interest bankers in the project and the directors of
the French railway company might be persuaded to reduce their
charges if it were proved to them that this would be to their own
advantage. If they only made five francs profit on each balk, they
would be hundreds of thousands of francs to the good even after
deduction of all expenses. "It is worth while thinking the matter
over."

There is, perhaps, no need to record that this final offspring of
Balzac's speculative genius never got further than the stage of
preliminary discussion.

⟡⟡∘⟡⟡

During the months he spent at Wierzchownia Balzac allowed
himself to be pampered. One of his descriptions of a trip to Kiev
with the young ladies tells how he was overwhelmed with atten-

tions in the Ukrainian capital. There was a rich Russian there who
lit a candle for him every week and promised Madame de Hanska's
servants considerable largesse if they would let him know when
Balzac intended to return, so that he might make a point of seeing
him. In the house he was allotted for his own use

> a delightful apartment consisting of a salon, a study, and a bed-
> room. The study is adorned with pink stucco-work and contains
> a fireplace, superb carpets, and comfortable furniture. The
> windows are made of large, clear panes of plate-glass, so that I
> have a view over the landscape in every direction.

He planned further excursions and longer journeys to the Crimea
and the Caucasus, journeys which unfortunately were never carried
into effect. So far as work was concerned, he did practically nothing. During these last years he had never been able to settle down
to serious writing while he was with Madame de Hanska, for whom,
as for her daughter and her son-in-law, he had become "*le bilboquet*", a waggish companion who helped them to pass their hours
of boredom. With the Carrauds or the Margonnes he was always
treated with the respect due to his artistic genius. They did not
encroach upon his time, but left him to himself unless he wished
for their company. When he had stayed with them he had been able
to work. At Wierzchownia it was different. In the atmosphere
surrounding these spoilt and indolent women, who had never lifted
a finger in their lives to help themselves, there was something that
made it difficult to concentrate on creative writing.

In January, in the depths of the Russian winter, with twenty-
eight degrees of frost on the ground, he suddenly set out on the
return journey to Paris, ostensibly in order to attend to some
supplementary payments he had to make in connection with his
wretched railway shares. He may also have been uneasy about his
new house. Madame de Hanska, it goes without saying, allowed
him to travel alone. There was no further mention of engagement
or marriage. Her hesitation appears to have increased with familiarity. In the Ukraine she could live without a care in the world, and
she had probably come to the conclusion that she would hardly
find Paris a haven of peace and tranquillity with a husband whose
extravagant ways and gambling instincts she had learned so well
to know. So she let him go without much demur, in ill-health as

he was, merely covering his shoulders with a thick Russian fur as
she bade him farewell.

◇◦◌

Whenever Balzac returned home after an absence of any duration he was accustomed to being met by the news of fresh trouble
even before he had crossed the threshold. His return from Wierzchownia was no exception, but this time the trouble was not of his
own making. Scarcely had he stepped once more on the soil of
France when the revolution of February, 1848, broke out. The
monarchy was swept away and with it, in view of his publicly
expressed legitimist opinions, disappeared any chance he might
have had of launching on a political career. He did, indeed,
announce in the *Constitutionnel* on the 18th of March that he was
prepared to stand as a candidate for the Chamber of Deputies if he
were asked to do so, but as was to be expected, no serious invitation
was forthcoming. A Parisian club called the *Fraternité Universelle*
was the only organisation that displayed an inclination to include
him in its list of candidates, on condition that he submitted his
political confession of faith, but this he proudly declined to do on
the grounds that those who wished him to represent them in
parliament must already have deduced his political convictions
from his collected works. It was typical of Balzac that though in his
writings he foresaw so clearly the social changes that were about to
take place, and revealed such discernment in his depiction of the
circumstances that had made them inevitable, when the political
crisis came he placed himself in a false position just as he always did
in his business affairs.

Disappointment followed on disappointment. His railway shares
had fallen to a new low level and the theatre was no kinder to him
than it had been before. He was unable to keep his promise to
deliver the play *Pierre et Cathérine*, but he had brought from Russia
instead a "*drame intime*" entitled *La marâtre*, which was produced
on the 25th of May at the Théâtre Historique. Paris was still in the
throes of political unrest and the piece did not awaken any particular interest. His most important play, *Mercadet*, was accepted
"unanimously" by the reading committee of the Comédie Française, but its production was postponed for the time being. We hear

very little at this period about novels or plans for novels, and it
seems that Balzac was completely taken up with the theatre. One
of the ideas he had formed was the establishment of an association
of all outstanding dramatists for the joint writing of plays where-
with to enrich the French stage.

It is probable, however, that his mind was not really absorbed in
these matters. He was no longer inspired by literary ambition. The
only thing that interested him was his house. Much had been done
there during his absence, but it was still not ready. The contrast
between the luxury with which he was having it installed and his
own personal poverty was extraordinary. The publishers had
buttoned up their pockets more tightly than ever, he had no new
manuscripts to offer them, and he was still deeply committed to his
latest publisher, Souverain. The journalists remained hostile; and
he must sometimes have had the feeling that the public had forgotten him. Girardin, to whom he had repaid the advance on his
unfinished novel *Les paysans* before setting out for Russia, with
the exception of a trifle of seven hundred and twenty-one francs
eighty-five centimes still outstanding, demanded the final settlement of his account as soon as he heard of Balzac's return. A
fortnight later he sued Balzac for non-payment, and the court
upheld his claim. The day had gone when Balzac could charge sixty
centimes a line. His short story, *L'initié*, had to be disposed of for a
paltry fee to the *Musée des Familles* so that he could get enough to
eat. He was poorer than ever he had been, for owing to his long
absence all his sources of revenue had dried up. He was deterred by
a certain sense of shame from trying to borrow while he was throwing money away like water on his house in the rue Fortunée, where
the walls of the reception room were being hung with gold damask
and the doors were being carved or inlaid with ivory. For a book-
case in his library, a dreadful piece of furniture inlaid with tortoise-
shell, he gave fifteen thousand francs. At the auction in the Hôtel
Drouot it was with difficulty that a purchaser was found to take it
for five hundred. The staircase was covered with costly carpets,
while every vacant space was filled with Chinese vases and malachite bowls. His chief pride, however, was the "great gallery",
which was the reason why he had chosen this particular house. The
ground-plan of the *Pavillon Beaujon* was of awkward design, and
the gallery consisted of an oblong rotunda roofed with glass, the

walls being painted in white and gold. Fourteen statues stood in a circle and a variety of bric-à-brac was displayed in ebony cabinets, genuine *objets d'art* being mixed up with obvious counterfeits. On the walls hung the sixty-six pictures that constituted the Balzac collection, including his alleged Sebastiano del Piombino, an even more dubious landscape by Hobbema, and a portrait which Balzac without hesitation pronounced to be a Dürer.

The contrast between crazy extravagance and personal poverty was a source of vexation to his family. Instead of being honest with them he was always inventing new explanations for Madame de Hanska's repeated postponement of the expected wedding. On one occasion he asserted that he had written direct to the Tsar to solicit his consent, but that this had been refused. Or he would talk of complicated lawsuits that prevented Madame de Hanska from leaving Russia. He pretended all the time that she was in grave financial difficulties, attributing these at first to the fact that she had assigned her property to her daughter and therefore had no control over it herself, but later on he put them down to the harvest having been destroyed by fire. His object was to diminish in the eyes of his family the discrepancy between Madame de Hanska's position and his own. Neither family, in fact, regarded the other with favour. Madame de Hanska's relatives were headed by the implacable Aunt Rosalie, who was constantly trying to dissuade her niece from throwing in her lot with that untrustworthy spendthrift of a French writer, who would only end in compromising her and flinging the de Hanski fortune into the gutter. Old Madame Balzac and her daughter saw in Honoré's future bride only a haughty, conceited aristocrat, a cold, egotistic creature who would keep him dancing attendance on her and let him go chasing half across Europe without any consideration whatsoever for his poor state of health.

Though Balzac's mother had patiently assumed the duties of watchdog at the house in the rue Fortunée, a thankless task which demanded all the old woman's reserves of courage and energy, she had no illusions as to the treatment she would receive when the new abode was ready and the bridal couple were comfortably installed. She was well aware that there would be no room for her amid the splendours of the *Pavillon Beaujon* and that she herself would be swept out with the last speck of dust. She did not expect even to be allowed to welcome the newly married pair at the threshold—and her misgivings were not belied when the time came. Madame de Hanska had never taken the slightest notice of her existence, either by a line of conventional greetings or a word of thanks for the trouble she was taking. It is therefore understandable if the resentment she felt towards her future daughter-in-law simmered more hotly as the days went by. The question was continually cropping up whether she could afford to take the omnibus from the rue Fortunée to visit her daughter at Suresnes. While she supervised the spending of tens of thousands of francs on Madame de Hanska's behalf, the expenditure of a couple of sous represented a considerable item in her personal budget. Balzac had not yet repaid the loans he had received from his mother, and neither he nor Madame de Hanska apparently thought of at least providing her with an annuity as a way of meeting his obligation. His devious excuses did not blind her to Madame de Hanska's obvious reluctance to seal the union, which she put down to hauteur. On the other hand, it cannot be expected that Madame de Hanska should have looked forward with any degree of pleasure to the prospect of a permanent move to Paris, where she would be brought into contact with Balzac's mother and sister, to say nothing of the rest of his bourgeois relations. The gilded luxury of Balzac's new house was to offer him little genuine enjoyment.

Any hopes that Balzac may have entertained during all these months of a speedy change of mind on Madame de Hanska's part once the house was ready must have been damped by the increasingly clear indications that his desire for a permanent union was not shared by her, and that she had not the slightest intention of exchanging the amenities of Wierzchownia for the dubious prospects of the *Pavillon Beaujon*. So he had for good or ill to make up his mind to return to Russia at the end of September, before the intense cold set in which had caused him to suffer such misery when he made the journey to Paris in the previous January. He must make yet one more attempt, by a personal visit, to persuade his protesting mistress to accompany him to the altar.

Before starting out he tried his luck once more with the Académie

Française. The death of Chateaubriand and another immortal
whose name has now vanished into limbo had created two vacan-
cies, and Balzac announced his candidature. According to custom
it was necessary for him to call upon each of the thirty-eight
remaining Academicians in turn in order to solicit their support,
but he had no time to do this, since he had to be in Wierzchownia
before the onset of winter, so he left the election to the whims of
Fate. The result was lamentable, though from our point of view it
was a lamentable reflection not on Balzac but on the Academy.
The creator of the *Comédie humaine* received two votes in all. The
seats under the dome and the coats decorated with palms were
awarded to the Duc de Noailles and another gentleman whose
imperishable services to literature have escaped the memory of
posterity. To Balzac's credit it must be recorded that he accepted
this third rebuff with dignity and composure. He merely asked one
of his friends to discover the identity of the two courageous members who had dared to give him their support, so that he might
offer them his thanks.

⟨⟩∘⟨⟩

In October he was once more in Wierzchownia, but this time his
enthusiasm was remarkably subdued. It was no longer a paradise,
but "a desert". He wrote to his mother: "Oh, if you were to spend
a fortnight here in the Ukraine, you would think the rue Fortunée
a delightful place." He was at pains to emphasise the warmth of his
welcome, but one can detect an almost apprehensive tone in his
insistence on this point:

> The people with whom I am living here are extraordinarily
> charming to me, but, after all, I am no more than a pampered
> guest and a friend in the literal sense of the term. They know all
> the members of my family and take the greatest interest in all
> the cares by which I am beset, but what can one do against the
> impossible?

So it appears that Madame de Hanska had deigned to take cognisance of the fact that he had a mother and sister living in Paris,
but one can read between the lines, where it is not stated quite
openly, that something had gone wrong at Wierzchownia. The

reference to "the impossible" seems to have been wrung from him chiefly by Madame de Hanska's horror at the crazy sums he had expended on a house that she would probably never occupy. Her attitude was not unjustified, and Balzac began to pull on his reins. He wrote to his mother:

It is enough if I say that there are limits to the sacrifices one is willing to make, and one must not impose a burden even on those who are nearest to one. These everlasting debts in connection with the house have not been incurred without making an unfavourable impression, and if any further difficulties were to ensue my whole future might, in certain circumstances, be placed in question.

Madame de Hanska did not always conceal her annoyance:

She is chagrined at my having expended such a large sum.

She had again been taught her lesson, that Balzac's powers of speculative calculation needed to be brought under control. Instead of the hundred thousand francs at which he had originally estimated the outlay that would be required on the house, it had already cost three times that amount, and even a woman of Madame de Hanska's resources could not help feeling disquieted. The irritable atmosphere at Wierzchownia became infectious. Balzac wrote home in ill-humour and his mother answered in the same tone. When one of her letters fell into the hands of Madame de Hanska there was a further embroilment, with the result that Balzac tried to put the blame for the misfiring of his wedding plans on the shoulders of his family. There was talk of the house in the rue Fortunée being put up for sale:

Here she is rich, loved, and respected, and she wants for nothing, so she is reluctant to exchange her environment for one in which she sees nothing but upset, debts, the spending of money, and strange faces. Her children are trembling for her.

Balzac too grew anxious and was seized by a fit of economy. He suddenly instructed his mother to dismiss the servant-girl because he could not afford her wages and food. Only François, his valet, was to be kept on to look after his treasures. He went to even more ludicrous extremes, writing to his sister in Suresnes to ask whether she could not send him her cook every Monday after his return to Paris, so that enough meat could be prepared to last himself and his servant for the ensuing week. His budgetary calculations were reduced to very modest figures:

I shall have no more than two hundred francs left, and when that is gone there will be nothing apart from what I may receive from my plays. In the theatre, too, I can see the day coming when there will be no money to be made even with masterpieces.

Discouragement of this kind was something we have not met before in Balzac, and it shows that his self-confidence had been sapped. He was no longer himself. His vitality had been seriously weakened and his constitution was at last succumbing to the strain to which he had subjected it for so long. The warnings had gone unheeded until his physical condition was such that it would take little more to bring about complete collapse. Even his second journey to Wierzchownia had been unwise, for as a son of Touraine he was not used to Russian winters. An attack of bronchitis left no doubt about the state of his heart, which had caused his good friend Dr. Nacquart to shake his head seven years before. When he was eventually able to leave his bed he found that he was unable to move about freely. He had to catch his breath after every step, and even talking was an effort. He had become "as thin as in 1819", his illness had made him "as weak as a child", and there could be no thought of settling down to work. "For a whole year I have not earned a penny." It was symbolic that he had to put aside even his beloved monkish robe: "During my illness I have worn a dressing-gown—which will now permanently take the place of my white Carthusian garb."

There could be no thought of his returning to Paris during the Russian winter, and even the journeys he had planned to Kiev and Moscow had to be abandoned. He was in the hands of two German physicians, a Doctor Knothe and his son, whose ideas on healing seemed to be in advance of their time, for they tried a lemon cure. This brought only a temporary relief, since various physical organs were affected. He had trouble with his eyes, ran a temperature again, and suffered a recurrence of the inflammation of the lungs which had laid him low shortly before.

Though there is little evidence to show how Madame de Hanska behaved while Balzac was on his sick-bed, one thing is certain. The famous author whom she had once greeted with gushing enthusi-

asm and whose adoration had flattered her vanity had become
merely an amusing companion. When he was no longer in a condition to entertain them with his drolleries, he became simply a
nuisance. The two pleasure-loving women, mother and daughter,
had been looking forward for months to visiting the great annual
fair at Kiev. They had taken an apartment in the town, servants
had been sent ahead with carriages and furniture, and they had
refurbished their wardrobes for this important social occasion.
Owing to Balzac's illness their plans had to be postponed, though
perhaps the impassable state of the roads was partly responsible for
their disappointment, and the only amusement that either he or
they could extract from the situation was when they put on their
new frocks for his inspection as he lay in bed.

In his letters to his family he continued to write enthusiastically
about his divine Eva and her simple-minded daughter, but he must
have felt a chill atmosphere of loneliness encompassing him. He
must have felt that he was in an alien environment, with these
spoilt women who thought only of their own selfish pleasures, for
all at once he began to remember his old friends. For years Madame
de Hanska had occupied the foremost place in his thoughts. He had
almost ceased to write to Zulma Carraud, the most loyal and
understanding of the women to whom he had been attached, but
as he lay on his sick-bed he recalled once more her tender solicitude,
and thought how she would have looked after him in his hour of
need. She had been absent from his mind for so long that the words
"*chère*" or "*cara*", with which he had been wont to address her, no
longer came easily to his pen, and he commenced his letter, "My
very dear and kind Madame Zulma," as though the intimacy of
long ago had cooled into a conventional friendship. Yet he soon fell
into the old confidential tone, and the lines in which he told her of
his hopes and illusions are pervaded by a mood of melancholy:

I have twice received very saddening news about you from my
nieces and my sister, and if I did not write it was because I was
simply not in a condition to do so. I was very near to death . . .
it is a matter of a dreadful heart trouble occasioned by fifteen
years of over-exertion. And so I have been living here for the
past eight months under the care of a doctor who, astonishing
as it may seem in the wilds of the Ukraine, is a great physician
and has attached himself to the estate of the friends with whom

I am residing. The treatment he has been giving me was interrupted by one of those ghastly fevers that are called "Moldavian fevers". They come from the marshes of the Danube, spread to Odessa, and from there they ravage the steppes. The type of fever by which I have been attacked is called an intermittent affection of the brain, and it lasts for two months. It is only a week since I recovered sufficiently to resume the treatment of my chronic heart trouble.

The day before yesterday I received from my nieces a letter telling me that you, dear Zulma, were hoping to be able to keep on your house at Frapesle, though you are selling your land there. The words "Frapesle" and "Madame Carraud" revived all my memories as strongly as ever, and though I have been forbidden any exertion, even that involved in writing letters, I wanted to tell you why I had not written to you since last February, apart from some communications on business matters. I had to tell you that you must not believe one forgets one's true friends, and I should like you to know that I have never ceased to think of you, to love you, and to speak of you even here, where they have known our mutual friend Borget since 1833! ...

How differently one looks at life from the summit of fifty years! And how often do we find that we are still far distant from the goal we had hoped to reach! Do you remember how I sent Madame Desgrès to sleep at Frapesle? I think I have sent many people to sleep since then. But how much, and how many illusions, I have cast overboard since those days! And believe me! Apart from my affection for you, which is still growing, I have progressed very little farther. How swiftly misfortune can unfold itself, and how numerous are the obstacles that place themselves in the way of our happiness! Truly, life fills one with revulsion. For three years I have been building myself a nest. It has already, more's the pity, cost me a fortune—but where are the mating birds that were to occupy it? When are they going to move in? The years are passing, we are growing old, and everything is beginning to fade, even the furnishings of my little nest. You see, my dear, that not everything is rosy even for those who appear to be living in the lap of fortune. . . .

He wrote, too, to Madame Delannoy, who had so often helped him with his debts and whom he had never adequately thanked. He seemed to be haunted by an unconscious desire to settle his still outstanding obligations of affection and gratitude before it was too late. Perhaps he realised that his time was short.

25

CHAPTER XXV

Marriage and Homecoming

Whether or not Balzac realised the gravity of his condition, there was no doubt in the minds of his doctors that he would never recover, and it must be assumed that they informed Madame de Hanska of the opinion to which they had come. In the certainty that their marriage would be only of short duration she decided to grant his last wish to the man who had wooed her for so many years. There was no longer any danger of his being able to give way to his gambling instincts or to indulge his spendthrift nature. "*Le bon Balzac*" had become "*le pauvre Balzac*", and she was swayed by a certain condescending sympathy such as a great lady might feel for a faithful retainer who had grown old in her service. The wedding was fixed for the month of March, 1850.

The ceremony was to take place at Berdichev, the nearest provincial town of any size, after which they would set out for Paris, where the *Pavillon Beaujon* was at last ready for occupation. Nothing could be more characteristic of Balzac's impatience than the detailed instructions he conveyed to his mother with regard to the preparations she was to make for the reception of his bride in her new home:

> In the large Chinese bowl that stands on the brown cabinet in the first room on the top storey, next to the inlaid salon, you will find the address of a florist in the Champs Elysées. He came to see me in 1848, when we discussed the question of his delivering flowers

372

to decorate the house once a fortnight, and he told me what his charge would be for a yearly subscription. It was a matter of six to seven hundred francs a year. Since I was on the verge of leaving Paris I postponed the making of arrangements which could only be entered into when I had enough money and when the lady concerned was agreeable. I know she is fond of flowers. Once the florist has undertaken the decoration of the house you will have a basis on which to bargain with him for a favourable price. See to it that he supplies really handsome blooms and let him know exactly what is wanted.

The following decorations are to be carried out. First, the flower table in the first room; secondly, the one in the Japanese salon; thirdly, the two flower-stands in the room with the dome; fourthly, the small flower-containers of African wood on the mantelpiece of the grey room under the dome; fifthly, the two large flower vases on the staircase landing; and sixthly, the small wooden flower holders standing in the two bowls that were fitted by Feuchères.

These were the instructions given by Balzac before he was married, some weeks prior to the date on which he expected to take possession of the home he had furnished for his bride. Sick man though he was, his imagination was as keen as ever and his memory retained the photographic quality that enabled him to recall the minutest details. Every piece of furniture, every vase, every flower-stand was recorded in his mind and he knew where each of them stood. The wedding and the long journey home were still to come, but he had flown on the wings of thought and in his waking dreams he was already installed in the rue Fortunée.

◇⊃∘⊂◇

On the 14th of March, at the Church of St. Barbara in the Ukrainian town of Berdichev, Balzac and Madame de Hanska were married. The ceremony was strictly private, for they did not want to attract attention. There were no guests and nobody was informed. It was seven in the morning and the skies were still grey. The Bishop of Zhitomir, who had been expected to conduct the service, failed to put in an appearance, but Balzac at least had the satisfaction of being joined in holy wedlock by an aristocratic abbé, a certain Count Czaruski. The only witnesses were a kinsman of the abbé and Count Mniszech, who now became Balzac's son-in-law. Immediately after the ceremony the couple returned to Wierzchownia, where they arrived dead tired about eleven o'clock the same night.

Two or three days afterwards Balzac sat down to compose the communiqués of his last and greatest victory. Happiness seemed to have restored his health, and he wrote to his mother, his sister, Dr. Nacquart, and Zulma Carraud. Zulma was once more assured that "when I was asked about my former friendships, yours was always the first name I mentioned", and he informed her of his marriage in the following terms:

> I was married three days ago to the only woman I have ever loved, whom I love now more than ever, and whom I shall continue to love until my dying day. This union is, I believe, the reward that God has kept in reserve for me as compensation for so many vexations, so many years of toil and of difficulties that I have encountered and overcome. My childhood was not happy and my spring was not decked with flowers, but now I shall enjoy a radiant summer and the most delightful of autumns. And perhaps my happy marriage will, from this point of view, provide you with some personal consolation, since it proves to you that after long suffering providence does hold treasures in store which it is willing in the end to distribute.

When he had sealed his letters he had but one thought left in his mind—to follow them as quickly as possible and cross the threshold of his own home. He was still unable to enclose a single line of greeting from his wife, who even now could not be coaxed into showing this small courtesy to his mother, and he had to make the lame excuse:

> My wife intended to add a few lines at the end of this letter, but the courier is waiting and she has moreover to keep to her bed. Her hands are so swollen with rheumatism that she cannot hold a pen. She will convey her respects to you in my next letter.

Balzac had to pay for his new-found happiness. It was impossible to start out for Paris, since the roads were deep in snow and impassable. Even if this obstacle had not presented itself he could not have undertaken the journey in his then state of health. He had ordered the flowers too soon for his house in the rue Fortunée. His weakened constitution was subjected to further trials:

> I have had a serious recurrence of my heart trouble, as well as of the lung inflammation. I have lost much of the headway I had made when it really looked as if there had been considerable progress. . . . I have a black screen before my eyes that will not disperse and veils everything, so that it keeps me from writing. . . . This is the first time I have taken up my pen since the thunderbolt fell from a clear sky.

It might have been expected that now at least his wife would utilise the opportunity to write a few lines to his mother with a view to calming her fears about her son, but Balzac had to add apprehensively:

> My wife has not a single free moment at her disposal, apart from the fact that her hands are so dreadfully swollen. It is the damp which is the cause of it. . . .

A fortnight later, on the 15th of April, he again had to make the effort of writing to his mother:

> I can hardly distinguish the letters as I write these words. The state of my eyes practically prevents me from either writing or reading.

To his sister, who was ill in bed and being nursed by their old mother, he was also compelled to make halting excuses, though he did add that his wife had asked him "to send you her regards". Of himself he said:

> I am not very well. My heart and my lungs are both giving me trouble. I have to catch my breath after every step and am unable to speak.

⊷⊐◦⊏⊷

At last they made up their minds to start off. They had a terrible journey. At Brody, on the Polish frontier, Balzac was overcome by extreme weakness. He lost his appetite and kept breaking out into profuse perspiration, which lowered his strength still further. Acquaintances who saw him at the time almost failed to recognise him.

On the 11th of May he reported from Dresden:

> It has taken us a full month to get as far as this, instead of the normal six days. Not once, but a hundred times, our lives were in danger. We often had to obtain the help of fifteen or sixteen men with winches to drag us out of bogholes in which we had sunk to the carriage windows. But we arrived here in the end, and are still alive, though we are tired and ill. A journey like this adds ten years to one's age. You can imagine what it means to be in constant fear that one of us will die in the other's arms— particularly when one is as much in love as we are.

In a state of complete exhaustion and half blind, he had managed to hold out until they reached Dresden. He was unable to climb steps, and began to doubt whether he would have the strength to continue on to Paris: "I am in a parlous condition. . . . This dreadful journey has made my illness worse." In spite of his failing sight he had to write this letter himself, and once more he made excuses for his wife:

> She is very grateful for everything you have said about her in your letters, but the state of her hands makes it impossible for her to write to you herself.

Strangely enough, her rheumatism did not deter her from visiting the jewellers of Dresden, where she bought a handsome pearl necklace for twenty-five thousand francs, and her swollen fingers did not prevent her from writing to her daughter in a clear, round hand, with full details of her purchase. That she could concentrate her thoughts on a pearl necklace while Balzac lay on his hotel sick-bed can only be a sign of heartlessness, and it is characteristic that she should refer to him in this letter as "*le bon, cher ami*". He was a burden that she tolerated because she knew that she would not be inconvenienced for very long.

We can only dimly suspect the clash of temperament that may have taken place during their enforced sojourn at Dresden, but Balzac had to play his part to the end. He instructed his sister: "I am counting on you. You must impress on mother that she is not to be at the rue Fortunée when I arrive." He was filled with apprehension at the prospect of a meeting between the two women, which he explained under the clumsy pretext: "Mother's dignity would suffer if she were to be present and helped us while we are unpacking our things." The old woman's mistrust had been more than justified. During all these months she had kept a watchful eye on their treasures, supervised the domestic staff, and looked after business matters, though she was firmly convinced that the haughty Russian aristocrat would expect her to clear out of the house before her son's arrival. One task was left to her. Once the flowers were arranged for the bridal couple's reception, there was nothing more for her to do but silently to close the door behind her. François could stand at the threshold and lead his new mistress into her princely home. All the lights would be burning in the rooms and at the entrance steps in readiness to receive the bride, but Balzac's old mother knew that there was no place there for her and she slipped away to Suresnes as soon as her task was finished.

⊲⊃○⊂⊳

The curse that rested on Balzac's fortunes did not desert him at his homecoming. Every fragment of happiness that fell to his lot exacted its tribute. One more item remained to be added to the sum total of his lost illusions, for his homecoming to the *Pavillon Beaujon* was the occasion of a gruesome scene that would have been worthy of his own pen. The last stretch of the journey had been made by rail, and the train was delayed. It was late at night when their carriage drove up to the door of the house in the rue Fortunée. Balzac was impatient to see whether his instructions had been carried out to the last detail, with the flowers, the lights, and François standing in the doorway with a branched candlestick in his hand.

At last the carriage stopped. François had obeyed his orders. The house was brightly illuminated from roof to basement. Balzac rang the bell, but no one came to open the door. Again and again he tore at the bell, but the house remained silent behind its blazing windows. A few neighbours began to gather round and Balzac asked questions which none of them could answer. His wife remained seated in the carriage while the coachman hurried off to fetch a locksmith. When the door was eventually broken open a macabre scene met his eyes.

François, his servant, was crouching in one of the rooms—stark mad. Fate had chosen the very moment of his master's homecoming to deprive him of his reason, and he had to be taken in the middle of the night to a madhouse. While the raving François was being overpowered and carried away, Balzac led his bride into the house he had prepared for her.

CHAPTER XXVI

Finale

he law that governed Balzac's destiny held good to the end. His dreams could be transmuted into reality only in his books, not in his own life. With unutterable toil, desperate sacrifices, and glowing hopes he had provided a home in which to spend his last "twenty-five years" with the wife at his side who had at long last yielded to his wooing. When all was ready, he moved in, only to die. He had designed for himself the perfect study in which to complete the *Comédie humaine*, fifty further volumes of which were already planned, but he never wrote a line in it. His eyesight failed completely and the only letter we possess from the rue Fortunée, addressed to Théophile Gautier, is in the handwriting of his wife, with a single line of postscript scrawled laboriously by Balzac himself: "I can no longer read or write." He had fitted up a handsome library in which he never opened a book. His drawing-room was hung with gold damask for receptions to Parisian society that were never held. The physicians forbade him the slightest exertion, even that of speaking. His beloved picture-gallery, that was to be the sensation of Paris when it was seen what an incomparable collection he had been able to gather together, was to have been displayed and explained to friends, authors, and artists item by item, but when Victor Hugo came to see him he had to ask his wife to show his friend round. He had dreamed of a palace and it had become a prison. He lay alone in the vast house, where now and then his mother would flit into the room like a shy shadow to

attend to his wants. His wife—and all witnesses are agreed on this point—showed the same lack of genuine solicitude, the same cruel indifference which she had demonstrated on the journey from Wierzchownia and during their stay at Dresden.

Her attitude is irrefutably proved by the letters she wrote to her daughter at this time. She chatted naively about lace, jewels or new clothes, and there was hardly a line that betrayed sincere anxiety about her dying husband. Even now she referred to him by the nickname he had been given when he amused the family with his droll ways: "Bilboquet arrived here in a worse condition than ever. He can no longer walk and is subject to continual fainting fits."

No one who saw him could doubt that the end was near, but he himself refused to believe it. His unshakable optimism discerned the prospect of recovery where others saw only the certainty of death. He was accustomed to mocking at difficulties and making possible the impossible, and he did not abandon the struggle. When an occasional slight improvement gave him back his voice he would summon up his waning strength and converse with a visitor, discussing political matters, expressing confidence that he would soon be on his feet again, trying to persuade others, as he was persuading himself, that he still possessed reserves of his old vigour. A last gleam of his former vivacious spirit would even break through at times.

Before the summer was well on its way the doctors had delivered their verdict. From a report of a joint consultation between four physicians, Drs. Nacquart, Louis, Roux, and Fouquier, it is clear that all they could now recommend was palliatives and occasional light stimulants. For the rest it appears that they had no hope. Balzac himself began to grow anxious. He lamented that he would not be able to finish the *Comédie humaine*, and spoke of what was to happen about his works after his death. He pressed Dr. Nacquart to tell him frankly how much time he had left, and from the expression on his old friend's face he realised how things stood. It may be truth or it may be merely a pious legend, but it has been related that in his confusion of thought he called for Horace Bianchon, the physician whom he caused to work scientific wonders in the *Comédie humaine*: "If Bianchon were here, he would save me!"

The process of dissolution made rapid progress. In his memoirs

Victor Hugo has described the last visit he paid to the dying Balzac:

I rang the bell. The moon was shining through a mass of cloud. The street was empty. No one answered, and I rang a second time. The door was opened. A maid appeared holding a candle. "Whom do you wish to see, sir?" She was weeping. I gave my name and was shown into the salon on the ground floor, in which David d'Angers' colossal marble bust of Balzac stood on a console opposite the fireplace. A light was burning on a richly decorated table in the centre of the room, the pedestal of which consisted of six gilt statuettes in the finest taste. Another woman, who was also weeping, entered and said: "He is dying. Madame has retired to her room. The doctors have given him up since yesterday. He has a wound on his left leg and it has become gangrened. The doctors are at a loss what to do for him. They say that dropsy has brought on fatty degeneration, that his flesh and skin have turned tallowy, and therefore it would be impossible to tap him. A month ago he struck himself against an ornamental projection on a piece of furniture. . . . He has not spoken since nine o'clock this morning. Madame sent for a priest, who came and administered the last unction. He made a sign to show that he knew what was happening. An hour later he offered his hand to Madame de Surville, his sister. Since eleven o'clock there has been a rattling noise in his throat. He will not survive the night. If you wish it I will fetch Monsieur de Surville. He has not yet gone to bed." The woman left me and I waited for a few moments. The light scarcely illumined the furniture in the salon and the magnificent paintings by Porbus and Holbein that were hanging on the walls. The marble bust shimmered as if it were the ghost of the man who lay dying. The house was filled with a corpse-like odour. Monsieur de Surville appeared and confirmed all that the maid had told me.

We walked along a passage, ascended a staircase that was covered with a red carpet and richly adorned with works of art, statues, vases, pictures and enamelled bowls, and passed through another corridor in which I noticed an open door. I heard a loud, ominous rattling sound. I was in Balzac's room. His bed stood in the centre of the chamber. It was of mahogany, and at the head and foot was an apparatus of straps and cross-bars for enabling the sick man to be moved. Balzac lay with his head supported on a mass of pillows to which had been added red damask cushions from the settee. His face was purple, almost

black, and inclined towards the right, he was unshaven, his hair
grey and cut short, his eyes open and staring. I saw him in
profile, and he looked like the Emperor. An old woman (the
novelist's mother), the nurse and a servant were standing on
either side of the bed, behind which a light was burning on a
table, with another on the chest by the door. On the night-table
there stood a silver vase. The nurse and the servant stood in a
kind of horrified silence as they listened to his dying rattle. The
light by the bed cast a vivid glimmer on a picture of a fresh-
faced, smiling young man that hung near the fireplace. An overpowering, sickening odour was wafted from the bed. I lifted the
coverings and grasped Balzac's hand. It was covered with
perspiration. I pressed it, but the pressure was not returned. . . .

The nurse said to me: "He will die at dawn." As I descended
the stairs I carried away in my mind the picture of this livid
figure. On my way through the salon I again saw the bust,
immobile, unfeeling, exalted, and with a vague radiance eman-
ating from it, and I could not help drawing a comparison between
death and immortality.

Balzac died at half-past ten on the evening of August the 17th,
1850. His mother was the only person present, his wife having long
since retired. His end was terribly lonely.

The funeral was on the 22nd, the service being held at the
Church of St. Philippe de Roule. In pouring rain the body was
accompanied to the cemetery. His wife could have had little understanding of Balzac's secret heart, for the pall-bearers, apart from
Victor Hugo, were Alexandre Dumas, Sainte-Beuve, and the
Minister Baroche. None of these three had ever been on terms of
intimate friendship with Balzac. Sainte-Beuve had even been his
most bitter enemy, the only one whom he had really hated. The
cemetery was Père Lachaise, a place that Balzac had always loved.
It was from here that his Rastignac had gazed out over the city
and issued his challenge to Paris. It was Balzac's last home, the
only one, as has been said, in which he could take refuge from his
creditors and find peace.

Victor Hugo pronounced the final words at the graveside:

The man who has now been lowered into the tomb was one of
those who are accompanied by the grief of a nation. . . . Henceforth men's eyes will be turned towards the faces not of those who
are the rulers, but of those who are the thinkers, and the whole

nation trembles when one of these faces disappears from their ken. To-day the people grieve for the death of a man of talent, the nation mourns the loss of a man of genius. The name of Balzac will join the gleaming trail that our epoch will bequeath to the future. . . .

Paris has been dazed by his death. It is but a few months since he returned to France. He felt that he was about to die and wished to see his native land once more, as on the eve of a long journey one comes to embrace one's mother. His life was short, but it was full. It was richer in works than in days. Alas! This tremendous, unwearying worker, this philosopher, this thinker, this poet, this genius experienced during his sojourn among us that life full of storms and struggles which is the lot of all great men. To-day he rests in peace. Now he is lifted above the plane of conflict and hatred. On the day he enters the tomb he enters also into the halls of fame. Henceforth he will shine among the stars of this land of ours, far above the clouds gathering over our heads. All you who stand here, are you not tempted to envy him? Yet however great our grief may be at such a loss, let us resign ourselves to these misfortunes. Let us accept them, with all the cruel affliction that they signify. It is perhaps good, it is perhaps necessary, in an age like ours, that from time to time the death of a great man should cause a wave of religious emotion to pass through our spirits, consumed as they are with doubt and scepticism. Providence knows what it is doing when it confronts the nation in this way with the supreme mystery and leads it to think of death, in which all are equal and all are free. There can be room in our minds for none but austere and earnest thoughts when a lofty spirit enters majestically upon another life, when a being who has long hovered above the crowd on the visible wings of genius suddenly spreads those other wings that have hitherto remained hidden from our sight and vanishes into the unknown. No! It is not the unknown. As I have said once before on a similar sorrowful occasion, and as I shall never tire of saying—it is not night, but light. It is not the end, but the beginning. It is not nothingness, but eternity. Do I not speak truth, all you who are listening? Tombs like this are a proof of immortality.

These were words such as had never been spoken of Balzac while he was alive. Like the hero of his own novel, he was to set out from Père Lachaise to conquer Paris.

FINIS

BALZAC'S LIFE AND WORK

A Survey

Life.	*Work.*
The family Balzac, originally Balsa or Balssa, of peasant stock from the Albigeois.	
1797 Bernard-François Balzac (1746–1829) marries Anne-Charlotte-Laure Sallambier (*d.* 1854).	
1799 Honoré, born May 20th in Tours, rue de l'Armée d'Italie.	
Educated, Collège des Oratoriens, Vendôme; Institut Lepître, Paris; and Institut Ganser et Beuzelin, Paris.	Described in *Louis Lambert.*
1816 Student at the Ecole de Droit; articled to Maître Guillonet-Merville.	
1818 With Maître Passez.	*Note sur l'immortalité de l'âme; Notes sur la philosophie et la religion.*
1819 First examination for baccalauréat du droit.	
Decides to become a writer. Living in Paris: 9, rue Lesdiguières.	Described in: *La peau de chagrin.* Poetry: *Saint-Louis; Robert de Normandie; Livre de Job;* tragedy *Sylla.*
His family domiciled in Villeparisis, near Paris.	Novels: *Coqsigrue; Sténie.* Tragedy: *Cromwell.*
1820 Acquaintance with Auguste le Poitevin de L'Egreville.	
1821 Joint authorship with le Poitevin, under various pen-names.	*Les deux Hectors,* by Auguste de Viellerglé.
Meets Madame de Berny, née Hinner (1777–1836).	*Charles Pointel,* under the same nom-de-plume.
1822 Further novels in joint authorship with le Poitevin.	*L'héritière de Birague,* by A. de Viellerglé et Lord R'hoone; under the same nom-de-plume. *Jean-*

Life.	*Work.*
First dramatic plans.	*Louis* and *Clotilde de Lusignan*. *Le centennaire* and *Le vicaire des Ardennes*, by Horace de Saint-Aubin.
1823 First visit to Touraine. **1824** Failure in his attempt at starting a career as writer of thrillers.	*La dernière fée*, by Horace de Saint-Aubin; *Annette et le criminel*, under the same pseudonym. Pamphlets: *Du droit d'aînesse*, by M.D. . .; *Histoire des jésuites*.
1825 Last thriller published anonymously; collaboration with the journalist Horace Raisson; series of *"Codes"* started. First commercial speculation: Balzac starts publishing, jointly with the publisher Urbain Canel and two other shareholders; the money being lent by his mother and Madame de Berny. Failure of this venture.	*Wann-Chlore*, anonymous; *Le Code des gens honnêtes*, by Horace Raisson. *Molière, oeuvres complètes*; *La Fontaine, oeuvres complètes*, both with preface by Balzac, published by H. Balzac et Sautelet.
1826 Balzac meets the Duchesse d'Abraptès. The publishing firm dissolved: loss of 15,000 francs. Second speculation: Balzac buys, with fresh capital, a printer's firm; in June licensed as printer, printing novels, pamphlets, and prospectuses.	Pamphlet: *Petit dictionnaire critique et anecdotique des enseignes de Paris, par Un batteur de pavé*.
1827 In September the printers' shop closed down. Third speculation: Balzac buys, again with fresh capital, a type-foundry.	More *" Codes "*: *L'art de mettre sa cravate*; *L'art de payer ses dettes*.
1828 In spring the type-foundry liquidated; final collapse of all commercial speculations, resulting in debts of about 90,000 francs. Balzac living rue Cassini, under an assumed name.	Further *"Codes"*: *Code civil*; later *Code pénal, Code galant, Code conjugal, Code du commis-voyageur*, all jointly with Horace Raisson.
1829 First novel published under his own name. Meets Madame Zulma Carraud.	*Le dernier Chouan* (later: *Les Chouans*), by Honoré Balzac; *Physiologie du mariage, par un jeune célibataire*.
1830 First fame. Intensive activity as journalist.	*Scènes de la vie privée*, 2 vols. (cont. a.o. *La Vendetta, Gobseck, Le bal de sceaux, La maison du chat-qui-pelote*): articles and essays in *Le Voleur, La Mode, La Caricature, La Silhouette, Revue de Paris*.

Life.	*Work.*
1831 Balzac adds the prefix "de" to his name; new apartment, No. 1, rue Cassini; valet, horses, and carriage. First political ambitions. Letter from Madame de Castries. Visits to Saché (M. de Margonne) and Angoulême (M. and Madame Carraud).	*La peau de chagrin*, by M. de Balzac; *Romans et contes philosophiques*, 3 vols. (sec. ed. of *La peau de chagrin*, and twelve stories, a.o. *Sarrasine, El Verdugo, Le chef-d'oeuvre inconnu, Jésus-Christ en Flandre*); contributions to *La Caricature, Le Voleur, Revue de Paris*. Political pamphlet: *Enquête sur la politique des deux ministères.*
1832 Madame de Castries; Balzac in aristocratic circles; loyalist candidate (unsuccessful). First letter from Madame de Hanska. In August in Aix-les-Bains with Madame de Castries; trip to Italy planned; clash and departure. In October, visit to Madame de Berny in the country; in December, back in Paris.	*Contes drolatiques*, 1st dizain; *La femme de trente ans*; *Maître Cornelius*; *Madame Firmiani*; *Louis Lambert*; *Le curé de Tours.* Journalism: contributions to *La Caricature, Revue de Paris, Le Renovateur* (the organ of the loyalists.).
1833 In April–May again in Angoulême with M. and Madame Carraud. In September, first meeting with Madame de Hanska in Switzerland (Neuchâtel); in December, with Madame de Hanska in Geneva.	*Contes drolatiques*, 2nd dizain; *Le médecin de campagne*; new series of novels: *Etudes de moeurs au 19me siècle*, including the *Scènes de la vie de province* (*Eugénie Grandet, Le message, L'illustre Godissart* a.o.). Contributions to *L'Europe littéraire.*
1834 In January in Geneva, departing on Feb. 8. In April in Frapesle (Madame Carraud). In October in Saché (M. de Margonne).	*Scènes de la vie parisienne*; *L'histoire des treize*; *La recherche de l'absolu*; *La duchesse de Langeais.* In *Revue de Paris*: *Lettre aux écrivains français.*
1835 Apartment in Chaillot, rue des Batailles, under the assumed name of "veuve Durand". In May–June visit to Vienna; meeting with Madame de Hanska.	Series *Etudes philosophiques* (intended to comprise twenty volumes): *Un drame au bord de la mer*; *Le père Goriot*; *Séraphita*; *Le contrat de mariage.*
1836 The *Chronique de Paris* founded. In prison from April 27 to May 4 after refusal to serve with the National Guard. Struggle with Buloz (unauthorised reprint of Balzac's *Le lys dans la vallée*). Countess Sarah Visconti-Guidoboni. Journey to Italy in company of Caroline Marbouty.	In *Chronique de Paris*: *La messe d'athée*; *L'interdiction*; *Le cabinet des antiques*; *Facino Cane.* *Le lys dans la vallée*; *Melmoth reconcilié.*

26

Life.	*Work.*
1837 In spring, again two months in Italy (Milan, Venice, Florence). Financial difficulties; Balzac living in the house of the Viscontis, 54, Avenue des Champs Elysées. *Chronique de Paris* insolvent.	*Etudes de moeurs* and *Etudes philosophiques* continued. *La vieille fille*; *Les illusions perdues*, 1st part; *Une passion dans le désert*; *César Birotteau*. *Contes drolatiques*, 3rd dizain.
1838 New speculation: the silver mines in Sardinia. In March, departure from Marseilles, via Corsica, to Nurra in Sardinia; failure and return to Paris. Balzac living at *Les Jardies* near Sèvres.	*La maison Nucingen*; *La femme supérieure* (afterwards: *Les employés*); *La Torpille* (afterwards: *Splendeurs et misères des courtisanes*, 1st part).
1839 Collapse of the newly erected walls of his garden at *Les Jardies*. Balzac sponsors the cause of the notary Peytel; failure.	*Gambara*; *Une fille d'Eve*; *Massimilla Doni*; *Béatrix*, 1st and 2nd parts; *Un grand homme de province*.
1840 Balzac living for some time in the house of his tailor, Buisson, rue de Richelieu; then in Passy, 19, rue Basse. March 14, first performance of Balzac's play *Vautrin* at the Théâtre Porte-Saint-Martin. In July, *Revue Parisienne* founded.	*Pierrette*; *Pierre Grassou*; *Vautrin*; *La princesse parisienne* (afterwards: *La princesse de Cadignan*). *Code littéraire proposé à la société des gens de lettres*.
1841 November, Count Hanski dies.	*Physiologie de l'employé*; *Z. Marcas*; *Le curé de village*. Draft for a law of copyright.
1842 In March, *Les ressources de Quinola* played at the Odéon. Arrangements for a collected edition of his novels under the new title: *La comédie humaine*.	*Ursule Mirouet : Mémoires de deux jeunes mariées*. *La comédie humaine*, vols. 1–3.
1843 July, August, September in St. Petersburg with Madame de Hanska. In September his play *Paméla Giraud* at the Théâtre à la Gaîté.	*Une ténébreuse affaire*; *La muse du département*; *Le martyr calviniste* (afterwards: *Cathérine de Médicis*, 1st part). *Comédie humaine*, four more vols. published.
1844 Balzac buying furniture and bric-à-brac for his new house. Illness.	*Un début da.is la vie*; *Honorine*; *Splendeurs et misères des courtisanes*, 1st and 2nd parts. Three more vols. of *La comedie humaine* published. *Modeste Mignon*. *Les paysans* (partly) in serial publication.

Life.	*Work.*
1845 Madame de Hanska and her daughter in Dresden; visit of Balzac there in May. Travels to South Germany, Paris, the Netherlands. Parting in Brussels. In autumn Balzac travelling with the Hanskis to Italy. At the end of the year, back in Paris.	*Béatrix*, 3rd part; *Petites misères de la vie conjugale.* *Comédie humaine,* 2 more vols.
1846 Again in Italy with Madame de Hanska. In September preparations for marriage in Metz. A child born at the end of the year. Balzac buys the *Pavillon Beaujon,* rue Fortunée, for Madame de Hanska. The child dies in December.	*Splendeurs et misères des courtisanes,* 3rd part. *Comédie humaine,* last four vols.
1847 Balzac furnishing the house in the rue Fortunée. In October, voyage to Wierzchownia in the Ukraine to Madame de Hanska. Four months in Russia.	*Splendeurs et misères des courtisanes,* 4th part; *Les parents pauvres,* consisting of *La cousine Bette*; *Le cousin Pons.*
1848 Return to Paris, shortly before the outbreak of revolution in February. May 25, first performance of his play *La Marâtre* at the Théâtre Historique. In autumn, second journey to Russia.	
1849 Staying in Wierzchownia; severe illness.	
1850 March 14, marriage ceremony with Madame de Hanska in the parochial church of St. Barbara at Berdichev. In April, departure for Paris. Last illness. August 18, Victor Hugo's visit. Death of Balzac during the night of August 18–August 19. August 22, funeral service.	
1882 Death of Eva de Balzac.	

Posthumous Works.

1851   First performance of Balzac's play *Mercadet* at the Théâtre du Gymnase: adaptation by d'Ennery.
Story *La filandière* (supplement to *Contes drolatiques*).

1853   *Théâtre complet,* in 1 vol.
Novel *Le député d'Arcis* published, the last part by Charles Rabou.

1854 *Les petits bourgeois* (probably also edited by Charles Rabou).

1855 *Les paysans.*
La comédie humaine, three vols., supplement.

1870–2 *Oeuvres diverses,* 4 vols. (first collected edition of Balzac's essays, sketches, articles, etc.), as vols. 20–23 of his *Oeuvres complètes.*

1876 Correspondence, 1 vol.

1899 sq. *Lettres à l'Etrangère* (Madame de Hanska), 3 vols.
1907 *L'école des ménages, tragédie bourgeoise,* published by Vicomte de Lovenjoul (first performance 1910 at the Odéon).

1912 sq. *Oeuvres complètes,* critical edition, edited by Marcel Bouteron.

1925 *Cromwell,* first edition, in facsimile, by W. S. Hastings, Princeton.

BIBLIOGRAPHY

ONLY a selected list of publications can be given here. For a full survey of books on Balzac, see: William Hobart Royce, *A Balzac Bibliography*, Chicago, 1929 (supplements 1930–37).

The story of Balzac's works in their original editions has been told by Vicomte de Spoelberch de Lovenjoul: *Histoire des oeuvres de H. de Balzac*, Paris, 1879; 3rd edition, 1888. The huge collection of Balzac manuscripts formerly in his possession now forms part of the *Musée de Chantilly*.

COLLECTED WORKS

Oeuvres complètes, 20 vols., Paris 1853–5. *Edition définitive*, 24 vols., Paris, 1869–75. The modern critical edition, edited by Marcel Bouteron and Henri Longnon, Paris, has been in course of publication since 1912 (38 vols. have so far appeared).

Oeuvres de jeunesse: 10 vols., Paris, 1866–68; illustrated edition in 2 vols., in 4to., Paris, 1868.

TRANSLATIONS INTO ENGLISH (*Collected Editions*)

The Comedy of Human Life, translated by Katherine Prescott Wormeley, Boston, Roberts Bros., 1885–93; London, Routledge & Sons, 1886–91.

Novels (The Human Comedy), now for the first time completely translated (by Ellery Sidgwick, G. B. Ives a.o.), London, printed by H. S. Nichols, 1895, 11 vols.; reissued in 22 vols. by Leonard Smithers, London, 1897–9.

The Human Comedy, translated by Clara Bell, Ellen Marriage, James Waring and R. S. Scott, introductions by G. Saintsbury, London, Dent, 1895–98, 40 vols.

CORRESPONDENCE

Correspondance, Vol. 24 of *éd. définitive*, Paris, 1876.

Lettres à l'Etrangère (Madame de Hanska), vol. I, Paris, 1899; vol. II, 1906; vol. III, 1935.

Balzac : Letters to his Family, 1809–1850, ed. W. S. Hastings, Princeton University Press, 1934.

Correspondance inédite avec Madame Zulma Carraud, ed. M. Bouteron, Paris, 1935. M. Bouteron has also edited various smaller volumes of correspondence, with Madame de Berny, Madame de Castries, Dr.

Nacquart a.o. (Cahiers Balzaciens, Paris, since 1923). In the same series several fragments and sketches, hitherto unpublished, have been printed (*Fantaisies de Gina*; *Fragments des contes drolatiques*; *Lettre sur Kiev*, 1847).

BIOGRAPHY, CRITICISM, ETC.

(a) Contemporaries.

Laure de Surville (Balzac's sister): *Balzac, sa vie et ses oeuvres*, Paris, 1858.

Sainte-Beuve's essay, first printed in 1850, was reissued in *Causeries du lundi*, vol. II.

Victor Hugo's funeral oration: first printed in *Les femmes de Balzac*, Paris, 1851. His description of Balzac's death in *Choses vues*, 1887.

Théophile Gautier: *H. de Balzac*, Paris, 1859.

E. Werdet (Balzac's publisher): *Portrait intime de Balzac*, Paris, 1859.

L. Gozlan: *Balzac en pantoufles*, Paris, 1856; *Bazlac chez lui*, 1862.

H. Taine: essay on Balzac, 1858; reprinted in *Essais de critique et d'histoire*.

(b) Later Publications.

Spoelberch de Lovenjoul: *Un roman d'amour* (Madame de Hanska), Paris, 1899; *La genèse d'un roman de B.* (*Les paysans*), 1901; *Une page perdue*, 1903. A Cerfberr et J. Christophe: *Répertoire de la Comédie Humaine*, Paris, 1887; preface by P. Bourget. Dr. A. Cabanès: *Balzac ignoré*, Paris, 1899. E. Biré: *H. de B.*, Paris, 1897. F. Wedmore: *Balzac*, London, 1890 (*Great Writers* series). F. Brunetière: *Balzac*, Paris, 1906. G. Hanotaux et Vicaire: *La jeunesse de Balzac*, Paris, 1904. G. Ruxton: *La Dilecta de Balzac* (Madame de Berny), Paris, 1909. A. Lebreton: *Balzac, l'homme et l'oeuvre*, Paris, 1905.

(c) Modern Publications.

L. J. Arrigon: *Les débuts littéraires* and *Les années romantiques de Balzac*, Paris, 1924, 1927. P. Abraham: *Balzac*, Paris, 1927, and *Créatures chez Balzac*, 1931. E. R. Curtius, *Balzac*, Bonn, 1923. J. H. Floyd: *Les femmes dans la vie de Balzac*, Paris, 1926. E. Preston: *Recherches sur la technique de B.*, 1926. A. Prioult: *B. avant la Comédie Humaine*, Paris, 1936. R. Bouvier: *B., homme d'affaires*, Paris, 1930; R. Bouvier et E. Maynial: *Les comptes dramatiques de Balzac*, Paris, 1938. A. Billy, *Vie de Balzac*, 2 vols., Paris, 1944.

INDEX